Methods for Teaching Science as Inquiry

TENTH EDITION

Allyn & Bacon
is an imprint of

Boston   New York   San Francisco
Mexico City   Montreal   Toronto   London
Madrid   Munich   Paris   Hong Kong
Singapore   Tokyo   Cape Town   Sydney

Methods for Teaching Science as Inquiry

JOEL E. BASS
Late of Sam Houston State University

TERRY L. CONTANT
Science Curriculum and Instruction Specialist, LEARN

ARTHUR A. CARIN
Late of Queens College

Vice President and Executive Publisher: Jeffery W. Johnston
Publisher: Kevin M. Davis
Editor: Meredith D. Fossel
Development Editor: Bryce Bell
Editorial Assistant: Maren Vigilante
Senior Managing Editor: Pamela D. Bennett
Project Manager: Mary Harlan
Production Coordination: S4Carlisle Publising Services

Design Coordinator: Diane C. Lorenzo
Photo Coordinator: Valerie Schultz
Cover Design: Candace Rowley
Cover Image: Fotosearch
Operations Specialist: Susan W. Hannahs
Director of Marketing: Quinn Perkson
Marketing Manager: Erica M. DeLuca
Marketing Coordinator: Brian Mounts

For related titles and support materials, visit our online catalog at www.pearsonhighered.com.

Between the time website information is gathered and then published, it is not unusual for some sites to have closed. Also, the transcription of URLs can result in typographical errors. The publisher would appreciate notification where these errors occur so that they may be corrected in subsequent editions.

Library of Congress Cataloging-in-Publication Data
Bass, Joel E.
    Methods for teaching science as inquiry / Joel E. Bass, Terry L. Contant, Arthur A.
Carin. -- 10th ed.
        p. cm.
    Rev. ed. of: Methods for teaching science as inquiry / Arthur A. Carin. 9th ed. 2005.
    Includes bibliographical references and index.
    ISBN 978-0-13-235329-8
    1. Science--study and teaching (Elementary) I. Contant, Terry L. II. Carin, Arthur A.
III. Carin, Arthur A. Methods for teaching science as inquiry. IV. Title.
    LB1585.C27 2009
    372.3'5044--dc22

                                                            2008002458

Photo Credits: EyeWire Collection/Getty Images–Photodisc, p. 2; Arthur A. Carin, pp. 7, 80 (*top*); Thinkstock, p. 9; Anthony Magnacca/Merrill, pp. 28, 45 (*both*), 86, 89, 119, 190, 208 (*both*), 236, 244; Barbara Schwartz/Merrill, p. 60; Scott Cunningham/Merrill, p. 80 (*center, bottom*), 92, 252, 262; Valerie Schultz/Merrill, p. 96; Laura Bolesta/Merrill, p. 110; Getty Images–Stockbyte, p. 136; Krista Greco/Merrill, p. 139; Richard T. Nowitz/Photo Researchers, Inc., p. 184; Getty Images, Inc., p. 206; David Buffington/Getty Images, Inc.–Photodisc, p. 209; Andersen Ross/Getty Images, p. 230; Richard Haynes/Prentice Hall School Division, p. 263. All color insert photos by Helen Bass.

Printed in the United States of America

5 6 7 8 9 10   EB   17 16 15 14 13

Dedication

THIS BOOK IS DEDICATED to the memory of Dr. Joel E. Bass, who passed away after completing this edition. Dr. Bass inspired many science educators during his 35 years at Sam Houston State University, and he touched thousands more through his work on the ninth, tenth, and eleventh editions of *Teaching Science as Inquiry*. Joel, your passion for teaching science lives on in our memories, and in this book.

THIS BOOK IS ALSO DEDICATED to the memory of Dr. Arthur A. Carin, author of the first eight editions of *Teaching Science as Inquiry* (then called *Teaching Science as Discovery*). Through five decades of exemplary writing, teaching, research, and service, Dr. Carin had a significant, positive impact on science education. Art, you are remembered and honored.

Preface

THE RAPID ADVANCE of cognitive learning theories in the past few years has led educators to realize the need for students to be more actively engaged in their own construction of knowledge. This research tells us that an inquiry approach to science teaching motivates and engages all types of students, helping them understand the relevance of science to their lives, as well as the nature of science itself.

Inquiry is both a way for scientists and students to investigate the world and a way to teach. In this instructional environment, teachers act as facilitators of learning, guiding students in asking simple but thoughtful questions about the world and finding ways to engage them in answering their questions.

Inquiry incorporates the use of hands-on and process-oriented activities for the benefit of knowledge construction while building investigation skills and habits of mind in students. Inquiry encourages students to connect their prior knowledge to observations and to use their observations as evidence to increase personal scientific knowledge and explain how the world works.

But is there a manageable way for new and experienced teachers to bring inquiry into their science classrooms?

Drawing on a solid understanding of inquiry with a teaching framework that builds in accountability for science content learning, and using inquiry-based activities, teachers can create and manage an engaging, productive science classroom. By integrating an inquiry approach, science content, teaching methods, standards, and a bank of inquiry activities, the 10th edition of *Methods for Teaching Science as Inquiry* demonstrates a manageable way for new and experienced teachers to bring inquiry successfully into the science classroom.

The Inquiry Framework

In this edition we have used the National Science Education Standards (NSES) and the 5-E Learning Cycle model of instruction to create an inquiry framework for science teaching. *Methods for Teaching Science as Inquiry* lays the foundation for teaching standards-based elementary science, scaffolding an understanding of an inquiry lesson model and how to use it to teach science.

National Science Education Standards

Many years of work and research in the science education community have provided a coherent, research-based vision for a new era of science education. As a result, the *National Science Education Standards* (NSES) were created to coordinate the goals and objectives for science instruction.

Throughout this edition, you will have an opportunity to become familiar with the *National Science Education Standards* through margin notes and lengthier features quoting from the *Standards* document, showing the *Standards'* relationship to chapter content. This integrated coverage in all chapters highlights the importance of using the *National Science Education Standards* to inform instruction.

 STANDARDS ABOUT ORGANISMS AND CONCEPTS AND PRINCIPLES THAT SUPPORT THE STANDARDS FOR GRADES K–4

NSES Standards

Students should understand:

• Characteristics of Organisms (K–4)
• Life Cycles of Organisms (K–4)

Concepts and Principles That Support the Standards

• Organisms have basic needs. For example, animals need air, water, and food; plants require air, water, nutrients, and light. Organisms can survive only in environments in which their needs can be met.
• Each plant or animal has different structures that serve different functions in growth, survival, and reproduction.
• Plants and animals have life cycles that include being born, developing into adults, reproducing, and eventually dying. The details of this life cycle are different for different organisms.

Source: Reprinted from *National Science Education Standards* by The National Academy of Sciences, with permission courtesy of the National Academies Press, Washington DC.

5-E Model

The text follows the 5-E model of instruction, which frames activities in terms of engaging, exploring, explaining, elaborating, and evaluating. This learning cycle model, introduced early in the text, reflects the NSES *Science as Inquiry Standards*, seamlessly integrating inquiry and the *Standards* to create a science teaching framework best suited for engaging students in meaningful science learning while providing accountability opportunities for teachers.

Highlights of This Edition

This text scaffolds the understanding of science concepts; investigation procedures; concepts of teaching, learning, and assessment; and the 5-E and other instructional models to help readers understand the inquiry approach to teaching. Among the many highlights of this revision, you will find

- attention given to strategies for teaching with inquiry methods in a high-stakes testing environment;
- a revised assessment chapter, based on Bloom's taxonomy of educational objectives, including the interpretation of high-stakes testing results and linking standards to both learning objectives and assessment items;
- critical thinking questions at the end of each chapter to practice application of chapter content;
- updated, research-based coverage on meeting the needs of English Language Learners (ELLs) and strategies for diverse learners;
- full integration with additional online material found on MyEducationLab (www.myeducationlab.com) to complement chapter content;
- a strong focus throughout the book on the 5-E model of instruction;
- a comprehensive discussion of conceptual change and how to use conceptual change strategies within the 5-E model of instruction;
- margin notes that link readers to activities that model standards-based inquiry and developmentally appropriate science content;

- suggestions on how to construct and use performance assessments and how to use traditional assessments in new ways;
- the presentation of exciting new advancements and trends in educational technology and how they apply to the science classroom;
- clarification of various ideas important to inquiry, including aspects of the nature of science and constructivist principles of learning;
- classroom scenarios that illustrate strategies of inquiry instruction and introduce readers to important science concepts; and
- a look at descriptive investigations, classificatory investigations, and experimental investigations, three main ways children can learn to investigate the world.

The changes made to this edition help build a clearer understanding of teaching science as inquiry and practical methods for implementing an inquiry approach to science education.

Instructor Supplements

Instructor's Manual

Free to adopters, this manual provides chapter-by-chapter supplements to enrich each class meeting. You will find an extensive test bank, as well as suggested activities, objectives and overviews, suggested readings, and other tools for teaching.

PEARSON myeducationlab

"Teacher educators who are developing pedagogies for the analysis of teaching and learning contend that analyzing teaching artifacts has three advantages: it enables new teachers time for reflection while still using the real materials of practice; it provides new teachers with experience thinking about and approaching the complexity of the classroom; and in some cases, it can help new teachers and teacher educators develop a shared understanding and common language about teaching. . . ." [1]

As Linda Darling-Hammond and her colleagues point out, grounding teacher education in real classrooms—among real teachers and students and among actual examples of students' and teachers' work—is an important, and perhaps even an essential, part of training teachers for the complexities of teaching today's students in today's classrooms. For a number of years, we have heard the same message from many of you as we sat in your offices learning about the goals of your courses and the challenges you face in teaching the next generation of educators. Working with a number of our authors and with many of you, we have created a website that provides you and your students with the context of real classrooms and artifacts that research on teacher education tells us is so important. Through authentic in-class video footage, interactive simulations, rich case studies, examples of authentic teacher and student work, and more, **MyEducationLab** offers you and your students a uniquely valuable teacher education tool.

MyEducationLab is easy to use! Wherever the MyEducationLab logo appears in the margins or elsewhere in the text, you and your students can follow the simple link instructions to access the MyEducationLab resource that corresponds with the chapter content.

Go to the Homework and Exercises section in Chapter 1 of MyEducationLab to view the five part set of videos called "Water Wheels." These videos provide a view of a third grade class as they investigate, construct, and test water wheels. These videos provide a good example of the application of both the technological design cycle and the science as inquiry tasks. A video guide for this video is included in the *Online Professional Development* section at the end of this chapter.

---

[1]Darling-Hammond, L., & Bransford, J., Eds. (2005). *Preparing Teachers for a Changing World*. San Francisco: John Wiley & Sons.

These include:

Videos: Authentic classroom videos show how real teachers handle actual classroom situations.

Homework & Exercises: These assignable activities give students opportunities to understand content more deeply and to practice applying content.

Building Teaching Skills: These assignments help students practice and strengthen skills that are essential to quality teaching. By analyzing and responding to real student and teacher artifacts and/or authentic classroom videos, students practice important teaching skills they will need when they enter real classrooms.

Case Studies: A diverse set of robust cases drawn from some of our best-selling books further expose students to the realities of teaching and offer valuable perspectives on common issues and challenges in education.

ONLINE PROFESSIONAL DEVELOPMENT

Pretests and Posttests to assess your knowledge of chapter content, along with exercises to enhance your understanding, can be found on MyEducationLab at www.myeducationlab.com.

Video Guides

Video clips on MyEducationLab selected for this chapter include *Teacher Discussion of Moon Phase Lessons* and *Investigating Goldfish—Parts 1, 2, 3,* and *4.*

Accessing the Videos

1. Go to the Homework and Exercises section in Chapter 4 of MyEducationLab to select and view videos for this chapter.
2. Videos might be viewed individually, by small groups of colleagues, or by the whole class.
3. As you watch each video, use the **Questions for Reflection** to guide your thoughts and note taking for personal use and group discussion.
4. Discuss your answers to the questions about each video with classmates.

Video: Teacher Discussion of Moon Phase Lessons

Overview

In this video we listen to the two fourth- and fifth-grade teachers we saw in the moon phase videos of Chapter 3 as they reflect on what they were trying to accomplish in the moon phase lessons.

Questions for Reflection

1. What examples of student records of observations do you see in the investigations of moon phases?

2. What evidence do you see that the 5-E model (or a similar model) forms the structure for the moon phase lessons?

Videos: Investigating Goldfish, Parts 1, 2, 3, and 4

The first three videos in the *Investigating Goldfish* video set follow kindergarten students as they investigate goldfish. In the fourth part, the classroom teacher reflects on her purposes for the lesson and the children's investigations. In this part, the teacher also discusses how the goldfish lesson followed the 5-E model of inquiry instruction.

Questions for Reflection

1. What Connecticut standards does the kindergarten teacher say the science lessons emphasize?
2. What questions did the teacher ask to engage the children in inquiry?
3. During the explore phase, what observations of the goldfish were made in response to the questions from the engage phase?
4. What conclusions about goldfish did the children reach in the explain phase of the lesson? What was the basis for the children's explanations?
5. How well do you think the teacher followed the 5-E model in designing and implementing the goldfish lesson?

Annenberg Videos

Video Series: Science K–6: Investigating Classrooms

Video: Completing the Circuit

To access Annenberg videos, follow the instructions given in the Online Professional Development section in Chapter 1 on page 26.

Simulations: Created by the IRIS Center at Vanderbilt University, these interactive simulations give hands-on practice at adapting instruction for a full spectrum of learners.

Student & Teacher Artifacts: Authentic student and teacher classroom artifacts are tied to course topics and offer practice in working with the actual types of materials encountered every day by teachers.

Individualized Study Plan: Your students have the opportunity to take pre- and post-tests before and after reading each chapter of the text. Their test results automatically generate a personalized study plan, identifying areas of the chapter they must reread to fully understand chapter concepts. They are also presented with interactive multimedia exercises to help ensure learning. The study plan is designed to help your students perform well on exams and to promote deep understanding of chapter content.

Readings: Specially selected, topically relevant articles from ASCD's renowned *Educational Leadership* journal expand and enrich students' perspectives on key issues and topics.

Other Resources

Lesson & Portfolio Builders: With this effective and easy-to-use tool, you can create, update, and share standards-based lesson plans and portfolios.

MyEducationLab is easy to assign, which is essential to providing the greatest benefit to your student. Visit www.myeducationlab.com for a demonstration of this exciting new online teaching resource.

Acknowledgments

Science education is a dynamic field. Application of new research findings, technological advances, and state and national initiatives result in a gradual evolution of learning theories, instructional and assessment strategies, state content, and inquiry standards. Application of these current ideas in practice occurs most directly in the classrooms of our nation's schools. Our goal in writing and revising this textbook is to provide you an accurate view of contemporary science education, with specific suggestions, guidelines, and examples as you prepare to teach science to children and early adolescents so they become scientifically literate citizens of the future.

The revisions and modifications incorporated in the tenth edition would not have been possible without insightful reviews of the previous edition and suggestions for improvement from our colleagues. We acknowledge and express our gratitude to the following reviewers: James D. Ellis, The University of Kansas; Wendy Frazier, George Mason University; Violetta Lien, Texas State University, San Marcos; Leann Steinmetz, University of Texas, San Antonio; and Senay Yasar, Arizona State University.

We want to thank the many editors at Pearson who have helped make this edition possible, especially Meredith Sarver Fossel and Bryce Bell, whose amiable advice and support has enriched the efficacy of this text. The creation of classroom video segments to illustrate the content of the text would have been impossible without Meredith's support and the talents of videographer Carl Harris. We are also grateful for our collaboration with Autumn Benson, which led to the on-line components of the text through MyEducationLab. We also wish to thank Mary Harlan, our supportive project manager at Pearson. For their help in bringing the book to production, we appreciate the assistance of Mary Tindle and Amy Gehl at S4Carlisle Publishing Services.

Contents

"Messing About in Science"

An Introduction

SCIENCE IS FUN! The geneticist Barbara McClintock was one of the few women in American science in the 1930s. When asked 40 years later why she chose science as a career, she said: "I did it because it was fun! I couldn't wait to get up in the morning. I never thought of it as 'science.'" (Judson, 1980, p.4). Expressions of the sheer enjoyment of science appear again and again in scientists' reflections on their work. In doing science, the excitement of pursuing the unknown, the joy of discovery, the achievement of elegance in an explanation, and the satisfaction of accomplishment are almost what matters most.

The developers of the Elementary Science Study (ESS) program drew on the adventures of Rat and Mole in The Wind in the Willows *to express the spirit of "fun" they wanted to incorporate into science for children. Rat and Mole found pure joy in "messing about in boats." The ESS developers sought to design science activities that would create similar feelings in young learners. Thus, they adopted "messing about in science" as a metaphor for their program activities. Written by Kenneth Grahame in the early 1900s,* The Wind in the Willows *still enchants young readers today. Read this delightful excerpt from Mole's first river adventure and see how Rat and Mole can serve as models for you and your students as you freely engage in scientific inquiry and encounter, once again, the wonders of science.*

As the narrative begins, Mole and Water Rat are eyeing each other cautiously across a great river.

"Hullo, Mole!" said the Water Rat.

"Hullo, Rat!" said the Mole.

"Would you like to come over?" inquired the Rat presently.

"Oh, it's all very well to *talk*," said the Mole, rather pettishly, he being new to a river and riverside life and its ways.

The Rat said nothing, but stooped and unfastened a rope and hauled on it; then lightly stepped into a little boat which the Mole had not observed. It was painted blue outside and white within, and was just the size for the two animals; and the Mole's whole heart went out to it at once, even though he did not yet fully understand its uses.

The Rat sculled smartly across and made fast. Then he held up his fore-paw as the Mole stepped gingerly down. "Lean on that!" he said. "Now then, step lively!" and the Mole to his surprise and rapture found himself actually seated in the stern of a real boat.

"This has been a wonderful day!" said he, as the Rat shoved off and took to the sculls again. "Do you know, I've never been in a boat before in all my life."

"What?" cried the Rat, open-mouthed. "Never been in a—you never—well I—what have you been doing, then?"

"Is it so nice as all that?" asked the Mole shyly, though he was quite prepared to believe it as he leant back in his seat and surveyed the cushions, the oars, the rowlocks, and all the fascinating fittings, and felt the boat sway lightly under him.

"Nice? It's the *only* thing," said the Water Rat solemnly, as he leant forward for his stroke. "Believe me, my young friend, there is *nothing*—absolutely *nothing*—half so much worth doing as simply messing about in boats. Simply messing," he went on dreamily: "messing—about—in—boats: messing—"

"Look ahead, Rat!" cried the Mole suddenly.

It was too late. The boat struck the bank full tilt. The dreamer, the joyous oarsman, lay on his back at the bottom of the boat, his heels in the air.

"—about in boats—or *with* boats," the Rat went on composedly, picking himself up with a pleasant laugh. "In or out of 'em, it doesn't matter. Nothing seems to matter, that's the charm of it. Whether you get away, or whether you don't, whether you arrive at your destination or whether you reach somewhere else, or whether you never get anywhere at all, you're always busy, and you never do anything in particular; and when you've done it there's always something else to do, and you can do it if you like, but you'd much better not. Look here! If you've really nothing else on hand this morning, supposing we drop down the river together, and have a long day of it?"

The Mole waggled his toes from sheer happiness, spread his chest with a sigh of full contentment, and leaned back blissfully into the soft cushions. "What a day I'm having!" he said. "Let us start at once!"

In the words of the Mole, "Let us start at once" to explore the *whats, whys,* and *hows* of teaching children science as inquiry and see for ourselves why children find such joy in messing about in science.

Source: From *The Wind in the Willows* (pp. 3–5), by Kenneth Grahame, 1908/1981, E. Shepard, illus. New York: Charles Scribner's Sons.

1

From *the earliest grades, students should experience science in a form that engages them in the active construction of ideas and explanations and enhances their opportunities to develop the abilities of doing science. Teaching science as* inquiry *provides teachers with the opportunity to develop student abilities and to enrich student understanding of science.*

(*National Science Education Standards*, National Research Council, 1996, p. 121)
(Emphasis added.)

Children, Science, and Inquiry: Some Preliminary Questions

CHILDREN ARE NATURALLY CURIOUS. Their curiosity shows itself as they watch and wonder about the world around them. If we are careful to listen to them, we can hear young children ask such questions as: *Do ants make tunnels under the ground? Where does the rain come from? Where does the puddle go after the rain?* As children grow and mature, their questions become more complex: *Why can astronauts go to the moon but not to the sun? Why does the moon look different every night but the sun always looks the same?*

A childlike curiosity remains in adult scientists, but it has erupted into a passion, an urge—even rage—to know and understand the universe (Judson, 1980). A lone scientist, driven primarily by an intense desire to know, might spend years researching different aspects of mosquitos: *How do mosquitos sense their prey? Do they smell it? If so, how does the olfactory sense work?* It may take a large team of scientists to answer some questions: *What is the moon's surface like? What are the causes of different cancers?*

How we as teachers view science and the learning of science is critical to the ways we build on and nurture our students' inborn curiosity. If the meaning teachers attach to science is "finding the right answer," they will probably focus on providing factual answers to children through a direct instruction and reading approach to science (Rowe, 1996, p. 164). Taught in this way, however, students are not likely to remain interested in questioning, collecting information, and generating explanations, because that is not the approach to science they encounter. On the other hand, if teachers view science as inquiry and children as constructive learners, they will want to teach science in ways that engage students in the active construction of ideas and explanations and enhance their abilities to inquire.

The vision of science education we present in this book is one in which all children have the opportunity to engage in science as inquiry—to explore and construct ideas and explanations of the natural world within a supportive community of learners (Loucks-Horsley, Hewson, Love, & Stiles, 1998). The realization of this vision for each of your students depends on what you choose to teach in science, how you teach and assess it, and how you arrange your classroom environment for learning. Solid scientific knowledge is necessary, but you don't need to be a science major to teach science effectively through an inquiry approach. What you do need is contagious curiosity, a willingness to explore with your students, and a commitment to personal excellence and continued learning. Your own science knowledge will grow as you teach.

This chapter provides background and guidance as you begin to explore teaching science as inquiry to children and adolescents. When you have finished studying this chapter, you should be able to answer these questions:

- *What do scientist do when they inquire? What should students learn to do when they inquire? What does it mean to teach science as inquiry?*

- *Why should children learn science from the earliest grades? What does it mean to be scientifically literate? What is the NCLB Act, and why is early science education important for this federal law?*

- *What are the National Science Education Standards? How are standards connected to curriculum, instruction, and assessment? What approach to science teaching and learning do national and state standards recommend?*

- *What is meant by conceptual understanding in science? How are facts, scientific concepts, principles, and theories interconnected?*

- *What are the tasks of scientific inquiry? What can we do to help students develop inquiry abilities?*

- *Why is it important for students to understand the nature of science and scientific inquiry? What are some specific understandings about science and inquiry that chilldren and adolescents should learn?*

- *How does technology differ from science? What are the steps in the technological design cycle? How can the tasks of inquiry and the technological design cycle be used together in classroom investigations?*

Science is a way of knowing the natural world. As a way of knowing, "science is both a body of knowledge that represents current understanding of [the natural world] and the process whereby that body of knowledge has been established and is being continually extended, refined, and revised" (Duschl, Schweingruber, & Shouse, 2007, p. 2). Understanding science requires an understanding of both elements.

Inquiry instruction is a method of teaching that parallels what scientists do when they do science. *What do scientists do when they do science?* No single "scientific method" invariably works for scientists. Rather, there are many methods. But scientists typically ask questions, find ways to investigate the questions through observations and experiments, collect and organize data, and construct models, theories, and explanations based on observational evidence, existing knowledge, and clear arguments. Scientists' imagination also plays a critical role in this process. Through participating in inquiry like scientists, students learn to raise questions, gather data through observation and investigation, acquire scientific knowledge, and use the knowledge in making sense of and explaining observational data.

Constructive Learning

Inquiry instruction supports a *constructivist* approach to learning science. According to this approach, learning is a construction based on the learner's prior knowledge. Students take in information from many sources, including personal discoveries and acquisition from teachers, books, videos, and other resources. But in constructing understanding, students must connect new information to their existing knowledge and experiences, reorganize

Scientific knowledge is always tentative; if a prediction fails, theories must be modified to fit new evidence.

their knowledge structures and assimilate new information to them, and construct meaning for themselves (Loucks-Horsley et al., 1998).

Although learners are the ones who construct knowledge, in inquiry instruction teachers are active in the process. Teachers provide for new experiences of the natural world, encourage wonder, help students form questions that can be investigated, help them plan investigation strategies, provide materials for investigations, interact with students as they investigate, assist them in organizing and making sense of the data, provide direct instruction on concepts, principles, and theories, and guide them in constructing scientific explanations.

Consider this example of an inquiry lesson in science in first grade.

An Invitation to Inquiry Science: Leaves

To begin an inquiry lesson on leaves, Debbie Wu talked with her first graders about trees, leaves, and the seasons. She pointed out that since this was the fall season, the trees were losing their leaves and the leaves were accumulating on the ground. She also discussed what season would come next and asked the children what the trees would look like when winter came, what the weather would be like then, and how they would dress for it. Through this dialogue, Ms. Wu helped the children begin to focus their curiosity and attention on particular aspects of the world. It also helped her to assess the children's prior knowledge and to adjust her instructional plans accordingly.

At the next science time Ms. Wu gave each child a small basket containing about 10 leaves. She arranged the class into pairs and instructed the children in each pair to place leaves from their baskets together into a pile on their table. "What do you notice about the leaves? What do you wonder about? What would you like to *investigate* about leaves?" Ms. Wu asked. The children observed the leaves and talked with each other and Ms. Wu about what they saw. Most children were first drawn to the different colors of the leaves. One child said, "Leaves are usually green. Why are these leaves brown and red?" A second child wondered why one part of a leaf was white and another part red. Another child noticed the "spines" of the leaves (the stem). "It's straight," the child exclaimed, feeling a stem, "with little bumps on it." This little observer also commented on the "bones" of the leaves (the veins) sticking out from the spines.

Acknowledging the children's questions and comments, Ms. Wu guided them to explore the questions: *Which leaves are alike? How are they alike? How do they differ from the other leaves?* After a discusson of how the children might investigate this question, the children sorted their piles of leaves into groups based on likenesses. As the children worked on sorting the leaves, Ms. Wu went around the classroom, observing the children, discussing the similarities and differences of the leaves with them, and providing assistance as needed. Since there were four different kinds of trees in the yard where the teacher gathered the leaves, most groups of children ended up with four piles of leaves (see Figure 1-1).

Back in a whole-class configuration, Ms. Wu reminded the children of the initial question, *How are leaves alike and different?* The students then discussed what they noticed about the leaves in the different piles and what their observations made them wonder. Building on their observations of leaves, Ms. Wu helped the children begin to recognize that leaves from the same tree are alike; they have similar properties such as similar shapes and structures of veins and points along their edges. Extending their generalization that leaves from the same tree are alike, the children also concluded that leaves from different trees have different shapes and structures of veins and edges.

Go to the Homework and Exercises section in Chapter 1 of MyEducationLab to read "A Conversation on Leaves," an interesting report on the observations and reflections of pre-school learners about leaves.

A variety of additional activities on leaves can be found on pages A-138 and A-139 of *Activities for Teaching Science as Inquiry,* the activities volume that accompanies this book.

Many topics in elementary school science can be addressed at any grade level, K–6. In early grades, emphasis is primarily on observaton and classification, as in the leaves lesson. In upper grades, emphasis on observation and classification continues, but activities that lead children to use their data as evidence in constructing complex explanations are typically added.

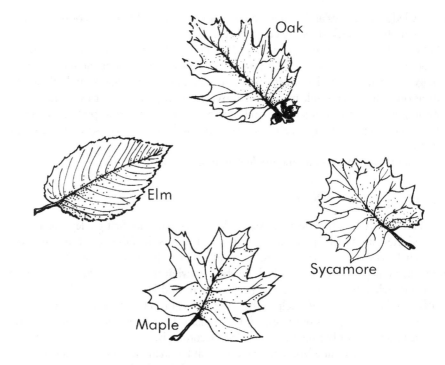

Features of the leaves lesson are found in most inquiry lessons in science. These features include:

* A question about some aspect of the natural world that could be investigated was asked.
* The children, aided by the teacher, found ways to gather observational data relevant to the question.
* The observations were then used as evidence to form generalizations, interpretations, and explanations to answer the question.

Through their own inquiry, the children were beginning to learn an approach to observing and understanding that would serve them well as they watched and wondered about the world. Teachers of science in grades K–8 should make a coordinated effort to teach science concepts and inquiry processes simultaneously.

Are you beginning to see the importance of inquiry experiences for children? Can you see yourself incorporating genuine inquiry into your own science lessons?

Why Should Science Be Taught in Elementary School?

In the modern world, some knowledge of science is essential for everyone (Duschl et al., 2007). But, why should students begin to learn science in the elementary grades? There are several reasons to support early science education.

Learning to Think and Understand

Developing understanding in science involves various processes of inquiry, including observing, raising questions, engaging in meaningful investigations, combining, comparing, and reflecting on data, and using existing knowledge to make sense of what is seen. Jean

* What were the questions investigated by the children in the lessons on leaves?
* What did they do to gather data relevant to these questions?
* What generalization did they develop?
* How were the generalizations connected to the children's observational evidence?
* How did the children use the new generalization to answer the questions raised?

Piaget has shown that such processes of thinking develop gradually over a long period of time from infancy through adolescence. Piaget was concerned with the spontaneous development of thought. Contemporary research by educators and psychologists highlights the important contribution that interactions with peers, teachers, and others can make in the development of thinking. Learning to think scientifically and to understand the scientific view of the natural world takes time. Science experiences from the earliest grades are essential for helping students learn to think and understand.

Scientific Literacy

A second reason to teach science in elementary school is to begin early to build *scientific literacy*. Some of your students will likely choose to work in a scientific, technical, or health-care profession, but *all* of them will need to be scientifically literate to take an active role in recognizing problems, contributing to solutions, and making informed decisions about local, state, national, and global issues.

The *National Science Education Standards* (National Research Council, 1996) define **scientific literacy** as

> the knowledge and understanding of scientific concepts and processes required for personal decision-making, participation in civic and cultural affairs, and economic productivity. (p. 22)

According to the *National Science Education Standards* (National Research Council 1996, p. 114), "Lifelong scientific literacy begins with understandings, attitudes, and values established in the earliest years."

Science Education and National Concerns

Many people believe that what happens in elementary science today can have potentially dramatic effects, not only on the lives of children, but also on the economic future of our

Go to the Homework and Exercises section in Chapter 1 of MyEducationLab to read the "Science Literacy for All in the 21st Century" article detailing why science literacy is such an important goal for our nation.

"Lifelong scientific literacy begins with understandings, attitudes, and values established in the earliest years." (National Science Education Standards, National Research Council, 1996, p. 114)

nation. A prestigious panel sponsored by the National Academies of Science produced a report, *Rising Above the Gathering Storm* (National Academies of Science, 2006), that details some of the global issues our nation faces.

The report noted that the "high quality of life" in the United States, "our national security, and our hope that our children and grandchildren will inherit ever-greater opportunities" is derived, in large part, from "the steady stream of scientific and technological innovations" produced in this country since World War II. But there are indications that our global leadership position in science and technology is changing. Among the findings of the committee are these:

- Since the early 1990s, the United States has become a net importer of high-technology products.
- Other nations are graduating considerably more engineers, computer scientists, and information technologists than the United States.
- Lower labor costs and the availability of highly trained scientists and engineers have led to the location of factories by U.S. companies in foreign countries and the outsourcing of many jobs.
- International assessments in math and science indicate that U.S. K–12 students lag behind students from other countries.

In response to such findings, the committee recommended, among other things, that the United States vastly improve science and math education to increase the pool of students prepared to choose science as a career. Improving science and math education must begin in the early grades.

Language Literacy and Mathematics Competency

Science provides a rich context for children to apply and further develop their language and mathematics skills. In the process of acquiring information, students have opportunities to improve the skills needed in reading expository texts. For example, children learn to apply their skills of reading expository texts as they read about the many interesting treatments of science in trade books and children's literature (see Figure 1-2). Skills of reading in the content area are not only necessary in acquiring new information, they are essential in preparing for and taking standardized tests in reading, science, and other content areas.

Writing on prepared observations sheets and in science journals, editing collaboratively, refining procedures, and rewriting at each stage of the inquiry process can be an effective ways to enhance inquiry and to improve writing skills (Champagne & Kouba, 2000).

Science can also provide a context in which children can apply and practice their math skills, such as counting, estimating, measuring, putting data into tables, and constructing and interpreting graphs.

Early Science and the NCLB Legislation

Responding to growing concerns about the quality of education for all students in our nation, Congress passed the *No Child Left Behind* (NCLB) Act in 2001. Science education was an important part of this legislation. According to the NCLB Act, by the 2007–2008 school year, every state had to administer annual assessments of reading, math, and science at elementary, middle school, and high school levels. Results of these assessments provide information for determinations of whether schools are demonstrating adequate

Teachers of science at all grades, K–8, need to make a coordinated push—with teachers of mathematics and literacy—to connect science, math, and language arts instruction at all grades.

Currently, only the results of reading and math tests are used in the adequate yearly progress determinations at the federal level, but congressional leaders periodically present addendums to the NCLB Act that would include science in demonstrations of AYP. However, some states already include the results of the science tests in high-stakes evaluations of students and teachers.

Children's Literature and Science

There are many wonderful books that connect science and literacy. For example, when studying *astronomy* in science, read some of the following books during language arts time.

A cricket looks for another insect that is just like himself. This and other Eric Carle books, The Very Hungry Caterpillar, The Very Busy Spider, *and* The Very Clumsy Click Beetle, *delight children with surprising interactive elements. All of these stories launch children into wanting to find out more about insects, patterns, and the natural environments where survival is dependent on interdependency.*

- *Follow the Drinking Gourd* by Jeanette Winter (Grades K–6). Runaway slaves followed the "Drinking Gourd," another name for the Big Dipper, north to Canada and freedom. In science, children can learn how to use the Big Dipper to tell time and find the North Star.

- *The Magic School Bus Lost in the Solar System* by Joanna Cole (Grades K–6). A fantasy trip to the moon, sun, and planets, noting their colors, sizes, and unique features. In science, construct scale models of the solar system and charts of planetary features.

- *Sky Songs* by Myra Cohn Livingston (Grades 5–12). Poems about various aspects of the sky.

- *To Space and Back* by Sally Ride with Susan Okie (Grades 4–7). An astronaut's fascinating description of what it's like to travel in space—to live and work in conditions unlike anything we know on earth. In science, students can access and study NASA's website, including real-time data.

- *The Way to Start a Day* by Byrd Baylor (Grades 3–7). The many ways people of the world have celebrated the dawn. In science, construct models of the earth-sun system that explain why the sun rises each morning. Also, observe the changing positions of sunrise and sunset throughout the seasons.

Figure 1-2 Children's literature connections to science.

Source: "Children's literature connections to science" is based on material in the Great Explorations in Math and Science (GEMS) teacher's handbook entitled *Once Upon a GEMS Guide: Connecting Young People's Literature to Great Explorations in Math and Science,* copyright by The Regents of the University of California, and is used with permission. The GEMS series includes more than 70 teacher's guides and handbooks for preschool through eighth grade, available from: LHS GEMS, Lawrence Hall of Science, University of California, Berkeley, CA 94720-5200. (510) 642-7771. For more information, visit our website at www.lhsgems.org

---

yearly progress (AYP) toward the goal of 100% proficiency for all students. Schools that do not maintain adequate yearly progress are subject to severe sanctions. Many believe that the best way to prepare elementary and middle school students for the science portion of these statewide examinations is a coordinated K–8 effort built around inquiry approaches to science.

You will likely have some students with disabilities and students who are English Language Learners (ELLs) in your inclusion classroom. Although different learning pathways may be necessary for some individuals, the goals of science instruction are the same for all students. With the exception that about 30% of students with special needs take an alternative form of the test, according to the NCLB, most students with special needs must take the same statewide assessments as regular education students. Assisting all learners to achieve proficiency in science, as well as in language, mathematics, and other subjects, is a national challenge.

What do you think? Do you agree that early experiences in science are essential for children today?

Ways to modify science activities and instruction for students with disabilities and for ELL students are discussed in Chapter 10.

U.S. Science Education: Where Have We Been, Where Are We Now, Where Are We Going?

Where Have We Been in Science Education?

Off and on since at least the 1950s, national concern has focused on the quality of U.S. science education. An early stimulus to these concerns was the successful launching of an earth-orbiting satellite, *Sputnik*, by the Russians in 1957. In response to *Sputnik*, the federal government began to commit more and more tax money to the development of exemplary science programs in the United States.

Most of the newly developed science programs were widely known by acronyms. At the elementary school level, the most successful programs funded by the National Science Foundation (NSF) were SAPA (Science—A Process Approach), SCIS (Science Curriculum Improvement Study), and ESS (Elementary Science Study). These programs, which were developed beginning in the 1960s, represent three very different approaches to science education. SAPA focused on the processes involved in doing science, SCIS on broad concepts for organizing scientific ideas, and ESS on investigation as a way to develop science knowledge.

The various "alphabet soup" programs were widely used in school districts across the nation. But it was the common, hands-on spirit of these new approaches to learning science that most influenced science education in the 1960s, 1970s, and 1980s. In these federally funded elementary science programs students did not just read about science, they did science. Science was more than a noun; it was also a verb—*sciencing*.

The late 1980s saw national movements toward establishing common goals and standards of excellence for science education and other subjects. The American Association for the Advancement of Science (AAAS) established Project 2061 to begin to explore what all U.S. students should know and be able to do in science in the 21st century. The year 2061 marks the next return of Halley's comet to our region of the solar system. By including this distant date in the project title, AAAS implied that it intended to take a very long view indeed in determining what students will need to know and be able to do to be scientifically literate throughout a new century.

Project 2061 published a number of pivotal documents, including *Science for All Americans* (Rutherford & Ahlgren, 1990), *Benchmarks for Science Literacy* (AAAS, 1993), and the *Atlas of Science Literacy*, *Volume 1* (AAAS, 2001) Volume 2 (2007). These documents have effectively expressed and clarified ideas about the nature and importance of science and science teaching. They have also laid the foundation for the development of national standards for science education.

Where Are We Now in Science Education?

Building on the work of Project 2061 and other groups, a distinguished panel coordinated by the National Research Council (NRC) worked on standards for science education throughout the early 1990s. In 1996, the *National Science Education Standards* (NSES) were published. The NSES offer the U.S. public a coherent vision of what it means to be scientifically literate.

There are six categories of standards in the *National Science Education Standards*, including Science Content Standards, Assessment Standards, Teaching Standards, Professional Development Standards, Science Education Program Standards, and Science Education System Standards. For teachers, the heart of the standards is the Science Content Standards, which include (1) standards related to conceptual knowledge and under-

You can read the *National Science Education Standards* on the website of the National Academies Press. For the URL to access the standards, see Table 1-1.

standing in physical science, life science, and earth and space science; (2) specific abilities of scientific inquiry; and (3) understandings about the nature of scientific inquiry.

The *National Science Education Standards* do not prescribe curriculum; that is a state and local responsibility. Rather, they describe what all students must understand and be able to do in science as a result of their cumulative learning experiences.

The central message that the NSES content standards convey, and the other types of standards support, is that students should be engaged in an *inquiry* approach to learning science that basically parallels the procedures scientists use and the attitudes they display in doing science. The standards emphasize that inquiry can involve many different approaches to science instruction, including hands-on–minds-on investigations, reading books, using Internet resources, talking and listening to scientists and teachers, and direct teacher instruction on the concepts, principles, and procedures of science. A common feature of all inquiry methods of instruction is a shift from a teacher-centered to a student-centered classroom. Through engaging in the many forms of inquiry, students learn how to investigate on their own and to work cooperatively with others. They learn important science knowledge and the process of generating science knowledge. And, they learn to use science knowledge in understanding the objects, organisms, and events in their environments. It is clear why the *National Science Education Standards* have declared, "inquiry into authentic questions generated from student experience is the central strategy for teaching science" (National Research Council, 1996, p. 31).

Where Are We Going in Science Education?

Although much has been accomplished in science education, much remains to be done. Recently, the National Research Council commissioned a distinguished panel chaired by science educator Richard Duschl to examine the state of science education in elementary and middle schools in our nation. In the report, *Taking Science to School: Learning and Teaching Science in Grades K–8* (Duschl et al., 2007), the panel critiqued and evaluated the standards movement and made recommendations about science education for the future. The panel also reviewed contemporary studies from psychologists and educators about how children develop understanding in science. Among the recommendations of the committee was the call to reduce the K–12 science content taught and to emphasize fewer well-chosen core concepts to focus more on understanding rather than just accumulating knowledge.

The National Science Teachers Association (NSTA) has recently initiated a new project, *Science Anchors,* that focuses on reducing the broad range of science topics and skills taught in the schools. Science Anchors seeks to help bolster student achievement in science by emphasizing the essential skills and topics in science that must be taught, given the limited amount of time teachers have with students. Achieving this objective will aid all of our nation's education stakeholders in the alignment of curriculum, instruction, and assessment practices and help teachers better manage their instruction, making teaching and learning more effective and efficient.

Research and best practices clearly show the importance of an inquiry approach to science teaching and learning. Yet many teachers are more comfortable with traditional approaches to science instruction that rely largely on telling and reading about science. The implementation of new approaches to science depends now on teachers like you. Will you join the growing body of teachers who are committed to the idea that children are constructive learners and learn best through approaches that involve them in doing science?

The No Child Left Behind Act requires states to have high-quality state standards in science. The statewide tests administered in each state are based on that state's standards. In most cases, state science standards reflect the *National Science Education Standards,* but go well beyond them in specificity and detail. You will be expected to use the standards in your state in planning instruction, guiding learning, and preparing students for statewide tests.

TABLE 1-1 NATIONAL SCIENCE EDUCATION REFORM PROJECTS

Documents	Description
Science for All Americans Project 2061 http://www.project2061.org/	• describes the nature of science and technology, including historical perspectives and their impact on society • describes understandings and ways of thinking that are essential for all citizens
Benchmarks for Science Literacy Project 2061 http://www.project2061.org/	• builds on *Science for All Americans* • states what all students should know and be able to do in science by the end of grades 2, 5, 8, and 12
Atlas of Science Literacy, Volumes 1 and 2 Project 2061 http://www.project2061.org/	• presents conceptual strand maps that show how K–12 students' understanding at the ideas and skills that lead to scientific literacy interconnect
National Science Education Standards National Research Council http://www.nap.edu/catalog.php?record_id=4962	• defines science education standards for science content, teaching, professional development, assessment, programs, and systems • emphasizes scientific literacy • focuses on inquiry approaches to teaching
Inquiry and the National Science Education Standards National Research Council http://www.nap.edu/catalog.php?record_id=9596	• provides a learning research foundation for the science standards • serves as a companion volume to the science standards
Federal No Child Left Behind Act of 2001 http://www.ed.gov/nclb/landing.jhtml	• requires that states must have their own standards and statewide assessments
Rising Above the Gathering Storm (2006) National Academies of Science http://www.nap.edu/catalog/11463.html	• provides a view of science in the national economy and the growing precariousness of our nation's leadership in the global economy • recommends that U.S. K–12 science and math education be vastly improved
For state standards and released tests, see state education agencies or departments. You can access links to many state standards and released tests through the Chapter 1 Resources for this text at http://www.prenhall.com/bass	• provides access to state standards • provides access to released tests from different states
Duschl, R. S., Schweingruber, H. A., & Shouse A. W. (2007). *Taking Science to School: Learning and Teaching Science in Grades K-8.* Washington, DC: National Academies Press, http://www.nap.edu/catalog/11625.html	• provides a critique and evaluation of the science standards movement • presents new research on how children learn science • suggests that science content should be further reduced to concentrate only on core conceptualizations in science

Direct links to the URLs in Table 1-1 are given in Chapter 1 of MyEducationLab.

Table 1-1 briefly describes several reform programs and documents that can impact the "whats and hows" of your science education program. For additional information, you are invited to access the Internet sites listed in Table 1-1.

What Shall We Teach in Science?

A synthesis of recommendations by science education leaders (Bybee et al., 1989; Duschl et al., 2007; National Research Council, 1996; National Research Council, 2000) suggests that major outcomes of science instruction should include the following goals or proficiencies:

- *Proficiency 1: Conceptual knowledge and understanding in science.* Students should acquire facts, build organized and meaningful conceptual structures, and use these conceptual structures in interpreting observations and constructing theories and explanations (Duschl et al., 2007, p. 37).
- *Proficiency 2: Abilities to carry out scientific inquiries.* Students should learn to gather, organize, and communicate observational data and use the data in developing knowledge, forming explanations, and answering questions.
- *Proficiency 3: Understandings about the nature of science and scientific inquiry.* Students should understand science as a way of knowing, the nature of scientific knowledge, and the connections between theory and evidence in science (Duschl et al., 2007, p. 37).

Duschl and his colleagues have emphasized that these proficiencies are not independent but should always be interconnected in learning science. We will examine each of these major science proficiencies in the following sections.

Proficiency 1: Conceptual Knowledge and Understanding in Science

As they engage in inquiry, students develop conceptual knowledge and understanding in science. The specific knowledge and understandings in physical science, life science, and earth and space science that elementary and middle school students should achieve are identified in national and state science standards.

Knowledge and understanding in science are composed of facts, concepts, principles or laws, models, theories, and explanations (National Research Council, 1996; Duschl et al., 2007).

Facts. A **fact,** in science, is a statement about an observation that has been repeatedly confirmed. Facts are not mere collections of random observations of the world. We make observations and generate facts selectively, based on prior knowledge and assumptions about what is valuable and what might be disregarded.

Concepts. **Concepts** are abstract ideas derived from experience around which new experiences may be organized. Concepts go beyond observations and facts and reflect the larger *ideas* of science. By reducing many observations to fewer categories, concepts bring a measure of coherence and simplicity to the world. Concepts are developed gradually, from many experiences and reflections on them.

Examples of concepts encountered in elementary science include stems and veins of leaves, magnets, magnetic poles, birds, minerals, cotyledons, and light reflection. Each of these concepts is a class in which the members of the class have some common attributes. Birds, for example, have two legs, wings, and feathers. Some birds lay eggs in nests and live in trees. Some birds, but not all, fly. Concepts enable us to interconnect past experiences so that we can better use them to begin to make sense of new experiences.

From the constructivist viewpoint, concepts are not simply passed from teachers or books to students; in order to *understand* a concept, children must be actively engaged in making sense of their experiences. Understanding of concepts begins to take place as students actively learn and use them to guide their own observations and extend their prior knowledge.

Principles. **Principles** are ideas about relationships among concepts. They are formed from investigations and observations of a few situations and generalized through inductive reasoning to other similar events and situations. In reasoning inductively, learners move from particular instances to generalizations about all cases.

As an example of principles, consider a science principle related to how things change with heat. Expanding (getting larger), contracting (getting smaller), hot (having a high temperature), and cold (having a low temperature) are all concepts in science (Vitale & Romance, 2000). These concepts are related to one another in the principle "objects expand when heated and contract when cooled." This relationship might be found in individual investigations and then generalized to a universal principle that holds in all cases. This principle can be used to explain, for instance, why concrete sidewalks are poured in sections with "expansion gaps" between the sections.

Well-established principles in science are sometimes referred to as *laws*, though there are no clear-cut guidelines in science for elevating principles to the status of laws. Examples of laws in science include the laws of reflection and refraction of light, the laws of motion, and the law of gravity.

Students should be guided to organize facts, concepts, and principles into conceptual structures or networks. Conceptual structures are important to students in developing theories and explanations of what is seen in the natural world.

Theories. In everyday language, people sometimes say, "I have a theory about that," or "Well, that's only a theory, not a fact." In the language of science and science education, the term **theory** has two, more precise, meanings. First, a scientific theory is an explanation of some aspect of the natural world that has undergone considerable testing and refinement. Examples of theories in this sense include Newton's theory of motion, the theory of light, and the theory of plate tectonics. Scientific theories generally use existing conceptual structures. But sometimes, new theories require the construction of new concepts and principles.

In the second meaning, theories are tentative explanations that serve to make observations of the world meaningful. Children of all ages watch the world, wonder about what they see, and form "theories" that help them make sense of what they encounter.

For example, in the leaves lesson described earlier in this chapter, young children theorized that leaves are like animals and have spines and bones. As another example, many, if not most, early grade children observe the earth around them, perceive that it is flat, and theorize that they live on a flat earth. It will take careful instruction, with evidence from various sources, such as photographs from space, to convince them that their flat-earth theory is unsatisfactory and that the earth is spherical, with plains, hills, valleys, mountains, and canyons scattered about on its surface.

Models. Scientists find that the use of models often makes it easier to think about physical reality. A **model** is a representation of objects and interactions in a physical system. Types of models include *physical models* (such as a model airplane or a model of the arrangement of planets and the sun in our solar system), *mathematical models* (such as an equation for principles of levers and balances), and *propositional models* (such as a set of rules for how magnets interact with other magnets and with different kinds of materials).

Through science instruction, teachers help students develop understanding by integrating facts, concepts, principles, models, and theories into coherent conceptual structures. An example of an inquiry approach to helping students construct integrated networks of the properties of water is given next.

Investigations will sometimes show that there are exceptions to a principle. For example, contrary to the general principle that materials expand when heated and contract when cooled, water expands rather than contracts when it is cooled to its freezing point. That is why automobile radiators must have antifreeze added—to prevent damage that would be caused by expansion if water in the radiator froze.

A glossary containing definitions of important terms used in this chapter can be found on MyEducationLab.

Seven-year old Rick stared out the car window for mile after mile as his family traveled across the endless plains of the American southwest. Finally he said, "The earth really is round, isn't it?" He was attempting to accommodate his own perceptions that the earth is flat with the theory of a round earth presented to him in school.

Activity 1-1: Observations of Water Phenomena

1. Fill a 30 ml medicine cup all the way to the top with water. Use a dropper to add water drop by drop to the cup until it is heaping full and starts to overflow. How many drops of water from a dropper do you think you can add to the medicine cup before it overflows? Make a prediction. Try it and see. What does the surface of the water look like as drops are added? What happens to each drop of water as it is added to the cup? What do you observe happening when the water overflows the rim?

2. Use the dropper to add some water back into the cup so that it is almost ready to overflow again. How many paper clips do you think you can add to the filled medicine cup before it overflows? Make a prediction. Now, gently slide paper clips into the cup, one at a time down the edge of the cup. How many paper clips could you put in the water?

3. How do you explain your observations of the behavior of water in these two cases?

Building Conceptual Understanding: Properties of Water. Scientific understanding begins with observations of the real world. Through engaging in activities with water, children have opportunities to make many new observations and learn many new facts, as well as to raise questions, generate new conceptual knowledge, and form some explanations to answer their questions. Activity 1-1 provides an example of an investigation of the properties of water. This investigation may be new to you. Before reading on, obtain the necessary materials and try this activity for yourself.

The water drop investigation supports NSES standards about properties of objects and materials, as is shown in the accompanying NSES box.

Hands-on investigations like these arouse our curiosity, raise our interest level, and increase our motivation to learn. What did you observe and what *facts* did you learn about water from Activity 1-1? It is a fact, for example, that when water is added drop by drop to a small plastic medicine cup, the water will tend to heap up a surprising amount before it starts to spill over the edge of the cup. It is also a fact that as many as 30 paper clips can be

    See *Activities for Teaching Science as Inquiry,* pages A-19–A-27 for a variety of additional activities for children on properties of water.

gently slid along the edge into a filled cup without the water overflowing. Such facts are the data or products of our observations that we organize and attempt to explain. How would you explain this puzzling behavior of water?

Children spontaneously form theories to explain what they see in the world. In a field test of an ESS unit called Kitchen Physics, some sixth-grade children explained the heaping effect of water by theorizing that water is "grabby" or "sticky." According to the grabbiness model of heaping, drops of water added to a cup *grab* on to or *stick* to water already in the cup, thus allowing the water to "heap."

Educational research indicates that teachers should recognize children's explanations and treat them with respect but go beyond them by providing learners with scientific explanations (Duschl et al., 2007). The scientific explanation for heaping is not so very different from the children's grabbiness explanation, but it is more powerful. Scientists model water as tiny particles (molecules) that attract or bond to one another. The attractive bonds between water particles account for heaping. Water heaps up in a cup until the gravitational forces pulling on the water that is above the rim of the cup overcome the attractive forces of the water particles for one another.

Since the children's concept of "grabbiness" comes close to capturing the essence of the bond theory, teachers can build on the children's conception when teaching them the scientific theory of attractive bonds between particles of the liquid.

Many other activities about the properties of water can be used to deepen and extend the knowledge and understanding of children about the properties of liquids. Activity 1-2 illustrates some additional facts about the properties of water. Before reading on, obtain the necessary materials, do this activity for yourself, and generate a possible explanation for what you observe.

To explain why water drops bead up on wax paper and spread out on aluminum foil, two concepts—cohesive bonds and adhesive bonds—are needed. *Cohesive bonds* bind water drops to one another; *adhesive bonds* bind water drops to different surfaces, such as wax paper or aluminum foil. Applying these new principles of cohesive and adhesive bonds, we might theorize that water beads up on wax paper because the cohesive forces within drops are greater than the adhesive forces between the drops and the wax paper. In contrast, water spreads out on aluminum foil because the adhesive forces between water drops and the aluminum are greater than the cohesive forces within the drops. Children might come up with this theory on their own. However, children's theories need to be refined and extended through instruction, including instruction on scientific terms. Just remember to build on concepts already developed and stay close to the observations of the real world made in investigations.

"Inventing hypotheses or theories to imagine how the world works and then figuring out how they can be put to the test of reality is as creative as writing poetry, composing music, or designing skyscrapers."

Science for All Americans, Rutherford and Ahlgren, 1989

Water drop phenomena may also be modeled in terms of *the skinlike* effect at the surface of a container or drop of water. Water acts as if it has a skin across its surface. Water heaps up in a medicine cup until the skin of the water becomes stretched too much and breaks. This skin like effect has been called *surface tension*; the term *tension* is a British term for force. Surface tension is a force acting at the surface of a container or drop of water.

Activity 1-2: Water Drops on Different Surfaces

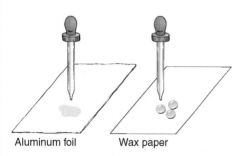

Aluminum foil   Wax paper

Using a dropper, put drops of water on wax paper and aluminum foil, as in the illustration. Make large drops and small drops. How do drops of water on wax paper compare with those on aluminum foil? What do the drops look like? Can you lead a drop around with a toothpick on each surface? What happens to small drops of water when led to interact with other drops of water on wax paper? What happens when you try to combine small drops of water on aluminum foil?

How can you explain your observations of what happens to water drops on the different surfaces?

TABLE 1-2 ANALYZING SCIENCE TOPICS IN TERMS OF FACTS, CONCEPTS, PRINCIPLES, AND THEORIES		
Knowledge Component	**Definition**	**Examples Related to Water**
Facts	objectively confirmed statements about observable objects or events	water heaps in medicine cups and beads up on wax paper
Concepts	classes of things or ideas that serve in the organization of experiences	bonds between particles, adhesion, cohesion
Principles	generalizations about the relationships among concepts	the closer the water particles, the stronger the bonds
Theories	networks of terms, assumptions, concepts, principles, and inferences that can be used to form tentative explanations of observations	at the surface of water the particles bond, forming a skinlike effect that can be applied to explain heaping and beading

Table 1-2 summarizes how scientific knowledge about water can be analyzed in terms of facts, concepts, principles, and theories.

Proficiency 2: Abilities to Carry Out Scientific Inquiry

Science is both a body of knowledge and a way of knowing (Duschl et al., 2007). Scientific inquiry—asking questions, gathering and analyzing observational data, and using the data as evidence in forming theories and building explanations—provides the basis for scientific knowledge. Thus, scientific inquiry and conceptual knowledge in science are intimately linked.

The *National Science Education Standards* (National Research Council, 1996) have captured the way that scientists inquire in a set of inquiry tasks that students should learn. Through engaging in scientific inquiry, students should learn to:

- *Ask a question about objects, organisms, and events in the environment.* In elementary and middle school science, questions should come (in so far as possible) from the experiences and activities of learners. Children need ample time to simply watch and wonder about the world around them—to observe and compare leaves, tend to mealworms, watch ants in their underground homes, find out about air, observe weather changes, and on and on. It is from such experiences that interesting and productive questions about the natural world can be generated.
- *Plan and conduct a simple investigation.* When inquiring scientifically, children investigate to gather evidence to use in answering their questions. In their investigations, children might observe what things are like or what is happening within a system, collect specimens for analysis, or do experiments (American Association for the Advancement of Science, 1993).
- *Use appropriate tools and techniques to gather data.* As students investigate, they use simple tools, such as thermometers, rulers and meter sticks, and hand lenses, and practice simple skills, such as observing, measuring, recording data, graphing, inferring, and predicting.
- *Use evidence and scientific knowledge to develop explanations.* As they develop explanations to answer their questions, children should reflect on the evidence they obtained and draw on existing and developing scientific knowledge to support their thinking. Most children have personal theories and explanations of objects, organisms, and

Chapter 2 describes and provides examples of three types of investigations—descriptive, classificatory, and experimental investigations—that students should understand and be able to carry out.

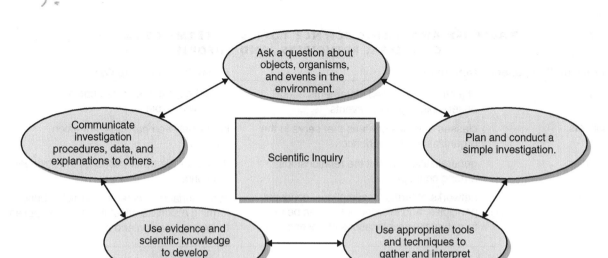

Figure 1-3   Tasks of scientific inquiry.

events but will need some degree of assistance from teachers in constructing scientific explanations.

- *Communicate investigations, data, and explanations to others.* Throughout the inquiry process, students engage in discourse with one another and their teachers about questions, investigations, findings, and explanations. Students should use different means, including speaking, writing, and drawing to represent and communicate their procedures, observations and data, and explanations to others.

Figure 1-3 graphically depicts the tasks of scientific inquiry.

The NSES (National Research Council, 1996, p. 121) emphasize that the inquiry tasks of Figure 1-3 should not be interpreted as the "scientific method." The tasks suggest some common characteristics of scientific investigations and a logical progression, but they do not imply a rigid approach to solving problems. Like inquiry in scientists' studies of the natural world, inquiry in elementary and middle school science classes can take many forms, but each form generally involves some level of use of each of these inquiry tasks.

In the various chapters of this book and in the video series that accompanies the book, we will be examining what you can do to help children and adolescents develop these tasks of inquiry. What you can do to help them form questions for inquiry is treated in the following section.

Questions for Investigations

The very first task in inquiry, according to the *National Science Education Standards,* is to ask a simple question about objects, living things, and events in the environment. In this stage, inquiry can be initiated from a wide range of activities (National Research Council, 1996, p. 33):

- Something puzzling that children may notice in their everyday experiences may trigger inquiry.
- Some questions for inquiry grow out of hands-on activities involving observations, data collection, data organization, and reflection.

"Full inquiry involves asking a simple question, completing an investigation, answering the question, and presenting the results to others."

(*National Science Education Standards,* National Research Council, 1996, p. 122)

"Scientific inquiry is not easily described apart from the context of particular investigations. There simply is no fixed set of steps that scientists always follow, no one path that leads them unerringly to scientific knowledge."

(Rutherford and Ahlgren, 1990, p. 5)

- Questions may come from the critical analysis of information gathered from books, CD-ROMs, the Internet, and other sources.
- Novel or discrepant events demonstrated by the teacher or presented through pictures and videos may also generate questions for inquiry.
- Questions might even be raised in lecture, if they are authentic and relate to the students' own experiences.

Children wonder about many things, and they can ask many questions. But which questions can be investigated through their own activities? A teacher brings several hundred earthworms into his fourth-grade classroom. He places them in some soil on paper plates and distributes the plates to each small group in the class. Some students let the earthworms crawl on a finger, while some others find the earthworms "yucky" and will not touch them. But all are curious and thoughtful. Wondering about how they move, one child says, "I think they are made up of two parts. One part moves forward and then pulls the second part up to it." The teacher asks, *"Which part has the head, and which part has the tail?"* Another child observes that the earthworms use their "legs" to move forward. *"Are they really legs? How could we find out?"* asks the teacher. "We could look in a book," one child suggests. "Yes, but how else could we find out? *What could we do on our own to find out if earthworms have legs?"* A child says, "We could use a hand lens to watch them move and see how they use their legs."

In this classroom episode, curiosity grows into *wonder*, wonder results in *thinking*, and, with the teacher's assistance, thinking *produces new questions* that can be investigated. Children can learn to improve their questioning skills. As you emphasize the importance of questions for investigations, ask the students how they could investigate the questions they ask. Also guide them to reformulate some of the questions they ask, and provide them many good models of scientific questions.

Figure 1-4 describes some characteristics of good questions for initiating scientific inquiry.

Following is an example of an inquiry lesson in which children use the tasks of scientific inquiry as they discover facts and build concepts and principles about magnets and how they interact with different materials

An Invitation to Inquiry Science: Magnetic Interactions

To begin a lesson on magnets, Julie Clark arranged her second-grade class in cooperative learning groups and gave each group sets of materials consisting of magnets and an assortment of

Teaching for scientific literacy includes helping students "ask, find, or determine answers to questions derived from curiosity about everyday experiences."

(National Research Council, 1996, p. 22)

Good questions for initiating inquiry:

- lead to interesting new knowledge about the world
- lead to a deeper understanding of the nature of science and scientific inquiry
- require students to gather observable evidence and use it with developing knowledge to generate answers
- require a variety of science processes to answer them
- may require students to observe, compare, and classify objects and organisms
- may require students to infer and predict
- may require students to identify and measure variables
- may require controlled experiments

Figure 1-4 Characteristics of good questions for initiating inquiry.

metal and nonmetal objects. She challenged the students to find out how magnets interact with each other and with the various objects.

The curious children eagerly explored the magnets and materials. Holding up two magnets, one surprised child said, "Look, Ms. Clark, these push apart and they are not even touching." Another child noted, "Put them like this and they come together." "It won't pick this thing up," a third child observed. Going beyond the materials given to them, several children found that the magnets would stick to the metal filing cabinet, but not to the teacher's wooden desk. One surprised child observed that the magnets did not attract a cola can. Another child explained, "The cola can is not made of iron." Through their observations and descriptions, the children were learning many new *facts* about magnets and magnetic interactions.

Ms. Clark then asked the children what they wondered about magnets and what they wanted to find out about them. Among the things the children wanted to know were: *What are magnets? Why do they stick to some things?* From the children's watching and wondering, Ms. Clark helped them form a question that they could investigate: *How do magnets interact with one another and with other materials?*

To address this question, the children decided they should test all of their various materials to find out if they were attracted to a magnet. While the children worked on this question, Ms. Clark circulated among the small groups, asking and answering questions, supplying terms, and suggesting some procedures. To help the students organize their findings and communicate them to others, she challenged them to sort their materials into groups according to how they interacted with magnets. As she went about the room, she asked each group of students to explain how they had sorted the objects. Some children had grouped the objects by color or size. After some prompting, these children began to understand how to classify the objects, not by their more obvious attributes but by the ways they interacted with the magnets. Most children ended up with two piles: things that were attracted to a magnet and things that were not attracted to a magnet.

In a whole-class discussion, Ms. Clark asked the children to report what they had found out. Collectively, the children's knowledge from their explorations of magnets and magnetic interactions was quite complete. To summarize the children's observations and discussion about how magnets interact with other magnets and with various materials, Ms. Clark wrote these "magnet rules" on the chalkboard.

1. Two magnets can *attract* (pull) one another, but they can also be made to *repel* one another (push one another apart).
2. Magnets will not attract nonmetal objects.
3. Magnets attract some metal objects but not all.

Each of the magnet rules was based on observational evidence the children had discovered as they investigated. Through the magnet rules, the teacher introduced some new *concepts*, including *attract* and *repel*. The rules themselves were *principles*, because they showed how concepts were related to one another.

To help the children remember and understand the rules, Ms. Clark pointed to each rule in turn and asked the teams to search for and hold overhead one example of objects that fit each rule. In each case, the class decided whether the objects selected were correct examples. This "game" continued until every object of every team had been held aloft. To further help children to understand and apply the rules of magnetism, children went about the room making predictions and then testing them with different materials.

Many interesting activities on magnetism that you can use to involve your students in inquiry can be found on pages A-97–A-105 in *Activities for Teaching Science as Inquiry*, the companion volume to this text.

Why are the rules of magnetic interaction rightfully considered to be scientific principles?

Because magnets can damage computer monitors and TV screens, before this activity the teacher put stickers announcing "NO MAGNETS HERE!" on all the classroom computers and the TV.

This inquiry lesson on magnetism incorporates each of the tasks of inquiry identified previously in Figure 1-3. First, a question about magnetism was asked (Inquiry Task 1). Then, an investigation plan was formulated to address the question, and the students followed the plan to gather observational data relevant to the question (Inquiry Tasks 2 and 3). Observations were then used as evidence in formulating rules and generating explanations to answer the initiating question (Inquiry Task 4). In the course of the investigation, the students discussed their investigation results and conclusions with the teacher and other class members (Inquiry Task 5).

In inquiry teaching, assessment is a continuing process, occurring during a lesson series (formative assessment), as well as at the end of the lessons (summative assessment). Assessment is directed toward determining how well students are attaining lesson objectives. Information on student achievement is used to modify instruction and improve learning approaches.

Successful inquiry teaching depends on a host of additional teaching variables. Successful teachers establish communities of learners focused on understanding and provide instructions to students about working together in groups. They apply planned classroom management procedures strategically and fairly. They emphasize safety rules, provide opportunities for practice, rehearsal, and review, and attend to various other classroom variables. We will discuss many of these in the different chapters of this book.

Are you beginning to see the importance of inquiry experiences for children? Can you see yourself incorporating genuine inquiry into your own science lessons?

Proficiency 3: Understandings About the Nature of Science and Scientific Inquiry

Understanding the nature of science and scientific inquiry is also an important goal of science education (National Research Council, 1996; National Research Council, 2000). Emerging research suggests that children's abilities to engage in inquiry and form new conceptual understandings are enhanced when they grasp the nature and construction of scientific knowledge. Following is a discussion of some of the specific aspects of the nature of science and scientific inquiry that elementary and middle school students should begin to understand.

Science Is Something People Do and Create. From this idea follows the understanding that scientific knowledge is not based on the authority of scientists, teachers, or books, nor is it simply a copy of reality. Science is a product of the activity of knowing. Science knowledge is based in scientists' investigations, observations, and explanations (Duschl et al., 2007).

Further, virtually all people are involved in science in some way. Scientists generate new knowledge through their investigations. All of us are consumers of products developed from scientific knowledge. We are all affected by issues involving science and technology, such as issues related to pollution, global warming, and other environmental changes that result from decisions about how to use scientific and technological knowledge.

Many people find science to be a rewarding career. Scientists are involved with fascinating puzzles to be solved, innovative methods and instruments to be developed, contacts with colleagues around the world to keep up, reports to write, and scientific meetings to attend. The pursuit of science is, for most scientists, sheer *fun* (Judson, 1980). "And," as the science writer Gary Zukav (1979) observed, "the clever rascals get paid for doing it" (p. 3).

- What question about magnetism was asked to initiate the magnets investigation?
- What investigation plan was formulated to address the question?
- What did the students do to gather observational data relevant to the question?
- How were observations used as evidence in formulating principles and generating explanations to answer the initiating question?

Science Is a Way of Answering Questions About the Natural World. Science is a special way of thinking in the modern world, but students should understand that science is only one way humans seek understanding. Knowing what types of questions science can investigate and those it cannot is important in the inquiry process.

Science deals only with questions about the natural world that can be answered, even if tentatively, through data gathering, logical reasoning, the use of scientific knowledge, and the formation and testing of explanations. Consider, for example, the question: *Why did the boy speak up in the story of the Emperor's New Clothes?* Providing satisfying answers to this question may require personal interpretation and empathy. Reflecting on the question may yield valuable new understandings of people and new self-knowledge. But the question simply cannot be answered through scientific investigation, description, and explanation.

As another example, science cannot answer questions involving religious beliefs, such as: *Does God exist?* We must answer questions about things we simply cannot see, but hope for, through personal faith, not through scientific investigations. Similarly, questions about beauty, ethics, and moral choices generally involve personal interpretations and beliefs and cannot be answered through scientific data taking and analysis.

Sometimes teachers can help children reformulate their questions so they can be investigated scientifically. The question *Why do birds fly?*, which is a question of motivation and purpose, might be revised so it can be investigated scientifically. For example, *How do bird bones differ from mammal bones?* can be a productive scientific question. A follow-up question might ask: *How do birds' bones make it easier for them to fly?*

Scientific Knowledge Is Generated Through Questions, Investigations, Observations, and Explanations. As portrayed in the five tasks of scientific inquiry (Figure 1-3), in generating science knowledge, scientists and students ask questions about the natural world and plan and conduct investigations to provide evidence to be used in answering the questions. Logical reasoning, scientific knowledge, and imagination must be used in the construction of explanations of observational evidence. The interplay among the *evidence of investigations, scientific knowledge,* and *explanations* provides the basis for scientific advances. Figure 1-5 provides a model of how observation, scientific knowledge, and explanations are linked in scientific inquiry.

Scientific Knowledge Is Tentative. Because science is a human construction and depends on limited observations and incomplete explanations, scientific knowledge is subject to change as new evidence becomes available (National Research Council, 1996). Even in the best of circumstances, the theories and explanations of children and scientists must be considered tentative. No matter how well a widely accepted theory fits observations, a new theory might fit them just as well or better or might fit a wider range of observations (American Association for the Advancement of Science, 1993). Thus, science knowledge is never fixed, never complete, always tentative, and subject to revision or even rejection with new evidence.

Scientists Present Their Investigations and Explanations to the Scientific Community for Critical Evaluation. Establishing science knowledge is a social process involving the community of scientists (Duschl et al., 2007). Scientists make the results of their investigations public. To evaluate scientific studies, other scientists review experimental procedures, examine evidence, identify faulty reasoning, point out statements that go beyond the evidence, try out investigations for themselves, and suggest alternative explanations. Children also should present their procedures and findings to their classmates and teachers for evaluation.

The many videos in the Homework and Exercises section at www.myeducationlab.com, directed by Dr. Terry Contant, can help illustrate and extend the concepts presented in each chapter. Now would be a good time for you to watch the first video, *What Do Scientists Do?* A video guide is provided in the section on Online Professional Development at the end of this chapter.

The *Benchmarks for Science Literacy* (American Association for the Advancement of Science, 1993) remind us that even though science knowledge is subject to change, students should understand that it also has an enduring quality. Some science knowledge is several hundred years old and remains applicable today.

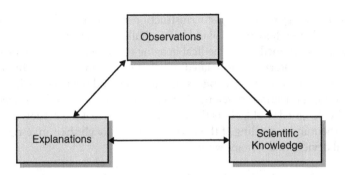

Figure 1-5 In understanding the natural world, scientists and students link obervations, scientific knowledge, and scientific explanations.

Scientists Display Certain Attitudes and Habits of Mind in Doing Science. Doing science with integrity requires that scientists display certain attitudes as they engage in science. Children should also acquire and display scientific attitudes and habits of mind as they do science. Some of these attitudes are (National Center for Improving Science Education, 1989, pp. 18–19):

1. *Curiosity.* an enduring interest and fascination about the natural and human-constructed worlds.
2. *Desire for Knowledge*—an urge, even "rage" (Judson, 1980), to know and understand the world.
3. *Placing a Priority on Evidence*—using data as the basis for testing ideas and respecting the facts as they accrue.
4. *Willingness to Modify Explanations*—changing initial conceptions and explanations when the evidence suggests different ones.
5. *Cooperation in Investigating Questions and Solving Problems*—working in collaboration with others is fundamental to the scientific enterprise.
6. *Honesty*—presenting data as they are observed, not as the investigator expects or wishes them to be.

The nature of science and scientific inquiry is *implicit* in the inquiry activities of students but must be made *explicit* to them. To teach students about how scientific knowledge is generated, for example, teachers can involve students in inquiry and discuss with them how what they have done is like what scientists do. In small group and whole class discussion of students' investigations, teachers can emphasize the importance of observation and data gathering, how simple instruments such as magnifiers and thermometers extend observations, how data is used as evidence in forming explanations of what is observed and why results are communicated to others for evaluation.

Especially good problems for investigation can be found from applications of science in technology. Application opens up the opportunity for students to explore the natural and technological world more deeply and to realize how extensively science and technology are interactive and affect people.

"Experiences in which students actually engage in scientific investigation provide the background for developing an understanding of the nature of scientific inquiry."

(*National Science Education Standards*, National Research Council, 1996, p. 179)

Science and Technology

As stressed in the *National Science Education Standards*, science and technology are closely related, but they differ in goals. The goal of *science* is to understand the natural world; the goal of *technology* is to make modifications in the world to meet human needs (National Research Council, 1996, p. 24).

The term *technology* refers not just to instructional technology, but also to innovations that enable people to adjust to the world better. Pulleys, levers, telescopes, bridges of different designs, modern medicines, medical imaging techniques (such as x-rays, MRIs, and CT-scans), and computers and associated peripherals are important technologies, as are light bulbs, electric motors and generators, automobiles, and the latest high-tech products.

Investigating applications of science in technology provides students opportunities to connect to the designed world, offers them experiences in making models of useful things, and extends their understanding of the laws of nature through their investigations of how technological devices and systems work.

Tasks of Technological Design. Paralleling the five tasks of scientific inquiry given in Figure 1-3, the *National Science Education Standards* (National Research Council, 1996, p. 137) identify five *tasks of technological design* that students should learn to do:

- *Identify a simple problem.* Students identify a specific need, problem, or task and explain it in their own words.
- *Propose a solution.* Students should make proposals to build something or to make something work better.
- *Implement a proposed solution.* Children should work individually and collaboratively and use simple materials, tools, techniques, and appropriate quantitative measurements when solving the problem.
- *Evaluate a product or a design.* Students should evaluate their own results or solutions as well as those of other children by considering how well a product or design met the challenge to solve a problem.
- *Communicate a problem design and solution.* Students should prepare oral, written, and pictorial communication of the design process and products. The communication might involve show-and-tell, group discussions, short written reports, pictures, or multimedia computer presentations.

Implementing the technological design cycle requires that students observe, measure, draw inferences, make hypotheses and predictions, conduct controlled investigations, and apply scientific knowledge. A graphic illustration of the tasks of technological design is provided in Figure 1-6.

Here is an example of applying science concepts and principles in the course of the technological design cycle. In a unit on water quality, students in one Florida middle school studied local water resource issues and created public service announcements (PSAs) to convey the message of water conservation to their community. In creating the PSAs, student teams had to clearly identify a simple problem, propose a solution to the problem in terms of the intended PSA, create a PSA and evaluate it, and show their PSA to their teacher, peers, and public for their examination and comments. It is clear from the ways students engaged in this project and their reactions to it that they were beginning to understand, appreciate, and care about the real-world interactions of science, technology, and society. Read about this innovative approach to studying issues involving science, technology, and people in an article by Stokes and Hull (2002) in *The Science Teacher*.

Teachers and Inquiry

Teachers have preferred styles of instruction. Some prefer more student-centered classrooms. Others want more control of activities and prefer teacher-centered activities, such as is the

Go to the Homework and Exercises section in Chapter 1 of MyEducationLab to view the five part set of videos called "Water Wheels." These videos provide a view of a third grade class as they investigate, construct, and test water wheels. These videos provide a good example of the application of both the technological design cycle and the science as inquiry tasks. A video guide for this video is included in the *Online Professional Development* section at the end of this chapter.

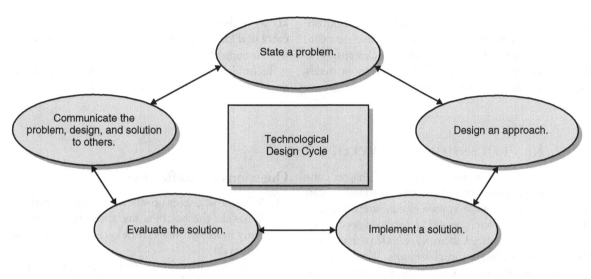

Figure 1-6 Tasks in designing a technological solution to a problem.

case in most direct instruction models. Some see the overriding goal of instruction in subject matter as the development of language literacy and thus prefer a reading approach to science.

In this text we take the position that inquiry-constructivist approaches to science best enable students to develop the three main goals of science education—conceptual understanding, abilities to inquire, and understanding of science and scientific inquiry. Although we emphasize inquiry approaches, we show you in Chapter 4 how to use inquiry as a framework in which direct instruction and reading approaches to science can fit together with inquiry.

Teaching science as inquiry provides many opportunities for you to interact with each of your students, to guide and challenge them to acquire and understand a scientific view of the world, and to develop the abilities and attitudes they need to inquire on their own.

Are you beginning to understand why inquiry approaches are so important for teaching science?

SUMMARY

• Inquiry instruction is an approach to science teaching focusing on understanding the world by questioning, investigating, observing, and explaining the order of the world around us.

• There are several advantages to science being a part of the school day at the elementary level. Science in the elementary school lays a foundation for children to develop abilities to understand the world scientifically; it can help ensure that students can successfully engage in scientific, technological, and medical careers and participate in a scientific society; it can support the learning of reading, writing, and math skills; and it is important for student success on statewide assessments required by the NCLB Act.

• According to the *National Science Education Standards,* all students should be engaged in an inquiry approach to science that basically parallels the procedures scientists use and the attitudes they display in doing science.

• Inquiry involves asking questions, planning investigations, gathering data, learning and using scientific knowledge to make sense of observational data, and communicating results to others.

• Scientific understanding is based in observations of the natural world and involves abilities to construct and apply concepts, principles, and theories.

• Through engaging in inquiry, students can begin to understand the nature of science and scientific inquiry. Scientific knowledge should always be considered tentative. Scientists must adjust their ideas when investigations produce new evidence that no longer supports previous conclusions. The study of science can build and reinforce important attitudes and habits of mind. Curiosity—the urge, even rage, to know—is the driving force for science. Scientists are skeptical of new ideas; they always insist on examining evidence offered in support of conclusions.

• Technological design seeks to apply science knowledge to the design of technological innovations.

ONLINE PROFESSIONAL DEVELOPMENT

Pre- and post-tests to assess your knowledge of chapter content, along with exercises to enhance your understanding, can be found on MyEducationLab at www.myeducationlab.com.

Throughout this book, you will be provided opportunities through MyEducationLab to view videos that show children engaged in inquiry in classrooms. Watching and reflecting on these videos can extend your understanding of chapter concepts and ideas and confront some of the issues and decisions facing science teachers. The process of observing and reflecting on teachers' actions and on students' learning and thinking can lead to changes in the knowledge, beliefs, attitudes, and ultimately the practice of pre-service and in-service teachers.

Video Guides

Video clips on MyEducationLab selected for this chapter include "What Do Scientists Do?" and "Water Wheels"—Parts 1, 2, 3, 4, and 5.

Accessing the Videos

1. Go to the Homework and Exercises section in Chapter 1 of MyEducationLab to select and view videos for this chapter and compute the questions.
2. Videos might be viewed individually, by small groups of colleagues, or by the whole class.
3. As you watch each video, use the **Questions for Reflection** to guide your thoughts and note taking for personal use and group discussion. Also, go beyond the Questions for Reflection, and reflect on the many different aspects of instruction and learning that interest you.

Video: What Do Scientists Do?

Overview

In this video excerpt, we watch fifth-grade students as they investigate pin-hole cameras. We also hear from second-, third-, and fifth-grade teachers about how the implementing of inquiry in classrooms can help students understand what scientists do.

Questions for Reflection

1. What do scientists do when they do science?
2. What do the teachers say about how classroom inquiry investigations can help children learn what scientists do?
3. What activities do the fifth-grade students do in investigating pin-hole cameras? How do the activities relate to what scientists do?

Video: Water Wheels: Parts 1, 2, 3, 4, and 5.

Overview

In this five-part series of videos, we watch as a third-grade class investigates water wheels. As the students design, construct, and test their own water wheels, we can see application of science in the technological design cycle (Figure 1-6).

Questions for Reflection

1. What do the children say that water wheels do? How do they describe how water wheels work?
2. What examples do you see in the videos that are related to the five tasks of technological design? What examples do you notice that show the students using the five tasks of scientific inquiry?
3. What does the teacher do to facilitate the investigations by the children?

Annenberg Videos

The Annenberg/CPB Foundation has made a wealth of 30- to 90-minute professional development videos on science learning and teaching available to you on the Web. We have selected a number of these for you to view in connection with various chapters in this book. This chapter features a video entitled, *What Is Inquiry and Why Do It?* This video is part of the Annenberg series called **Learning Science Through Inquiry.**

Websites change periodically, and we cannot guarantee that the selected video will be available on the Annenberg website when you wish to see it. Because of the potential importance to your professional development, we recommend that, if available, you take advantage of the invitation to view the Annenberg videos and learn about the Annenberg website.

Instructions for Accessing and Watching Annenberg Videos

1. Access the Annenberg website at http://learner.org/. Follow the instructions for registering the first time you access the Annenberg videos.

2. Go to *Browse Teacher Resources: Science*. Click on *Go*.

3. Click on the video series of interest.

4. Go to *Individual Program Descriptions*. Click the *Videos on Demand (VoD)* icon for the video you wish to watch.

2

I n the vision presented by the Standards, inquiry is a step beyond "science as process," in which students learn skills, such as observation, inference, and experimentation. The new vision includes the "processes of science" and requires that students combine processes and scientific knowledge as they use scientific reasoning and critical thinking to develop their understanding of science.

(*National Science Education Standards*, National Research Council, 1996, p. 105)

Processes and Strategies for Inquiring

ONCE STUDENTS (AND SCIENTISTS) have formed questions that can be investigated scientifically, they collect data, decide on ways to record and report the data, and interpret the data using logical reasoning and prior scientific knowledge. In investigating the natural world, children use simple tools such as thermometers, meter sticks, and hand lenses and practice simple skills such as observing, measuring, recording data, graphing, inferring, and predicting. The skills used in investigating are called *processes of science*.

Elementary and middle school teachers have traditionally taught specific processes of science in isolation from other processes and science content. However, the *National Science Education Standards* emphasize that the real value of a process approach to science comes as students learn to incorporate them into scientific investigations.

In this chapter, we focus on both processes of science and strategies of investigation. First, we describe individual processes and show you some examples of their use in elementary and middle school science. Then, we describe and provide examples of three particular investigational strategies—descriptive, classificatory, and experimental investigations. These special ways of investigating incorporate various processes of science. As you work your way through this chapter, reflect on these questions:

- *What specific processes of science are featured in elementary and middle school classrooms?*

- *What activities might be useful in teaching children how to apply specific processes of science?*

- *How can teachers help children use their natural curiosity to develop questions to investigate?*

- *What are the main features of descriptive, classificatory, and experimental investigations?*

- *How can you help students learn to apply these investigational strategies?*

- *How are different processes of science used in these three ways of investigating?*

- *At what grade level or grade span might each of the three kinds of investigations best be introduced?*

Processes of Science

Although the processes of science are especially characteristic of the work of professional scientists, everyone can exercise them in thinking about various matters of interest in everyday life (Rutherford & Ahlgren, 1990). They are the same skills that will serve children as

Teaching science processes parallels a well-known proverb: Give a man a fish and he eats for a day. Teach him how to fish and he eats for a lifetime.

Many good activities for teaching science process skills can be found in Rezba, Sprague, Fiel, and Funk (2003) and Ostlund and Mercier (1999).

adults, "when they measure their floor for a carpet, try to figure out why their automobile didn't start, or decide which presidential candidate to vote for. These are the thinking skills they will use when separating evidence from opinion while listening to someone's side of a story, or when looking for evidence and contradictions in written or spoken opinions" (Mechling & Oliver, 1983, p. 8).

A variety of science processes that are emphasized in elementary and middle school science classes are described in Table 2-1 and in the following sections.

Observing

Observation is the process of gathering information using all appropriate senses and instruments that extend the senses, such as hand lenses and microscopes. Children use their senses

TABLE 2-1 SOME PROCESSES OF SCIENCE EMPHASIZED IN ELEMENTARY AND MIDDLE SCHOOLS

Process of Science	Procedure	Example
Observing	Gather information using all appropriate senses and instruments that extend the senses.	Visually observe a melting ice cube as it changes phase, feel the water to determine its coldness, or use a hand lens to watch a snowflake melt.
Classifying	Group objects or organisms according to one or more common properties.	Classify rocks as igneous, sedimentary, or metamorphic.
Inferring	Draw a tentative conclusion about objects, organisms, or events based on observations and prior knowledge.	Infer that when water evaporates, it goes into the air; infer that heat caused the ice cube to change to water.
Measuring	Quantify variables using a variety of instruments and standard or nonstandard units.	Measure the length, width, thickness, and weight of bean seeds before and after they soak in water; use a clock to determine the number of minutes for an ice cube to melt; weigh ice cubes and water before and after melting.
Communicating	Record observations, measurements, inferences, experiments, etc., in multiple ways, and present them to others.	Draw pictures of, write about, and give an oral report on observations of amphibians; use a data table and a graph to display the number of children in a group who are wearing each of several different color shoes; use a data table and a graph to display the temperature of water every 5 minutes as it cools.
Predicting	Make a forecast of a possible outcome of an investigation based on known patterns in data.	Based on this investigation data, I predict that a 30-gram ice cube placed in 300 ml of water will melt in 50 minutes.
Hypothesizing	Make a statement to guide an investigation of a question.	The greater the amount of water in which an ice cube is placed the more time it will take to melt.
Experimenting: Controlled Investigating	Investigate by deliberately manipulating one variable at a time and observing the effect on a responding variable, while holding all other variables constant.	Conduct an experiment to determine the effect of the amount of water on the time it takes an ice cube to melt in water while keeping the size and shape of the ice cube and the initial temperature of the water the same.

to explore the world from the day they are born—or perhaps earlier. In preschool and kindergarten, they begin to discover the part each of their senses plays in making observations.

"What can you tell me about this?" a kindergarten teacher asks her class as she holds up a flower. "Yes, it is a flower. But can you tell me more about it? What color is it? What part of your body tells you that?" Then she asks the children to touch and smell the flower and to identify which sense they use to acquire their information (Minnesota Mathematics and Science Teaching Project, 1970).

Young children tend to observe globally and, thus, to miss potentially relevant details. They often see what they expect to see, and they may focus more on differences than similarities. As they develop skills in observing, children learn to observe for detail, to see what is actually there, and to pay attention to both similarities and differences (Harlen & Jelly, 1990).

Science provides children many opportunities to observe, to wonder, and to seek their own answers to questions through discovery and testing. Almost any objects, organisms, or events are suitable as a base for developing observing skills. For example, observing popcorn—including observing characteristics of the uncooked kernels, observing the popcorn as it is being popped, and observing the cooked popcorn—provides an excellent context for children to consider how each of their senses provides different information.

Take a moment to examine Activity 2-1. This activity can be used to test your own observation skills or as an activity to help your students develop their observation skills while learning some significant science knowledge. Do this activity on observing candy before reading further.

Did you make a variety of observations about the candy in Activity 2-1? Use the components of good scientific observing shown in Table 2-2 as a checklist to see how comprehensive your list of observations is.

* Did you use all appropriate *senses,* and perhaps a hand lens, in observing your candy?
* Did you make quantitative observations? For example, did you measure the size and the weight of the pieces of candy in standard or nonstandard units?

A glossary containing definitions of important terms used in this chapter can be found on MyEducationLab.

Many good activities using a variety of materials to teach and assess different processes of science are available on the PALS (Performance Assessment Links in Science) website at http://pals.sri.com.

Using a Magnifier

To observe an object through a magnifier or magnifying lens, hold the magnifier close to the object, look through the magnifier at the object, then lift the magnifier toward your eye, stopping when the object begins to blur.

Many science classrooms have magnifiers with three lenses. The large lens usually provides a twofold magnification, the medium-sized lens provides a sixfold magnification, and the small lens an eightfold magnification. To provide increased magnification, two or even three magnifiers can be fitted together and used as a single magnifier.

Activity 2-1: Observing Candy

Obtain several pieces of hard candy, such as sour balls or M&Ms of different colors. Write down all of the qualitative and quantitative observations of the candy you can make.

Safety Precaution: Stress the importance to students of their not tasting anything that has not been approved by an adult!

TABLE 2-2 COMPONENTS OF GOOD SCIENTIFIC OBSERVING

Component	Description
Senses	Use all appropriate senses as well as instruments that extend the senses in gathering extensive and clear information.
Measurements	Make quantitative observations—that is, measurements—to supplement qualitative observations when it matters.
Questions	Ask questions about the objects that can lead to new investigations and observations.
Changes	Make deliberate alterations in the objects that can help answer new questions and observe the responding changes.
Communication	Report your observations clearly, using verbal descriptions, charts, diagrams, drawings, and other methods as appropriate.

- Did you ask *questions* about the candy that might be investigated through further observations or experiments? For example, did you raise questions about what happens to the candy when you crush it?
- What *changes* did you make to the candy? For example, did you crush a piece or place it in water?
- How did you *communicate* your observations? Did you make a written list or perhaps a chart that might facilitate comparisons? Did you include drawings?

Learning to be a good observer is a lifelong task. Under your guidance as a sensitive teacher, students can begin to develop effective observation skills.

In an article titled "Unlocking the Power of Observation," Anderson, Martin, and Faszewski present a useful set of criteria for good observations and provide a checklist and rubric for evaluating them. You can find the article in the September 2006 issue of *Science and Children* (pp. 32–35).

Classifying

In **classifying**, people sort objects according to their common properties (characteristics, attributes, or features). Classifying is an important process in science. Why do we classify objects or organisms?

Classifying things requires not only that we observe properties but also that we look for relationships among the properties. This enhances our understanding of the structure and function of the things. Also, placing an object or organism within a group means you already know something about it, if you are familiar with the characteristics of the group. Additionally, grouping things with other things gives us an added way to search for information about them, by direct observation, in the library, or through the Internet (National Aquarium in Baltimore, 1997).

In the magnets lesson described in Chapter 1, children learned more about magnetism by classifying or sorting objects into piles based on whether or not they were attracted to magnets.

Special ways of classifying often introduced in elementary science are binary and multistage classification. In a *binary classification system*, a set of objects is divided into two groups on the basis of whether each object has a particular property. For example, a set of buttons might be classified into two groups based on the number of holes they have. One group might consist of all the buttons that have four holes; the other group would be made up of all buttons that do not have four holes.

In a *multistage classification system*, the objects in the original set are sorted again and again so that a hierarchy of sets and subsets is formed. For example, the four-hole buttons in our example of binary classification might be further classified as being round or not round. Four-hole, round buttons might then be classified as being plastic or not plastic.

Figure 2-1 shows an example of a multistage classification of button properties. What might a multistage classification of living things in a terrarium look like?

As another example of multistage classification, organisms might be described and classified based on similar characteristics. At a first level, the organisms might be classified as plants or animals. Animals might then be classified according to number of body parts. At a third level, animals with three main body parts might be further classified according to number of legs. Animals with three main body parts (head, thorax, and abdomen), six legs attached to the thorax, and two antennae attached to the head are classified as "insects."

Focusing on similar properties in classifying can lead to understandings about the most significant properties of objects and their functions. For example, a focus on the four-hole property of buttons might lead to a question about why some buttons have holes and others do not. What is the function of the holes? Do buttons without holes have some characteristic that substitutes for the holes (such as another means to attach them to garments)?

A variety of activities about observing, describing, and classifying buttons are provided in the activity titled "How Are Buttons Alike and Different" on pages A-16 through A-19 in *Activities for Teaching Science as Inquiry*.

Classifying according to only a few properties can lead to classification problems. For example, lobsters also have three main body parts, six legs, and two antennae. Why are they not classified as insects? What are some of the other critical properties of insects and lobsters that exclude lobsters from the insect class?

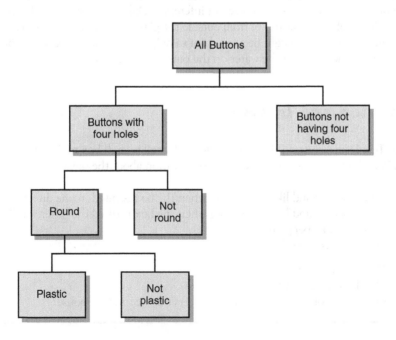

Figure 2-1 A multistage classification of button properties.

Inferring

Observations are statements about information that is available directly through the five senses; inferences are interpretations of these observations. In inferring, we use experiences and knowledge to fill in gaps about observed events and information. An **inference,** then, is an *interpretation* of observations based on prior knowledge and experiences.

Children often experience difficulties in distinguishing between their observations and their inferences (Duschl et al., 2007). Students should be especially encouraged to make explicit the observations and prior knowledge on which their inferences are based. When they claim that a statement is an observaton, you might ask, "What sense did you use in making that observaton?" When they draw inferences, you might ask: "What is your evidence?" and "Why do you think so?" Helping children distinguish between observations (evidence of the senses) and inferences (conclusions based on evidence) is important to their understanding of science.

In one popular activity designed to teach the skill of inferring, students are supplied with closed boxes in which mystery objects have been placed. They lift, shake, and tilt the boxes to gain information about the mystery objects. A student might observe, for instance, that the object rolls when the box is tilted one way and slides when it is tilted differently. What is the shape of the object? A good inference is that the object is cylindrical. The goal of this activity is not just for children to find out what is in the box, but to help them learn to distinguish between observations and inferences.

Activity 2-2 shows a sample test item to assess student understanding of the differences between observations and inferences. The item is similar to ones that might appear on statewide tests of science. Work through the activity and discuss it with a group of colleagues.

What answer did you choose for the item? Choices A, B, and C are all observations based on the sense of hearing or the sense of smell. Choice D is an inference based on observations of the content of the box and prior experience with rolling and sliding cylinders.

Moisture sometimes appears on the outside of a glass full of ice water, as is illustrated in Figure 2-2. Some people might say, "The glass is sweating." Is this statement an observation or an inference? It is, of course, an inference. Did the moisture on the glass come from inside the glass (sweating) or from outside the glass (perhaps from water vapor in the air)? What investigations might be carried out to help students decide between the two inferences about the source of the water on the outside of the glass?

One way to gather evidence about where the moisture on the outside of the glass of ice water came from is to put red food dye in the water and, when moisture forms, check it carefully for any hint of red. The observation that the moisture contains no sign of red supports the inference that it likely came from the air surrounding the glass, rather than from the water in the glass.

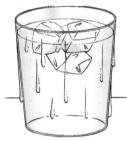

Figure 2-2 Where does the moisture on the outside of a glass of ice water come from? What is your evidence?

Activity 2-2: Observation and Inference

Sample Test Item. Four children tilt, rattle, and smell a small box to discover the object inside. Which of the following is NOT an observation about the object?

A. "It makes a sound like it is sliding when the box is tilted in one direction."
B. "It makes a sound like it is rolling when the box is tilted the other way."
C. "It smells like peppermint."
D. "I think it is candy."

- What is your answer choice?
- Why did you select that answer?
- Why is each of the other possible answers not a correct response?

Measuring

It is often important in science to quantify observations through measurement. For example, knowing the length of the roots and stems of developing plants and how these variables change from day to day can be important for understanding plant growth. Accurate measurements not only enhance descriptions, they can improve the quality of predictions and explanations of natural phenomena.

Measuring is founded on processes of observing and comparing. "Children naturally make comparisons" (National Science Resources Center, 1996, p. 3). They stand back to back to see who is taller, line up their feet to see whose are longer, and match their bodies to different size clothing to see what will fit.

The need to make comparisons leads to the notion of units of measure. At first, children may use nonstandard units to make comparisons. For example, they stretch out their own arms, use their own bodies, or use handy objects like pencils or plastic spoons as nonstandard units to measure length. However, nonstandard units have a main disadvantage. Because spoons and pencils, as well as children's arm spans and bodies, vary in length, it is difficult to use them to consistently compare objects that cannot be held side by side.

Science lessons at different grade levels can help students learn different aspects of the measuring process. First-grade lessons on measuring should be designed to enable children to understand (National Science Resources Center, 1996):

- Comparing involves observing similarities and differences.
- One way to make comparisons is by matching.
- A common starting line is required to make fair comparisons.
- Using beginning and ending points and placing units end to end are important factors when measuring.
- Nonstandard units of measure can be used in comparing.
- Standard units of measure produce more consistent results than nonstandard units.

By second grade, children should use standard units—centimeters, grams, and degrees Celsius or Fahrenheit—marked on rulers, balance scales, and thermometers to measure objects and events. Standard units enable consistent descriptions and comparisons of measured objects that are not side by side and cannot be directly compared.

Through activities in grade 3–6 science *and* mathematics classes, students should begin to understand:

- the meaning of each property that is being measured, such as volume or temperature;
- how to use a variety of measuring instruments;
- the meaning and use of a variety of standard units of measurement;
- the meaning and relationships among the various prefixes used with metric measurement units, such as *milli-, centi-,* and *kilo-;*
- how to interpolate between numbers in reading thermometers, rulers, and other instruments;
- how to express measurements in terms of decimals when appropriate; and
- how to estimate measurements and determine when estimation is appropriate.

In elementary and middle school science, children should be afforded a great deal of practice in using and reading metric rulers, metersticks, thermometers, balances, spring scales, timers of various kinds, graduated cylinders, measuring cups, and other measuring instruments.

Appendix B describes some important tools and skills for measuring length, area, volume, mass, weight, and temperature at the elementary and middle school level. Take a few minutes to read through this appendix.

Communicating

Recording, organizing, and reporting observations, measurements, experiments, findings, and conclusions is also an essential process of science. According to the *Benchmarks for Science Literacy* (American Association for the Advancement of Science, 1993, p. 10), "An important part of students' explorations is telling others what they see, what they think, and what it makes them wonder about. Children should have lots of time to talk about what they observe and to compare their observations with others." In addition to oral discourse, communications might take the form of drawings, written reports, journal entries, data tables, and graphs. Children might even use music, art, and role playing to communicate their understanding.

In science activities, once data have been obtained, they must be organized and interpreted. Data tables and graphs are common means of displaying data. Data tables display data in column form and facilitate the discovery of patterns within the data. Table 2-5 shows an example of a data table used in an investigation of white powders. Putting measurement data into graphs better enables students to discover relationships and patterns that help them make sense of the data. Graphs also facilitate the construction of precise predictions.

The types of graphs most often used in scientific applications in elementary and middle schools are bar graphs, histograms, and line graphs.

Bar Graphs. Bar graphs visually show *differences* in data collected. Bar graphs can be used, for example, to show the number of children with each different type of eye color. Data about how many students in a class have blue eyes, brown eyes, green eyes, and so on, may be displayed visually in bar graphs.

Some good examples of bar graph activities may be found in a *Science and Children* article by Susan Pearlman and Kathleen Pericak-Spector (1995) called "Graph That Data!"

An example of a bar graph is shown in Figure 2-3. This graph depicts the number of children in a group wearing shoes of different colors. The bottom line, or *horizontal axis*, shows different shoe colors worn by the children. The left side, or *vertical axis* of the graph, shows the number of children wearing a particular color shoe. Four children in the group wear black shoes, six children wear white shoes, three children wear red shoes, and two children wear blue shoes.

Histograms. Histograms display the *number of times* a *number event* occurs in a large set. Histograms differ from bar graphs in that the *x*-axis on a bar graph simply names a category, while the *x*-axis on a histogram is a number line representing a continuous variable. A familiar example of data that might be displayed in a histogram is how many students made each score on a test. Here, all possible scores are arranged in a number line on the *x*-axis;

Figure 2-3 Bar graph of number of children with different color shoes.

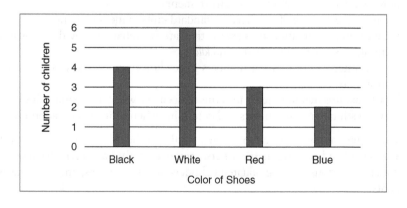

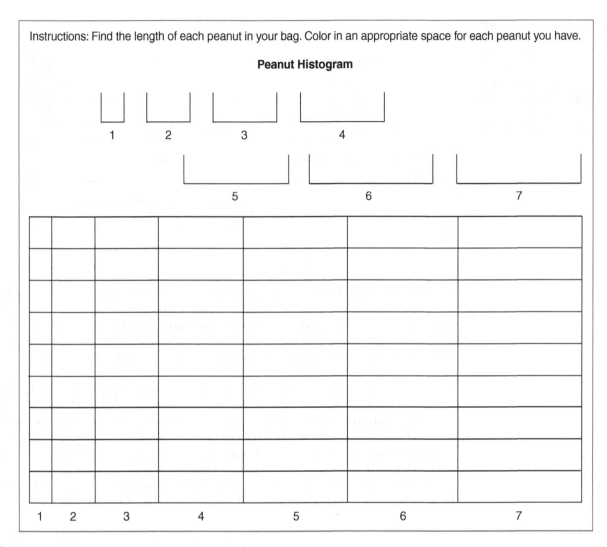

Figure 2-4 A histogram for graphing the lengths of unshelled peanuts.
Source: Used with permission from Larry Malone, Lawrence Hall of Science, University of California, Berkeley.

the frequencies, or number of occurrences, of scores are arranged in a number line on the y-axis. As an example, Figure 2-4 shows how many unshelled peanuts in a large bag there are of each designated length (or small range of lengths).

Line Graphs. Line graphs are more advanced; students from about fourth grade can learn to construct and interpret them. With line graphs, your students can graphically show numerical data about variables that are continuous. A line graph displays visually the changes in a *responding or dependent variable* in an investigation corresponding to changes in the values of a *manipulated or independent variable*.

As an example, suppose students wished to investigate the rate of cooling of a sample of hot water contained in an uncovered Styrofoam cup. Specifically, how does the temperature of the water vary with time? In gathering data to answer this question, students

A discussion of how measurement and graphing might be used to connect science and mathematics in the classroom is included in Chapter 9.

Figure 2-5 Graph of how the temperature of water changes with time as the water cools. The small squares represent the water temperature each time it was measured, then a best-fit curve was drawn to show the cooling trend over time.

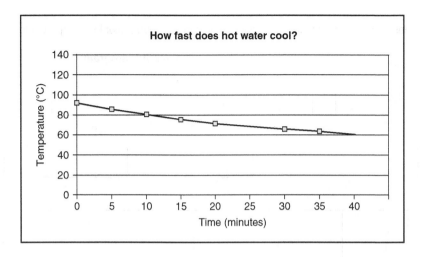

might begin with a cup of hot water. They might measure the initial temperature of the water and then measure the temperature every 5 minutes as the water cools. Figure 2-5 shows a graph for an investigation of temperature versus time for water as it cools. The graph indicates that the temperature decreases in a regular (predictable) way with time. Using the graph, students can predict the temperature of the water at different times.

Keeping Records in Science. One useful format for record keeping is the "*I Notice / I Wonder*" chart. The left column of this two-column chart should be labeled "I Notice." In this column students write their observations and discoveries as they explore objects, organisms, and events. The right column should be labeled "I Wonder." In this column students write questions that come to mind as they are exploring. These questions often begin with *What*, *Why*, or *How*. Such questions can lead to further inquiry investigations.

As you view the many classroom videos of children's investigations provided with this book, notice how often teachers and children use the I Notice/I Wonder chart.

I Notice	I Wonder
The cat's fur is black and white.	Are most cats black and white? Were this cat's parents black and white? What percent of this cat's fur is each color?
The pupils of the cat's eyes change shape as the brightness of the room changes.	Why the cat's eyes look different than human eyes?
The cat purrs when I pet him.	Does petting make the cat happy or angry?

Teachers help students turn their "I Wonder" questions into questions that they can investigate. For example, in lessons on light, such as the one seen in the video *What Do Scientists Do?*, featured in Chapter 1, students might ask, *Why does light travel in straight lines?*

It would be difficult, if not impossible, for children to answer this *why* question from their own investigations. Teachers can help them form this question that can be investigated: *What happens to the image of an arrow when seen in a pinhole camera?* Writing this focus question in their science notebooks or journals helps the students to clarify their purposes and keep those purposes in mind as they continue to investigate.

Scientists keep accurate records of data collected, so they are prepared to recall data taken, make comparisons of the data, draw inferences, make predictions, and generate explanations. For similar reasons, students should also keep accurate records.

During an activity, provide time for students to record their findings. Recording data will be a natural part of the work of some students; other students will need encouragement to stop and record their findings. Initially allow the students to use their own methods of recording data. Many will use sentences in making records. If so, encourage them to use labeled drawings and lists (Fulton & Campbell, 2003).

After discussions with the class about which of their observations are likely to be useful in answering the focus question and which are likely to be less useful, you might prepare a data sheet for students to fill in. An example of a class discussion about data is given in the Annenberg video *Bring It All Together: Processing for Meaning*. This video is featured in the Online Professional Development section of Chapter 3. An example of a prepared data sheet for white powder investigations can be seen in Figure 2-11 later in this chapter.

In making the transition from observational data to explanations, students might first reflect on their data and write about any patterns they see. For example, students might use writing and drawings to indicate that both vertical and horizontal arrows are inverted when seen in pin-hole viewers.

At the explanation phase of inquiry, students might be asked to explain why they think an arrow appears inverted when observed through a pin-hole viewer. With appropriate scaffolding, including introduction to some new concepts and principles through direct instruction, students can succeed with this task. In developing explanations, students should use writing and drawing to connect their observations with new conceptions and explanations that are developed through discussion or introduced by the teacher.

Through writing, students make their thinking visible, both to themselves and to teachers (Fulton & Campbell, 2003). Writing helps students to reflect on their data, offer their own interpretations of it, and better understand the new conceptions and explanation given by teachers. Further, writing gives teachers an important performance product to use in formative assessment.

Predicting

It is often important in science to predict future occurrences. A **prediction** is a forecast of a future outcome based on knowledge of patterns and relationships in data. Predictions look forward to what might happen. Inferences, in contrast, look backward; inferences are types of explanations of what has already happened.

Predictions are greatly enhanced when measurement data is organized into graphs to illustrate a trend. As an example, use the graph in Figure 2-5 to predict the temperature of the water after 25 minutes. What do you predict would be the temperature after 40 minutes? To make these predictions, determine what temperature would continue the trend already established by the data. A good prediction for the first case (after 25 minutes) is about 104°F, while a good prediction for the second case (after 40 minutes) is about 90°F. Some estimation from the graph is necessary in both cases. The first prediction in the water temperature example is called an *interpolation* because it is between (*inter-*) available

Go to the Homework and Exercises section in Chapter 2 of MyEducationLab to watch the video *Keeping Observation Records*. In this video we observe kindergarten and fifth-grade children involved in activities that help build the process skills of observation and record keeping.

See Hand and Keys (1999) for a well-designed science writing heuristic for developing reports on inquiry investigations in science. A discussion of inquiry reports is also included in our discussion of seed germination and plant growth later in this chapter.

Go to the Homework and Exercises section in Chapter 2 of MyEducationLab to watch the *Identifying Variables* video, highlighting the process skills of observation and record keeping. Each activity also helps students to attain writing standards for the state and introduces children to important science concepts.

Activity 2-3: Predicting

Sample Test Item. It is a cloudless, sunny day. A student measures the temperature of the air outside every hour. She collects the following data.

Time	Air Temperature
8:00 a.m.	18°C
9:00 a.m.	19°C
10:00 a.m.	21°C
11:00 a.m.	23°C

What will the air temperature outside most likely be at noon?

A. 18°C
B. 21°C
C. 25°C
D. 32°C

Source: National Assessment of Educational Progess (NAEP) released test item, grade 4, 2005.

data points; the second prediction is called an *extrapolation* because it is outside (*extra-*) the collected data points.

Activity 2-3 contains a sample test item involving predicting. The item is from the National Assessment of Educational Progress but is like those that might appear on statewide tests. Take some time to work through the activity.

What is your answer to the question in the activity? How did you arrive at it? To answer the item, students would first have to determine the trend of the data from the data table. They should determine that the air temperature increases about 1° or 2°C every hour. From this pattern, they could then predict that the temperature at 12:00 noon would be closest to 25°C, which is answer choice C.

Hypothesizing

The process of formulating and testing hypotheses is one of the core activities of scientific investigations. A **hypothesis** is a statement about a possible answer to a question that might be found through investigating. Hypotheses are often stated in an *if . . . then* form. For example,

> *If* more magnets are added to the magnets stack, *then* more washers will stick to the stack.
> *If* more weights are added to the bottom of the string, *then* the pendulum will make more cycles in 15 seconds.

Hypotheses guide scientists in choosing what data to collect, what available data to pay attention to, what additional data to seek, and possible ways to interpret the data in an investigation. To be useful, a hypothesis should suggest what observational evidence would support it and what evidence would refute it.

To test a hypothesis, students will typically need to conduct an experiment. For example, suppose children asked how the temperature of water affects the time for an effervescent tablet to dissolve in it. They might hypothesize, "If the water is warmer, a tablet will dissolve in it more quickly." To test this hypothesis, the children could conduct an in-

See the April 2001 *Science and Children* article by Louise Baxter and Martha Kurtz titled "When a Hypothesis Is Not an Educated Guess" for an interesting perspective on teaching children the similarities and differences among predictions, hypotheses, and theories.

vestigation in which the temperature of the water is systematically varied. For example, water temperatures of 40°F, 60°F, and 80°F might be used. Then, the time for the tablet to completely dissolve would be measured for each temperature. All other variables, such as the type of container, the volume of water, and the size and type of tablet, remain fixed. The data would be examined to see whether or not the hypothesis is supported.

Experimenting

Sometimes scientists or students can control circumstances deliberately and precisely in an experiment to obtain evidence to test hypotheses and arrive at explanations. Scientists may, for example, control the temperature while changing the concentration of chemicals in an experiment. In a variation of the experiment on water cooling, students may keep the room temperature and size and type of the container the same, while varying the volume of water to see if volume affects the rate of cooling. By controlling all other conditions and varying just one condition in the experiment, they can hope to identify its effects on what happens, uncomplicated by changes in other conditions (Rutherford & Ahlgren, 1990).

Controlled experiments involve (1) deliberately changing one variable at a time, (2) observing the effect on another variable, while (3) holding all other variables constant. A controlled investigation might be used to answer questions such as these:

- What factors affect the rate of swing of a pendulum?
- How does milk in a hamster's diet affect its health and growth?
- Which brand of paper towel is the best buy, considering such factors as absorbency, wet strength, quality, and cost per sheet?

Elementary and middle school students seem to understand controlled experiments better when they think of them as **fair tests**. If a test of a hypothesis is a fair one, then all variables are kept exactly the same except that one variable is changed intentionally. For example, if you wanted to conduct a "fair test" to find out how water temperature affects how quickly an ice cube melts, all of the following variables (the controlled variables) should be kept exactly the same (held constant): volume of water, size and shape of container, size of the ice cube, and air temperature. The water temperature is the variable that is changed intentionally on (the manipulated variable). You might use water at 35 degrees, 45 degrees, and 55 degrees. You would measure how long it takes each ice cube to completely melt, since melting time is the responding variable.

How would you design a fair test to determine which boy in your fourth-grade class is the fastest? What conditions would make this investigation a fair test? Would it be fair to give smaller children a headstart in determining who is fastest?

Working with variables is a particularly important part of controlled investigations. A **variable** is a property of objects or events that can change, has variations, or has differing amounts. The changing height and weight of a growing child, the time a candle can burn under a glass jar, and the amount of rainfall in a day are all examples of variables. The different colors of children's shoes is also an example of a variable.

Three types of variables are important in scientific investigations:

- A **manipulated variable** (also called an **independent variable**) is a variable that the experimenter deliberately changes or manipulates in an investigation.
- A **responding variable** (also called a **dependent variable**) is a variable that changes in an investigation in response to changes in the manipulated variable.
- **Controlled variables** are variables that are deliberately kept constant or unchanged in an investigation in order not to confound the results—that is, so the investigation is a fair test.

Here is an example to illustrate experimenting and the three types of variables. The students in a fifth-grade class wondered why NASA chose white as the color for astronauts' space suits. Several students thought the reason might relate to the sunlight absorbed by the space suit. Challenged by the teacher, the students reformulated their question to: "Do different colored materials absorb sunlight differently?" The teacher then guided the students as they designed and carried out a controlled experiment to help answer their question.

Working in cooperative groups, each team took two identical, empty vegetable cans and wrapped one with black construction paper and the other with white construction paper, filled the cans with equal amounts of water, and placed them side by side in sunlight for a period of time. What were the manipulated, responding, and controlled variables in the sunlight absorption investigation? The manipulated variable in the investigation was the color (light or dark) of the can; the color of the can was the variable that the investigators deliberately changed. The responding variable was the change in temperature of the water in the cans; the change in temperature was the outcome variable the investigators measured for each trial. To make the temperature test a fair one, in each investigation trial the teams would have to control such variables as the size of the cans and materials they were made from, the amount of water in each can, and the time the cans were left in sunlight.

Noting that the water in the dark can got warmer in the investigation of each team, the children, with the teacher's scaffolding assistance, concluded that it had absorbed more sunlight. In answer to their original question, the color of a material does make a difference in the absorption of sunlight. Generalizing from their observations, the children stated this principle: *Darker colored materials absorb more heat from sunlight than lighter colored materials.*

Returning to their initial question, the fifth graders reasoned that NASA chose white for astronauts' suits because white suits absorb less heat in sunlight than darker-colored suits. Follow-up reading activities and direct instruction from the teacher confirmed this inference.

Table 2-3 gives the meaning and examples of each of the three types of variables in the sunlight absorption experiment.

Children can learn to observe, measure, classify, infer, predict, and perform fair tests as part of isolated exercises, but these science processes become more meaningful when used together as intellectual tools in the context of full scientific inquiry. In the following sections, we will look more closely at how children learn processes of science through inquiry activities.

State tests typically include questions involving responding, manipulated, and controlled variables. Often students taking these high-stakes tests are called on to go beyond a multiple-choice format and provide written responses to questions.

How would you find out how stirring affects the time for the complete dissolving in water of three white powders—salt, sugar, and corn starch? What would be your manipulated and responding variables, and what variables would you control? (National Aquarium in Baltimore, 1997)

Go to the Homework and Exercises section in Chapter 2 of MyEducationLab to watch the *Identifying Variables* video. In this video, we see students in a dual-language classroom participating in a study of the variables associated with the most effective design of sails for "skimmers."

TABLE 2-3   DEFINITIONS AND EXAMPLES OF MANIPULATED, RESPONDING, AND CONTROLLED VARIABLES

Variable Type	Definition	Example
Manipulated or independent variable	Variable that is deliberately changed	Color of paper wrapped around the cans in color and sunlight absorption investigation
Responding or dependent variable	Variable that responds to manipulated changes	Change in temperature of the water in each can
Controlled variable	Variable that remains unchanged in an experiment	Type of container; amount of water in each can; time each can was left in sunlight

Investigation Strategies

Although recognizing the value of students knowing how to use individual processes of science, the authors of the *National Science Education Standards* called for "more than 'science as process'" (p. 2). The *Standards* stress that children should learn to use science processes within a framework of inquiry.

Consider, for example, how observation is used in inquiry in the process of generating scientific understanding. Kathleen Roth (1993), an educational researcher who has drawn much of her research data from teaching fifth graders in science and social studies, has suggested that:

> A scientist who observes well . . . is not one who spends endless hours documenting and describing every possible detail that can be observed about a particular phenomenon. . . . In contrast, good scientific observation focuses on key features in ways that will contribute new knowledge, increase the explanatory power of a particular conceptual framework, generate new understandings of relationships among concepts, or raise significant questions about accepted conceptual frameworks. . . . The importance of the observations is not how accurately the scientists can detail and describe all facets of the observed phenomenon, but how the scientists use the observed phenomenon to develop more powerful and complete explanations. (pp. 31–32)

Types of Investigations

There is no fixed set of steps that scientists always follow in doing science, no one path that leads them unerringly to scientific knowledge (Rutherford & Ahlgren, 1990). However, there are some specific types of investigations that children should experience. According to the *National Science Education Standards*, *three* types of investigations children should learn to conduct include:

* descriptive investigations;
* classificatory investigations; and
* experimental investigations.

In *descriptive investigations*, students gather observational and measurement data to answer questions about the properties and actions of objects, organisms, events, and systems. *Classificatory investigations* focus on using classification processes to organize collected information by sorting and grouping it according to one or more properties. Organizing data through classification and other procedures is an important step in identifying the defining properties of the objects and organisms of interest and in answering questions. *Experimental investigations* use experimental procedures, including controlled experiments, to provide evidence needed in forming and testing hypotheses and generating explanations.

Table 2-4 identifies the main characteristics and provides examples of each of these ways of investigating.

These three main approaches to investigating involve the application of processes of observing, measuring, classifying, inferring, predicting, experimenting, and communicating. When you make processes of science explicit to students during scientific investigations, you help them to develop skills for doing science, better understand how science is done, and appreciate more fully the real-world basis of all scientific knowledge.

Each of these three ways of investigating—descriptive, classificatory, and experimental— involve the five tasks of inquiry identified in Figure 1-3. In each type of investigation, students identify a queston or problem to investigate, conduct investigations, collect relevant data, analyze the data, form conclusions and explanations, and communicate their investigations and findings to others for review.

"Scientists use different kinds of investigations, depending on the questions they are trying to answer. Types of investigations include describing objects, events, and organisms; classifying them; and conducting a fair test (experimenting)."

(*National Science Education Standards*, National Research Council, 1996, p. 123)

TABLE 2-4   TYPES OF INVESTIGATIONS

Types of Investigations	Investigative Procedures	Example Science Topics	Example Engagement Questions
Descriptive Investigations	Gather observational and measurement data to answer questions about the properties and actions of objects, organisms, events, and systems.	White powders Seeds and plants	What are the visual properties of different kinds of white powders? What is the sequence of germination and growth for a bean seed?
Classificatory Investigations	Organize collected information by sorting and grouping it according to one or more properties in order to identify relationships and better define properties.	Rocks and minerals	Which mineral is hardest? How can you tell the difference between igneous and sedimentary rocks?
Experimental Investigations	Conduct experiments, including controlled experiments, to determine how variables are related and to isolate causal factors in natural phenomena.	Color and sunlight absorption Seeds and plants	Do different colored materials absorb sunlight differently? Do plants take in water through their leaves or their roots?

The theoretical and practical foundations for the grade placement of different types of investigation are considered in Chapter 3. Many activities in elementary science can be adapted to different grade levels. This is true for the many different activities provided in this chapter. In general, grade 1–3 children can readily carry out simple descriptive and classificatory investigations with moderate teacher assistance. With greater teacher assistance, children at this level might also carry out simple experimental investigations. Grade 4–6 students continue to conduct descriptive and classificatory investigations. They can also conduct more complex experimental investigations. However, they will likely need considerable teacher assistance to identify variables, plan and conduct controlled investigations, and interpret the results of investigations.

Sometimes statewide tests in science include items in which students are required to formulate and write out their answers. Activity 2-4 provides a sample item related to fair tests that might appear on a statewide test. Take some time to work through this activity. Follow the directions given. Compare your answers with those from a group of your colleagues.

Following are some examples of classroom inquiry involving the three types of investigations.

Go to the Homework and Exercises section in Chapter 2 of MyEducationLab to watch two videos, *Designing Experiments* and *Controlling Variables*. Together, the videos reveal the difficulties that even older students have with controlled experiments and how students can remarkably improve their understanding of a control of variables task through discovery activities and teacher instruction.

Activity 2-4: Experimenting with Soils: A Fair Test

Sample Test Item. James and Maria noticed three different types of soil, black soil, sand, and clay, were found in their neighborhood. They decided to investigate the question, "How does the type of soil (black soil, sand, and clay) under *grass sod* affect the height of grass?"

Plan an investigation the students could use to answer their question.

In your plan, be sure to:

1. Identify the manipulated, responding, and controlled variables for the investigation.
2. Describe the steps to do in the investigation.
3. Tell how often measurements are to be taken and recorded.

Mealworms are the larval stage of various beetles. They can usually be purchased from a local pet store. Talk to your pet store about how to feed, care for, and humanely dispose of mealworms. A bed of oatmeal on newspaper provides a good environment for students to observe mealworms.

To observe mealworms, student groups will need newspaper, oatmeal, crackers, plastic forceps, petri dish (for water), hand lenses, and their journals.

Investigating Mealworms: Descriptive, Classificatory, and Experimental Inquiries

The *National Science Education Standards* emphasize that "different kinds of questions suggest different kinds of scientific investigations" (National Research Council, 1996, p. 148). An investigation of mealworms can involve all three types of investigation strategies, depending on the question asked. Figure 2-6 provides a number of questions for mealworm investigations. Study the questions given in the figure and decide which type of investigation—descriptive, classificatory, or experimental—is most suitable for investigating each one.

What kind of investigation strategy is called for by the different questions for investigating mealworms? Questions 1 and 2 call for descriptive investigations about the body characteristics

Mealworms are the larval stage of beetles. They go through complete metamorphosis, with four different life stages: egg, larva, pupa, and adult.

1. What are the main body characteristics of mealworms?
2. How many legs does your mealworm have? Where on the body are the legs located?
3. Do mealworms have the general characteristics of insects? What are the similarities and differences between mealworms and other insects?
4. How does a mealworm move? How do its legs work together when it moves? How does it turn corners?
5. What kinds of food do mealworms prefer to eat?

Figure 2-6 Questions for investigating mealworms.

Figure 2-7 What are the main body parts of a mealworm?

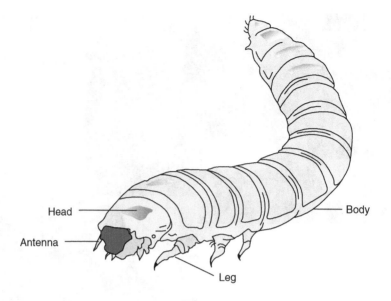

Head

Antenna

Body

Leg

of mealworms. To answer the question, students must observe the mealworms carefully, including observation with a magnifying lens. They can observe that mealworms have a segmented body with six legs attached to the body. Two antennae are attached to the head. Children might communicate this information through labeled drawings (see Figure 2-7).

Question 3 calls for a classificatory investigation. In response to question 3, for example, students can find out from their teachers, or through their textbook, a trade book, or the Internet that insects have three main body parts, six legs, and two antennae. By comparing their observations of the characteristics of mealworms with their findings from outside sources, they can conclude that mealworms should be classified as insects.

Question 4 calls for a descriptive investigation with an experimental component. In the experiment, students might work together to discover different ways the six legs of a mealworm might be used in moving (see Figure 2-8). Through observing whether meal-

Figure 2-8 How do mealworms use their legs when they walk and turn corners?

worms actually use their legs in the proposed way, students can test the different models of mealworm movement. The psychomotor involvement of the students helps them to understand the complexity and appreciate the wonder of mealworm movement.

Question 5 calls for an experimental investigation. One way to investigate question 5 is for student teams to draw a small circle (about 5 cm in diameter) in the center of a paper plate and draw four equally spaced lines straight from the edge of the inner circle to the edge of the plate. Different foods, including bran, sugar, lettuce, and potato are then placed equidistant from the center within the four segments created by the four lines. A number of mealworms are then placed in the inner circle. Students can observe how many mealworms move to each segment, note whether they eat the foods in the segments, and infer which foods they prefer. What is the manipulated variable in this experiment? What is the responding variable? What variables should be controlled?

Mystery Powders: A Descriptive and Classificatory Investigation

In classificatory investigations, students find out more about objects and organisms by discovering ways of grouping them according to their properties or traits. By focusing on properties, classificatory investigations tend to incorporate descriptive inquiry procedures. Investigating the properties of white powders forms the basis for an exciting descriptive and classificatory inquiry for children in about grade 3.

In this series of activities, children investigate common white powders, including sugar, table salt, baking soda, and cornstarch (see the accompanying Lesson Activities: Investigating White Powders). The powders are similar in color but differ in other properties. Through investigation, the children learn several indicator tests they can use to identify properties of the powders. For example, they learn that salt dissolves in water and baking soda fizzes in vinegar. Table 2-5 shows a chart of the properties of some common white powders.

Once children learn to identify each white powder through tests, they are given "mystery powders" consisting of mixtures of *two* powders.

A comprehensive set of activities on the properties of white powders can be found on pages A-30–A-33 in *Activities for Teaching Science as Inquiry*.

To connect science and social studies, you might ask children in social studies to investigate which white powders pioneer settlers would have carried with them on wagon trains and why they would need them.

TABLE 2-5 PROPERTIES OF WHITE POWDERS

Observations	Powder 1 Granulated Sugar	Powder 2 Table Salt	Powder 3 Baking Soda	Powder 4 Cornstarch
Visual (Magnifying Glass)	White crystals	White box-shaped crystals	Fine white powder	Fine yellowish white powder
Water Test	Dissolves in water	Dissolves in water	Forms milky mix	Makes water cloudy
Vinegar Test	Dissolves in vinegar	Has no reaction with vinegar	Fizzes with vinegar	Gets thick, then hard with vinegar
Iodine Test	Turns yellow with iodine	Has no reaction with iodine	Turns yellow-orange with iodine	Turns red, then black with iodine

Lesson Activities: Investigating White Powders

Materials

Salt, sugar, baking soda, and cornstarch; containers of water, vinegar, and iodine; medicine droppers; plastic spoons; toothpicks; blank data table for recording data; laminated blank data table to use as an investigation tray; magnifying lenses; safety goggles.

Safety Precautions

- Wear safety goggles for these investigations with powders.
- Do not taste any of the powders or liquids.
- Wash your hands after you test each powder.

Initiating Question

What are the identifying properties of some common white powders?

Preparation

Laminate copies of the blank data table shown and use one as an investigation tray for each group. Prepare an additional, unlaminated data table for each team to use for recording data.

Investigation Procedures

1. *Visual Observations:* Use a plastic spoon to place a small amount of each powder in the appropriate cells of your investigation tray. Use a magnifying glass to observe each powder. Write down your observations on a paper copy of the data table.
2. *Water Test:* Use a clean plastic spoon to place a small amount of each powder in a row on your investigation tray. Add several drops of water and mix with a toothpick to see what happens. Record your observations in your data table.
3. *Iodine Test:* Use a clean plastic spoon to place a small amount of each powder in a row on your tray. Add a drop or two of iodine to each powder. Write down the results in your data table. Be careful! Iodine can stain your hands and clothing.
4. *Vinegar Test:* Use a clean plastic spoon to place a small amount of each powder in a row on your tray. Add several drops of vinegar to each powder. Write down the results in your data table.

Explanations

Write your answers to these questions on your data record sheet.

5. What do the rows in your data table indicate?
6. What do the columns indicate?
7. How are the four powders alike?
8. How are the powders different? What is the best test for identifying each powder?

Communication

Throughout the activity, keep accurate written records of the array of data collected. Also, be prepared to present and discuss your investigation procedures, your data, and your explanations of the data with the whole class.

Clean Up

Throw away toothpicks. Return powders, test supplies, and the cleaned laminated data table to teacher-designated spot. Clean and dry anything dirty, including your hands. Do not put powders in the sink as they might harden and clog the drain.

DATA TABLE FOR INVESTIGATING WHITE POWDERS				
	Powder 1 Granulated Sugar	Powder 2 Table Salt	Powder 3 Baking Soda	Powder 4 Cornstarch
Visual Observations				
Water Test				
Iodine Test				
Vinegar Test				

Useful commercial guides to this activity can be found at: http://www.csulb.edu/~lhenriqu/mysterypowder.htm.

Scientists keep accurate records of data collected, so they are prepared to recall data taken, make comparisons of the data, draw inferences, make predictions, and generate explanations. For similar reasons, students should also keep accurate records. You can use the student records to assess understanding and decide next steps in instruction.

During this activity on white powders, provide time for students to record their findings. Recording data will be a natural part of the work of some students; other students will need encouragement to stop and record their findings.

Take some time to discuss with students the design of data record sheets. For example, column 1 of the data sheet used in the white powders investigation shows the types of investigation tests carried out. These include visual examination, water tests, and so on. The rows describe the results of each test with each of the white powders. Seen together, the columns and rows provide a display of data that allows patterns to be found and used in further investigations.

The teacher gives each pair of students a mixture of two powders. Working together, each pair uses visual and tactile observations to form hypotheses about their mixture. They then perform the various tests on the mixture to test their hypotheses. Here is what some of the children do and say during their mystery powders investigations:

Student 1: *Put a little bit here.*

Student 2: *(Student 2 pours some of the mystery powder on a piece of white paper, and the pair look at it and feel it.)*

Student 3: *You do the water (test); I'll do the vinegar. (One of the partners in this pair drops water from a small bottle on a bit of the mystery powder. The other one puts a few drops of vinegar on another small amount of the powder. The children observe the resulting reactions.)*

Student 4: It's fizzing a little!

Student 3: Fizzing, yeah! Try one more time. (The partner puts more drops of vinegar on the powder.)

Student 4: There's definitely baking soda in there.

Student 3: Big time!

Student 5: I think it's not salt.

Student 6: I don't know. What would be the best way to find out if it is not salt? (Pauses and ponders for a moment.) All right, let's try water.

Student 7: We thought it was cornstarch. We did the iodine test and we're positive that it is cornstarch. We want to move on to a really, really, hard one, a challenge. We want to put four (powders) in.

Teacher: Do you think you can solve that?

Students: Yes!

(Annenberg/CPB Foundation, 1997)

Go to the Homework and Exercises section in Chapter 2 of MyEducationLab to view the video, *Investigating Particles: Parts 1 and 2*. This video features second-grade children investigating a variety of particles, including different kinds of beans, rice, and cornmeal.

In performing the various tests on their mystery powders, the children take their role as scientists very seriously. They are thoughtful, respectful of one another, but excited.

Through these lessons, the child-scientists develop well-structured and grade-level-appropriate knowledge about matter. These lessons on matter align well with the *National Science Education Standards* for grades K–4 (see the NSES box on standards and concepts and principles related to matter). The children also have many opportunities to practice and extend their science process skills—but always within a context of inquiry and significant concepts and principles.

In the white powders lesson, the inquiries are primarily descriptive and classificatory. Next, let us look at a classroom investigation involving descriptive and experimental investigation procedures.

NSES STANDARDS ON MATTER AND CONCEPTS AND PRINCIPLES THAT SUPPORT THE STANDARDS

NSES Standards

Students should understand:

• Properties of objects and materials (K–4).

Concepts and Principles That Support the Standards

• Objects have many observable properties, including size, weight, shape, color, temperature, and the ability to react with other substances.
• Some properties can be measured using tools, such as rulers, balances, and thermometers.
• Objects are made of one or more materials, such as paper, wood, and metal. Objects can be described by the properties of the materials from which they are made, and those properties can be used to separate or sort a group of objects or materials.
• Materials can exist in different states—solids, liquids, and gases. Some common materials, such as water, can be changed from one state to another by heating or cooling.

Activity 2-5: What Are the Parts of a Seed?

1. Obtain several lima bean seeds. Make as many observations and measurements as you can about the bean seeds.
2. Soak some of the bean seeds for at least 48 hours.
3. Gently break a soaked lima bean seed open into its two halves. Observe the two halves carefully, including with a magnifying lens.
4. Communicate your observations to others using writing, charts, and drawings.

Germinating Seeds and Growing Plants: A Descriptive amd Experimental Inquiry Project

There is nothing like being around children to rekindle our own interest in the natural world. Children love to study living things. They especially enjoy planting seeds and watching and caring for plants as they grow. Forming good questions that can be empirically investigated and that lead to significant knowledge is the first step in scientific inquiry. Some questions children ask are not easily investigated, for example, *Why do plants develop from seeds?* and *How do plants grow? What* questions (questions about *what* might happen in an investigation) are more easily investigated in the classroom than *why* or *how* questions. If students ask *why* or *how* questions, teachers can help them rework the questions into forms that can be investigated. In this series of lessons on seeds and plants, the teacher helped the students formulate this question: *What happens to the seeds and plants during plant growth?* As the children began to investigate and collect data related to this question, through group discussion the teacher helped them focus on these additional questions:

- What are the parts of a seed?
- What happens to the different parts of the seed as the plants grow?
- What is the sequence of germination and growth for a bean seed?

These questions fit investigations that can be carried out at almost any grade level, K–6. Investigating questions such as these can be instrumental in helping children attain the K–4 NSES Content Standards related to organisms (see accompanying NSES box).

What Are the Parts of a Seed? Activity 2-5 is directed toward the first question, concerning the parts of the seed. Do this activity before continuing.

This activity reveals that once bean seeds are soaked and broken into two halves, three main parts can be observed. Through instruction, students can learn that the three parts are called a *seed coat*, the *cotyledon* (the pulpy mass in a seed), and a small plantlike structure—the *embryo plant*. The beginnings of a leaf and root are clearly observable in the embryo plant (see Figure 2-9).

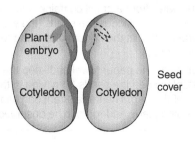

Figure 2-9 A bean seed has three main parts: a seed covering, the cotyledon, and an embryo plant.

In inquiry, children must plan investigations carefully and use their science process skills selectively in collecting data. The investigation procedures and the science processes used depend on the inquiry questions asked. What types of investigations—descriptive, classificatory, or experimental—are called for by the questions in the seed and plant study?

Once children identify the parts of a seed, they might engage in brainstorming and raise their own questions about the functions of the seed parts, such as *What is the seed coat for?* or *What does the cotyledon do?*

These and other questions lead to more investigation and research.

What Is the Sequence of Germination and Growth of Bean Seeds? This question calls for a descriptive investigation. Children cannot just place the seeds underground in moist soil, because then they would not be able to see them germinate. However, they can use a transparent germination bag like the one shown in Figure 2-10. The germination bags should be attached to a bulletin board or some other flat, vertical surface.

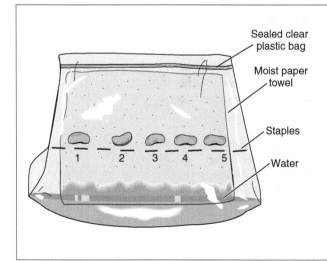

- Line a 7 inch × 8 inch (quart size) sealable, transparent storage bag with a moist paper towel.
- Place nine staples across the bag about 4 to 5 cm from the bottom, as shown in the diagram.
- Position the seeds to be germinated above the line of staples.
- The seeds may be presoaked for about 24 hours.
- Gently pour water from a small container into the bag, being careful not to dislodge the seeds (the water should bulge slightly at the bottom of the bag to about a finger's thickness).

The water will soak the paper towel and keep the seeds moist. The staples keep the seeds from lying in the water at the bottom of the bag. The transparent bag allows the seeds, developing plant, and roots to be observed.

Labels in figure: Sealed clear plastic bag; Moist paper towel; Staples; Water

Figure 2-10 How to construct a seed germination bag.

	Descriptions			Measurements		
Date	Changes in seeds	Changes in roots	Changes in stems	Length of roots	Length of stems	Drawing
Monday March 5						
Wednesday March 7						
Friday March 9						
Monday March 12						

Figure 2-11 Sample data sheet for recording seed germination data.

Children should observe their germinating seeds and developing plants regularly for 2 or 3 weeks. What should they observe? Initially, in this investigation children recorded their observations of a wide varierty of changes through words and drawings in their journals and on data sheets. As the children *reflected* on their question and data through class discussion, they found that they needed some additional observations. They also found that there were some observations that they would likely not use in drawing conclusions. The children decided to use a new data sheet like the one in Figure 2-11. The data sheet provides for recording data on changes in color, size, and apprearance that might occur in the seeds and in the emerging roots, stems, and leaves.

In investigating the process of germination, children might observe that first the seed becomes moist and softens. Early in the process, a "sprout" begins to emerge from the bean seed near where the embryo plant is located. As children observe further, they can see that the tip of the sprout becomes the root. The stem grows upward from the root carrying the cotyledon with it. Because the root has emerged from near the location of the embryo plant, children might infer that the growing plant develops from the embryo.

During the germination process, the seed coat comes off. Although they cannot know for sure from observation alone, children might infer that the seed coat protected the seed to ensure that it did not become moist earlier than desired. Instruction and reading can confirm this inference.

As the plant develops, the cotyledon shrivels and sometimes falls off the stem. Building on this observation, children might learn from instruction that the cotyledon is an energy or food source that is used by the young plant as it is germinating, before the leaves develop and the process of photosynthesis begins to take place. Your students can investigate further by trying to germinate each of the two halves of a cotyledon, one with the embryo plant and one without.

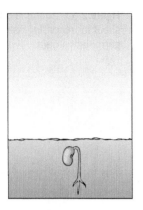

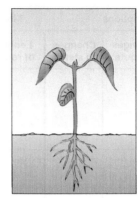
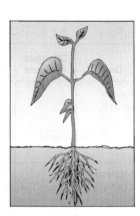

Figure 2-12 The developmental sequence from a bean seed to a young bean plant.

Eventually as the bean plant develops, green leaves begin to grow. Figure 2-12 summarizes the developmental sequence of a bean seed into a young bean plant.

Observation of the seeds and developing plants in the baggie suggest that the plant takes in and uses the water in some way. The children wanted to know, *How does the plant take in water?* The teacher helped the children reformulate this question to, *Do plants take in water through roots or leaves?*

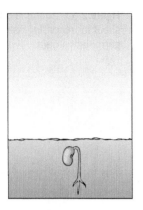
Additional activities about seeds and plants can be found on pages A-124–A-150 in *Activities for Teaching Science as Inquiry.* Also, see the delightful resource, *GrowLab: Activities for Growing Minds* (1992), published by the National Gardening Association (see Appendix B for address).

Do Plants Take in Water Through Roots or Leaves? To gather evidence to use in answering this question, children might carry out an experimental investigation like the one illustrated in Figure 2-13. This investigation involves two plants. The manipulated variable is how the plants are watered. The responding variable is the resulting condition of each plant. The variables that are controlled or kept constant are the amount of water each plant gets and environmental conditions such as temperature and light exposure. In the investigation, water is added to the soil of one plant so that it can reach the roots. The same amount of water is sprinkled on the leaves of the second plant, with a plastic bib keeping the water from reaching the soil and roots (National Gardening Association, 1992).

Children should keep daily records of their observations. Teachers might prepare data sheets for chldren to use, or students might be required to construct their own record

Figure 2-13 Do plants get water through their roots or their leaves?

plastic "bib"

dish

Pot A
Water soil

Pot B
Water leaves

sheets. After about 2 weeks, the teacher might guide the children as they use the data sheets to remember and review their observations as a basis for any discussions of their findings. In guiding discussion, the teacher might ask:

- What did you do in the investigation?
- What did you observe? How did your findings compare with your predictions?
- What can you infer about the role of leaves and roots in taking in water? What makes you confident in your inference that water is taken in by roots?
- Did you actually see roots taking in water? (National Gardening Association, 1992)

Through this investigation the children were able to conclude that water was taken into the plant by the roots, rather than through the leaves. This finding led to an additional question, *Is water carried to the leaves through the stem?*

Is Water Carried to the Leaves Through the Stem? Answering this question requires an experiment, though it is different somewhat from a true controlled investigation. Here are the investigation procedures:

- Obtain two clear drinking glasses.
- Fill the glasses about two-thirds full of water.
- Add blue food coloring to the water in one glass.
- Cut a small slice off the bottom of a celery stalk. Set the stem into the glass of colored water as in the left side of Figure 2-14(a).
- Cut a small slice off the bottom of a second celery stalk. Set the stem into the glass of plain water as in the right side of Figure 2-14(a).
- Allow both glasses with celery stalks to sit in a sunny area for 2 hours. At the end of this period, cut across both stalks as in Figure 2-14(b).
- To help the children organize and make sense of their observational data, teachers might ask: *Do both stalks look the same? What has happened to the celery stem? What parts of the stem appear to contain the colored water? How do you know? What can you conclude about the function of a stem? How is water carried to different parts of the plant?*

Through instruction, media, textbooks, or other means, teachers can provide the following information that will help students organize their developing knowledge:

- All organisms have basic needs. Plants need light, air, water, and nutrients. Animals need air, water, and nutrients.
- Plants and animals can survive only in environments in which their needs are met.

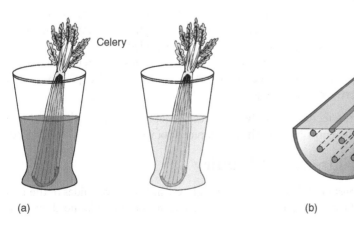

Celery

(a)   (b)

Figure 2-14 "What is the function of the stem of a plant? Why do you think so?"

- Roots absorb water and nutrients through small root hairs. Water and nutrients are carried from the roots to the leaves through small tubes, called capillaries, that are inside the stem.
- Plants get their energy for survival and growth directly from sunlight through a process called photosynthesis.
- Animals live by consuming the energy-rich foods initially synthesized by plants (*National Science Education Standards*, National Research Council, 1996).

Through inquiries like these—asking questions, conducting investigations, collecting and recording observational data, and using the data and science knowledge to generate theories and explanations—students build integrated conceptual structures that can be used in further descriptive, classificatory, and explanatory studies.

Communicating Investigation Results. Full inquiry involves asking a simple question, completing an investigation, answering the question, and communicating the results to others. In one kindergarten class, at the conclusion of a unit in which they planted seeds and investigated plant growth, the children communicated what they learned by acting out seed germination and plant growth. As the teacher read aloud from a children's book about seeds and life, the children solemnly played the roles of seeds, moisture, and sunlight. At first, each seed-child rolled into a tight ball close to the floor. The water-child then went about, sprinkling blue crepe-paper "rainwater" on the seed-children, and they began, one by one, to shake themselves and gradually spring to life. When the seed-children popped up through the "ground," they looked around for the sun-child, who held a large yellow circle with rays drawn on it. With the warming rays of the sun, the seed-children began to stretch and grow to their full heights. The children's understanding of seed germination and plant growth could be inferred from the seriousness of their role playing, the ways their actions paralleled the teacher's reading, and the connections between each seed-child's actions and the actions of the growth factors of moisture and sunlight.

Questions, investigations, observations, and explanations/conclusions might be communicated through a science journal or notebook, or orally to the class. The written records should be developed as the investigation unfolds, with questions, data, and conclusions recorded. The presentation might include the following components:

A. *Questions. What I want to find out.* (The focus question for investigation is expressed in writing.)
B. *Investigation Plans: What I will do to answer my questions* (Investigation procedures are described.)
C. *Observations: What I found out from my observations and measurements.* (Data sheets, verbal information, measurement data, graphs, labeled diagrams, and pictures, perhaps from digital cameras, would be included here.)
D. *Conclusions: What I concluded.* (In drawing conclusions, children should use their observational data as evidence to support their answers to the questions raised in the Questions section of the journal.)

The use of written records not only improves conceptual understanding and inquiry skills in science, it also contributes to the development of writing skills (Klentschy, 2005).

Teachers, Children, and Inquiry

Effective teachers must be skilled observers of children and effective guides of the inquiry process. Teachers who can match their teaching actions to the particular needs of students are essential in inquiry learning: deciding when and how to guide; when to encourage more exploration; how to scaffold learning through prompts, hints, questions, and other means; when to demand more rigorous grappling by the students; when to provide information; and when to connect students to other sources (National Research Council, 1996).

Teaching and learning science through an inquiry approach is challenging but well worth the effort!

SUMMARY

• Processes of science are skills that scientists and children apply in collecting, organizing, and using data to interpret and make sense of the world. Specific processes emphasized in elementary and middle school science include observing, measuring, classifying, inferring, hypothesizing, conducting controlled investigations, predicting, explaining, and communicating. These science processes are much like the mental processes we all use in solving everyday problems.

• Sometimes processes of science are taught in elementary classrooms primarily through isolated activities. But the *National Science Education Standards* have called for more than science as process, emphasizing that processes should be embedded and integrated in inquiry.

• Elementary and middle school students can be expected to engage in descriptive, classificatory, and experimental inquiries. In grades K–4, investigations are largely based on systematic description and classification of material objects and organisms.

• By grade 5 or 6, and even earlier with a great deal of teacher guidance, children begin to engage in experimental inquiries. In controlled investigations, students work to understand some phenomenon by determining the effect of a manipulated variable on a responding variable, while controlling all other relevant variables.

• Participating in investigations that incorporate processes of science is essential to the science learning and cognitive development of elementary and middle grade students. All of these ways of investigating involve the application of the various processes of science. By making processes of science explicit to students during scientific investigations, you help them to develop skills for doing science, to better understand the nature of scientific inquiry, and to appreciate more fully the real-world basis of all scientific knowledge.

ONLINE PROFESSIONAL DEVELOPMENT

Pre- and post-tests to assess your knowledge of chapter content, along with exercises to enhance your understanding, can be found on MyEducationLab at www.myeducationlab.com.

Video Guides

Video clips on MyEducationLab for this chapter include: *Keeping Observation Records, Identifying Variables,* and *Investigating Particles—Parts 1 and 2.*

Accessing the Videos

1. Go to the Homework and Exercises section in Chapter 2 of MyEducationLab to select and view videos for this chapter and answer the questions.

2. Videos might be viewed individually, by small groups of colleagues, or by the whole class.
3. As you watch each video, use the **Questions for Reflection** to guide your thoughts and note taking for personal use and group discussion.
4. Discuss your answers to the questions about each video with classmates.

Video: Keeping Observation Records

Overview

In this video we watch kindergarten and fifth-grade children involved in activities that help build the process skills of observation and record keeping. Each activity also helps students to attain state writing standards and introduces children to important science concepts.

Questions for Reflection

1. What does the kindergarten teacher say about the goldfish lesson and the Connecticut Science Standards? On what specific standards does the lesson focus?
2. What examples of observation do you see in the goldfish, pin-hole viewer, and moon phases lessons? What kinds of observation records do the children make in the different lessons?
3. How do the different observation records represent a means of developing the process skill of communicating? How do you think the different records also relate to the state writing standards?

Video: Identifying Variables

Overview

In this video, students watch a demonstration by two teachers, aided by students, of the variables associated with the most effective design of sails for "skimmers." Students respond excitedly to the demonstration and to the teachers' questions.

Questions for Reflection

1. What differences do you see in the two sails being tested?
2. What are the manipulated and responding variables in the investigation, and what variables are controlled?

What examples do you find of children naming or discussing the various variables?
3. What do the teachers do to help make sure the children are thinking about the different variables as they watch the demonstration?

Video: Investigating Particles, Parts 1 and 2

Overview

In these two videos, we watch as second-grade children investigate a variety of particles, including lima beans, mung beans, pinto beans, rice, and corn meal. For example, they investigate how the size of particles affects the size of the hills that can be made from them.

Questions for Reflection

1. What questions about particles do the children investigate in these videos?
2. How are observation skills used in investigating the different questions?

Annenberg Videos

Case Studies in Science Education: Jean

To access Annenberg videos, follow the instructions given in the Online Professional Development section in Chapter 1 on page 26.

3

L earning science is something students do, not something that is done to them.

(*National Science Education Standards*, National Research Council, 1996, p. 20)

Learning Science with Understanding

ONCE STUDENTS INVOLVED in inquiry have formulated questions that can be investigated and collected and organized data, they face the challenge of using the data as evidence in generating new knowledge, forming theories, and constructing explanations that can be used in answering their initial question. In learning science with understanding, most students will need considerable assistance from their teachers.

Fortunately, there is a growing body of research available on teaching and learning science with understanding. Teachers who know and use this research can greatly enhance the learning of science by their students. Consider how such research might be used in the following lesson scenario.

During a series of investigations on properties of light, Don Roach's fifth grade students pointed out one morning that they could see their "reflections" in a plate-glass door. Mr. Roach had studied children's theories about light in an in-service workshop and knew that his students would have a variety of conceptions and misconceptions about mirrors and images.

Through class discussion, Mr. Roach guided his students to think about what an image is and where it appears to be in mirrors and other reflecting surfaces. Most of the students knew that the image was just a copy of the real thing, but thought that it was on the surface of a mirror or just behind it (Shapiro, 1994). A few thought it might be deeper in the mirror. Drawing on their ideas and their knowledge of light reflection gained in previous lessons, Don helped the students form a simple question that might be investigated scientifically: *Where is my image in a mirror?*

The children decided to search for evidence to answer the question by investigating their own images in a glass door near the classroom. In the investigation, students worked in small, cooperative groups. One student, called the *object partner,* stood on one side of the glass door so she could see her image in it (see Figure 3-1). Another student, the *image partner,* went to the other side of the door, and after some direction stood right on top of the image of the partner's shoes.

One group decided to use the classroom meter sticks to measure each partner's distance from the door. Soon other groups were also measuring the distance from the door of the object and image partners. Mr. Roach suggested that the groups combine their data into a class data table (see Figure 3-2). When each group had entered its measurements in the data table, Mr. Roach asked the groups if they could discover a pattern in the data. Some of the students noted that in the data table the object distance and image distance were always

Figure 3-1 A child examines the image of herself formed in a glass door.

Figure 3-2 Data table for mirror images activity. What are some things you might conclude from the data?

Group	Distance of Image from Door (cm)	Distance of Object from Door (cm)
A.	200	190
B.	350	365
C.	250	238
D.	225	225
E.	300	320

about the same. Based on this discovery, the class generalized that an image appears to be just as far inside a mirror as the real object is in front of the mirror.

The teacher in this lesson used a number of research findings on how children learn, including findings related to knowledge construction, prior knowledge, knowledge organization, scaffolding assistance, learning communities, and naive theories. As a teacher, you need to know how children learn and develop so you can adjust instruction to meet the needs of all your students. This chapter describes some of the abundant research on learning and development that can provide a strong theory base for you as you guide children's learning of science with understanding.

As you study the chapter, keep these questions in mind:

- *What is meant by constructivism? What is the role of prior knowledge in new learning? What does it mean to learn science with understanding?*

- *How do various internal and external factors, including access to prior knowledge, knowledge organization, scaffolding, and learning communities affect science learning?*

- *What is meant by transfer? How can you help students learn to transfer their knowledge to new situations?*

- *How do students' naive theories and alternative conceptions affect their science learning? How can you use inquiry instruction to promote conceptual change and deeper understanding of science?*

- *What is meant by development? How does development differ from learning? How does development affect learning?*

- *What are some of Piaget's findings on the development of thinking that are relevant to science teaching?*

- *How do cognitive development, prior knowledge, and the availability of teacher scaffolding affect the learning of science with understanding?*

The New View of Learning

Contemporary research findings and theories on learning are well summarized by Bransford, Brown, and Cocking (1999) in *How People Learn* and by Duschl, Schweingruber, and

Shouse (2007) in *Taking Science to School: Learning and Teaching Science in Grades K–8*. Both of these important reports were sponsored by the National Research Council, the group that also sponsored the *National Science Education Standards*.

The traditional view of learning is that knowledge is discovered through the manipulation of objects or acquired from others when learners listen to what they say. However, we now accept that learning is more complex than that. Knowledge cannot be passed intact from a teacher or book to a learner, nor is it simply discovered in the real world. Students must *construct* new knowledge for themselves.

This view of learning is called *constructivism*. In the constructivist perspective, new knowledge is always based on the prior or existing knowledge that learners bring to learning situations. Students take in information from many sources, but in building their own knowledge, they connect information to prior knowledge and experiences, organize it, and construct meaning for themselves (Loucks-Horsley et al., 1998). Without an adequate level of prior knowledge, new learning and its transfer to new situations cannot be expected (Bransford et al., 1999). What learners already know influences what they attend to, how they organize input, and how they are able to integrate new constructions to expand their knowledge bases.

Constructing Knowledge with Understanding in Science

To *know* something implies to be able to remember or recall it so that it can be accessed and used when needed. *Understanding* is based in knowledge, yet it involves more than mere recall. What does it mean for a student to understand an idea? Contemporary researchers insist that when students truly understand an idea, they can do something with it. They can:

- interpret questions for investigation and express them in their own words;
- interpret what they learn and express it in their own words;
- relate concepts to real-world experiences;
- plan and conduct investigations to answer investigation questions;
- interpret data collected, relate it to real-world activities, find patterns in the data, compare and contrast their data with that of others; and
- apply their knowledge and their investigation findings in drawing inferences, making predictions, constructing explanations, and solving novel problems (Bransford et al., 1999; Wiggins & McTighe, 1998; Wiske, 1998).

As an example of the differences between knowledge and understanding, if students have knowledge of the facts, concepts, and principles of water introduced in Chapter 1, they should be able to describe what happens in heaping and other water phenomena, define important terms, such as cohesive bonds, and recall what they learned about the role of cohesive bonds in explaining why water heaps up in cups. On the other hand, if students truly *understand* the nature of water, when they encounter a new event, such as the beading of drops on wax paper or the spreading of drops on aluminum foil, they should be able to apply the concept of cohesion and the concept of adhesion between water and different types of materials to explain why the drops bead up on one surface and spread out on another.

Students often have limited opportunity to develop understanding because the curriculum, textbooks, and tests emphasize memory and recall. Too much emphasis on memory results in knowledge that is fragmented, incomplete, and tied to specific situations. In contrast, understanding in science must be based in knowledge that is integrated rather than fragmented, that is growing in completeness, and that can be transferred to a wide

"The new view of learning is that people construct new knowledge and understanding based on what they already know and believe."

(Bransford, Brown, and Cocking. 1999, p. 10)

Figure 3-3 Levels of student understanding.

1. *Proficient understanding.* Students use the knowledge, methods, evidence, and arguments involved in a topic as powerful tools in new problem situations.
2. *Satisfactory understanding.* Learners' understanding enables them to succeed with new tasks with only minimum amounts of teacher scaffolding support.
3. *Limited understanding.* Students succeed on new tasks, but only with considerable support from teachers and peers in the form of prompts, hints, series of questions, and direct instruction.
4. *No understanding.* Students fail to succeed on new tasks, even with a great deal of assistance from teachers and peers.

range of contexts and situations. Through its emphasis on investigations, such as the investigations of water, magnets, mealworms, common white powders, and seeds and plants described in previous chapters, inquiry instruction provides an excellent context in which to foster children's science understanding.

Levels of Understanding

Understanding is not an all or nothing proposition; rather, it develops gradually through different levels of understanding (Wiggins & McTighe, 1998). The rubric in Figure 3-3 suggests a continuum for thinking about the different levels of student understanding.

In the following sections we consider ways teachers can assist learners to develop higher levels of understanding.

Enhancing the Understanding of Science

Bransford, Brown, and Cocking (1999) have emphasized a variety of internal and external factors that affect children's learning with understanding. Each of the factors suggests something specific you can do in teaching to influence your students' understanding.

One important way to enhance learning with understanding is to provide for student access to previously acquired knowledge.

Provide for Access to Prior Knowledge

Students may have learned particular knowledge of concepts, principles, and strategies in the past but fail to access and use this knowledge when needed. Teachers can use a number of strategies to enhance access to prior knowledge. One thing teachers can do is to help students recall what they already know.

Another way to enhance access to prior knowledge is through frequent review in the form of rehearsal. *Rehearsal* is often contrasted with *practice*. Practice means to do something over and over again the same way to improve a performance (Ormrod, 2004). What is learned in practice is an item of knowledge or a specific skill applicable in a specific context. Rehearsal, in contrast, takes place "when people do something again in similar but not identical ways to reinforce what they have learned while adding something new" (Lowery, 1998a, p. 28). When the focus is on rehearsal rather than just practice, children's knowledge is less likely to be bound to specific tasks and more likely to be transferable and useful in a variety of ways (Lowery, 1998a).

Research on learning indicates that abstract representations of knowledge, in terms of concepts and principles rather than facts, promote access and transfer (Bransford et al., 1999). In the chapter-opening lesson scenario on light reflection, Mr. Roach was careful to guide his students to go beyond observations and data and to develop an abstract principle about image formation: *An image in a mirror appears to be just as far inside the mirror as the object is outside the mirror.* Stated in this form, the principle can promote both access to and transfer of knowledge about images and reflection.

Sometimes the problem with learning with understanding is not that children cannot access knowledge they already have, but that they simply have never had opportunity or occasion to acquire the knowledge needed in a task. In that case, teachers must provide learning activities that enable students to develop needed knowledge. The construction of new knowledge may come from a preliminary sequence of investigations or through direct instruction and reading, provided the new knowledge is firmly anchored in real-world activities and students are given opportunities to make the new knowledge their own.

Provide for Transfer of New Knowledge

An important way to enhance understanding is to include transfer tasks as part of science lessons. **Transfer** refers to the use of previously learned knowledge in new situations. As an example, in a follow-up to the lesson on reflection and images described in the chapter introduction, Don Roach guided his students to transfer their newly constructed principle on images to predict where a candle should be placed inside an empty aquarium so that the candle appeared lit when a burning candle was placed a few centimeters away outside the aquarium (see Figure 3-4). Transferring the principle on images to a new situation, each group of children correctly predicted and then empirically verified that the first candle had to be just as far inside the aquarium as the second candle was outside the aquarium.

Assessment tasks provide an excellent framework for students to use what they know to solve new problems. Such an assessment item is given in Activity 3-1. It pertains to the second-grade lesson on magnetism described in Chapter 1. Do Activity 3-1 for yourself before reading on.

Did you decide that the object in the item must be another magnet because it was repelled by a test magnet? Iron is attracted to magnets, but is not repelled by them. Copper and glass are neither attracted to nor repelled by a magnet.

> *"Knowledge that is overly contextualized can reduce transfer; abstract representations of knowledge can promote transfer."*
>
> (Bransford et al., 1999, p. 41)

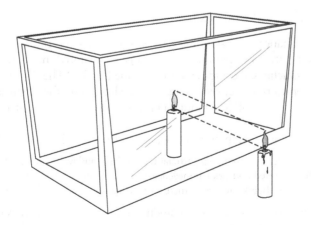

Figure 3-4 Although the candle inside the aquarium is not lit, it appears to be burning.

Activity 3-1: An Assessment Item about Magnetism

An object is placed on a table. A magnet is slowly moved toward it. The object moves away from the magnet. The object is most likely

A. another magnet.
B. a piece of glass.
C. a copper coin.
D. a piece of iron.

- Select an appropriate answer for the item.
- Using the rules for magnetic interactions, briefly explain why you chose the answer you did and why the other choices are not suitable.

"Tests of transfer that use graduated prompting provide more fine-grained analysis of learning and its effects on transfer than simple one-shot assessments of whether or not transfer occurs."

(Bransford et al., 1999, p. 54)

This item requires the transfer of the magnet rules learned in the magnets lesson—that is, their application in a new context. In individual interviews, children might be asked to select an answer and then to talk about why they chose that answer rather than one of the other choices. If their answer choice was incorrect, they might be given a prompt, hint, question, or information to help them solve the problem. For example, asking children to remember the rules of magnetism they had learned helps some children to use knowledge they already have but fail to access. Simply clarifying terms used in the item helps some other children to access needed knowledge and solve the problem. Further, to help children apply their knowledge in problem solving, they might be asked how the magnet rules could be applied to determine if an object found on the school campus contained iron (Rowe, 1973).

Some second graders are able to solve problems like these spontaneously. Other children succeed on the item with some level of teacher assistance. But, some children will have a hard time solving this problem even with a great deal of prompting. These results illustrate that teaching and learning science for recall and understanding so that "no child is left behind" is a challenging task.

Providing students opportunities to encounter concepts and principles in diverse circumstances not only results in more useful knowledge that can be transferred to new situations, it enhances the recall of knowledge.

A glossary containing definitions of important terms used in this chapter can be found on MyEducationLab.

Enhance Knowledge Organization

Another way to enhance understanding is to assist students in organizing new knowledge. Psychologists today theorize that useful knowledge is organized into connected networks called *knowledge structures*. According to Rosenshine (1997), "The size of these structures, the number of connections between items of knowledge, and the organization and richness of the connections are all important for processing knowledge, constructing meanings, and solving problems" (p.1).

From his review of research on learning, Rosenshine (1997) concluded:

When the knowledge structure on a particlar topic is large and well-connected, new information is more readily acquired and prior knowledge is more readily available for use . . . (S)tudents have more points in their knowledge structures to which they can attach new information. (p.1)

"Education is a process of developing, enlarging, expanding, and refining our students' knowledge structures."

(Rosenshine, 1997, p. 1)

One way you can enhance the organization of knowledge is through using and teaching your students to use graphic organizers. A variety of graphic organizers have been proposed

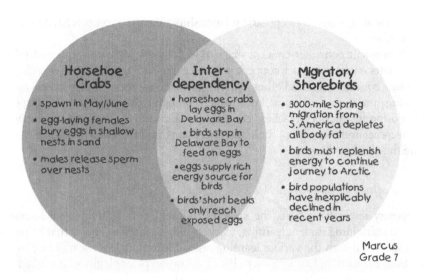

Figure 3-5 Graphic organizers such as Venn diagrams help students to organize their developing knowledge.

"Concepts, principles, and generalizations are the markers on a conceptual map. These markers become connected into a complex network of mental highways over which the student travels during problem solving."

(Rowe, 1973, p. 305)

To learn more about how to construct and use concept maps, go to http://cmap.ihmc. us. This site provides access to software you can download and use to make your own concept maps. An informative article about concept maps by Joseph Novak is available on the site.

to portray and facilitate the organization of knowledge in memory, such as outlines, spider maps, webs, and Venn diagrams. Figure 3-5 shows how a Venn diagram can help learners organize information about animals.

Joseph Novak (1995) and his colleagues (Mintzes, Wandersee, & Novak, 1998) have advocated the use of *concept maps* to enhance the knowledge organization and science understanding of students. A **concept map** is a visual representation of a major concept and its relations to subsidiary concepts.

In constructing concept maps, teachers and students enclose specific concepts in circles or boxes. They draw lines between these concepts to indicate connections and hierarchical relationships. Words or phrases written on or near the connecting lines specify the type of relationship that might exist between two concepts. Main ideas are generally placed near the top of the concept map and subsidiary concepts below. Figure 3-6 provides

Figure 3-6 To be useful, scientific knowledge must be well structured and interconnected.

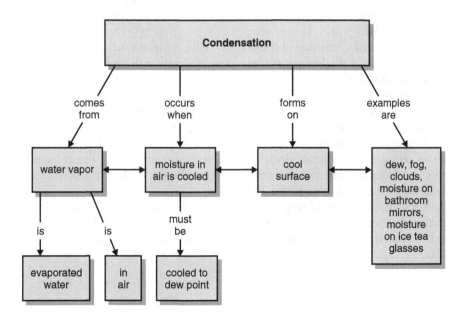

a concept map that shows concepts and relationships among concepts related to the condensation of water.

Teachers might construct concept maps to highlight specific concepts and relationships. Students might construct concept maps to express and enhance their understanding. By using concept maps and other graphic organizers in instruction, teachers can help students organize their developing knowledge. Through examining students' graphic organizers during instruction, teachers can discover and provide feedback to students on their conceptual understandings, their misconceptions, and the kinds of links in cognitive structure they are building.

Provide Scaffolding Support

Contemporary research supports the value of the deliberate scaffolding of learning by teachers. In **scaffolding** student learning, teachers supply external support that helps learners to be successful with the various learning tasks. The rationale for scaffolding has been derived from the work of Lev Vygotsky (1962), a Russian psychologist who worked in the early years of the twentieth century. Vygotsky translated Jean Piaget's works on intellectual development into Russian. He accepted the developmental nature of knowledge as proposed by Piaget, but, whereas Piaget focused on constructing a general theory of intellectual development, Vygotsky was concerned mainly with how schooling affects cognitive development.

In investigations of the relationship between learning assistance and level of cognitive development, Vygotsky (1962) gave two children of the same age (say, 8 years) problems that were harder than they could manage on their own. The investigator also gave some assistance to the children, such as the first step in a solution, a leading question, or some other form of help. Vygotsky discovered "that one child could, with cooperation, solve problems designed for twelve-year olds, while the other could not go beyond problems intended for nine-year olds" (p. 103).

Vygotsky referred to the difference in what children can do with assistance and what they can do on their own without assistance as the *zone of proximal development*. For Vygotsky, the goal of instruction is to assist all children to reach their potential as defined by this zone. "What the child can do in cooperation today," he concluded, "he can do alone tomorrow" (p. 104).

Thus, for Vygotsky, instruction needs to be challenging, running ahead of the actual level of knowledge of the learner. If students are to learn with understanding when instruction runs ahead of their level of knowledge, they will need varying degrees of teacher and peer assistance, or *scaffolding*.

To scaffold the learning process for students, inquiry teachers might provide suggestions, questions, prompts, or hints. They might also guide students to clarify, elaborate, or justify their investigation procedures and findings. Teachers might even choose to provide necessary terms, concepts, and principles to students through formal, direct instruction. Textbooks, videos, the Internet, and other means might also be used to help students develop knowledge needed to support understanding.

Just as scaffolds in a building project are designed to be taken down when the building walls are strong, scaffolding support in teaching should be gradually removed or "faded" (Ormrod, 2004) as students gain facility with science knowledge and inquiry processes.

Nancy Gallenstein has written an interesting article titled "Never Too Young for a Concept Map" that suggests a variation for young children. Rather than using only words, young learners can create concrete concept maps by using objects or pictures. Connections between concepts are made through the use of paper arrows, string, yarn, pipe cleaners, etc. Read this article in the September 2005 issue of *Science and Children*.

"Ideally, an individual spontaneously transfers appropriate knowledge without a need for prompting. Sometimes, however, prompting is necessary. With prompting, transfer can improve quite dramatically."

(Bransford et al., 1999, p. 54)

Information from ongoing informal and formal assessments provides the basis for decisions about who, when, and how to scaffold. Inquiry teaching provides teachers with many opportunities to gather assessment data. Teachers can gather information on students' learning and understanding through listening carefully to their discourse, asking students questions and listening to their responses, watching children as they work, and examining their work products. Through such means, teachers seek information from students about what they know and can do, including information related to such questions as:

- What do students already know about activities before they begin?
- Do students connect data they have collected to real-world activities?
- Are students using science knowledge to provide plausible explanations for their observations? Are the students' reasons becoming more detailed? Do students provide more than one reason for their explanations?
- Do students use their data to make inferences and predictions? How well are students able to provide reasons for their inferences and predictions? Are the reasons plausible?
- What do students do to test their inferences, predictions, and explanations?

Teachers use assessment data related to such questions as a basis for decisions related to scaffolding assistance.

> More information, including examples, related to ongoing, formative assessments are provided in Chapters 5 and 6.

Build Learning Communities

Vygotsky found that students can learn at higher levels in cooperation with others than occurs when they work alone. Thus, learning is enhanced when teachers work to establish a shared understanding of a learning task among a community of learners (Hogan & Pressley, 1997). According to Brown and Campione (1998),

> A community of learners reflects a classroom ethos different from that found in traditional classrooms. In the traditional classroom, students are perceived as relatively passive learners who receive wisdom from teachers, textbooks, or other media. In the community of learners classroom, students are encouraged to engage in self-reflective learning and critical inquiry. (p. 153)

One role of a teacher within a community of inquirers is to organize the learning environment to encourage an underlying cooperative culture that centers on thinking. Just as communication among scientists is central in the construction of scientific knowledge, students learn by talking among themselves and writing about and formally presenting their ideas. Teachers, as part of the classroom community of learners, make students' ideas more meaningful by commenting and elaborating on them and asking students to clarify, expand, and justify their own emerging conceptions and those of others. Conversational partnerships with the teacher allow students to build on and use the teacher's thinking processes to support their efforts to think in more flexible and mature ways. In addition, the give and take among learners in a learning community enables them to scaffold one another's learning.

> Forming cooperative teams and assigning job functions (Principal Investigator, Recorder, Maintenance Manager, etc.) to each team member is discussed in Chapter 5.

Table 3-1 provides a summary of factors that affect learning with understanding.

Children's prior knowledge not only facilitates understanding, it can also interfere with it. In the next section, we will examine the effect of children's existing alternative conceptions on their understanding of new concepts.

TABLE 3-1 ENHANCING THE LEARNING OF SCIENCE WITH UNDERSTANDING	
Teaching Actions That Enhance Learning	**Description and Rationale**
Provide for access to prior knowledge.	• Students take in information from many sources. In building new knowledge, they connect information to relevant *prior knowledge*, organize their developing knowledge, and construct meaning for themselves. • Failure to access prior knowledge interferes with new learning. Reminding students of what they already know is one way to provide for access to prior knowledge.
Provide for the transfer of new knowledge to new situations.	• Using new knowledge in new situations enhances its transferability and access. • Constructed knowledge is refined, expanded, and elaborated as learners transfer it to new situations in trying to understand the world. • Teachers should provide many opportunities for students to transfer their developing knowledge to new situations.
Provide for knowledge organization.	• The size of cognitive structures, the number of connections between items in the structures, and the organization and richness of the connections are important for accessing prior knowledge, processing information, constructing meanings, and solving problems. • Using and teaching students to use graphic organizers, such as spider maps, Venn diagrams, and concept maps, promotes knowledge organization.
Provide scaffolding support.	• Scaffolding the learning process for students effectively reduces the complexity of knowledge construction and enables students to learn at higher levels. • In scaffolding, teachers might provide suggestions, questions, prompts, or hints; guide students to clarify, elaborate, or justify their investigation procedures and findings; or provide necessary terms, concepts, and principles to students through formal, direct instruction or the use of textbooks, videos, the Internet, and other means.
Build learning communities.	• Being a member of a collaborative community allows students to cooperatively work and think together and to scaffold one another's learning. • You can support learning communities by encouraging cooperative learning and teaching students how to work cooperatively. • Arranging for students to investigate in small groups is another way to promote learning communities.

Children's Alternative Conceptions and Science Learning

Children are busy learning every day, processing and organizing information from many sources (Rutherford & Ahlgren, 1990). Consequently, when they come to science classes, children already have formed many ideas about the world from their daily experiences. The prior knowledge children bring to new learning situations is often fragmented, incomplete, and naive, and their ideas are typically not congruent with accepted scientific views. Children's partial understandings, naive theories, and alternative conceptions must be recognized and dealt with by teachers if students are to learn science with understanding.

Children's ideas about the world have received a great deal of attention by researchers. Here are two humorous examples of students' spontaneous notions (Paulu & Martin, 1991):

- "Fossils are bones that animals are through wearing."
- "Some people can tell what time it is by looking at the sun, but I have never been able to make out the numbers."

Table 3-2 presents other example of children's alternative conceptions of science topics.

Roth (1991) described an interesting example of children's alternative conceptions from her research with fifth-grade students. Children may know the word *photosynthesis*, but they

TABLE 3-2 ALTERNATIVE CONCEPTIONS OF CHILDREN RELATED TO SCIENTIFIC TOPICS

Science Content Area	Students' Naïve Conceptions	Scientific Conceptions
Biology	• Animals are living because they move, but plants are nonliving.	• Living things are composed of cells that carry out life processes such as the extraction of energy from nutrients and energy release. • Plants and animals are living organisms, composed of living cells.
Physical Science	• Anything that pours is a liquid, including powders. • When liquids evaporate, they just disappear. • Electric current is used up in bulbs and there is less current going back to a battery than coming out of it. • Light rays move out from the eye in order to illuminate objects. • Loudness and pitch are the same thing. • Suction causes liquids to be pulled upward in a soda straw.	• Powders are solids, composed of individual solid particles. • In evaporation, molecules in a liquid break free from molecular bonds and go into the surrounding air. • Electric current is the same throughout a continuous series circuit. • Light from other sources reflects off objects to our eyes, enabling us to see them. • Loudness and pitch are different variables associated with sound. • When the air pressure in a soda straw is reduced, atmospheric pressure pushes liquid up into the straw.
Earth and Space Science	• The earth is flat, like a pancake. • The phases of the moon are caused by shadows of the earth falling on the moon. • Seasons are caused by the changing distance of the earth from the sun (closer in the summer, more distant in the winter).	• The earth is spherical, as is shown by lunar eclipses and photographs from space. • The sun illuminates half of the moon at all times. Phases of the moon result from the way light from the sun reflects off the moon to the earth. • We experience seasons because light from the sun reaches the earth at a steeper angle in the summer than in the winter.

Source: Compiled by the authors from different sources.

have a lot of alternative ideas about where plants get their energy for life processes and growth. They may have the conception, for instance, that plants get their food from the soil through their roots. Plants do absorb nutrients from the soil, but this alternative conception conflicts in critical ways with the scientific view that plants use sunlight to make food from carbon dioxide and water. Students have arrived at their explanations through their own experience with plants, and the explanations work for them. Furthermore, common language usage about "plant food" that is mixed with the soil to "feed" plants reinforces erroneous beliefs. Personal theories are not easy to give up, especially when they are so commonly reinforced.

For conceptual change to occur, students must be challenged to recognize that their personal theories and explanations are in conflict with accepted scientific views. As Roth (1991) explained,

> They need to be convinced that their own theories are inadequate, incomplete, or inconsistent with experimental evidence, and that the scientific explanations provide a more convincing alternative to their own notions. (p. 49)

Convincing children that they should change their conceptions does not come from "telling" or threats. Roth proposed that to change their beliefs, students need repeated opportunities to struggle with the inconsistencies between their own ideas and scientific explanations, to reorganize their ways of thinking, and to make appropriate links between their own ideas and scientific concepts.

A Strategy for Conceptual Change: Moon Watching

Anderson (1987) proposed a strategy for conceptual change. According to Anderson, for conceptual change to occur, teachers must

- identify students' alternative conceptions,
- promote student dissatisfaction with them,
- introduce scientific conceptions, and
- provide for application and integration of the new conceptions.

An inquiry approach to science is especially compatible with this *conceptual change strategy*. Inquiry teachers have many opportunities to interact with students, observe and listen to them, and recognize their conceptions that are incomplete and inadequate and need further development. Understanding students' misconceptions and naive theories, teachers are then better prepared to "structure learning experiences that assist the reconstruction of core concepts. New constructions can then be applied to different situations and tested against other conceptions of the world" (Trowbridge & Bybee, 1996, p. 214).

As an example, consider a conceptual change emphasis in an inquiry lesson on moon watching. In the moon watching lesson, students observe and record the appearance and position of the moon each day or night for one month. They organize their observations in a table, on a calendar, through narrative descriptions, using drawings, or in some other way. Then they attempt to discover and explain the pattern of the phases of the moon they observe (see Figure 3-7). The first step in a conceptual change strategy is for the teacher to identify students' misconceptions.

Identify Alternative Conceptions. One advantage of an inquiry approach to science teaching is that it allows teachers to uncover what students already know or think about a topic. In inquiry lessons, students are encouraged to talk and frequently write about their understandings of the natural world and to illustrate them through drawing pictures and diagrams. As discussed previously, by paying close attention to student ideas, you can begin to gain some insight into their prior knowledge, including their misconceptions (Anderson, 1987).

Figure 3-7 The moon displays a pattern of phases in its monthly cycle.

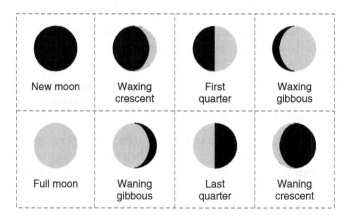

For example, when asked to explain why the moon shows phases, research and experience suggest that children and adolescents ages 9–16 are likely to give these explanations about why lunar phases appear:

- Clouds cover part of the moon so that we cannot see all of it (cloud viewpoint).
- The shadow of the earth falls on the moon so that we cannot see all of the moon (eclipse viewpoint).
- The shadow of the sun falls on the moon.
- Planets cast shadows on the moon.
- Only a portion of the sunlight illuminating the moon is reflected to earth (scientific viewpoint) (Stahly, Krockover, & Shepardson, 1999).

Up to 70% of subjects in research studies explain the phases of the moon from the "eclipse viewpoint."

The second step in the conceptual change strategy is to promote dissatisfaction with alternative concepts.

Promote Dissatisfaction with Alternative Conceptions. In teaching for conceptual change, it is not enough to just discredit misconceptions, nor is it sufficient to merely provide correct explanations. Rather, teachers should encourage students to test their own ideas through observation and investigation.

If children think that lunar phases are caused by clouds, for instance, you might lead them to add information on "cloud conditions" to the daily and weekly moon-watching charts they keep. Students can then examine their data and see if there is evidence to support the theory of a connection between clouds and moon phases. This process can help students develop awareness of and dissatisfaction with their own inaccurate and incomplete explanations.

Sometimes students have inadequate conceptions simply because they lack relevant information. For example, students may have difficulty in explaining lunar phases due to their lack of knowledge about earth-moon-sun distance relationships. On the National Assessment of Educational Progress (NAEP) for 2000, only about one-half of eighth-grade students tested knew that the moon is always much closer to the earth than it is to the sun. One-third of the eighth-grade students thought the earth's moon is sometimes closer to the sun than it is to the earth and sometimes closer to the earth than it is to the sun.

Most models of the sun-earth-moon system that are illustrated in science texts or assembled by students for science projects do not show relative sizes and distances on the same scale. One way for students to begin to understand the size and distance relationships of the earth, moon, and sun is to do the math involved in the relationships and build a scale model. If a basketball were used to represent the earth, the moon would be a softball placed about 10 meters (30 feet) away. On this scale, the diameter of the sun would be represented by a 10-story building about 2 miles away from the basketball and softball. Such a model can help students realize that the earth and moon are near neighbors that orbit the distant sun together.

When students' misconceptions have been identified, and they have been guided to become dissatisfied with their own explanations, you are ready to introduce scientific conceptions.

Introduce Scientific Conceptions. According to Anderson (1987), exploratory and discovery activities are useful but do not in themselves lead to conceptual change. Left to their own devices, children may discover many interesting things about the world, but they will develop scientific ideas "about as rapidly as the human race: in other words, not in a single lifetime . . . Therefore," Anderson (1987) asserted, "scientific concepts need to be explicitly introduced and taught to students" (p. 86).

When students have become dissatisfied with their own conceptions about the causes of the moon's phases and have collected a great deal of data and information at the descriptive level, it is time to formally teach key scientific concepts, principles, and explanations related to the topic. You should build on observational activities in ways that can be meaningfully understood by students. Guide students to examine and contrast misconceptions with scientific conceptions. At each point in instruction, assist students to modify, restructure, or abandon their existing conceptions in favor of new understandings of scientific concepts and explanations.

Realizing that clouds and eclipses are not satisfactory explanations for moon phases and that the earth and moon are near neighbors that are a great distance from the sun can help prepare children for a scientific explanation. Then, through expository instruction, diagrams, physical models, computer planetarium displays, and discussion, the scientific explanation for phases is presented. According to this explanation, light from the distant sun strikes the moon, but only a portion of that sunlight is reflected to the earth, resulting in the appearance of moon phases.

It is through applying new conceptions in new situations that students integrate and make sense of the new conceptions.

Provide for Transfer of New Conceptions. A physical model of the sun-earth-moon system provides an excellent approach to understanding phases of the moon. Provide each student with a Styrofoam ball. Instruct students to stand facing a central light source, but caution them not to look directly at the light. Give these instructions:

1. Imagine that the Styrofoam ball is the moon, that the light source is the sun, and that your head is the earth.
2. Place your Styrofoam ball on a stick or pencil. Hold your Styrofoam ball away from you at arm's length, slightly above your head, with the ball between you and the light. Look at the ball. Notice how much of the ball is lighted from where you are standing. Does the visible lit part of the ball look like any of the phases of the moon you have observed? (See Figure 3-8.)

Figure 3-8 How can different phases of the moon be illustrated in this model?

3. Stay in one spot. With your arm extended, slowly move your arm and the ball 90 degrees to your left. Look at the ball again. How much of the ball's visible surface is lighted from where you stand? Is this like another phase of the moon you have seen?

4. Rotate another 90 degrees to the left and look at the ball. How much of the visible surface of the ball is lighted now? Is this like another phase of the moon you have observed?

5. Rotate your arm 90 degrees more to the left and look at the ball. Compare what you see to the phases of the moon you have seen in the sky.

6. Can you see some of the phases of the moon? When is the Styrofoam "moon" full? What position creates the new moon? Why can't you see the new moon? (The new moon occurs when the lighted side of the moon is turned away from the earth.)

7. Try to identify the positions of the moon relative to the earth and sun when you see the waxing crescent moon, the first quarter moon, the waxing gibbous moon, the full moon, and the waning phases.

For all students to attain real understanding of scientific conceptions remains a challenging ideal. Nevertheless, as Anderson (1987) reported from his studies, when teachers use conceptual change approaches with inquiry methods, the percentage of students attaining real understanding jumps from the 0 to 20% range to the 50 to 80% range. This is clearly a great improvement, helping to close the performance gap that so often exists among groups of learners.

Next, we examine cognitive development and its effect on science understanding.

Go to the Homework and Exercises section in Chapter 3 of MyEducationLab to watch the videos, *Investigating Moon Phases: Parts 1, 2, 3, 4,* and *5,* and follow fourth- and fifth-grade students through a set of activities on moon phases.

Development, Learning, and Science Teaching

The growth of understanding of the natural world by children and adolescents is a product of both learning and development. The term **learning** refers to the construction of knowledge in specific situations. **Development**, in contrast, refers to the general growth and change of cognitive structures that allow knowledge to be extended from particular to general cases (Brown, Bransford, Ferrara, & Campione, 1983). Development occurs over time and requires abundant learning experiences.

The period of time from age 5 to 13, encompassing grades K–8, is marked by very dramatic developments in children's cognitive capabilities. These changes greatly affect what is appropriate to teach in science at the various grade levels. Piaget's theory of cognitive development is a rich source of details about children's cognitive development and their theories of the world. Consequently, this theory provides a basis for helping teachers make decisions about developmentally appropriate science.

Piaget's Theory of Cognitive Development

Through investigations carried out over nearly 60 years, Jean Piaget and his colleagues found that the understanding of science tasks grows and develops across the childhood and adolescent years. Piaget (Inhelder & Piaget, 1958) proposed that the development of understanding takes place across four age-related stages called the sensorimotor, preoperational, concrete operational, and formal operational stages. The characteristics of children's and adolescents' thinking at the preoperational, concrete operational, and formal operational stages greatly influence what is appropriate to teach in science at different grade levels.

The age spans given here in the descriptions of each stage are based on research studies, but should be considered approximations. Individual children may show characteristics of a given developmental phase at earlier or later ages than their peers.

Go to the Homework and Exercises section in Chapter 3 of MyEducationLab to watch the video, *Conservation of Matter, Volume X.* As you watch the video, reflect on the differences in the ways younger learners and older learners approach tasks. Also consider how effective you think teacher scaffolding and direct instruction would be in helping young learners develop higher-order reasoning skills needed for the tasks.

Preoperational Stage. Piaget found that children from about age 2 to age 7 display characteristics of *preoperational* thinking. At this stage, children tend to make judgments on the basis of perceptions rather than conceptions. Furthermore, they tend to focus on one, main perception of a situation and do not tend to shift back and forth *reversibly* or flexibly from one aspect of a situation to another. Because of their difficulties with reversible thinking, children at this level of development do not tend to mentally group elements into coherent wholes. This is shown, for example, through various *conservation* tasks.

Conservation. **Conservation** refers to the recognition that if an object or situation is transformed in some way, there may still be aspects of the object or situation that remain the same. Piaget and others have investigated the thinking of children and adolescents across a number of different conservation tasks. In a conservation of liquid amount task (see Figure 3-9), subjects are presented with two identical glasses filled with equal amounts of liquid. The liquid from one of the glasses is poured into a taller, narrower container. Subjects are then asked if there is now more, less, or the same amount of liquid in the new container.

In the conservation of liquid amount task, children at the preoperational stage tend to focus on only one aspect of the situation—the heights of the original and new containers. Noting that the level of liquid in the new container is higher, they conclude that there is more liquid in it. While focusing on the heights of the liquid in the two containers, they fail to simultaneously consider the widths.

In a conservation of length task, subjects are presented with two strings of the same length. One of the two strings is transformed into a curving, snakelike form. Learners classed as preoperational do not coordinate perceptions about the two end points of the strings and the pathways joining the end points (whether straight or curved). Thus, they fail to reason that the transformed piece of string has a constant length, regardless of how it is configured.

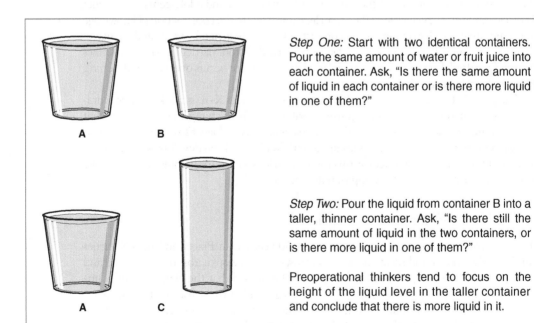

Step One: Start with two identical containers. Pour the same amount of water or fruit juice into each container. Ask, "Is there the same amount of liquid in each container or is there more liquid in one of them?"

Step Two: Pour the liquid from container B into a taller, thinner container. Ask, "Is there still the same amount of liquid in the two containers, or is there more liquid in one of them?"

Preoperational thinkers tend to focus on the height of the liquid level in the taller container and conclude that there is more liquid in it.

Figure 3-9 Task for assessing conservation of liquid volume.

Children's failure to consistently conserve variables, such as length, leads to difficulty in their conception of different variables and in their learning to measure them with understanding. For instance, in measuring length, young learners fail to correctly align the end point of a ruler with the end point of the object being measured; they do not understand the importance of units of measurement and the meaning of the numbers associated with measuring length; and they fail to count accurately the number of units, (such as centimeters or inches) in a measured length.

Because considering multiple aspects of a situation and forming holistic combinations is hard for young children, they have difficulty in science with such essential processes as identifying variables, measuring, classifying, inferring, and predicting. They also have difficulty forming and understanding principles.

Concrete Operational Stage. The gradual development of reversible thinking enables children in grades 3, 4, and 5 to form some new types of knowledge, including *series*, *classes*, and *relationships*. These three special ways of combining information are critical tools for the construction of knowledge in elementary science. The ability to form serially ordered groups, coupled with conservation, enables students to identify variables and measure them with understanding. The development of class logic enables students to organize their perceptions so they can think about them more clearly. The ability to form relationships enables an understanding of simple scientific principles and cause-and-effect relationships.

Piaget investigated the order of children's success across three different conservation tasks, including the conservation of substance, the conservation of weight, and the conservation of displacement volume. The conservation of substance task involves comparisons between the amount of clay in an original lump and the amount when an equivalent lump is transformed into a pancake, sausage, or hot dog. Conservation of weight involves comparions between the weight of an original lump of clay and its weight when it is transfomed into a different shape. Conservation of displacement volume involves judgment of the water level rise for an original lump of clay when it is placed in water compared with the water level rise when the lump is transformed into a new shape and immersed in water.

Piaget found that the age level for success is about 7 for the conservation of substance task, about 9 for the conservation of weight task, and about 11 for the *conservation of displacement volume* task (Piaget, in Gruber and Voneche, 1997). The order of these findings has been supported by other investigators, though the age ranges found in these investigations show some differences with Piaget's findings.

The realization that a variable may be conserved is essential to understanding the variable, measuring it with understanding, forming relationships involving the variable, identifying manipulated and responding variables, and carrying out controlled investigations.

Given the chance through hands-on, minds-on inquiry activities and teacher guidance, concrete operational thinkers begin to organize investigations in terms of concepts and variables, measure variables meaningfully, and arrange data in tables and graphs. They can also form and understand simple principles, use what they know to make inferences and predictions, and generalize from common experiences. The concrete operational years can be especially exciting times in science for children and their teachers.

Formal Operational Stage. The formal operational level is characterized by higher-order thinking with the concepts, variables, and principles formed at the concrete operational level. The cognitive advances at the formal operational level are revealed as adolescents engage more independently in thinking tasks such as

- planning and conducting controlled experiments or fair tests that involve *responding* (dependent), *manipulated* (independent), and *controlled* variables, as described in Chapter 2;
- organizing and thinking about complex numerical data sets in terms of ratios, proportions, and equations;
- constructing theories and models that coordinate facts, concepts, and principles; and
- coordinating evidence and knowledge in forming complex explanations of puzzling phenomena.

These formal operational advances better prepare learners to seek answers to their questions through designing and carrying out more complicated investigations.

As a word of caution, Duschl and colleagues (2007) report studies of cognitive psychologists and educational researchers that indicate that through continual assessment, proper scaffolding, and judicious direct instruction, students can learn much more about science than previously suspected. Nevertheless, instruction should take place within the context of development of children and adolescents.

Table 3-3 presents a summary of children's developmental characteristics that affect science learning.

TABLE 3-3 CHARACTERISTICS OF CHILDREN'S THINKING IN PIAGET'S FOUR COGNITIVE STAGES

Cognitive Stages and Approximate Age Spans	The Child at This Stage
Sensorimotor (0–2 years)	• adapts to the external world through actions • coordinates actions related to substance, space, time, and causality
Preoperational (2–7 years)	• maintains sensorimotor capabilities • develops extensive physical knowledge of objects, organisms, and events • begins to represent objects and actions with words and sentences • does not think "reversibly" • makes judgments on the basis of perceptions, not conceptual considerations
Concrete Operational (5–11 years)	• maintains capabilities of previous stages • thinks reversibly • groups elements into coherent wholes • conserves substance, liquid, volume, length, and area • identifies *variables* and measures them • forms *classes* and uses them to organize perceptions and experiences • forms and uses *relationships*, including simple scientific principles and cause-and-effect relationships
Formal Operational (12 + years)	• maintains capabilities of previous stages • engages in higher-order thinking • forms hypotheses, carries out controlled experiments, and relates evidence to theories • deals with ratios, proportions, and probabilities • constructs and understands complex explanations

Next, as an example, we look at children's development related to their understanding of floating and sinking.

Children's Theories of Floating and Sinking

When young children are given an array of objects and asked to predict whether the objects will float or sink, they rely primarily on past experiences. When asked why they think something will float or sink, they tend to focus on salient characteristics of the objects. Their answers are generally inconsistent. For instance, they may say one object floats because it is large and a second thing floats because it is small.

As children mature, their thinking about floating and sinking becomes more consistent. By grades 3–5, many children begin to realize (with appropriate scaffolding from their teachers) that weight (mass) and size (volume) are not the same thing and that both variables make a difference in whether an object floats or sinks. Applying the logic of serial ordering, the children can describe the weight of objects as heavy or light; they also describe the volume or size of objects as large or small. Applying the logic of relationships allows children to understand (with scaffolding) the concrete operational principle that *objects sink in water if they are too heavy for their size.*

It is not until adolescence that students typically add numerical considerations about weight and volume to their judgments and explanations. Some adolescents, but by no means all, begin to use proportions and ratios to think of floating and sinking in terms of the density of the object. **Density** is the mass per unit volume of a substance; that is, it is the ratio of the mass to the volume. Quantitatively, the dividing line for whether an object sinks or floats in fresh water is the density of water, which is 1 gram per cubic centimeter (1 g/cc). Thus, *objects float in fresh water if their density is less than that of water.*

Centimeter-gram cubes—small cubes that are 1 cm on each side and have a mass of 1 g—are often used in elementary and middle school math and science. The volume of each of these cubes is exactly 1 cc; the density of the cubes is then 1 g/cc. The density of fresh water is also 1 g/cc. Thus, these cubes float just under the surface of fresh water because their density is exactly the same as the density of water. If a small bit of clay is added to a cube, its density goes above 1 g/cc and the cube sinks in fresh water.

A lesson plan on floating and sinking is included in Chapter 5 (pages 122–126).

Developmentally Appropriate Science

As we have seen, the period of time spanning ages 5 to 13, which encompasses grades K–8, is marked by very dramatic developments in children's cognitive capabilities. These changes greatly affect what is appropriate to teach in science at the various grade levels.

According to the *Benchmarks for Science Literacy* (American Association for the Advancement of Science, 1993),

> Overestimation of what students can learn at a given age results in student frustration, lack of confidence, and unproductive learning strategies, such as memorization without understanding. Underestimation of what students can learn results in boredom, overconfidence, and poor study habits, and a needlessly diluted education. So it is important to make decisions about what to expect of students and when on the basis of as much good information as possible. (p. 327)

It is essential, then, for teachers to select types of science investigations, as well as concepts, principles, theories, and explanations, that are *developmentally appropriate* for their students.

Table 3-4 provides a summary of some characteristics of learners that affect inquiry learning in different grade spans. The items in this list are derived from the experience of

TABLE 3-4 CHARACTERISTICS OF LEARNERS IN DIFFERENT GRADE SPANS

Grade K–2 Learners

* Have a natural interest in almost everything around them.
* Work best with common objects, living things, and events within familiar contexts.
* Observe the world using all of their senses, but do not construct consistent explanations of it.
* Push, pull, and transform objects by acting on them.
* Observe, sort, group, and order objects.
* Carry out simple descriptive and classificatory investigations.
* Form concrete concepts based on their own observations.
* Make judgments and explanations primarily from perceptions and descriptions rather than conceptions.
* Make simple inferences with assistance.
* Can solve problems through trial and error, if guided to work step by step.

Grade 3–4 Learners

* Tend to create larger, more complex organizations, instead of being satisfied with grouping and ordering objects by limited attributes.
* Discover and understand simple rules of classification.
* Carry out simple classificatory investigations.
* Design simple comparative tests, carry out the tests, analyze the results, and communicate their findings.
* Carry out simple controlled investigations, with considerable teacher scaffolding.
* Record data and keep simple journals.
* Use data and knowledge to make inferences and predictions.
* Develop and use more abstract concepts and simple cause-and-effect principles in constructing explanations.
* Understand cycles (life cycles, seasons, water cycles) as continuous, repeatable chains of events.

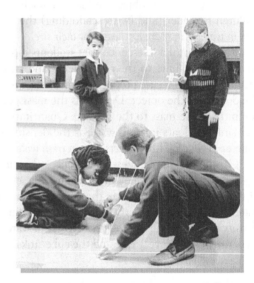

Grade 5–6 Learners

* Effectively use cause-and-effect relationships in constructing more complex explanations.
* Engage in experimental inquiries that are more advanced than simple descriptive and classificatory investigations.
* Generate simple hypotheses, conduct "fair" tests, and record and analyze data to find evidence to support or not support the original hypotheses.
* Have difficulty controlling all the variables in an experiment.
* Can keep extensive journals, diaries, records of information over time, and prepare written reports based on these records.
* Have preconceptions and expectations that can influence interpretation of data, even in a fair test.
* Generate, interpret, and make predictions from graphs; understand that graphs describe two variables at the same time.

teachers, the cognitive development research of Jean Piaget and others, and the NSTA publication, *Pathways to the Science Standards: Elementary School Edition* (Lowery, 1997).

With teacher scaffolding, students are enabled to think in more complex ways and carry out the different investigations at earlier ages. The guidelines in Table 3-4 are useful whatever the science topic investigated, whether leaves, magnets, ants, pillbugs, seeds and plants, floating and sinking, or other topics.

Grade Placement of the Cartesian Diver

As an example of appropriate grade placement, consider the Cartesian diver. Explaining the *Cartesian diver* involves the principles of floating and sinking, along with principles related to air pressure. This fun phenomenon has been introduced in elementary science to children as young as second grade. However, as shown in the following discussion, it is more appropriate for older learners.

The Cartesian diver (see Figure 3-10) consists of a 1-liter clear, plastic bottle filled with water nearly to the top. A medicine dropper, partially filled with water so that it floats at the surface of a container of water, is placed in the bottle. A cap is screwed tightly on the bottle. When the bottle is squeezed, the dropper descends. When it is released, the dropper ascends to the surface.

You can learn a great deal for yourself about observation, evidence, and explanation by building and trying out a Cartesian diver.

Explaining the Cartesian diver requires two main principles. One principle is related to objects floating and sinking in water: *objects sink in water if they are too heavy for their size (volume)*. The other principle is related to air pressure: *if a space containing air is decreased, the pressure of the air will increase*.

Here are explanations of the Cartesian diver given by some second graders:

Student 1: *It's like a parachute going up and down.*
Student 2: *I think when the water goes in, then the air pushes it up with the metal thing.*
Student 3: *When you squeeze it, the water goes in the eyedropper and when you let it go, some water goes out of it.*
Student 4: *It gets heavier when it goes down and then it gets lighter and then it goes up.*

As teachers, we need to listen carefully to what children say, filter their ideas through theories of learning and development and our own experiences, and decide how we should respond. Let's use the theories introduced in this chapter to analyze these second-grade children's thinking about the diving dropper.

Student 1 provides a *description* of the actions of the dropper. Focusing on observations and descriptions in the absence of concepts that bind them together is a general learning characteristic of K–2 students.

Student 2 gives a somewhat confused explanation of the event. He mentions air and the water going into the dropper, but focuses on his observation of the "metal thing" (the cap screwed on the bottle.)

Student 3 observes the event more closely, noting that water goes into and then comes out of the dropper. Thus, evidence for part of the explanation is present, but the child does not use these ideas further in forming an explanation of the event, nor does he propose a principle that might govern it.

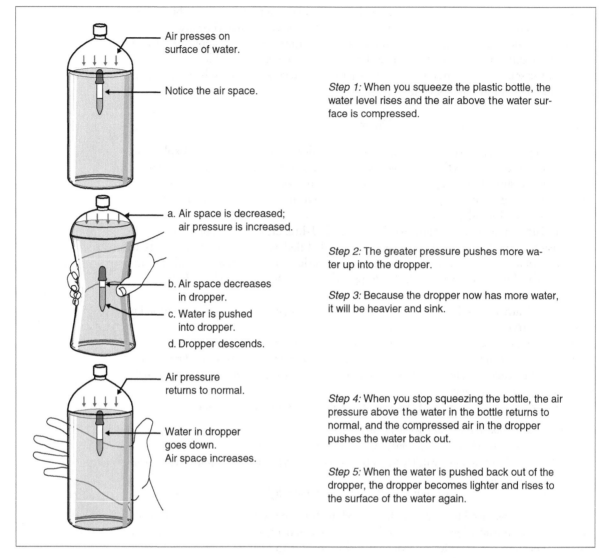

Air presses on surface of water.

Notice the air space.

Step 1: When you squeeze the plastic bottle, the water level rises and the air above the water surface is compressed.

a. Air space is decreased; air pressure is increased.

Step 2: The greater pressure pushes more water up into the dropper.

b. Air space decreases in dropper.

c. Water is pushed into dropper.

Step 3: Because the dropper now has more water, it will be heavier and sink.

d. Dropper descends.

Air pressure returns to normal.

Step 4: When you stop squeezing the bottle, the air pressure above the water in the bottle returns to normal, and the compressed air in the dropper pushes the water back out.

Water in dropper goes down. Air space increases.

Step 5: When the water is pushed back out of the dropper, the dropper becomes lighter and rises to the surface of the water again.

Figure 3-10 An explanation of the Cartesian diver demonstration.

Student 4 explains the phenomenon by stating that the dropper gets heavier and then gets lighter. But, she does not mention why the weight of the dropper changes or what the effect of the weight changes might be.

The thinking of students 3 and 4 is somewhat advanced for second graders, but they still do not recognize and connect: (1) their actions on the bottle, (2) the resulting changes in the air pressure in the bottle, (3) the changes in the amount of water in the dropper that is caused by the air pressure changes, and (4) the consequent change in weight of the dropper. In brief, these second graders deal with the descriptive aspects of the Cartesian diver, but fail to deal adequately with the explanatory aspects of the task.

Consider how you might provide scaffolding to advance the children's explanations. You could, for example, provide assistance through questioning. Hearing student 3's explanation, you might ask what causes the dropper to get heavier and then get lighter. Hearing student 4's explanation, you might ask why the water goes into the dropper and what happens to the dropper when the water goes into it. Even if students do not form complete scientific explanations initially, you can help them to make better connections between the various elements of the task and to think about them more flexibly.

From a Piagetian perspective, difficulties that young learners have in trying to explain the Cartesian diver are a result of their having not yet developed the cognitive structures required by the task. According to Vygotsky (1962), a primary distinguishing characteristic of children's spontaneous concepts learned through discovery is the absence of a system that holds the concepts together. Similarly, Ebenezer and Connor (1998) describe children's initial knowledge about the world as fragmented, made up not of organized theories but of a large number of fragments.

Because second-grade children generally have difficulties in constructing consistent explanations, the Cartesian diver is not a grade-level appropriate activity for most learners at this grade level. In Vygotskian terms, the explanation of the Cartesian diver is not one within the zone of proximal development for most second graders. It is not a phenomenon that children at this level are likely to understand well, even with good scaffolding assistance. Thus, it would be more appropriate to provide second graders with other experiences on the properties of air and floating and sinking and wait until about grade 4 to introduce the Cartesian diver. Further, at grade 4, to simplify the process, the teacher might decide to focus more on the qualitative principle of floating and sinking, without emphasizing the role of air pressure in the investigation.

SUMMARY

* Learning is a constructive process. In the process of constructing new knowledge, learners use prior knowledge to *organize* incoming information in various ways to form new knowledge, and they *integrate* new knowledge with prior knowledge to expand the knowledge base.

* Contemporary learning theorists emphasize the importance of enhancing learning through providing students ways to access prior knowledge, promoting the organization of knowledge, providing opportunities for transfer, providing scaffolding support, providing for formative assessment of student understanding, and establishing communities of inquirers.

* To scaffold student learning, set challenging and interesting learning tasks; simplify tasks for students; facilitate student talk in different settings; ask meaningful questions; lead students to clarify, elaborate, or justify their responses; and supply necessary information, concepts, and principles for learners.

* Students often come to science classes with pervasive alternative conceptions about how the world works. If students are to learn with understanding, teachers must help them recognize and deal with their incomplete and erroneous ideas.

* The term *learning* refers to the construction of knowledge or performance capabilities in specific situations. *Cognitive development,* in contrast, refers to the general growth and change of cognitive structures that allow knowledge and performance capabilities to be extended from particular to general cases.

* By looking closely at Piaget's theory, science teachers can get an idea of how scientific conceptions develop.

* Piaget's findings are important for science education, but they should not place a limit on what is appropriate for children to learn at each grade level. With prior knowledge and appropriate scaffolding assistance from their teachers, they can do more than previously expected.

ONLINE PROFESSIONAL DEVELOPMENT

Pre- and post-tests to assess your knowledge of chapter content, along with exercises to enhance your understanding, can be found on MyEducationLab at www.myeducationlab.com.

Video Guides

Video clips on MyEducationLab selected for this chapter include *Investigating Moon Phases—Parts 1, 2, 3, 4,* and *5.*

Accessing the Videos

1. Go to the Homework and Exercises section in Chapter 3 of MyEducationLab to select and view videos for this chapter and answer the questions.
2. Videos might be viewed individually, by small groups of colleagues, or by the whole class.
3. As you watch each video, use the **Questions for Reflection** to guide your thoughts and note taking for personal use and group discussion.
4. Discuss your answers to the questions about each video with classmates.

Video: Investigating Moon Phases: Parts 1, 2, 3, 4, and 5.

Overview

The first three videos in the five-part set of videos on Moon Phases, shows fourth- and fifth-grade children discussing their observations of moon phases and the different types of records they choose and learn to use. The fourth and fifth videos in the set show Terry Contant leading the children in using a physical model of the earth-moon-sun system to illustrate and explain the appearance of moon phases.

Questions for Reflection

1. What were some of the observations of the children of the moon phases?
2. What kinds of records did they keep? What was the purpose of the long record strip?
3. How did the activity with balls illustrate the connection between the positions of the sun, the moon, and the earth and the effect of these positions on the phases of the moon observed? How did the Internet pictures of moon phases on any date, past, present, or future, help to connect the 3-D model to the children's observations?
4. What did the teachers think was important for the children in the moon phase activities? What do you think the children were learning about observation, record keeping, and explanations? What do you think they learned about moon phases?

Annenberg Videos

Video Series. Learning Science Through Inquiry Video. Bring It All Together: Processing for Meaning During Inquiry

To access Annenberg videos, follow the instructions given in the Online Professional Development section in Chapter 1 on page 26.

4

Over the years, educators have developed many teaching and learning models relevant to classroom science teaching. Knowing the strengths and weaknesses of these models, teachers examine the relationship between the science content and how that content is to be taught. Teachers of science integrate a sound model of teaching and learning, a practical structure for the segment, and the content to be learned.

(National Research Council, 1996, p. 31)

Teaching Science for Understanding: The 5-E Model of Instruction

THE MAJOR PROFICIENCIES or goals of science instruction emphasized in the *National Science Education Standards* are conceptual understandings in science, abilities to carry out scientific inquiries, and understandings about the nature of science and scientific inquiry (National Research Council, 1996). These proficiencies are also reflected in the science standards developed by most states. A number of different instructional approaches are available to you for teaching science, including an inquiry approach, a textbook-based approach, direct instruction, and guided discovery. These approaches to science instruction differ in the opportunities they afford students to achieve each of the major proficiencies.

Textbook and direct instruction approaches have typically focused on students acquiring science knowledge. But they do not usually provide students with opportunities to develop the broad range of abilities necessary to inquire scientifically, nor do they deliberately provide opportunities for students to understand the nature of scientific inquiry. Further, they often fail to go beyond knowledge to understanding.

Discovery approaches have been very popular among science teachers. In carrying out discovery activities, students have opportunities to experience the processes and procedures of inquiry. Discovery activities provide students abundant opportunities for manipulating materials and observing what happens in the world, but they often do not focus on specific science knowledge and conceptual understanding that enable students to make sense of what they see and do.

On the other hand, inquiry methods of teaching science are designed to enable students to achieve each of the three main goals of science instruction. By providing opportunities for students to ask questions, gather, record, and reflect on data, and form their own theories and explanations, inquiry approaches help students to develop inquiry abilities and, at the same time, construct scientific knowledge and understanding. Further, the involvement of students in inquiring into the natural world provides a strong basis for them to develop understandings of the nature of science and scientific inquiry.

Just as the different teaching approaches vary in their treatment of the central goals of science education, they also differ in their attention to research on learning. Again, of these four approaches to instruction, inquiry is the only one especially designed to enable teachers to use a wide range of instructional factors that promote learning with understanding. In teaching science through inquiry methods, teachers enhance access to and transfer of science knowledge. By building in opportunities to transfer knowledge to new situations, inquiry teaching assists learners to go beyond knowledge and develop understanding.

Similarly, inquiry teaching provides many opportunities for teachers to assess and scaffold learning to assist students to develop understanding. Additionally, learning communities are a natural part of inquiry teaching approaches.

Teaching science through inquiry can be effective and rewarding, but it can also be complex. To help you simplify the process, we present in this chapter the 5-E model of inquiry instruction. We also examine the special features, advantages, and disadvantages of other approaches to science learning and how you can expand these approaches by setting them in the context of inquiry and the 5-E model.

As you study this chapter, consider these questions:

- *What are the main features of inquiry instruction?*

- *What are the phases of the 5-E model of instruction? How are they related to the the tasks of scientific inquiry? How do they relate to contemporary research on learning with understanding?*

- *What is the discovery approach to teaching science? What are the advantages and disadvantages of this method?*

- *What are the main features of textbook and direct instruction approaches to teaching science? What are the advantages and disadvantages of each of these approaches to science instruction?*

- *How can guided discovery, textbook-based instruction, and direct instruction be incorporated into the 5-E model for teaching science?*

Inquiry Instruction

A glossary containing definitions of important terms used in this chapter can be found on MyEducationLab.

In inquiry instruction, students build conceptual understandings, investigation skills, and understandings of the nature of science through inquiry procedures that mirror methods used by scientists. As inquirers, learners assume major responsibility for constructing their own knowledge and understanding. Teachers share in and facilitate this process, guiding children as they ask questions, conduct investigations, and use observational evidence and scientific knowledge to develop explanations and answer their questions.

Features of Inquiry Instruction

A number of special features characterize inquiry instruction and learning (National Research Council, 2000). These features include:

1. *Learners Are Engaged by Scientific Questions.* At every stage of inquiry, students are connected to objects, organisms, and events in the real world. An early stage in inquiry

---

NSES **TEACHING STANDARD B**

To *guide and facilitate learning, teachers should*

- focus and support inquiries while interacting with students;
- orchestrate discourse among students about scientific ideas;
- challenge students to accept and share responsibility for their own learning;
- recognize and respond to student diversity and encourage all students to participate fully in science learning; and
- encourage and model the skills of scientific inquiry, as well as the curiosity, openness to new ideas and data, and skepticism that characterize science.

Encourage students to collect, organize, and interpret data.

is the formulation of questions for investigation. Ideally, students would generate questions from their own real-world experiences. Many students, however, will need considerable assistance in learning to form questions that can be investigated scientifically. In many cases, the focus question or problem is formulated by the teacher.

2. Learners Give Priority to Evidence as They Plan and Conduct Investigations. In inquiry approaches, students devise ways to gather evidence to answer their questions. With varying degrees of assistance, students determine what data might be relevant, decide how to collect the data, how to represent it, and how to organize it in useful ways. Students use a variety of investigational approaches to gather evidence, including descriptive, classificatory, and experimental investigations and other approaches.

3. Learners Connect Evidence and Scientific Knowlege in Generating Explanations. Continuing in inquiry, students describe, classify, and explain their observations, and clarify and justify their work to themselves and to one another. Children gradually learn that explanations must involve scientific knowledge and always be based on observational evidence gathered through investigations. Students should reflect on their observations often, reexamining them, using prior and developing knowledge to draw inferences from their observations, and collecting more data if necessary. As they develop cognitive skills, students should learn to distinguish between explanations, which are ideas about *why* something happens, and descriptions, which are based on observations of *what* has happened.

4. Learners Apply Their Knowledge to New Scientific Problems. To develop and extend understanding, learners must have the opportunity to apply their new science knowledge to new circumstances. For example, in the magnets lesson of Chapter 1, students learned fundamental rules of magnetic interaction. To help them be able to access and apply the new rules in new circumstances, the children might be asked to apply the rules to interactions between magnets and other objects in new classsroom activities.

5. Learners Engage in Critical Discourse with Others About Procedures, Evidence, and Explanations. Children love to talk about their experiences. Inquiry science provides a rich context for all students to develop language and thought (Rowe, 1973), including students with special needs and English Language Learners (ELL). Communicating and justifying scientific procedures, collecting, recording, reporting, and reflecting on evidence, and generating interpretations focus the students on *what* they know, *how* they know it, and *how* their knowledge connects to the knowledge of other people, to other subjects, and to the world beyond the classroom (National Research Council, 1996).

The complex process of tending to these five features of inquiry while teaching a classroom of students can be a daunting task. However, inquiry instruction can be considerably simplified through use of the 5-E model of instruction.

Models of Instruction

Models of instruction involve some arrangement of phases, steps, actions, or decision points for teaching and learning. Different instructional models in science build on different points of view about the nature of inquiry, processes of science, scientific knowledge and understanding, and goals of science learning. They also incorporate different principles from research on learning and development.

According to Brown and Campione (1994), teachers cannot just import an instructional model, follow prescribed procedures, and expect to attain student understanding of complex subject matter. A teacher's use of a model must reflect the viewpoints and principles on which it is based.

One of the earliest models of inquiry instruction in science is called the *learning cycle*. The learning cycle was developed in the 1960s by Robert Karplus (Karplus & Thier, 1974) and his colleagues for the Science Curriculum Improvement Study (SCIS) program. The model has been widely used by science teachers since that time. As is shown in Figure 4-1, the learning cycle consists of three phases of instruction:

- *Discovery,* in which children explore materials and discover new knowledge
- *Concept invention,* in which teachers build on student ideas in formally teaching information, concepts, and principles that help students make sense of their discoveries
- *Concept application,* in which students construct new understandings by applying their discovered and acquired knowledge to new situations

Figure 4-1 The Karplus and Thier SCIS Learning Cycle.
Source: Modified with permission from Charles R. Barman, "An Expanded View of the Learning Cycle: New Ideas About an Effective Teaching Strategy." Monograph and Occasional Paper Series, no. 4 (Washington, DC: Council for Elementary Science International, 1990), 5.

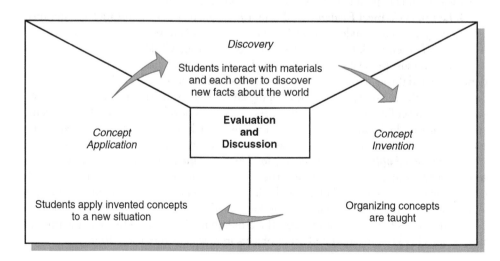

More recently, a model of instruction called the 5-E model has been designed to facilitate inquiry teaching.

The 5-E Model of Science Instruction

The 5-E model, which was developed by the Biological Sciences Curriculum Study (1989) group, builds on the learning cycle model. This model of instruction consists of five teaching phases: *engage, explore, explain, elaborate,* and *evaluate.* The five phases of the 5-E model and their functions are summarized in Table 4-1. One special value of the 5-E model in inquiry teaching is that the different phases of the model parallel the five tasks of inquiry identified in the *National Science Education Standards* (see Figure 1-3). Thus, Table 4-1 also shows how the different phases of the model are related to the tasks of scientific inquiry.

Notice that the middle three phases of the 5-E model—explore, explain, and elaborate—parallel the three phases of the learning cycle.

The 5-E model also facilitates the implementation of the research-based factors that influence learning with understanding presented in Chapter 3 (see Table 3-1), including accessing prior knowledge (at the engage phase), scaffolding (at every phase), building learning communities (in preparation for lessons and throughout the 5-E lesson phases), transfer (especially at the elaborate phase), and continual assessment (at every phase).

Let us examine each of the 5-E phases in more detail.

Phases of the 5-E Model

Engage. The first component in the 5-E instructional model, engage, is intended to pique curiosity and provide focus for the ensuing activities. It also provides an opportunity for teachers to identify the prior conceptions students have about the topic of study. Most important, at this stage, the question for investigation is formulated.

Chapters 1 and 2 provided many examples of questions that might be used in engaging students in inquiry.

Explore. At this phase of the 5-E model, teachers guide students as they devise ways to gather evidence to answer their questions. Students use a variety of observational and experimental investigational procedures to gather data. In planning investigations, they may

TABLE 4-1 THE FIVE PHASES IN THE 5-E MODEL OF INSTRUCTION, STUDENT ACTIONS IN EACH PHASE, AND THE TASKS OF SCIENTIFIC INQUIRY CORRESPONDING TO EACH PHASE

5-E Phase	Student Actions in Each Phase	Corresponding Tasks of Inquiry
Engage	Ask a question about objects, organisms, or events in the environment.	Ask a question about objects, organisms, and events in the environment.
Explore	Plan and conduct simple investigations to collect relevant data.	Plan and conduct a simple investigation. Use appropriate tools and techniques to gather data.
Explain	Use data and scientific knowledge to generate explanations.	Use evidence and scientific knowledge to develop explanations.
Elaborate	Extend strategies, concepts, principles, and explanations to new problems and questions.	Apply knowledge and skills in new situations.
Evaluate	Demonstrate knowledge, understanding, and ability to use inquiry strategies through formal and informal formative assessments.	Communicate investigations, data, and explanations to others. (Formative assessment helps to provide a basis for decisions about scaffolding and improving instruction. Helps to provide a basis for scaffolding.)

Encourage children to discover new knowledge through exploration.

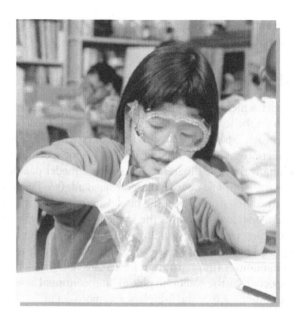

consider whether descriptive, classificatory, experimental, or some other approach to investigations would be most appropriate. In the process of gathering data, students develop simple process skills such as how to observe, measure, infer, and predict. They also learn how to cut, connect, switch, pour, tie, hold, and hook. Beginning with simple instruments, students learn to use rulers, thermometers, watches, spring scales, and balance scales to measure important variables. They learn to use magnifiers and microscopes to see finer details of objects and organisms (National Research Council, 1996).

Students should be encouraged to record their discoveries during the explore phase. One useful format for accomplishing this task and supporting future inquiry is the *I Notice/ I Wonder* chart. The left column of this two-column chart should be labeled "I Notice." In this column students write their observations and discoveries as they explore with the materials. The right column should be labeled "I Wonder." In this column students write questions that come to mind as they are exploring. These questions can lead to further inquiry investigations. Keeping records helps children to organize their findings and to remember them when they are needed in reflection, or during the explain and elaborate phases.

The explore phase of inquiry involves largely guided discovery by the students. It is in the explain and elaborate phases of inquiry that the 5-E model goes beyond discovery approaches to learning with understanding.

Explain. In the explain phase of the 5-E model, first, the teacher asks children to describe what they have noticed during the explore phase, reflect on their observations, and give their own theories and explanations that make sense of the observational data. Building on the activities and discussion of students, the teacher may use direct instruction, textbooks, and other means to formally introduce scientific knowledge (terms, facts, concepts, and principles) needed to make sense of the event. In presenting science knowledge, teachers should place an emphasis on students' understanding the natural world rather than just acquiring terminology and facts.

The teacher then assists students to use the new knowledge and the evidence from investigations during the explore phase to examine their initial conceptions and then to build accurate scientific explanations that help to answer the initiating question. At some point in the explain phase, the teacher may provide an explanation for the students.

Elaborate. It is not enough just to have knowledge. In developing understanding, learners must be able to access their knowledge and use it in new learning and problem solving. Failure to access knowledge at the appropriate time can severely constrain new learning and transfer (Bransford, Brown, & Cocking, 1999).

Mary Budd Rowe (1973), a distinguished science educator, has suggested that concept application is too often the neglected ingredient in science teaching. It is through concept application that understanding is generated. Rowe emphasized that children need to learn to view knowledge as procedures to be applied rather than just as information to be memorized and recalled.

Concept application takes place at the elaborate phase of 5-E instruction. At this phase, learners are presented with new learning tasks and called on to use their developing knowlege to negotiate the new task.

Evaluate. Assessment and evaluation always go hand in hand. *Assessment* is the process of gathering data on learning. *Evaluation* involves making decisions based on the assessment data. Assessment and evaluation in inquiry instruction are based on the objectives of the lesson taught. They provide a basis for decisions related to how to improve teaching and learning and are designed for the purpose of continual improvement of learning and teaching. In the 5-E model, assessment information is gathered through *formative* (ongoing) and *summative* (end of lesson or unit) assessments.

Self-assessment is an important aspect of the evaluation process. Brown and Campione (1994) argued that students should be taught metacognition strategies for planning, executing, monitoring, and adjusting their processes and products of learning.

As a summary view of the 5-E instructional model, Table 4-2 provides a chart that identifies teacher actions and student behaviors consistent with each phase of the model.

Teaching Electrical Concepts Through the 5-E Model of Instruction

Joyce Jackson used the 5-E approach to guide her fourth-grade class in a series of inquiry activities on electricity (see the accompanying 5-E lesson plan). When children learn about batteries and bulbs through the 5-E approach, they formulate initiating questions, explore electrical circuits, form generalizations about them, use the generalizations to explain why bulbs in different circuit arrangements do or do not light, and transfer the generalizations to new types of circuits.

Go to the Homework and Exercises section in Chapter 4 of MyEducationLab to watch the video clip *Teacher Discussion of Moon Phase Lessons*. In this video, we listen to two fourth- and fifth-grade teachers reflect on what they were trying to accomplish in the moon phase lessons, which appear to follow the 5-E (or a similar) model.

TABLE 4-2   APPLYING THE 5-E INSTRUCTIONAL MODEL

Stage of the Instructional Model	What the TEACHER Does	
	That Is Consistent with This Model	That Is Inconsistent with This Model
Engage	• Creates interest • Generates curiosity • Raises questions • Elicits responses that uncover what the students know or think about the concept/topic	• Explains concepts • Provides definitions and answers • States conclusions • Provides closure • Lectures
Explore	• Encourages students to work together without direct instruction from the teacher • Observes and listens to students as they interact • Asks probing questions to redirect students' investigations when necessary • Provides time for students to puzzle through problems • Acts as a consultant for students	• Provides answers • Tells or explains how to work through the problem • Provides closure • Tells students that they are wrong • Gives information or facts that solve the problem • Leads students step-by-step to a solution
Explain	• Encourages students to explain concepts and definitions in their own words • Asks for justification (evidence) and clarification from students • Formally provides definitions, explanations, and new labels • Uses students' previous experiences as the basis for explaining concepts	• Accepts explanations that have no justification • Neglects to solicit students' explanations • Introduces unrelated concepts or skills
Elaborate	• Expects students to use formal labels, definitions, and explanations provided previously • Encourages students to apply or extend the concepts and skills in new situations • Reminds students of alternative explanations • Refers students to existing data and evidence and asks: "What do you already know?" "Why do you think . . . ?" (Strategies from explore stage apply here also.)	• Provides definitive answers • Tells students they are wrong • Lectures • Leads students step-by-step to a solution • Explains how to work through the problem
Evaluate	• Observes students as they apply new concepts and skills • Assesses students' knowledge and/or skills • Looks for evidence that students have changed their thinking or behaviors • Allows students to assess their own learning and group-process skills • Asks open-ended questions, such as: "Why do you think . . . ?" "What evidence do you have?" "What do you know about x?" "How would you explain x?"	• Tests vocabulary words, terms, and isolated facts • Introduces new ideas or concepts • Creates ambiguity • Promotes open-ended discussion unrelated to the concept or skill

TABLE 4-2 APPLYING THE 5-E INSTRUCTIONAL MODEL

Stage of the Instructional Model	What the STUDENT Does	
	That Is Consistent with This Model	That Is Inconsistent with This Model
Engage	• Asks questions, such as: "Why did this happen?" "What do I already know about this?" "What can I find out about this?" • Shows interest in the topic	• Asks for the "right" answer • Offers the "right" answer • Insists on answers or explanations • Seeks one solution
Explore	• Thinks freely, but within the limits of the activity • Tests predictions and hypotheses • Forms new predictions and hypotheses • Tries alternatives and discusses them with others • Records observations and ideas • Suspends judgment	• Lets others do the thinking and exploring (passive involvement) • Works quietly with little or no interaction with others (only appropriate when exploring ideas or feelings) • Plays around indiscriminately with no goal in mind • Stops with one solution
Explain	• Explains possible solutions or answers to others • Listens critically to one another's explanations • Questions one another's explanations • Listens to and tries to comprehend explanations offered by the teacher • Refers to previous activities • Uses recorded observations in explanations	• Proposes explanations from thin air with no relationship to previous experiences • Brings up irrelevant experiences and examples • Accepts explanations without justification • Does not attend to other plausible explanations
Elaborates	• Applies new labels, definitions, explanations, and skills in new, but similar, situations • Uses previous information to ask questions, propose solutions, make decisions, and design experiments • Draws reasonable conclusions from evidence • Records observations and explanations • Checks for understanding among peers	• Plays around with no goal in mind • Ignores previous information or evidence • Draws conclusions from thin air • Uses in discussions only those labels that the teacher provided
Evaluate	• Answers open-ended questions by using observations, evidence, and previously accepted explanations • Demonstrates an understanding or knowledge of the concept or skill • Evaluates his or her own progress and knowledge • Asks related questions that would encourage future investigations	• Draws conclusions, not using evidence or previously accepted explanations • Offers only yes-or-no answers, memorized definitions, or explanation and answers • Fails to express satisfactory explanations in own words • Introduces new, irrelevant topics

Source: Teaching Secondary School Science, 6th ed. (pp. 218–219), by Leslie Trowbridge and Rodger Bybee, 1996, © Reprinted by permission of Pearson Education, Inc., Upper Saddle River, NJ.

5-E Lesson Plan for Batteries and Bulbs

All students should develop an understanding of:

National Science Education Standards

• Light, heat, electricity, and magnetism (Grades K–4)

• Electricity in circuits can produce light, heat, sound, and mechanical motion (Grades K–4)
• Electrical circuits require a complete conducting loop through which an electric circuit can pass (Grades K–4)

Concepts and Principles that Support the Standards

Young girls are as curious as boys about science and inquiry. Sensitive teachers nurture that interest.

Objectives

Through these lesson activities, students should be able to,

1. Demonstrate and explain through words and drawings how to make a bulb light in various ways, given one or two batteries, one or two bulbs, and one or two wires.

2. State, explain, and demonstrate the complete circuit rule. For a bulb to light:
   • the base of the bulb must be touched on the side and the bottom;
   • the battery must be touched on both ends; and
   • there must be a complete circuit or continuous path along the wires and through the battery and bulb.

3. Explain in their own words what a conductor is and demonstrate how to test a material to determine if it is an electrical conductor.

4. Identify and construct series circuits and use the complete circuit rule to explain why the other bulbs in a series circuit go out when one bulb is removed from its holder.

5. Identify and construct parallel circuits and use the complete circuit rule to explain why the other bulbs in a parallel circuit stay lit when one bulb is removed from its holder.

6. Understand, appreciate, and apply safety rules and procedures related to electricity.

Safety

• Respect electricity! Do not touch or go near frayed or broken wires. Do not insert anything but an electrical plug into an electrical outlet.

• Never try these activities with any battery larger than a 1.5 volt D cell (flashlight battery).

• Always wear goggles when you work with batteries, bulbs, and wires to protect your eyes from the sharp points of wires.

• If wires get hot, immediately disconnect them from the battery. This arrangement of the parts of the circuit will not light the bulb, so try a different arrangement.

Learning Activities	5-E Phases	Procedures

Learning Activities

Engage

Explore

5-E Phases

- Engage students in the learning task
- Discover what happens

- Show What You Observe

- Predict and test

Procedures

1. Tell a story of three campers lost in the dark. They have batteries, bulbs, and wires, but do not know how to light a bulb. Ask: Can you help the campers light the bulb?
2. Students work individually to light a bulb using one wire and one battery.
3. Find several ways to light the bulb (students may work individually or with team members on this and subsequent tasks).
4. Light a bulb using two wires, without the bulb touching the battery.
5. Draw pictures to represent the bulb-battery-wire arrangements for tasks 2 and 3.
6. Draw a picture to represent the arrangement of the bulb, wires, and battery in task 4.
7. Complete Prediction Sheet 1. Work frame by frame, going from one frame to the next using what you learn to move from one to another.
   - Make a prediction.
   - Test your prediction.
   - Learn from your test.
   - Apply what you have learned.

Prediction Sheet 1

Will the bulb light? If you are not sure, try it and see!

Explain
- Generalize
- Apply
- Use knowledge to infer and explain

8. Where must a bulb be touched in order for it to light? Where must a battery be touched? Write a general rule for what must be done to make a bulb light.
9. Apply your generalizations or rule to explain each frame in Prediction Sheet 1.
10. Examine a bulb with a magnifying lens. The coiled wire across the top of the bulb is called a *filament*. That is what uses electrical energy to produce light. Do you see the two wires that disappear into the base of the bulb? How do you think they are connected internally within the base of the bulb? Use your rule from task 8 in making your inference.
11. Examine a bulb holder. What are its parts? How is a bulb holder designed to touch the tip and metal side of the base of a bulb?

Elaborate
- Apply knowledge to new situations

12. Make the circuit shown in diagram A.
    - How many wires are needed?
    - Remove one of the bulbs from its holder. What happens? Why?
    - Replace the bulb. Remove another bulb. What happens? Why?
    - Add one or two more batteries. What happens? Why?
    - What would the label "series circuit" describe about the circuit in diagram A?
13. Make the circuit shown in diagram B.
    - How many wires are needed?
    - Remove one of the bulbs from its holder. What happens? Why?
    - Replace the bulb. Remove another bulb. What happens? Why?
    - Add one or two more batteries. What happens? Why?
    - What would the label "parallel circuit" describe about the circuit in diagram B?

Evaluate
- Formative assessment
- Summative assessment

- Through informal and formal assessments, the teacher should continually monitor understanding and adjust individual and group instruction accordingly.
- Develop a test card with new illustrations of battery and bulbs arrangements similar to those on Prediction Sheet 1. Give the test card to students. Have them work alone to answer the test card items.
- Use the test card as a basis for one-on-one interviews with students to assess their understanding of complete circuit ideas.

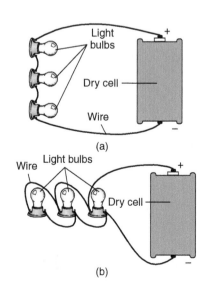

Diagram A. A series circuit.
Diagram B. A parallel circuit.
Source: Adapted from discovery activities in *Batteries and Bulbs*, Elementary Science Study, 1968, Cambridge, MA: Educational Development Center.

Engage. Ms. Jackson arranged her class in cooperative learning groups and assigned jobs, such as Principal Investigator, Materials Manager, Recorder, and Reporter, to different team members within each group. To *engage* the students in the learning task, she began with an improbable little story:

> Three campers had strayed deep into the woods, far from their campsite. Night had fallen and they had no flashlight to find their way back in the darkness. However, one camper had a spare battery in his backpack, another had a flashlight bulb, and a third had a few pieces of copper wire. Unfortunately, they did not know how to connect the battery, bulb, and wire to light the bulb.

Then, while interest was high, Ms. Jackson asked the class: "Can you use the materials in front of you to light a bulb and help the campers get back to their campsite safely?"

Explore. As she talked, Ms. Jackson had quietly given each group a box containing several 1.5-volt D-cell batteries, small flashlight bulbs, and pieces of wire. Now, she asked the Materials Manager in each group to place one battery, one bulb, and one piece of wire before each child. She had planned the engagement activities so that once the problem had been introduced and curiosity was high, students could begin to *explore* immediately, manipulating materials and making observations. The story helped the students comprehend and maintain focus on the task.

Initially, the students worked individually to light the bulb (see task 2 in the batteries and bulbs lesson). Many students lit the bulb within a few minutes; others took considerably longer. During the explore phase, Ms. Jackson resisted the temptation to give too much help. As students successfully lit a bulb, she acknowledged their success with a little cheer, a word or two, or a smile or gesture. But she cautioned those who had succeeded not to reveal to others what they had done to light a bulb and rob them of the joy and feeling of accomplishment of discovery and the opportunity to develop real understanding.

As students succeeded in the discovery task, she directed their attention to two additional tasks she had written on the chalkboard:

* Find several ways to light a bulb using only one battery and one wire.
* Light a bulb using two wires, without the bulb touching the battery.

These were tasks 3 and 4 from the lesson plan. Students either worked individually or with their team members on these tasks. Children freely exchanged information and ideas as they worked in their groups, but Ms. Jackson always noted whether each child could succeed on a task. She invited those who were content to learn from others to show her with their own materials how to do each task.

In the process of exploration, most students used trial and error. Some students thought about possibilities, made hypotheses and predictions, and tried out their ideas. Each cooperative group moved through the exploration activities at their own pace, with the teacher giving hints, adding information, posing questions, or providing additional activities and material as needed. Most of the groups were able to complete tasks 2 through 4 on the first day.

To start the next science time, Ms. Jackson turned out the lights in the classroom and asked the children to individually make a bulb light and hold it aloft to light the room. As she walked about the room watching what the children were doing, she was able to quickly assess the knowledge and skills of each child, to note who needed help, and to either supply assistance or ask someone in a cooperative group to help.

Back in a large group, she asked the children to talk about what they had done. Then, she directed the children, working individually, to draw pictures of the different ways they

You may need to study circuit ideas yourself before teaching batteries and bulbs activities. Good presentations on electricity and electrical circuits at an elementary level are available in many curriculum resources. Especially good treatments can be found in the STC (Science and Technology for Children) *Teachers' Guide for Electric Circuits,* and the FOSS (Full Option Science System) *Teachers' Guide for Magnetism and Electricity.*

Through the Annenberg video *Completing the Circuit,* which is recommended in the Online Professional Development section of this chapter, you can learn a great deal about electrical circuits as you watch a class of fourth-grade students learning electrical concepts and principles through their own investigations and teacher scaffolding. A study guide and instructions for accessing this video are given in the Online Professional Development section.

had found to light a bulb (tasks 5 and 6 of the lesson plan). This activity was designed to lift thought from a kinesthetic, hands-on level to a more abstract, iconic, or imaging level. As she went about the room assessing each child's drawings, she noted that some had not perceived exactly what it was they did to light a bulb. Again, she either provided assistance or asked another child to assist. Thus, the children's understanding was continually assessed and enhanced.

Ms. Jackson passed out Prediction Sheet 1 and gave directions for it (task 7). Circulating among the students as they worked in their groups, she encouraged them and supplied assistance as needed.

Explain. When all groups had finished the prediction sheet, Ms. Jackson led the students to shift from exploration to explanation. She began the third day with task 8 from the lesson plan. She posed the question for this activity by saying,

> "Suppose one of the campers lost in the woods had a cell phone and called you to find out how to light a bulb. What would you tell her? Write out your answer."

This task was intended to raise the children's level of thought from kinesthetic and imaging levels to a higher semantic level. Children worked individually, then as groups, to answer the question. Noting that the children had considerable difficulty with this more abstract task, Ms. Jackson decided to provide some direct instruction on the concept of circuits.

In formally presenting the new concept, Ms. Jackson followed these simple guidelines:

- First, she grouped her students near her so they could all hear what she said and see what she demonstrated or wrote on the chalkboard.
- She referred to tasks 2 through 6 that the students had done themselves during exploration.
- As she discussed the activities, she defined the circuit concept that she wanted to develop. Referring through gestures to the complete circuit in front of her, she said,

  A *circuit* is an arrangement of bulbs, batteries, and wires. A circuit is a complete circuit if the bulb lights. If the circuit is complete, there is an unbroken pathway around the circuit from one terminal of a battery, along the wires, through the bulb, and back to the other terminal of the battery.

- She wrote the word *circuit* on the board for all the children to see. (Writing the word gives visual as well as oral introduction of the new word.) Through questioning and verbal instruction, she led the students to apply their new knowledge of circuits to the circuit arrangements they had already encountered in tasks 2 through 6.

This instructional sequence referred to activities the students had already done or observed but added a new concept, *circuit*. With this new information, the children went back to the task of writing out a general rule for lighting a bulb. The class-as-a-whole, under Ms. Jackson's assistance, decided on these rules:

To light a bulb with one wire:

1. *Touch the tip of the bulb to one terminal of the battery.*
2. *Touch the wire to the metal on the side of the bulb.*
3. *Make a complete pathway for the electricity to flow by touching the other end of the wire to the other end of the battery.*

The children, working in their groups, then applied their new rule to each frame in Prediction Sheet 1, noting which circuits must be complete ones and identifying why other circuits pictured might not provide complete paths for the electricity (task 9).

Elaborate. Once they have been introduced, concepts, principles, and explanation must be applied or transferred to new situations to be understood. Through tasks 10–13 from the lesson plan, circuit concepts and principles were refined, extended, and linked to one another and to real-world experiences. Although all of the children enjoyed these activities and were able to learn a good deal more factual and conceptual information about electrical circuits from them, many of the children were not able to spontaneously apply the new circuit rules to understand what happened in each case. Because of their complexity and novelty, the new problem situations were challenging for the students. Yet, for many students, the challenges yielded to the application of complete circuit concepts developed through earlier activities.

Evaluate. Ms. Jackson used a combination of *formative* and *summative* assessments as a basis for evaluating student performance and understanding. She conducted formative assessments primarily through student responses to the various questions featured in the lesson plan. Teachers monitor students' performances during investigations, examine their products, such as drawings and notebook entries, and listen to discourse. The goal of formative assessment in this case was to determine and improve student understanding of electrical circuits. Ms. Jackson used the results of formative assessments to adjust instruction in order to improve learning.

Summative assessment was undertaken through a teacher-made test card that parallels Prediction Sheet 1. The teacher used the test card for whole-group assessment and as the basis of one-on-one interviews with students to assess their understanding of complete circuit ideas. The teacher also used the performance task and rubric shown in Chapter 6 in Figures 6-12 and 6-13 to assess understanding. Decisions about next steps in the teaching sequence were determined from these results.

Using the 5-E Model to Sequence Science Activities

In the previous example on electrical circuits, the teacher used the 5-E model to plan and implement an entire lesson. The 5-E model might also be used to sequence individual science activities within a lesson or unit.

Here are some important guidelines for using the 5-E model with individual activities.

- Plan each individual activity so that it involves the first three phases in the 5-E model—engage, explore, and explain. This means that explanation is implemented within each activity, rather than letting the data from exploration accumulate across different activities before the explain phase is introduced (as in the previously presented lesson sequence).
- Use the engage, explore, and explain phases of the 5-E model, with each succeeding activity to develop additional concepts, principles, and explanations.
- Also, use succeeding activities in a sequence as elaborations of previously learned concepts, principles, explanations, and procedures. Thus, succeeding activities require the transfer/application of previously learned ideas to new situations.
- Use formative assessment procedures within each activity to obtain information for improving learning and instruction.

Go to the Homework and Exercises section in Chapter 4 of MyEducationLab to watch the video *Investigating Goldfish: Parts 1, 2, 3, and 4*. In this set of videos, we watch kindergarten children as they raise questions about goldfish and observe live goldfish to answer their questions.

An Annenberg video entitled *Completing the Circuit* illustrates the engage, explore, and explain phases within each activity. This video is featured in the Online Professional Development section at the end of this chapter. In addition, each activity in the companion volume for this book, *Activities for Teaching Science as Inquiry*, uses the engage, explore, and explain phases of the 5-E model.

- Use summative assessment after the last activity as a basis for evaluating the students' conceptual understanding, use of inquiry abilities, and understandings of the nature of science and scientific inquiry.
- Keep in mind that summative assessments can serve as evidence for decisions about grades and for reports to students and parents.

Guided Discovery, Textbook, and Direct Instruction Approaches to Teaching Science

So far in this book, we have focused on using inquiry instruction to help students construct conceptual understanding in science, develop their abilities to do science, and further understand the nature of scientific inquiry. The emphasis on inquiry, however, does not mean that all science lessons should be inquiry oriented, nor does it imply that teachers should pursue a single approach to teaching. According to the *National Science Education Standards* (National Research Council, 1996), "Just as inquiry has many different facets, so teachers need to use many different strategies to develop the understandings and abilities described in the *Standards*" (p. 2).

Let us examine first the guided discovery approach to teaching science.

Guided Discovery

In guided discovery learning, children begin with interesting questions and concrete materials. Learners work individually or in small groups to explore materials, make observations, and discover answers to their questions about the natural world. The teacher serves as a facilitator and guide through the discovery process.

Discovery lessons are highly motivational. There is joy for children in probing into and finding out about the unknown. As children start to explore, they seem to suddenly awaken to exciting possibilities in the natural world and in themselves. Discovery allows students to find their own meanings and organize their own ideas. In discovery learning, children's imagination, hunches, and insight precede proof and instruction by teachers (Wiggins & McTighe, 1998). As young students engage in probing interesting questions, much open inquiry can take place if teachers allow students to explore. Students do not have to be scientifically mature, merely curious.

The Elementary Science Study (ESS) program developed in the 1960s with federal funds was one of the pioneers in the use of discovery approaches to learning science. The ESS group devised many activities and units and tested them in classrooms across the nation. Dozens of lessons from ESS modules such as *Kitchen Physics*, *Batteries and Bulbs*, *Bones*, *Mealworms*, *Gases and Airs*, *Rocks and Minerals*, *Mystery Powders*, and *Small Things* were developed.

The ESS philosophy was captured in the phrase "messing about in science," which was based on an expression in Kenneth Grahame's (1981) children's book *The Wind in the Willows*. In this delightful tale, Water Rat explained to Mole the joys of simply "messing about in boats" on a lazy afternoon. If you have not already done so, read the account of Mole and Water Rat's river adventure in the introduction to this book (page 2) and think about why it inspired the developers of ESS. As you read, consider how Water Rat's little speech at the end of the selection can also fit some of the purposes of discovery learning.

Through discovery learning, children enjoy simply messing about in science. But well-planned discovery materials and activities also give children opportunities and time to observe, investigate, and appreciate the order and diversity of the world.

Preparing for Guided Discovery. Although it is the students who engage in the discovery work, careful teacher planning is necessary for successful discovery lessons. Teachers must consider the kinds of introductory questions that can effectively set the stage for exploration. Here are some sample questions:

- What are some things you notice about butterflies? What colors are they and what patterns do you see? How might different color patterns serve to protect butterflies?
- How do mealworms respond to environmental conditions, such as moisture, light, and heat? What foods do mealworms prefer?
- What things live on the edge of the pond? How do they interact with one another? Why do they live on the edge of the pond and not in it?

Strategies for Guided Discovery. To teach by guided discovery, you should introduce the problem, distribute materials in an orderly way, and let the discoveries begin as soon as possible. Circulate among the children as they engage in discovery activities, spending no more than about 30 to 60 seconds with each student or small group. You should give only enough assistance to ensure that students do not become overly frustrated, experience undue failure, and give up.

Rather than telling the students what to do while investigating, teachers can scaffold children's discoveries by asking questions or giving hints that help them sense the direction for solving problems. You must be careful to respect the discovery process and not to supply too much information. Do not rob children of opportunities for thought and creativity in their investigations. Thus, in discovery lessons, you might choose to answer children's questions with "What do you think?" or "What are your ideas?" Deciding when to give assistance and when to withhold it is an important part of the art of discovery teaching.

At different points in the discovery process, you will want to hear from and talk with the class as a whole about their procedures and discoveries. You will be tempted to give students the "right" answer. However, a skilled discovery teacher listens to and uses the ideas of children in questioning and discussion to help them organize their thoughts and build more scientifically accurate understandings of the world (see Chapter 7).

As you probably have noticed, guided discovery is essentially the approach students and teachers should take in the explore phase of the 5-E model.

Guided Discovery in a Nutshell. We can summarize the teaching approach to discovery learning in the following way:

- Engage children in activities.
- Encourage them to explore concrete materials and reflect on what they find out.
- Engage children in conversations, listen to their ideas, and provide guidance to help them build and test their own explanations of what is happening (Koch, 1999).

Guided discovery is a wonderful approach to learning science that students and teachers have enjoyed for many years. Nothing raises the sense of wonder and joy of learning about the natural world like discovery. In teaching science, you should provide your students a variety of opportunities to experience the joy of discovery.

Discovery approaches to science instruction share several features of inquiry instruction. Yet, often missing in guided discovery teaching are careful attention to constructing and applying specific scientific knowledge, opportunities for students to develop conceptual understanding by attempting to transfer what they have learned to new problems, and a planned development of specific abilities of inquiry. Adding explain and elaborate phases to guided discovery can greatly enhance the science learning of students.

Go to the Homework and Exercises section in Chapter 4 of MyEducationLab to read an interesting and informative article, "Inquiring Scientists Want to Know." The article contrasts three approaches to science teaching: a laboratory verification method, a discovery approach, and an inquiry approach. This article extends and refines the comparisons of different teaching approaches to science discussed in this chapter.

Direct Instruction

Direct instruction is an approach to science instruction in which teachers present to learners the primary information to be learned. It emphasizes learning from being told. Hunter (1984) incorporated some behavioral principles of S-R learning into a direct instruction model called *lesson design*. Behavioral learning principles in Hunter's model focus on teacher stimulus (S), student response (R), teacher reinforcement of responses, and student practice.

Following are the instructional steps in Hunter's lesson design model of direct instruction. Note especially that learning input does not come from student activities but from teachers and other sources.

- *Anticipatory set.* In this phase, focusing activities are carried out that orient students to the lesson and lead them to access relevant prior knowledge.
- *Objectives and purpose.* Here, the students are informed of the objectives for the day. The teacher also explains how and why the ideas of the lesson are useful and important.
- *Instructional input.* The teacher uses a wide variety of methods—including lecture, media presentations, role playing, simulations, demonstrations, and even laboratory investigations—to help the students achieve the objectives. The specific content and processes to be learned are contained explicitly in the instructional input.
- *Modeling.* Through modeling, the teacher provides examples of the content knowledge and procedures to be learned.
- *Monitoring understanding and adjusting instruction.* The teacher elicits an active response from each student and assesses the response for evidence of understanding. The teacher adjusts instruction as necessary to improve understanding.
- *Independent and guided practice.* Because practice is essential to learning and retention, ample opportunity is afforded for students to practice the new content and processes.

Considerable content in elementary and middle school science is well suited to direct instruction, and you will want to use this method when appropriate. Direct instruction methods can be useful and effective for teaching well-defined performance skills or specific facts, concepts, and information to be remembered. Arbitrary conventions such as stoplight colors, measurement equivalencies, and vocabulary labels that cannot be logically deduced, as well as concepts and procedures that may be invented by some students but not by others, can be taught by direct methods. Also, direct instruction is more appropriate for content that we do not want students to learn by trial and error, such as safety precautions or how to focus a microscope.

Within inquiry contexts expository methods can be important, such as for providing background knowledge, giving directions, teaching specific skills, inventing concepts and principles in the explain phase of the 5-E model, applying them to new situations in the elaborate phase of the model, and summarizing inquiries (Wolfinger, 2000). You might recognize that in the classroom example of teaching science by the 5-E model, Ms. Jackson used direct instruction in the explain phase to teach the concept of complete circuits.

Yet, in light of the *National Science Education Standards* and contemporary learning research, there are several problems with the direct instruction approach to science teaching. It typically fails to provide opportunities for students to ask their own questions about the natural world, explore and collect data, and use the evidence of their own explorations and their prior or new scientific knowledge as the basis for their own theories and explanations. It does not provide the experiential base needed for learning processes of science and investigational strategies. Further, it does not typically build in discourse among students and teachers that promotes learning with understanding. Finally, direct instruction does not usually provide authentic opportunities for teachers to assess student understanding formatively and provide scaffolding assistance.

A Textbook Approach to Science Teaching

The textbook approach has traditionally consisted of textbooks and worksheets as the major instructional materials, supplemented with teacher lecture, class discussion, demonstrations, videotape presentations, or other short activities. Students may also read about and conduct some hands-on activities to provide a basis for science knowledge and explanations. Typically, teachers present information, students read text materials and examine pictures (such as pictures of circuits, switches, or electromagnets), and engage in independent and guided practice activities using worksheets. This approach generally places high demands on students' reading, language, and memory skills and presents large amounts of vocabulary to learn (Scruggs, Mastropieri, Bakken, & Brigham, 1993). As with other approaches, textbook methods should be well structured and involve daily review, active engagement by students, formative and summative evaluation of student products, and questioning.

In the past, because of an emphasis on reading about science rather than doing science, textbook series did not usually provide opportunity for children to investigate and to learn investigative procedures. Further, science textbooks tended to focus more on presenting specific concepts and principles to be learned.

However, contemporary textbook series are increasingly placing emphasis on inquiry. Inquiry lessons in textbook series typically include initiating questions, data gathering, and data interpretation, but investigations are largely directed or guided by the textbook, with little opportunity for student inquiry.

With the changing emphasis of textbooks, the question to be considered is not whether textbooks should be used in teaching science, but how the texts should be used. Lowery (1998) has explained that new, meaningful knowledge acquired from text materials is actually a construction based on prior knowledge and linguistic input. With something to work with, an author can help readers understand abstract ideas and make difficult connections. But if readers have inadequate prior knowledge related to the content, they will gain little from reading. Thus, *reading is more powerful in science when it follows experience and is based on prior knowledge*. Following this principle, the FOSS (Full Option Science System) has designed reading materials to be used after hands-on instruction.

An approach in which text reading is introduced only after inquiry would seem to work well with most textbook series. In that case, topics might be introduced through inquiry approaches, such as the 5-E approach, with textbook materials being read and text activities conducted after the 5-E lessons or during the explain phase of the model. The texts would then serve to supplement previous learning by filling in gaps, providing new information and concepts, reinforcing definitions, and summarizing what has been constructed through earlier inquiry lessons. Since readers would have some prior knowledge of a topic through their own activities, when they encounter textbook presentations, they should be able to read them with more comprehension.

For example, in the inquiry lesson plan on electrical circuits presented previously, students built series and parallel circuits. They predicted on the basis of the complete circuit rule what would happen to the other bulbs in the circuit if one of the bulbs were removed. Figure 4-2 shows a reading selection on series and parallel circuits that appears in a fourth-grade science textbook. In an *inquiry first, reading later* approach, children would carry out

Some specific suggestions on connecting reading and science instruction are given in Chapter 9.

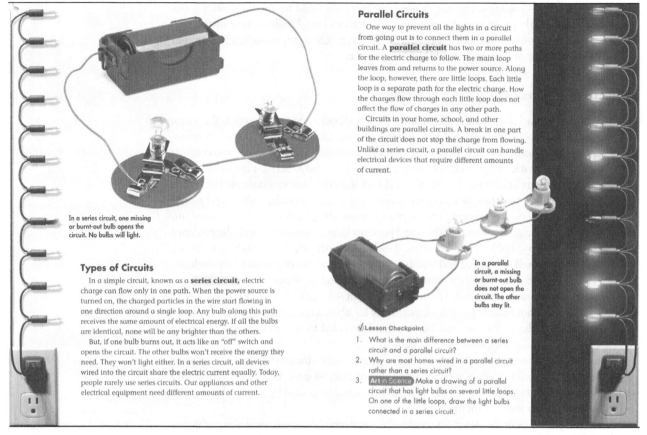

Parallel Circuits

One way to prevent all the lights in a circuit from going out is to connect them in a *parallel circuit*. A **parallel circuit** has two or more paths for the electric charge to follow. The main loop leaves from and returns to the power source. Along the loop, however, there are little loops. Each little loop is a separate path for the electric charge. How the charges flow through each little loop does not affect the flow of charges in any other path.

Circuits in your home, school, and other buildings are parallel circuits. A break in one part of the circuit does not stop the charge from flowing. Unlike a series circuit, a parallel circuit can handle electrical devices that require different amounts of current.

In a series circuit, one missing or burnt-out bulb opens the circuit. No bulbs will light.

In a parallel circuit, a missing or burnt-out bulb does not open the circuit. The other bulbs stay lit.

Types of Circuits

In a simple circuit, known as a **series circuit**, electric charge can flow only in one path. When the power source is turned on, the charged particles in the wire start flowing in one direction around a single loop. Any bulb along this path receives the same amount of electrical energy. If all the bulbs are identical, none will be any brighter than the others.

But, if one bulb burns out, it acts like an "off" switch and opens the circuit. The other bulbs won't receive the energy they need. They won't light either. In a series circuit, all devices wired into the circuit share the electric current equally. Today, people rarely use series circuits. Our appliances and other electrical equipment need different amounts of current.

✔ **Lesson Checkpoint**

1. What is the main difference between a series circuit and a parallel circuit?
2. Why are most homes wired in a parallel circuit rather than a series circuit?
3. **Art in Science** Make a drawing of a parallel circuit that has light bulbs on several little loops. On one of the little loops, draw the light bulbs connected in a series circuit.

Figure 4-2   In an *inquiry first, reading later* approach, children carry out activities on series and parallel circuits before they read about them in their textbooks.

inquiry activities on series and parallel circuits before they read about them in their textbooks. Because the students would have some prior knowledge of series and parallel circuits and complete circuit paths, they should be able to read the text selection with more comprehension and understanding.

Research on the Effectiveness of Different Approaches to Science Instruction

A key question asked in many research studies on learning and instruction in science has been: *What is the relative effectiveness of different approaches to teaching science?* Haury (1993), the National Research Council (2001), and Duschl and colleagues (2007) have reviewed a large number of research studies on the effectiveness of different approaches to teaching science. Although definitions of inquiry vary from study to study, research data indicate that inquiry instruction is effective in fostering problem solving, creativity, and independent learning and in improving reasoning, observing, and logical analysis. Research indicates further that students exposed to inquiry methods in science typically perform better than their peers in more traditional classes on measures of general science achievement, process skills, analytical skills, and related skills such as language arts and mathematics.

Studies consistently found that, when compared with students in more traditional, textbook-oriented science programs, students engaged in inquiry activities

- found science more exciting and interesting,
- had greater feelings of success, and
- had a more positive view of science and scientists.

Studies indicate that the advantages of inquiry-oriented instruction also extend to special student populations (Duschl et al., 2007). Research indicates that students with learning disabilities and English Language Learners (ELL) can successfully engage in inquiry and learn science concepts through inquiry instruction.

Research data on measurable cognitive and affective variables support the advantages of inquiry instruction over other methods. Yet, intangible achievements may outweigh tangible ones, as students learn through an inquiry approach to ask questions, place a priority on evidence, and use observable data, knowledge, and clear reasoning to arrive at explanations and evaluate claims.

Klahr and Nigam (2004) compared discovery and direct instruction models of instruction, although the researchers used somewhat unconventional definitions of discovery and direct instruction. Discovery instruction was defined in terms of pure discovery, with essentially no teacher guidance, rather than the guided instruction model presented in this chapter. Also, in contrast to the direct instruction approach described here, direct instruction as defined in Klahr and Nigam's study involved considerable hands-on activities, with appropriate teacher scaffolding.

The science topic treated in both methods was designing and constructing controlled investigations for problems involving balls rolling down ramps. Tests assessed *near transfer* (transfer to the design of experiments related to the balls and ramps problem, but requiring the testing of different variables) and *far transfer* (transfer to the evaluation of the design of totally new experiments). Results of the study by Klahr and Nigam strongly favored direct instruction (with hands-on activities) over discovery (with no teacher input).

The critical importance of teacher input in instruction can be shown through the Klahr and Nigam study. In the discovery approach tested, there was little if any scaffolding and no direct instruction on how to design and set up controlled investigations. In contrast, teacher scaffolding, including teacher instructions about controlled experiments, was a critical part of the researchers' direct instruction approach. Further, tasks involving the transfer of knowledge of experimental design were included in the direct instruction condition.

From one perspective, the discovery condition in the Klahr and Nigam study omitted the critically important 5-E phases of explain and elaborate. In contrast, the direct instruction approach emphasized the importance of teaching explicit concepts and skill in the explain phase of the model. Thus, the study by Klahr and Nigam indirectly demonstrates the value of the 5-E approach in learning and instruction.

Selecting Instructional Approaches for Teaching Science

In addition to inquiry, discovery, textbook, and direct instruction methods, a variety of other strategies available for use in science are presented in this book. The questioning strategies of Chapter 7 work well with teacher demonstration approaches to science. Learning centers are discussed in Chapter 5. Field trips to large public science institutions, such as aquariums, are treated in Chapter 5. Reading as a strategy for learning science is discussed in Chapter 9. Writing to learn science is discussed in Chapters 2 and 9. Web-based lessons are presented in Chapter 8. Computer simulations and virtual field trips as teaching methods are also introduced in Chapter 8.

There is no one best way to teach all science concepts to all children all the time. You cannot guarantee how effective any individual method will be. Students differ in prior knowledge, experiences, learning abilities, preferred learning approaches, and the amount of structure they need in learning. Classroom and environmental factors vary and can affect teaching and learning. Some science lessons might be planned to prepare students for future science learning. Other lessons might be intended to provide for reinforcement, practice, and review of topics. Lessons focusing on application of science concepts and principles are also important. That is why you need to use a variety of teaching techniques throughout the school year.

Regardless of the approach selected, it should involve knowledge of objectives, daily review, active engagement by students, a variety of practice activities, opportunities for transfer learning, teacher scaffolding, and regular evaluation of student products. When direct input is called for, effective teachers should also pay attention to such presentation variables as structure, clarity, redundancy, enthusiasm, appropriate rate of presentation, and maximum engagement through questioning and feedback. "If these variables are considered along with the specific needs of students during instruction," conclude Mastropieri and Scruggs (2004, p. 181), ". . . overall achievement will improve."

What conclusions are you beginning to form about science teaching models and strategies? Although there are many valuable methods for teaching science, all children should experience, at least two or more times a year, the joy and satisfaction of asking questions about the natural world, finding ways to investigate and gather evidence, and using their evidence and science knowledge to arrive at explanations that provide answers to their questions. In short, all children should have the opportunity to learn science through inquiry.

SUMMARY

* Inquiry instruction refers to teaching procedures focused on student investigations of the natural world. Through inquiry activities, students have opportunities to develop conceptual knowledge and understanding, inquiry abilities, and understandings about the nature of science and scientific inquiry.

* Throughout the inquiry process, teachers guide, focus, challenge, and encourage student learning, using their knowledge of students as well as their knowledge of science and how it is learned.

* The 5-E model of instruction is a second-generation version of the learning cycle model.

* The five Es in the model are engage, explore, explain, elaborate, and evaluate. The 5-E model provides a specific focus on the NSES tasks of inquiry.

* The 5-E model also provides opportunities for teachers to use the different factors that enhance learning with understanding, such as providing access to prior knowledge,

providing for scaffolding assistance, and building learning communities.

* Several different instructional strategies have been developed for teaching science. In guided discovery approaches, children are presented with interesting questions and concrete materials. They work individually or in small groups to explore materials, make observations, and discover answers to their questions about the natural world. The teacher serves as facilitator and guide of the discovery process.

* Direct instruction and textbook instruction strategies are teacher-directed methods in which teachers and textbooks present to learners the main information to be learned.

* The 5-E model incorporates guided discovery strategies in the explore phase. Building on student explorations and ideas can include the use of direct teaching of core concepts in the explain phase. In science, textbook reading should follow experiences with the concepts. This order enables

students to build prior knowledge useful in comprehending science texts. Science textbooks would then be used to supplement and summarize inquiry activities.

• No one method of teaching science is best for all teachers and all students, all the time, under all circumstances.

Inquiry models of instruction mirror inquiry procedures of science, are consistent with constructivist approaches to learning, and are motivational and effective in teaching science to children. All children should have the opportunity to learn science through inquiry.

ONLINE PROFESSIONAL DEVELOPMENT

Pre- and post-tests to assess your knowledge of chapter content, along with exercises to enhance your understanding, can be found on MyEducationLab at www.myeducationlab.com.

Video Guides

Video clips on MyEducationLab selected for this chapter include *Teacher Discussion of Moon Phase Lessons* and *Investigating Goldfish—Parts 1, 2, 3,* and *4*.

Accessing the Videos

1. Go to the Homework and Exercises section in Chapter 4 of MyEducationLab to select and view videos for this chapter.
2. Videos might be viewed individually, by small groups of colleagues, or by the whole class.
3. As you watch each video, use the **Questions for Reflection** to guide your thoughts and note taking for personal use and group discussion.
4. Discuss your answers to the questions about each video with classmates.

Video: Teacher Discussion of Moon Phase Lessons

Overview

In this video we listen to the two fourth- and fifth-grade teachers we saw in the moon phase videos of Chapter 3 as they reflect on what they were trying to accomplish in the moon phase lessons.

Questions for Reflection

1. What examples of student records of observations do you see in the investigations of moon phases?

2. What evidence do you see that the 5-E model (or a similar model) forms the structure for the moon phase lessons?

Videos: Investigating Goldfish, Parts 1, 2, 3, and 4

The first three videos in the *Investigating Goldfish* video set follow kindergarten students as they investigate goldfish. In the fourth part, the classroom teacher reflects on her purposes for the lesson and the children's investigations. In this part, the teacher also discusses how the goldfish lesson followed the 5-E model of inquiry instruction.

Questions for Reflection

1. What Connecticut standards does the kindergarten teacher say the science lessons emphasize?
2. What questions did the teacher ask to engage the children in inquiry?
3. During the explore phase, what observations of the goldfish were made in response to the questions from the engage phase?
4. What conclusions about goldfish did the children reach in the explain phase of the lesson? What was the basis for the children's explanations?
5. How well do you think the teacher followed the 5-E model in designing and implementing the goldfish lesson?

Annenberg Videos

Video Series: Science K–6: Investigating Classrooms

Video: Completing the Circuit

To access Annenberg videos, follow the instructions given in the Online Professional Development section in Chapter 1 on page 26.

5

Teachers are designers. An essential act of our profession is the design of curriculum and learning experiences to meet specified purposes. . . . We are not free to teach any topic we choose. Rather, we are guided by national, state, district, or institutional standards that specify what students should know and be able to do. These standards provide a framework to help us identify teaching and learning priorities and guide our design of curriculum and assessments.

(Wiggins & McTighe, 1998, pp. 7–8)

Planning and Managing Inquiry Instruction

BY DESCRIBING THE CONCEPTUAL knowledge and understandings, inquiry abilities, and understandings about the nature of science and science inquiry that children at different grade levels should learn, national and state standards provide a framework for instruction. Teachers, then, are responsible for selecting science content to be learned, developing lesson plans, and implementing them effectively to help students attain goals specified in the standards. Further, teachers plan how to group students for instruction, establish safety rules, and plan and implement fair and effective behavior management procedures that will help establish positive learning environments for students.

In Chapter 4, we showed you a 5-E lesson plan on electrical circuits. This chapter explores how you can develop your own instructional plans. We also discuss ways of organizing your class for instruction, deciding on safety rules and practices to emphasize, and managing student activities during instruction.

As you study this chapter and continue to build your background for teaching science, think about the following questions:

- *How can you select science content topics that are aligned with national and state standards?*

- *How can you develop and write learning objectives?*

- *How can you create and sequence activities that engage students in meaningful learning? How will you design the introductory activities so they initiate the lesson, establish focus questions, and pique the interest of children? How will you design activities for the body of the lesson that enable students to attain learning objectives?*

- *What will you attend to in designing assessments of student understanding?*

- *How can you effectively design the learning environment and group students for learning?*

- *What safety precautions should you and your students take in doing science?*

- *What strategies will you use to manage student behavior?*

- *How can you bring it all together to implement effective science instruction in your own classroom?*

Planning Science Lessons

In this chapter we emphasize these generic steps in planning well-designed science lessons:

- Select science content to be learned that is consistent with state or national content standards.
- Write learning objectives.
- Develop learning activities that enable students to achieve the objectives. Describe these activities in writing.
- Plan assessment tasks and procedures.

The accompanying NSES box summarizes some of the program standards related to planning and implementing science lessons.

Select Science Content to Be Taught and Learned

You can review the *National Science Education Standards* online. Go to http://www.nap.edu/readingroom/books/nses/html. Click on Chapter 6: Science Content Standards. A synopsis of content standards is available on the PALS (Performance Assessment Links in Science) website at http://pals.sri.com.

National standards in science are designed to specify broad goals but do not inform teachers specifically of what to teach. Usually specific content to be learned will be presented in state frameworks or district curriculum guides. These documents are typically developed based on the national standards and other resources, such as the *Benchmarks for Science Literacy* (American Association for the Advancement of Science, 1993) and scope and sequence charts of nationally developed science programs and textbook series. Classroom teachers must determine the teaching strategies and sometimes instructional materials suitable for enabling their students to master the required content.

As an example of how standards can guide the selection of science topics, consider Figure 5-1. This figure provides a list of NSES content standards and related concepts and principles on the topic of sound. The concepts and principles on sound are much more specific than is usually the case for other science topics. State standards are often more detailed than national standards. For example, many states include indicators that give specific concepts and principles to be learned and assessed relative to each science topic.

The FOSS (Full Option Science System) teachers' guide for *The Physics of Sound* (Full Option Science System, 2000) provides an excellent model to follow in selecting your own

---

NSES   NSES

According to the program standards of the *National Science Education Standards*:

- All students, regardless of gender, cultural or ethnic background, physical or learning disabilities, or future aspirations, should have the opportunity to experience the richness and excitement of knowing about and understanding the natural world.
- Clear goals and expectations for students must be used to guide the design, implementation, and assessment of all elements of the science program.
- Science content should be embedded in curriculum patterns and activities that are developmentally appropriate, interesting, and relevant to students' lives.
- The science program must emphasize inquiring into and understanding natural phenomena and science-related social issues.
- The science program should connect to other subjects.

NSES SCIENCE CONTENT STANDARDS

Science Content Knowledge Standards: Sound

As a result of their science activities, all students should develop an understanding of:

- Position and motion of objects (sound) (K–4)
- Sound as a form of energy (5–8)
- Transfer of energy (5–8)

Fundamental Concepts and Principles on Sound

As a result of their science activities, all students should develop an understanding of fundamental concepts and principles underlying the knowledge standards:

- Sound is produced by vibrating objects (K–4)
- The pitch of a sound can be varied by changing the rate of vibration (K–4)
- Vibrations in materials set up wavelike disturbances that spread away from the source. Sound waves and earthquake waves are examples. These and other waves move at different speeds in different materials. (*Benchmarks for Science Literacy,* 6–8)

Scientific Inquiry Standards

As a result of their science activities, all students should develop abilities to:

- Ask a question about objects, organisms, and events in the environment.
- Plan and conduct a simple investigation.
- Use appropriate tools and techniques to gather data.
- Use evidence and scientific knowledge to develop explanations.
- Communicate investigations, data, and explanations to others.

Figure 5-1 What students are expected to learn about sound in grades K–4 and 5–8, according to the *National Science Education Standards.*

content that fits state and national standards. This module is designed for grades 3 and 4. It focuses on this content:

- What the characteristics of sound are;
- What causes sound: vibrating sources;
- How sound travels;
- Where sound comes from, how it is transferred through various materials, and how it is received;
- How we hear sounds.

These topics of sound can be expanded into content descriptions, objectives, and lesson activities.

The Physics of Sound Module includes lessons with content descriptions, objectives, and instructional plans. Even if teachers are not using the commercial module, these topics provide a good outline of concepts that should be included.

Developing Teachers' Knowledge of Science. Teachers often feel that their science background is inadequate. But you do not need to be a science major to teach science effectively. Truth be known, many experienced teachers of science began to really understand science topics only after teaching them.

To develop your own background knowledge on a science topic you will be teaching, you should:

The federal government often funds programs at universities and colleges for teachers of science and mathematics at every level. A typical program focuses on a narrow range of content and uses hands-on approaches. Funds for tuition, fees, and books, abundant teaching materials, stipends, and expenses to a state science conference are often provided for teacher participants. We urge you to take advantage of these professional development opportunities. They are not only educational—they are great fun.

* Read widely, including textbook chapters, teachers' guides for nationally funded science projects, and especially books written for children; but be aware that children's books sometimes provide inaccurate information.
* Use an Internet search engine such as Google or Yahoo! to locate appropriate science content discussions.
* Talk to other teachers and science education specialists.
* Attend college courses and institutes for teachers.
* Attend relevant sessions at national, regional, and state conferences for science teachers.
* Visit websites of science education professional organizations such as http:// www.nsta.org.

When you have selected standards-based science content to be learned and understand that content yourself, you are ready to begin to develop and write objectives.

Write Appropriate Objectives

In planning for instruction, you must translate content descriptions into instructional objectives. Instructional objectives are specific intended learning outcomes. Clear objectives aid teachers in planning instructional activities and choosing instructional approaches. They serve as a guide in the process of teaching and facilitate the assessment of student learning. They also make clear to students the specific performances you will expect from them.

The ABCs of Objectives. An instructional objective typically contains three main components: the audience, the behavior, and the conditions. In these ABCs of objectives, the *audience* identifies who will be expected to achieve the objective, such as learners or students. The audience is often specified in a phrase placed before a list of objectives, such as, "Through the experiences of this lesson, the students will be able to." Here, the audience is "the students."

The *behavior* identifies the specific type of performance that will be expected of students and what actions they will be expected to take. Action words such as *compute, compare, identify, demonstrate,* and *predict* identify specific behaviors to be demonstrated by students. Table 5-1 defines several action words denoting different types of performances that are particularly useful for science instruction. Although objectives might be described in terms of specific behaviors, collectively they are intended to indicate understanding.

The *conditions* for an instructional objective specify the "givens"—that is, what the learner will have access to, if anything, in demonstrating the expected performance. For example, in the objective "*Given an array of boxes, cans, strings, rubber bands, etc., construct a simple stringed instrument,*" the material supplies available are the conditions.

The quality of performance that will be expected of students is sometimes stated within the objective, but more often today it is given in the assessment plan for the lesson. How to design assessment plans is considered later in this chapter.

As an example for your use, Figure 5-2 provides a list of instructional objectives for a third grade lesson on sound.

A glossary of definitions for important terms used in this chapter can be found on MyEducationLab.

TABLE 5-1 SOME ACTION WORDS ESPECIALLY USEFUL IN WRITING COGNITIVE OBJECTIVES FOR SCIENCE LESSONS

Cognitive Processes	Action Words
Remembering	**Identify.** To select (by pointing to, touching, or picking up) the correct object or designating the object property, in response to its name.
	Name. To supply the correct name for an object, property, or event.
	Define. To state the meaning of a term.
	State. To make a verbal statement that conveys a fact, concept, principle, or procedure.
Doing	**Distinguish.** To show how objects or events that might be confused are different.
	Describe. To give details of objects' properties, sequences of events, or relationships in a situation.
	Compare. To note similarities and differences among two or more things.
Understanding	**Classify.** To place objects into groups based on common properties.
	Interpret. To express the meaning, in one's own words, of a concept, principle, or model; or to find and express patterns and relationships in data.
	Explain. To draw conclusions about relationships involved in an event, giving special attention to links between observational evidence and prior knowledge that serve to support the conclusions.
	Apply. To use a concept, principle, or procedure to derive an answer to a question or problem.
	Demonstrate. To perform the operations involved in a given procedure, such as using instruments, collecting and organizing data, or carrying out a controlled investigation.

At the conclusion of the activities on sound, students will be able to:

1. *Ask* questions about sound, *plan* investigations, *collect* data, *record* data, *form* simple explanations, and *report* investigations and findings to the class.
2. *State, explain, and demonstrate* that all sound originates in vibrating sources.
3. *Given an array of boxes, cans, strings, rubber bands, etc., construct* a simple stringed instrument.
4. *Identify* the vibrating source of sound in each constructed musical instrument.
5. Given different sounds, *distinguish* between the pitch and loudness of the sounds.
6. *Demonstrate* and *explain* the production of different pitches of sound using the instrument.
7. *State* and *explain* that pitch is related to how fast or slow a sound source vibrates.
8. *Describe* the outer ear and *explain* its role in receiving sounds.
9. *Demonstrate appreciation* of the importance of safety rules related to hearing and sound through consistently *practicing* them.
10. *Show respect* for partners when working in cooperative groups by taking turns and by listening attentively and responding courteously to their ideas and suggestions.

Figure 5-2 Sample instructional objectives for lessons on sound at about grades 3–5.

Activity 5-1: Selecting and Writing Appropriate Objectives

1. Study the following lesson activity.
2. Write a set of learning objectives that fit the activity. Follow the guidelines for writing objectives given in this chapter. Be sure to include objectives related to conceptual understanding, inquiry abilities, and safety where appropriate.
3. Share and discuss your instructional objectives with a group of your classmates.

Sample Lesson Activity

Fourth graders constructed electromagnets by wrapping many turns of wire around a large iron core consisting of a nail or bolt. They connected the bare ends of the wire to a battery. The teacher cautioned the children not to leave the connection in place for very long as there were no bulbs or motors in the circuit, and the battery would run down within a few seconds.

The children learned to test the strength of their electromagnets by counting how many paper clips they could pick up. Noticing that some electromagnets picked up more paper clips than others, the children asked why was this so?

Through discussion, teacher guidance, and some direct instruction, the students theorized that the type of iron core, the number of turns of wire, and the number of batteries used determined an electromagnet's strength. The children designed and conducted a controlled investigation to test their theories. They concluded that all three of the variables made a difference in the strength of the electromagnet.

Activity 5-1 is designed to help you improve your ability to write learning objectives related to an inquiry science lesson. Spend some time with this activity before reading on.

Select and Design Lesson Activities

When you have selected content to be learned, checked its alignment with standards, and written clear instructional objectives, you are ready to develop lesson activities. In designing lesson activities, teachers determine what specific learning experiences relate to the content, lead to the attainment of specified objectives, and promote interest and understanding. Many good examples of science learning activities have been provided in the lessons and lesson plans described in previous chapters. Table 5-2 describes the content description, objectives, and synopsis of activities for the FOSS unit on sound.

Good lessons begin with good introductions.

Introduction to the Lessons. Introductory activities should be designed to engage the students in an activity or lesson. Consistent with the engage phase of the 5-E model, introductory activities should be designed to:

- create a "hook" that draws in the students,
- relate abstract academic knowledge to familiar experiences,
- motivate students,
- assess prior knowledge and identify current conceptions, and most importantly,
- engage students in a question that can be investigated.

TABLE 5-2 CONTENT, OBJECTIVES, AND ACTIVITIES FOR THE FOSS (FULL OPTION SCIENCE SYSTEM) MODULE ON THE PHYSICS OF SOUND

Science Content Description	Science Objectives	Synopsis of Activities
1. Characteristics and Causes of Sound • Objects can be identified by the sounds they make when dropped. • Sounds have identifiable characteristics. • Sounds can convey information. • Sound is caused by vibrations. • A sound source is an object that is vibrating. • A sound receiver detects sound vibrations.	Students should be able to: • *Describe* sounds made by objects when dropped. • *Communicate* with others using a code. • *Compare* sounds to develop discrimination.	**Dropping In** Students explore their ability to discriminate between sounds, by dropping objects into a drop chamber and identifying each object by the property of its sound. They develop a code by assigning letters to objects and send messages to one another by using their drop code.
2. Pitch and Vibrating Sources • Sound originates from vibrating sources. • Pitch is how high or low a sound is. • Differences in pitch are caused by differences in the rate at which objects vibrate. • Several variables affect pitch, including size (length) and tension of the source material.	Students should be able to: • *Demonstrate* that sound originates from a vibrating source. • *Compare* high-, low-, and medium-pitched sounds. • *Record* observations on sound. • *Relate* the pitch of a sound to the physical properties of the sound source.	**Good Vibrations** Students explore sound generators and musical instruments in mini-activities to find out what causes sound and what changes the pitch. They investigate variables that affect changes in pitch: the length of vibrating objects and the tension on vibrating strings.
3. How Sound Travels • Sound vibrations need a medium to travel. • Sound travels through solids, water, and air. • Sound that is directed travels better through air. • Our outer ears are designed to receive, focus, and amplify sounds.	Students should be able to: • *Describe* evidence that sound travels through solids, water, and air. • *Compare* how sound travels through different mediums. • *Record* observations on sound.	**How Sound Travels** Students work in collaborative groups on mini-activities that introduce a sound source and a medium of sound travel. They observe and compare how sound travels through solids, water, and air.
4. Sources, Mediums, and Receivers of Sound • Several variables affect pitch, including size (length), tension, and thickness of the source material. • Sound can be directed through air, water, or solids to the sound receivers. • The medium that sound passes through affects its volume and the distance at which it can be heard.	Students should be able to: • *Describe* the outer ear and *explain* that it is designed to receive sounds. • *Compare* different ways of amplifying sounds and making them travel longer distances. • *Record* observations of how sound travels. • *Report* findings in a class presentation.	**Sound Challenges** Students investigate the nature of our sound receivers, ears. They are challenged to put their knowledge of sound sources, sound travel, and sound receivers to work. They take one of the instruments they used earlier and change its pitch, make its sound travel farther, or make it louder.

Source: Adapted from FOSS® (Full Option Science System®) Physics of Sound, Overview. © The Regents of the University of California and published by Delta Education. Adapted with permission.

Introductory activities should be brief. Your goal is to open a door to learning. As soon as possible, escort your students through the door by moving on to the next sequence of activities. In the electric circuits lesson of Chapter 4, for example, the teacher told a story to engage the students. The story served as a good focus, but it was the hands-on investigations of batteries and bulbs that really served as the "hook."

A variety of introductory activities can be designed for science lessons. For example, to introduce lessons on weather, you might show brief segments of videos illustrating different weather conditions, including rain, snow, and violent winds. Include a video segment of a person measuring and recording weather factors and conditions and a segment of a TV weathercast. One purpose of the video segments is to bring the abstract topic of a school lesson into the familiar and interesting world of the student.

To stimulate discussion, ask such questions as: *What is weather? What factors are important in producing weather? How are these various factors measured? How are they used in predicting the weather?* In guiding discussion, be generally accepting of students' answers, recording them in your own notes and/or on the chalkboard. Remember that the purposes of the introductory activities are to engage the students in the content and skills to be learned, to create interest, to motivate, to determine prior knowledge, and to establish a question for investigation. There will be plenty of opportunities in later activities for students to confront and clear up misconceptions and construct new knowledge and understandings.

As another example, to introduce a series of lessons on food chemistry, you might ask: *What is healthy eating? Do foods that are good for you have to taste "yucky"?* (Wiggins & McTighe, 1998).

Because they usually fascinate students and enable you to probe what students already know and what they think, *discrepant events* make excellent introductory activities.

Discrepant Events. A discrepant event is some scientific phenomenon that has a surprising or unusual outcome for students to consider. Discrepant events may be demonstrated by the teacher, presented by video, or embedded within student activities. As an example, Activity 5-2 shows a puzzling discrepant-event, *The Floating Coin*, that can serve as an activity for lessons on light refraction. Try this activity for yourself before reading on. Why do you think the coin appears to float into view?

Activity 5-2: The Floating Coin

1. Anchor a coin to the bottom of an opaque container as in the illustrations.
2. Stand directly above the coin so that you can see it from above.
3. Step back gradually so the coin is just out of sight.
4. Ask another person to slowly pour water into the container. What do you see happening? (The coin will slowly appear to float into view.)
5. Why do you think this happens?

A few raisins placed in a glass of clear, carbonated soda water create a "raisin elevator."

Here is an explanaton of the floating coin phenomenon.

- Light ordinarily travels in straight lines.
- In refraction, light rays bend as they go from one medium, such as water, to another medium, such as air.
- Light refracts or bends outward when it goes from water into air.
- As the light rays reflected from the coin emerge from the water, they bend outward and follow a new path that carries them to your eyes.
- The illusion created is that the light rays followed a straight-line path and came directly from a coin floating high in the water.

After doing the activity and observing the phenomenon, ask students to discuss what they saw and their theories and explanations of why the coin floated into view. Use the discrepant event activity to assess students' prior knowledge. In the activities that follow in the explore and explain phases of inquiry, you can build on student ideas, investigations, and developing concepts and principles to construct an explanation of the floating coin phenomenon.

Activity 5-3 shows another example of a discrepant event, *The Raisin Elevator*. This novel event is sure to be interesting and puzzling to children. Try this activity yourself before reading further.

Activity 5-3: The Raisin Elevator

- Place a few raisins in a glass of clear, carbonated soda water. Shelled peanuts also work fine for this activity.
- Wait a minute or so.
- What do you observe?
- How would you explain the "raisin elevator" phenomenon?
- What scientific concepts and principles did you use in your explanation?

Have you formed an explanation about the phenomenon in Activity 5-3? Did you observe that the raisins initially sink to the bottom and then rise to the top of the liquid, stay a moment, then descend once more, only to rise again? How did you explain this phenomenon? If you had appropriate prior experiences and scientific knowledge about floating and sinking, you might have inferred that the raisins were initially too heavy for their size to float and, thus, sank. As the raisins sank, air bubbles became attached to them. The air bubbles served to buoy up the raisins.

Explanations in science need to be checked out through further observations and investigations. By looking very carefully, perhaps with a magnifying lens, children can watch the bubbles attaching themselves to the raisins when they are at the bottom of the carbonated drink and popping when the raisins reach the surface.

Use a Variety of Lesson Activities. Activities are learning experiences that enable students to attain the specified instructional objectives. Activities are at the core of science lessons. If you are using the 5-E model, activities appropriate for explore (data gathering), explain (interpretation), and elaborate (extension and transfer) phases should be selected here. Look again at Table 5-2 for an example of good lesson activities from the FOSS module on sound. Note especially how the lesson activities are aligned with instructional objectives.

A wide variety of activities you can include in your lesson plan are given in various science activity sources. *Activities for Teaching Science as Inquiry,* the companion volume to this book, contains about 140 activities related to more than 30 science topics. Elementary textbook series, kit-based science programs, and other books and documents provide access to a wide range of activities.

There are hundreds, if not thousands, of activities available on the Internet. But a word of caution is in order. Many of the Internet science activities, and some published traditionally, are merely "show and tell" or "vocabulary drill" activities. They are not designed to lead students to develop conceptual understanding and inquiry abilities. However, you can modify almost any science activity to make it more inquiry and constructivist oriented.

Although hands-on inquiry activities are essential in science learning, this does not mean that every science lesson activity must have students handle science materials and generate new data. Your lesson activities should include a variety of teaching and learning approaches, including listening and speaking, reading and writing, research in books and the Internet, and watching as well as doing. Films and videos, books, research reports, use of Internet sources, existing data sets, and field trips, including virtual field trips presented through websites, can also provide excellent learning opportunities for students.

But over the long term be sure that your lesson plans provide opportunities for students to learn inquiry skills through their own activities and better understand the nature of science and scientific inquiry.

Activities to Develop Inquiry Abilities. Exploration activities that incorporate *descriptive, classificatory,* and/or *experimental investigations* are ideal for developing inquiry abilities. But almost any activity that follows an inquiry or 5-E teaching approach can build inquiry abilities as well as conceptual understanding. For example, the electricity lessons of Chapter 4 do not use the investigational strategies introduced in Chapter 2, but they help students build inquiry abilities and understandings.

Open inquiries represent another type of activity that might be included in a lesson.

Open Inquiry Activities. In open inquiry, the teacher may provide the problem and materials for students but then allow them time and freedom to simply "mess about." In the 5-E

Many of the nearly 150 science activities in *Activities for Teaching Science as Inquiry* feature discrepant events, especially at the engage phase of inquiry. More examples of discrepant events for elementary science are given at:

http://tiger.coe.missouri.edu/ ~pgermann/DiscEvent/
http://physics.unco.edu/ sced441/demos99.pdf
Enter "discrepant events science" into a search engine for more examples of discrepant events.

model of instruction, this typically occurs in the explore stage. For example, you might give cooperative groups of students soft drink bottles and pitchers of water (and newspapers and plenty of paper towels to mop up spills). You might then ask the groups to discover what they can do to change the pitch of the sounds produced with the bottles. In producing sounds, some groups might try to strike the bottles with a wooden object. Others might blow across the open ends of the bottles. As they try different things, students may discover that putting different amounts of water in the bottles changes the pitch produced by their actions on the bottles.

After allowing students to explore for some time, collect the equipment and discuss with the students what they discovered. Students might also write in their journals and read about wind instruments, such as horns and flutes.

In classrooms where students actively engage in inquiry, learning centers can be a good way to present activities.

Science Learning Centers. Learning centers are created and directed by the teacher for independent activities of students. They can motivate, guide, and support the learning of individuals and small groups. Science learning centers will better enable you to meet individual needs and provide students with self-directed learning opportunities. They can also encourage student responsibility.

There are various types of science learning centers. A guided discovery learning center involves students in developing a better understanding of specific science concepts. For example, place materials in shoe boxes with a series of guiding questions on cards for students to read. An example of a question to guide activities on light at the learning center is: "How can you use a flashlight and the cards in the box to show that light appears to travel in a straight line?" Include a flashlight and a number of blank index cards with 1 cm holes punched in the center of each card. Children should discover that light from the flashlight will pass through the holes in the center of the cards only if they are all aligned as in Figure 5-3. This provides evidence that light travels in straight lines.

Field Trips. Field trips to zoos, discovery centers, museums, public aquariums, planetariums, natural areas, and even the school playground provide wonderful opportunities to create interest and serve as rich learning experiences for students. An important part of any field trip is the advance preparation that takes place in the classroom before the trip. Teachers should plan in advance for field trips, developing instructional objectives, well-planned learning activities for students before, during, and after the trip, and relevant assessments. Often discovery institutions have science educators on staff who can provide materials and assist in planning.

The accompanying photo essay on investigating aquatic life provides some examples of how students can get the most out of a field trip.

See Chapter 8 for a discussion of virtual field trips presented through Internet websites.

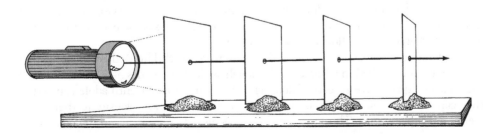

Figure 5-3 How does this activity show that light travels in straight lines?

Designing Assessment Experiences

In developing lesson plans, teachers should use both formative (ongoing assessments) and summative (end of lesson) assessments. As introduced in Chapter 4, *formative assessment* involves gathering assessment information during the process of instruction. A main function of formative assessment is to serve as a basis for adjusting instructional strategies to improve learning. For example, information from formative assessment is important for teachers in determining what kinds of scaffolding assistance to provide for students.

Summative assessment is assessment at the end of lessons or instructional units that provides important information for determining what the students learned and did not learn as a result of instructional activities. Summative assessment provides a basis for feedback to students and for grades and accountability.

Rubrics are often used in assessment of inquiry learning.

Rubrics. A rubric defines several different levels of knowledge and understanding in specific terms. Thus, teachers can use rubrics to specify the ideal levels of learning performance on lesson objectives and assess the actual level of student attainment. The number of levels in a rubric should be based on the needs of your class and your observations of what your students are actually doing in science activities. Four-level rubrics are frequently used.

- Level 3: Advanced, Excellent, Exceeds Expectations
- Level 2: Proficient, Satisfactory, Meets Expectations
- Level 1: Basic, Below Expectations
- Level 0: Unacceptable

Many examples of rubrics are treated in Chapter 6 on assessing science learning. Figure 5-4 shows a sample rubric related to two of the objectives for the sound lesson given in Figure 5-2. This rubric defines the level of expected performance of students on the two objectives.

In the next section, we will see how the different parts of a lesson plan fit together by examining how two preservice teachers developed a lesson plan for teaching a series of activities on floating and sinking to fourth-grade students.

A Lesson Plan on Floating and Sinking

In preparing a series of lessons for fourth graders, one pair of preservice teachers in a science methods class chose to focus on the properties of matter related to whether objects float or sink in a liquid. They were assigned to teach science in a fourth grade class in a rural elementary school. Each of the preservice teachers would be teaching the topic to one-half of the class for 5 days. They had already formed some ideas about the children's prior knowledge and developmental levels based on their experiences observing, assisting, and formatively assessing students in the classroom. They chose to prepare a series of lessons related to whether objects float or sink in a liquid.

In planning, the teachers considered Piaget's work on children's theories of floating and sinking as described in Chapter 3. Although students in grades 3–5 can understand the concrete, qualitative aspects of floating and sinking, it is not until adolescence that they can add numerical considerations about mass, volume, and density to their judgments and explanations. Thus, the preservice teachers chose to focus on the qualitative

Rubric Related to Objectives 3 and 6 of the Sound Unit

Objectives

Objective 3. Given an array of boxes, cans, strings, rubber bands, etc., construct a simple stringed instrument.

Objective 6. Demonstrate and explain the production of different pitches of sound using the instrument.

Criteria	3 Points Advanced	2 Points Meets Expections	1 Point Below Expectations	0 Points Unacceptable
Construction of instrument (Objective 3)	Instrument is sturdy, well constructed with attention to detail.	Instrument is sturdy and neatly constructed.	Instrument is not well constructed, but can be played.	Instrument is not sturdy, falls apart when played.
Demonstration of instrument (Objective 6)	Student plays a recognizable tune on instrument consisting of at least 4 different pitches.	Student plays instrument producing at least 4 different pitches.	Student plays instrument producing 2 or 3 different pitches.	Student plays instrument, but only 1 pitch is demon-strated, or no sound is produced.
Explanation (Objective 6)	Student explains what is vibrating and the relationship between the proper-ties (length, width, tension) of the rubber band and the pitch produced.	Student explains what is vibrating and how the different pitches were produced.	Student attempts to explain how instru-ment works, but explanation is incomplete.	Student does not explain how different pitches are produced or expla-nation is incorrect.

Figure 5-4 Rubrics can be used to define the level of expected performance of students.

rule: *Objects float in fresh water if they are not too heavy for their size; objects sink in water if they are too heavy for their size.*

Figure 5-5 provides an outline of the content knowledge and understandings to be developed in the lesson on floating and sinking. Before creating this outline, the preservice teachers consulted a variety of sources, including state frameworks and local curriculum guides, chapters within the science textbook adopted by the local district, the activities sections of science methods textbooks, and lessons developed by national curriculum groups.

They noted in their reading that any explanation of floating and sinking that uses the numerical concept of density (ratio of mass to volume) is generally beyond elementary and middle school children and should be introduced only in grades 8–12.

The preservice teachers focused on grade-level appropriate concepts of weight and volume (size) and the relationship between weight and volume for floating and sinking

Figure 5-5 Content
knowledge outline for
floating and sinking unit.

I. Floating and sinking
  A. Several variable factors contribute to whether an object floats or sinks:
    1. Volume (size)
    2. Weight
    3. Design
II. Some characteristics that affect floating and sinking can be measured and compared
  A. Volume (size)
  B. Weight
III. Theory/rules for floating and sinking in fresh water
  A. The weight and volume (size) of objects are compared in predicting whether they will float or sink.
  B. Objects float if they are light enough for their size.
  C. Objects sink if they are too heavy for their size.
IV. Investigating boat designs
  A. The buoyant force on a boat is increased when the amount of space of the boat underwater is increased.
  B. Boats can weigh the same but be designed so that they occupy different amounts of space underwater.
  C. Boats that occupy more space underwater can carry the largest cargo.

objects. By considering the design of boats, the content knowledge is expanded, related to technology, and applied to the children's real-world experiences.

Using the outline of content knowledge and understandings as a guide, the preservice teachers could then develop a lesson plan, complete with relevant standards, learning objectives, activities, and assessments. The lesson plan is shown in Figure 5-6. This lesson plan is appropriate for students in about grades 3–5.

Assessment and Evaluation Plan for the Floating and Sinking Lesson

The preservice teachers used a combination of formative and summative strategies to assess conceptual understanding and inquiry abilities of students during the floating and sinking lessons.

In formative assessment of student attainment of the learning objectives on floating and sinking, the teachers listened carefully to student responses to the various questions given in the lesson plan. They noted student performance during hands-on activities and demonstrations and checked students' written work and notebooks.

In summative assessment, the teachers used a rubric (see Figure 5-7) related to the objectives of the clay boat activity. Information gathered through formative assessment was used to provide a basis for scaffolding or feedback to students and to monitor and adjust instruction to improve learning.

As a part of summative assessment, the teachers demonstrated another discrepant event. They placed a can of regular Coke and a can of Diet Coke in a large container of water. The regular Coke sank, but, surprisingly, the Diet Coke can floated.

Before the Coke float demonstration was discussed, the children wrote their explanations for the activity on an assessment sheet. The teachers used a rubric similar to the one in Figure 5-7 to evaluate the children's explanations in terms of how they used concepts of *weight* and *size* to explain why one can floated and the other can sank. After the written explanations were collected, the group discussed the demonstration and how the floating and sinking rules applied. The can of Diet Coke floated because it was lighter, although

Details of the Coke float activity are given on pages A-186 and A-187 in *Activities for Teaching Science as Inquiry.* The emphasis of the activity in that section is on the sugar content of diet and regular soft drinks.

Instructional Objectives

As a result of the lessons on floating and sinking, students should be able to:

1. Demonstrate inquiry abilities, including asking questions, conducting investigations, and using observational evidence and science knowledge to construct logical explanations and communicate their findings.
2. Design and construct a clay boat that floats and holds as much cargo as possible.
3. Distinguish between size and weight.
4. Identify size and weight as variables related to the floating and sinking of clay boats.
5. Demonstrate ability to coordinate size and weight of floating and sinking objects by stating and applying the following rules.
   • Objects sink in water if they are too heavy for their size.
   • Objects float in water if they are light enough for their size.
6. Explain how the floating and sinking rules apply to clay boats and golf ball "floaters."

Activities and Procedures

1. **Engage.** Introduce the lesson by demonstrating the raisin elevator discrepant event.

   Ask: *Why do you think the raisin descended in the bottle and then rose to the surface again?* Ask more generally: *What factors do you think determine whether or not an object floats in water? How could we find out?* Note explanations, ideas, and prior knowledge of students, but do not provide any explanation at this point.

2. **Explore.** Arrange class in teams of two. Set up stations around the room, with objects that float and objects that sink at each station. Place a container of water at each station. Direct students to move in orderly fashion from station to station. Also, tell them to make predictions about whether objects will float or sink and give a reasonable basis for the predictions in each case. Provide a record sheet for students to record their predictions, explanations, and test results. Encourage students to go beyond experience to consider the variable attributes of the objects.
   • Place a different array of objects at each station.
   • At one station, include a number of centimeter-gram cubes, cubes that have a mass of 1 gram and are 1 cm on a side and thus have a volume of 1 cc.
   • At another station include two golf balls, one that floats and one that sinks in fresh water.

3. **Explain.** Ask: *What observations did you make at each station? In general, how did you decide whether an object would float or sink? Why did the cubes float just under the surface of the liquid? What would happen to a cube if you added a bit of clay to it and placed it in the container of water?* (Try it and see.) *Why did one golf ball float and the other one sink?*
   • Solicit student ideas and discuss them. Ask students to compare results and to give their own theories/ideas about why objects float or sink.
   • At some point, teach the two qualitative rules for floating and sinking by direct instruction. Write the rules on the chalkboard. Discuss with the students how the rules apply in each case they encountered.
   • Lead the children to suggest that one golf ball may have been lighter than the other. Ask: *How can we test this idea?* The explanation might be tested by comparing the weight of the two golf balls with a balance scale. Carry out the test.

4. **Elaborate.** Give each group two same size lumps of clay about 3 or 4 cm in diameter. Ask: *How can you design and construct a clay boat that floats and holds a large cargo of pennies?*
   • Each team designs and constructs two clay boats and tests them in the classroom "lake." If a boat floats, load it with pennies one by one until the boat sinks. Promote a competition in which the winning boat supports the largest number of pennies.
   • Guide students to talk about their boat designs and results. Note particularly any mention of the size or weight of the boat. Ask: *How do the floating and sinking rules apply to the clay boats?* Lead the students to recognize that the boats that supported the most cargo were those with the greatest effective size—that is, boats that floated with more of their volume under water.

5. **Evaluate.** See the accompanying assessment plan.

Figure 5-6 A lesson plan on floating and sinking.

Objectives

Students should be able to:

2. Design and construct a clay boat that floats and holds as much cargo as possible.

5. Explain how floating and sinking rules apply to clay boats of different designs.

Criteria	3 Points	2 Points	1 Point	0 Points
Design and Construction (Objective 2)	Boat is well designed and constructed and holds at least 25 pennies	Boat is well designed and holds at least 15 pennies, but has some flaws that limit cargo	Boat has major flaws	No boat constructed
Explanation (Objective 5)	Student clearly explains that the boat floats until the weight of the cargo becomes too heavy in relation to the size of the boat	Student uses notion of the size of the boat and the weight of the cargo in explaining floating and sinking, but explanation has some flaws	Unsatisfactory explanation of the role of size and weight in whether the boat floats or sinks	No attempt to explain floating and sinking of the clay boat

Figure 5-7   Rubric for assessing student performance and understanding on clay boats objectives.

Go to the Homework and Exercises section in Chapter 5 of MyEducationLab to watch the set of videos entitled *Pinhole Cameras: Parts 1, 2,* and *3.* In this series of videos we see fifth-grade children constructing pin-hole viewers. We also see how the children used the pin-hole viewers to observe, then generalizing about images seen when the viewers are pointed at illuminated arrows. Further, you can examine how the structure of the pin-hole viewer lessons is consistent with the principles presented in this chapter. A video guide for these videos is provided in the Online Professional Development section at the end of the chapter.

the two cans had the same volume. Regular Coke contains sugar, making it heavier than an equal volume of Diet Coke. The students compared the weights of the two cans on a balance scale. If children wished to, they were allowed to write revised explanations.

Throughout the lessons, the teachers took opportunities to read to the children about and discuss boats, submarines, life preservers, and other real-world experiences related to floating and sinking.

The preservice teachers' lesson plans were well designed and assisted them immensely as they taught. Keep in mind, however, that lesson plans are not scripts, and even the very best set of activities must be adjusted to your own objectives, the needs of the children, and classroom facilities.

Now let's turn to how you can best manage your classroom for inquiry learning and teaching.

Managing Inquiry Instruction and Learning

Establishing a classroom learning environment focused on learning with understanding is a critical factor for effective inquiry instruction. Research indicates that learning with understanding is enhanced when students are grouped in ways that provide them opportunities to discuss their investigations, findings, and conclusions with one another and with the teacher (Duschl et al., 2007).

Grouping Students for Learning

Expert teachers use a variety of classroom arrangements for science and other subjects. These include (Lowery, 1998):

- *Whole class structure* (e.g., the teacher lectures, demonstrates, or guides the whole class in discussion),
- *Cooperative group structure* (e.g., students in small groups cooperatively collect data, organize it, exchange ideas, and arrive at collaborative conclusions),
- *Pair structure* (e.g., two students work together to construct an explanation of some action in a demonstration), and
- *Individual structure* (e.g., each student works individually on an investigation, collecting data, recording it in a science journal, and answering relevant questions).

Cooperative groups—small groups of students working cooperatively—are especially important in contemporary upper elementary and middle school science classrooms. At the primary level, pairs often are more appropriate than small groups.

Whether working cooperatively or in small groups, students consider problems and assignments together, verbalize what they know, consider the multiple viewpoints of group members, collect data together, learn from one another, and come up with group solutions to problems. These group processes are the kinds of student interactions that help establish *communities of learners* in which students have opportunities to learn from and teach each other. The concept and rationale for communities of learners was discussed in Chapter 3.

Cooperative groups might be formed from children who sit near one another. More strategically, heterogeneous grouping strategies are often used. Heterogeneous grouping is used to maximize variety within groups. Factors considered in heterogeneous grouping include achievement or ability, interests, learning styles, ethnic or cultural background, age, attitude toward subject matter, and leadership ability (Watson & Marshall, 1995).

In addition to encouraging cooperative learning, using cooperative teams can facilitate classroom management by providing for group sharing of limited science materials and giving students responsibility to manage materials.

Pair structures often provide for more interaction between students. Some teachers use a *think-pair-share* strategy to lead students to express their own ideas and learn from one another, Jones and Carter (1997) described a verbal interaction between a pair of fifth- grade boys, in which one of the boys assisted the other in understanding written directions about a lever activity. The goal of the activity was to formulate a generalization about how to get a crossbar to balance. Larry was confused about the task:

> *Larry: Do we place the three blocks on the same side of this thing?*
> *Billy: No, we are supposed to figure out how to balance these two blocks using this other block.*
> *Larry: How do we know when it is balanced?*
> *Billy: The lever will be straight out. Neither side of the lever will be touching the table. That means it's balanced. (p. 265)*

In this exchange, Billy provided Larry with an interpretation of the problem and the meaning of the term *balance*, which enabled Larry to proceed toward constructing generalizations.

- **Principal Investigator.** In charge of team operations including checking assignments, seeing that all team members participate in activities, and leading group discussions.
- **Materials Manager.** Gets and inventories materials and distributes them to the team.
- **Recorder/Reporter.** Collects and records data on lab sheets and reports results to whole class orally or in writing on class summary chart posted on chalkboard.
- **Maintenance Director.** With the assistance of other team members, cleans up and returns materials and equipment to their appropriate storage space or container. Directs the disposal of used materials and is responsible for team members' safety.

Source: Richard M. Jones. (1990, December). *Teaming Up! The Inquiry Task Group Management System User's Guide*. LaPorte, Texas: ITGROUP.

A cooperative group structure might involve specific roles for group members, such as Principal Investigator (PI), Recorder/Reporter, Materials Manager, and Maintenance Director (see Figure 5-8). However groups are organized, students should share responsibilities within a small group. Throughout the year, each student should have an opportunity to take the responsibilities required of each of the cooperative learning jobs. The various small group structures described here are typically used during the explore and/or elaborate phases of the 5-E instructional model.

Teachers can also enhance student learning by bringing the whole class back together and giving groups opportunities to make presentations of their work. Deeper understanding is attained when students explain, clarify, and justify what they have learned (National Research Council, 1996, p. 30). As the students communicate their findings and explanations, they should be encouraged to accept and react to the constructive criticism of others. Communication of investigations and findings to others typically occur during the explanation and/or the evaluation phases of the 5-E instructional model.

Used thoughtfully and strategically, different types of grouping arrangements can be effective tools for promoting cooperation, discourse, and improving learning and instruction.

Safety in the Science Classroom

Safety in the science classroom is critical. Teachers are legally responsible for the safety of students in their classroom (Gerlovich, 1996). But the law does not require teachers to be superhuman in their efforts. It is only expected that teachers be reasonable and prudent in their judgment when performing their duties with students. Teachers must attempt to anticipate hazards, then eliminate or address them.

According to NSTA's current position statement on safety and school science instruction (2000), "Inherent in many instructional settings including science is the potential for injury and possible litigation. These issues can be avoided or reduced by the proper application of a safety plan." NSTA recommends that the responsibilities for the establishment and maintenance of safety standards be shared between school district authorities and teachers.

Safety in the science classroom is often closely tied to the room's size and arrangement. As you arrange your room, think out patterns of student movements and avoid overcrowding any area.

At the onset of the school year, you should generate and post a list of safety rules that students should always follow. Review these rules as appropriate throughout the year especially

You can read NSTA's recommendations about the shared teacher–school district responsibility by visiting http://www.nsta.org/about/positions/safety.aspx.

INVESTIGATING AQUATIC LIFE

Structure and Function

When you visit a public aquarium, observe the wide diversity of aquatic life. Notice how the different aquatic animals move, such as fish, jellies, and sea turtles. For example, sea turtles use their flippers to move forward, backward, and turn. Fish have caudal fins, dorsal fins, pelvic or ventral fins, and pectoral fins. Many fish swim forward by moving their *caudal fins* back and forth. They maneuver up and down by moving their *dorsal fins* and *pelvic* or *ventral fins*. They turn to the right or left by using their *pectoral* fins. Watch the fish closely to see how they use their fins in swimming.

Fish are adapted to living in water. Aquatic animals still need oxygen. Fish obtain oxygen through their *gills*, which take in water and filter out oxygen trapped in the water. Sea turtles are actually reptiles; they have no gills and must surface from time to time to obtain oxygen from the atmosphere.

A large school of multicolored fish swims by in an exhibit at Georgia Aquarium, Atlanta.

What do you observe in this photo about the fin structure of a fish?

How do you think jellies propel themselves in water?

Aquatic animals, such as this octopus at the South Carolina Aquarium in Charleston, seek protection in the nooks and crannies of corals.

Habitats

Aquariums provide habitats for a wide variety of aquatic life. A *habitat* is a place where animals or plants live. Aquatic habitats must provide food, shelter, and protection. Aquariums offer many examples of aquatic habitats and the animals or plants that are at home in them. With the wide variety of aquatic life and habitats available for you and your students to study, aquariums make wonderful places for field trips for science classes.

Coral Reefs. Many aquariums display coral reef habitats and the array of life in and around them. Corals are tiny animals that live in colonies that create complex structures resembling branching antlers, brains, knobby fingers, dinner plates, or giant fans. Reef animals find food and shelter within the nooks, crevices, crannies, and caves of the complicated coral structures. Sponges, anemones, and clams attach themselves to the coral surfaces and rocks they need to survive. Snails, shrimp, lobsters, sea stars, and crabs travel over and through the reef searching for food or shelter. Colorful fish swirl over and around the more sedentary inhabitants. The coral reef is a fragile world susceptible to destructive natural and human-made forces.

An Oil Platform Habitat. The Texas State Aquarium on the Texas Gulf Coast displays a model of a habitat formed from the bare steel legs of an abandoned oil platform. This habitat supports an amazing variety of life.

Preserving Biodiversity

Through different activities, people often cause permanent disruption or destruction of oceanic animal and plant communities and their habitats. Some important activities contributing to these changes are pollution, commercial fishing, physical alterations to the coasts, introduction of nonnative species, and human factors contributing to global climate change. The result is a serious decline in the abundance of most species of preferred edible fish and shellfish, reductions (or the total loss) of species, reduced aesthetic and recreational value of coastal habitats, unpredictable and serious changes to the structures and functions of ecosystems, and potentially harmful effects on human health and well-being.

What can you do to help reserve the biodiversity of our oceans, lakes, ponds, rivers, and streams?

An abandoned oil platform serves as a dynamic habitat for diverse aquatic life, Texas State Aquarium, Corpus Christi.

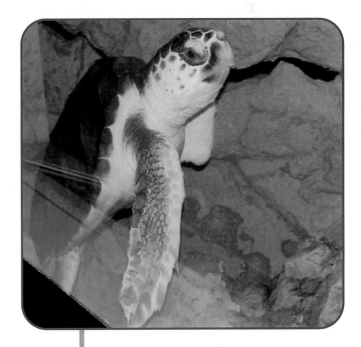

What are some differences you notice between sea turtles and land turtles?

How does coloration, as shown in an exhibit at the Texas State Aquarium, Corpus Christi, help preserve the life of aquatic animals?

An abundance of colorful life forms is found in the world's oceans and in the exhibits at public aquariums, such as this at Georgia Aquarium.

Some Questions to Guide Student Observations

- Can you find fish seeking protection through their coloration?
- Can you find fish seeking protection in the nooks, crannies, and caves of coral habitats in the aquarium tanks?
- How are the "models" of ocean habitats displayed in the large aquarium like the real thing? How are they different?

targeting rules that apply to the current lab activity. Here are some general classroom safety rules you might provide to students (Full Option Science System, 2000).

1. Always follow the safety procedures outlined by your teacher.
2. Never put any materials in your mouth.
3. Avoid touching your face, mouth, ears, or eyes while working with chemicals, plants, or animals.
4. Always wash your hands immediately after using materials, especially chemicals or animals.
5. Be careful when using sharp or pointed tools. Always make sure that you protect your eyes and those of your neighbors.
6. Wear American National Standards Institute approved safety goggles (with Z87 printed on the goggles) whenever activities are done in which there is a potential risk to eye safety.
7. Behave responsibly during science investigations.

As emphasized in the safety precautions, live animals in the classroom require special care and cautions.

Live Animals in the Classroom. In its 2005 position statement on Responsible Use of Live Animals and Dissection in the Science Classroom, NSTA supports including live animals as part of instruction in the K–12 science classroom because observing and working with animals firsthand can spark students' interest in science as well as a general respect for life while reinforcing key concepts as outlined in the NSES. NSTA encourages districts to ensure that animals are properly cared for and treated humanely, responsibly, and ethically. Ultimately, decisions to incorporate organisms in the classroom should balance the ethical and responsible care of animals with their educational value.

Teachers and students must be aware of their responsibilities and use precaution when keeping and caring for live animals in the classroom. Here are some directions to help students care for and adopt a humane attitude toward the living things they are observing.

Small animals, such as insects, frogs, and fish, may be kept for short periods of time, from 24 hours to several weeks, if the habitat in which they were found is simulated as closely as possible in captivity. Teachers should be aware that diseases such as salmonellosis can be transmitted to students who handle classroom animals. The small painted turtles that are frequently kept in elementary classrooms have been found to carry salmonella (Texas Safety Standards, 2002). Keeping the cages clean of fecal remains will reduce the presence of bacteria that may cause an illness.

Always insist that students wash their hands before feeding the animals and after they have handled the animals or touched materials from the animals' cage. They should research information about identification, characteristics, feeding habits, and values. The animals should eventually be released unharmed in their natural habitat or as prescribed in safety guidelines.

Managing Classroom Behavior

Maintaining an orderly learning environment is crucial in inquiry classrooms. During inquiry, students are naturally active—getting materials, performing investigations, discussing procedures and results with one another and with you, and moving into different group structures. Still, you must establish rules for behavior, monitor students' activities, and enforce disciplinary consequences when necessary.

Additional safety precautions for elementary and middle school science classrooms are given in Appendix A and in safety manuals produced by your district or state.

You can read NSTA's recommendations to teachers about including live animals in the classroom by visiting http://www.nsta.org/about/positions/animals.aspx.

Safety guidelines for keeping a variety of animals such as earthworms, mealworms, crickets, guppies, and butterflies can be also found in the FOSS (Full Option Science System), STC (Science and Technology for Children) and AIMS (Activities that Integrate Math and Science) teachers' guides.

Also consult the Science Store offerings on the NSTA website (http://www.nsta.org) for various helpful how-to publications on living things in the classroom.

Go to the Homework and Exercises section in Chapter 5 of MyEducationLab to watch the set of videos, *Managing Classroom Instruction, Parts 1, 2, 3,* and *4*. These videos illustrate and expand the discussion of classroom management strategies presented in this chapter. A video guide to these videos is provided in the Online Professional Development section at the end of this chapter.

Keep in mind that all misbehavior is not equal. Classify misbehavior as *off-task* (attention wandering, failing to attend to the task at hand), *inappropriate* (doing something that is against the agreed-on rules), or *disruptive* (inappropriate behavior that prevents learning or is potentially dangerous). Deal with each case in an appropriate way, such as regaining attention indirectly or stopping inappropriate behavior and cautioning the student.

Monitor the behavior of individuals or groups during science lessons to see if you need to address any of these obstacles:

- Some students may be too immature for group work. You may have to work with them individually while the rest of the class works in groups. The goal is to help each student develop strategies for following class rules and participating in activities effectively. Don't just give up on a student and stop trying to help him or her.
- If there is a chronic offender in your class, you might
  1. talk with the student;
  2. ask for the student's perceptions of the problem and schedule a student-parent-teacher conference to develop a plan; and
  3. if necessary, invite the principal, school psychologist, social worker, or other professional to attend the conference or observe the behavior of the student in the classroom.

Dealing strongly and consistently with disruptive students is essential if they and their neighbors are going to learn science effectively in inquiry settings. Here are some special actions you might consider:

- Prepare contingency plans for problem situations, for example, deliberate damage to science supplies or explosive student behavior (fighting and pushing).
- Consider beforehand the pros and cons of various methods of discipline, such as removing a student from the situation, so you can use the methods effectively if necessary. Consider developing routine procedures for handling improper actions so students understand beforehand the consequences of bad behavior. If it fits within your school/district policy, you might review the following policy with students and then display it in the classroom:

  First offense: warning addressed to student by name in clear, calm voice.

  Second offense: student given 10-minute time-out in an isolated part of the classroom, another teacher's classroom, or school office. Never use learning centers for time-out.

  Third offense: 15-minute time-out in isolation.

  Fourth offense: phone call to student's parents or guardian.

  Fifth offense: conference with student, parent or guardian, school principal, and/or school psychologist or counselor. (Baron, 1992)

If you feel the lesson is getting away from you, don't hesitate to end it. Assess what went wrong and plan the next lesson to eliminate the problem.

Despite your best efforts, some students may exhibit disruptive or asocial behaviors or be diagnosed as having serious emotional disorders. Because students with disorders may be included in your classroom, a few suggestions may be helpful.

As you work with students who have emotional or behavioral disorders, remember that your utmost concern is to provide a safe and supportive learning environment for all of your students. To work successfully with students whose conduct is often disorderly, try viewing their deficit in appropriate social behaviors just as you would academic deficits—skills that need to be taught. Don't condone inappropriate behaviors; teach alternative, appropriate ways to interact. With patience and guidance some students can learn to "correct" social behaviors just as they can learn to be more successful academically. One way to teach "correct" behavior is to use behaviorist principles.

Behavior modification is one technique that is often effective when other techniques are not, because (1) students know exactly what is expected of them; (2) through the gradual process of shaping, students attempt to learn new behaviors only when they are truly ready to acquire them, and (3) students find learning new behaviors usually leads to success.

These four steps are routinely used in behavioral modification:

1. Identify the problem behavior to be modified.
2. Log behavior with regard to how often and under what conditions it occurs.
3. Reinforce desired behavior(s) by initiating a system that reinforces or rewards appropriate, positive behavior.
4. Determine the type of positive reward to use: manipulatives (computer games, interactive videos, games); visuals (videos, CD-ROMs); physical (extra gym or recess privileges, dance); social (praise, attention, status); tactile (art time); edibles (food and drink); auditory (music as choices of audiotapes or CDs); and others selected by students. Positive (or negative) reinforcers can vary.

> The use of behavior modification with children diagnosed as emotionally disturbed is discussed in detail in Chapter 10.

Remember, the special education teachers in your building are prepared, available, and desiring to assist you with students identified as emotionally disturbed.

Implementing Learning Activities

In preparing to implement learning activities, an ounce of prevention is worth a pound of cure. Thinking and planning can help you spot many, though never all, potential challenges. Here are some things to keep in mind as you plan lessons, make teaching preparations, and move into that most important phase of teaching—implementing your lessons with students in the classroom.

Phase A: Teacher Preparation

- Formulate your objectives, activities, and assessment design into a lesson plan.
- Collect supplies and equipment you and the students will need.
- If possible, place materials into separate kits in sacks, baggies, or boxes, or on trays for each group. The organization and distribution of materials and the transition from one activity to another can make or break your science lesson.
- Practice all activities in advance to identify and then problem-solve to eliminate or reduce potential problems.
- Plan grouping structures for the lesson.

Phase B: Pre-Activity Teacher/Student Activities

- Establish with students a minimum set of rules and working directions that cover classroom and cooperative group behavior that is fair and courteous. Wherever possible, give students a reason for the rule. Post the rules so all students can see them.
- Establish beforehand a signal calling for quiet (e.g., putting lights out for a moment, ringing a bell, raising a hand in the air).
- Establish and consistently use a system for distributing and collecting science supplies and equipment, as well as cleanup procedures.

- Working within the framework of inquiry instruction, lead the students to pose questions that can be investigated and to suggest procedures for investigating them.
- Organize the class into learning groups.
- Before students move into groups, give them time to ask questions, discuss what will be done, and exchange ideas. It is important for students to internalize what will be done and to form working relationships with other students.

Phase C: Distribution and Collection of Science Materials

- Once students are in their groups, make sure each group knows exactly what is needed. Then ask the Materials Manager from each group to go to the supply stations, two or three at a time, and get the needed items (which you have prepackaged for each group).
- Work efficiently and quickly in all pre-activity tasks. Remember, time is of the essence. Students should be working in their cooperative groups within a few minutes after the start of the science period.

Phase D: Beginning the Activity

- With all the groups in place with their supplies, move quickly from group to group, checking once more to see that each group knows what to do. Sometimes it helps to check by asking the students on a team who have the most difficulty, so that you can be sure all team members understand the directions.

Phase E: During the Activity

- As your students engage in their group work, move about the room. Do not plant yourself in the front of the room, but move quietly to each group.
- Encourage communication among the students in each group.
- Be sure to spend only a brief time—less than a minute—with each group. When working with one group, keep an eye and ear on the other groups in the classroom. Remember, as a teacher you must have eyes in the back of your head.
- Assess the student behavior in each group and see if it's appropriate for the specific activity. If it's not, you might try these solutions:
  1. Use the preestablished signal for quiet. When everyone becomes quiet and attentive, remind the class that it was too noisy. Ask the students to work more quietly.
  2. Move to the offenders and quietly remind them to lower their voices.
  3. Temporarily remove individual students from their groups if they are displaying disruptive behavior and ask them to watch groups that are working well together. In a few minutes you might say, "Jason, I know you want to work with your group. Do you think you are ready to cooperate with your group, work quietly, and share your materials properly?" If Jason answers, "Yes," have him return to his group to work.
  4. Conclude the lesson if you feel the class is out of control or is not responding to your directions. Do this only as a last resort.
- Praise students who are working well instead of criticizing those who are not working well. Be specific so students know exactly the behavior you are praising, such as, "Notice how quietly Ann's group is discussing what effect the length of the pendulum string has on its swings."
- Show respect for students by speaking politely and listening to each student in an unhurried manner.

- Do not add to class noise by shouting above students' voices. Calm and quiet the students with a firm but soft voice.

Phase F: After the Activity

- At the conclusion of the hands-on phase of the activity, ask Materials Managers to inventory equipment and materials and return them to the collection stations. Remind students to clean up their group work area. This helps teach students to share responsibility in caring for equipment, materials, and the classroom environment.
- Assemble the whole group to share data, examine different ways data has been organized, discuss conclusions, and review what they have learned.
- Throughout the class discussion, focus deliberately on observations, the data students collect, things they notice, and things they wonder about before shifting the level of thought to interpretations. Accept, extend, and probe student responses, building toward understandable explanations. As an alternative or supplement to questioning, promote higher-level thinking through group presentations of their investigations, findings, and conclusions. Students from other groups should be encouraged to ask questions and make suggestions to the presenting group.
- Use the conceptual change strategies of Chapter 6 to deal with misconceptions and encourage conceptual change. Identify misconceptions and alternative theories; lead students to be dissatisfied with their alternate ideas; and use discrepant events that challenge alternative theories.
- Use direct instruction to teach terms and concepts. Guide students in using prior and acquired knowledge, along with observational data, in constructing explanations that help them make sense of the problems posed.
- Use science textbooks as resources after students have engaged in hands-on, minds-on activities that have helped them develop the knowledge base necessary for comprehending text materials.

School, district, or regional in-service sessions are often available to help beginning teachers handle classroom management; to guide them in choosing lessons and activities; to show them how to modify activities to meet their students' needs; and to show them how to manage science classrooms safely. If your district does not offer this kind of support, you might suggest it, along with a hands-on learning day that involves teachers in inquiry, making science discoveries just like students.

SUMMARY

- Working within a framework of national, state, and local district expectations for science learning, teachers are responsible for planning effective science lessons and managing learning environments.
- Designing science lessons is a complex task requiring professional knowledge and skills. In lesson planning, you must make decisions related to four generic lesson components: science content, instructional objectives, learning activities, and assessment procedures.
- Science content outlines specify and organize the science facts, concepts, principles, models and theories, and inquiry procedures to be taught.
- Objectives state what students will do to demonstrate the attainment of skills, knowledge, understandings, attitudes,

and values related to the content. Learning activities describe the opportunities you will provide for students to attain the objectives.

• Science learning centers can be an important part of lesson plan activities. Centers allow your students to explore, discover, and experiment on their own in structured or less-structured situations.

• Well-planned field trips can add to the quality experiences you provide for students in your classroom.

• Inquiry-oriented lessons can include a variety of types of teaching and learning methods, such as listening-speaking, reading-writing, and watching-doing. Examples are included in the chapter and other chapters to serve as models as you design your own lessons.

• Assessment procedures detail how you will use specific performances of students and the products they will develop to determine what they are learning during lessons and to adjust your instruction to improve learning.

• Building an effective learning environment centered on learning with understanding is an important task in preparing to teach. The way you group your students for learning is important to the success of cooperative learning in your classroom.

• Attention to safety standards and the safety of individual and groups of students is a must in science classrooms.

• How you manage your science classroom, including managing materials and student behavior, can make or break your science teaching. The main purposes of classroom management are to ensure safety and to facilitate learning. Specific practical examples of classroom management and discipline guidelines are highlighted in the chapter.

ONLINE PROFESSIONAL DEVELOPMENT

Pre- and post-tests to assess your knowledge of chapter content, along with exercises to enhance your understanding, can be found on MyEducationLab at www.myeducationlab.com.

Video Guides

Video clips on MyEducationLab selected for this chapter include: *Investigating Pin-hole Viewers: Parts 1, 2, and 3* and *Managing Classroom Instruction—Parts 1, 2, 3, and 4.*

Accessing the Videos

1. Go to the Homework and Exercises section in Chapter 5 of MyEducationLab to select and view videos for this chapter.
2. Videos might be viewed individually, by small groups of colleagues, or by the whole class.
3. As you watch each video, use the **Questions for Reflection** to guide your thoughts and note taking for personal use and group discussion.
4. Discuss your answers to the questions about each video with classmates.

Video: Pin-hole Cameras: Parts 1, 2, and 3

Overview

In this series of videos we see fifth-grade children constructing pin-hole viewers. We also see how the children used the pin-hole viewers in observing and generalizing about images seen when the viewers are pointed at illuminated arrows.

Questions for Reflection

1. How did the teacher assess the children's prior knowledge about light?
2. How were the pin-hole viewers constructed?
3. What questions did the teacher ask the children to engage them in the investigation task?
4. At the explore phase of the lesson, what observation records did the children make to describe what they noticed about the arrows when the viewer was pointed at them?
5. What patterns did the childen notice in their observaton records of the orientation of the arrow when seen through the viewer? How did the pattern-finding part of the activity fit the explain phase of the 5-E model?

6. What additional tasks did the teacher introduce for the children to investigate?
7. What did the teacher say about the objectives of pin-hole viewer lessons, the Connecticut science standards, the process skills of science, and the ways in which the lesson follows what scientists do?

Video: Managing Classroom Instruction

Part 1: Grouping

Part 2: Clear Directions, Grade 5

Part 3: Clear Directions, Kindergarten

Part 4: Time Management

Overview

In Part 1 of this four-part video, we have a chance to observe different grouping structures and how grouping students can affect inquiry learning. In Parts 2 and 3, we see examples of clear directions for children as they prepare to carry out inquiry tasks. In Part 4, we see some ways that teachers at kindergarten and grade 5 manage time in science lessons.

Questions for Reflection

1. What do the children in Part 1 say is the importance of working in teams?
2. What task assignments did the teacher use in building the teams? What did the children say about the role of each designated task in working together in teams?
3. In what different ways did the teacher in the Part 1 video group the children for learning?
4. How effective do you think the chosen grouping structures were in promoting dialogue among the children and in enhancing understanding?
5. How would you change the grouping structure in your own classroom?
6. In Parts 2 and 3, what do you think is the importance of clear directions for students in their successfully carrying out the different activities?
7. In Part 4, what did the teachers do in managing time effectively in the different lesson activities?

A ssessment and learning are two sides of the same coin. The methods used to collect educational data define in measurable terms what teachers should teach and what students should learn. And, when students engage in an assessment exercise, they should learn from it.

(National Research Council, 1996, p. 76)

Assessing Science Learning

LEARNING AND ASSESSMENT ARE CLOSELY linked in inquiry teaching. Consider how learning and assessment interact in these scenarios.

- *Students observe as a boy grasps a piece of paper and blows steadily across the top of it. Unexpectedly, the paper moves up rather than down. The students each draw a line down the middle of a page in their science logs. On one side, they list questions pertaining to the event that might be investigated; on the other side they propose explanations about why the paper went up rather than down. The teacher uses the results to assess the students' prior knowledge about Bernoulli's principle and the effect of rushing air.*

- *During a period of watching and keeping records on the moon every night for 2 weeks, students respond to their teacher's oral questions about any patterns they may have discovered in the data. The teacher recognizes the students' responses and decides what kinds of scaffolding assistance might help them improve their understanding.*

- *Later in the moon-watching lessons, students respond to multiple-choice questions about moon phases and their causes and justify their answers through drawings and in writing. Their teacher studies the answers and explanations to determine students' levels of understanding and misconceptions that might interfere with their continued learning about lunar phases. The teacher also uses the students' responses in making decisions about changes in instruction that might be needed.*

- *After a lesson in which students learned the investigation strategy of controlling variables, a teacher displays rolls of three different brands of paper towels to the class. She says: "Your job is to test these paper towel brands for a consumer magazine. What factors will you test? How will you determine which brand is the best buy?" Students work together in small groups to formulate and carry out a plan for investigation, write a brief report, and present their results to the rest of the class. As the students work, the teacher circulates among the groups, keeping notes and marking a check sheet.*

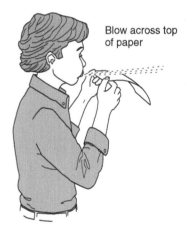

Blow across top of paper

What happens when the boy blows across the top of the paper?

What do these four situations have in common? All of them are examples of assessments used in the service of science learning. Assessment takes place at the beginning of instruction (the first case), during instruction (the second and third situations), and at the end of instruction (the fourth case). In the first situation, students' prior conceptions and misconceptions are being assessed. In the second and third situations, students' conceptual understanding is assessed through oral and written responses of students to teacher questions.

Inquiry skills and understandings about inquiry are being assessed with a performance task in the fourth situation. The first three assessments provide the teacher feedback for modifications in instruction to improve learning. The fourth situation provides for a summing up after the lesson on what students have learned. As these examples demonstrate, asessment is an ongoing process, not one that occurs just on tests given at the end of a period of instruction.

In the past, concern with assessment techniques took a back seat to learning theory and instructional reforms. Today, as is shown in the chapter opening quote, the assessment scenarios, and the discussion of formative and summative assessment in Chapters 3, 4, and 5, assessment is an integral part of the teaching-learning process. To participate in the assessment transformation, you will need to develop new assessment techniques and use traditional techniques in more creative ways.

In this chapter, we place the notions of assessment and evaluation into a broad framework and show how information from assessment is used in making evaluative decisions. We also provide many examples of informal assessments, performance tasks, and traditional assessments that you can use in formulating your own assessment plans.

As you study this chapter, reflect on the following questions:

- *How do assessment and evaluation differ? What are the purposes of assessment in science classrooms?*

- *What are the characteristics of diagnostic, formative, and summative assessments? How are formative and summative assessment linked to inquiry instruction?*

- *What are the characteristics of informal and formal assessments?*

- *What is performance assessment, and how does it differ from traditional assessment techniques?*

- *What are the components of an effective performance assessment task?*

- *What specific informal assessments, performance tasks, and traditional test items can be used to assess science knowledge, understanding, and inquiry procedures as described in national and state science standards.*

- *What are the characteristics of test items used on statewide tests of science?*

Assessment and Evaluation

Assessment is a process of gathering information about student learning for decision making. Teachers gather information on the learning of students through oral questioning, watching and listening to students, student entries in journals and record sheets, performance tasks, and formal tests. By emphasizing multiple means of collecting student data on a variety of variables, assessment goes beyond mere testing.

A glossary containing definitions of important terms used in this chapter can be found at MyEducationLab.

Assessment and evaluation are closely related concepts, but they are not the same. Assessment involves collecting data, while **evaluation** involves using that data in judging student performance and making decisions about learning and instruction. Teachers, students, parents, administrators, and legislators need different kinds of assessment information for different purposes (see Table 6-1).

Each of the assessment procedures and evaluation purposes listed in Table 6-1 is important. Our focus in this chapter is on the role of assessment and evaluation by the classroom teacher in the teaching-learning process.

TABLE 6-1 DIFFERENT AUDIENCES USE DIFFERENT TYPES OF ASSESSMENT RESULTS FOR DIFFERENT PURPOSES

Users of Assessment Data	Purposes	Frequency	Results	Assessment Types
Teachers	planning, monitoring, evaluating, and adjusting instruction; assisting students in learning; assigning grades	daily	immediate; gained through classroom observation of student performance and products	variety of assessment types, formal and informal performance assessment tasks, traditional tests
Students	feedback about learning performance and progress	daily	communicated directly from teacher or personally developed	traditional tests, performance tasks, teacher observation, self-assessment
Administrators and Legislators	accountability; budget, policy, and personnel decisions; student placement, promotion, and graduation	once each year	delayed; calculated outside of schools; made available at a later date	standardized tests; multiple-choice and short-answer items so many objectives can be assessed in a short period of time
Parents	feedback about their children's learning performance and progress	as needed; at least once each grading period	immediate or delayed; communicated directly from teachers or students	traditional tests; performance tasks; informal assessments

Assessment should help make students' work and progress understandable to students and parents. It should also guide further instruction.

Assessment and Inquiry Science

The interactive approach to teaching science as inquiry provides teachers with unique opportunities to teach science for understanding, to assess student learning in ongoing ways, and to make reflective judgments based on concrete evidence of students' accomplishments.

Think of classroom assessment as a tool used in the service of learning and instruction. By observing students while they work, asking key questions, examining the performance and products of students, and administering assessment tasks of various designs, teachers can ascertain the quality of students' conceptual understanding and ability to use inquiry strategies.

Student participation is a key component of successful assessment. If students are to participate successfully in the process, they need to be clear about the objectives and criteria for good work, to assess their own efforts in light of the criteria, and to share responsibility in taking action (National Research Council, 2001).

Key Questions to Guide Assessment in Inquiry Science

Assessment in inquiry science should be based on three guiding questions (National Research Council, 2001):

1. Where are students trying to go?
2. Where are students now?
3. How are students going to get there?

The first question leads to a consideration of standards and objectives. The second question involves assessing students' learning. The third question leads to the critical step of teachers using assessment results in making decisions about scaffolding, learning strategies, and instruction.

Where Are Students Trying to Go? There is growing consensus that the *National Science Education Standards* and the standards of the various states define the goals that should be achieved in science at different grade levels. As discussed in Chapter 5, it is the responsibility of district curriculum personnel and classroom teachers to determine the specific objectives that will lead to the attainment of the goals set forth in the science standards.

NSES   **Assessment Standard A**

Assessments must be consistent with the decision they are designed to inform.

- Assessments are deliberately designed.
- Assessments have explicitly stated purposes.
- The relationship between the decision and data is clear.

Assessment Standard B

Achievement and opportunity to learn science must be assessed.

- Achievement data should focus on the science content that is most important for students to learn.
- Equal attention must be given to the assessment of opportunity to learn and to the assessment of student achievement.

Teachers and districts develop specific objectives designed to guide the learning process. Then, teachers should provide students opportunities to attain the objectives and learn standards-based science in active ways.

Where Are Students Now? Students should be required to show evidence of their learning through formal and informal assessments. Assessment in the past centered too often on what was easy to measure with multiple-choice items: the recall of facts, concepts, principles, and theories. State and national science standards have not lost sight of the importance of a strong knowledge base, but they go beyond knowledge and place emphasis on students' understanding and applying science concepts and principles, as well as on their being able to use a variety of science processes and investigative procedures.

How Are Students Going to Get There? Assessments of any kind must always be related to standards and lesson objectives and have a clear purpose. The purpose of classroom assessment is to improve learning and instruction. Assessment results can be used to guide decisions about how modifications in instruction can help learners achieve agreed-on objectives. Classroom assessments can also be used to provide summative information on what students have actually learned through instruction.

Diagnostic, Formative, and Summative Assessment

Assessments can be diagnostic (before starting teaching), formative (during teaching), or summative (after instruction).

Diagnostic Assessment

Diagnostic assessment, sometimes called *preassessment,* is used before you start teaching to discover needed information about your students' knowledge, interests, abilities, and preferences. Diagnostic questions asked and observations made at the beginning of a lesson (in the engage phase of the 5-E instructional model, for example) can help you identify what students already know about a topic, what misconceptions and alternative theories they carry, and what they are interested in learning. By using informal assessments, performance assessments, paper-and-pencil tests, and inventories diagnostically before you begin teaching, you can decide what specific experiences will best encourage students' learning progress. Diagnostic data will help you adjust instructional strategies to students' individual differences.

Formative Assessment

Formative assessment is integral to inquiry learning and instruction. Formative assessment involves collecting data on student learning during a lesson. A combination of informal and formal assessment methods should be used in formative assessment.

Duschl and colleagues (2007) have emphasized the importance of linking formative assessment to scaffolding. A central theme in scaffolding is to make a process, concept, or principle more explicit for learners by enabling them to do something they could not do without some crucial element. For example, the crucial elements in the process of using evidence to formulate explanations include the claim, the empirical evidence in support of the claim, and the reasoning that connects the evidence and the claim (Duschl et al., 2007). Assessment of what students understand and can do provides support for further instruction, including scaffolding.

Go to the Homework and Exercises section in Chapter 6 of MyEducationLab, to read "Seven Practices for Effective Learning," an informative article on the uses of diagnostc (preassessment), formative, and summative assessment to measure student understanding. Read this article to extend your own understanding of these three forms of assessment.

Scaffolding of these crucial elements might come through teachers, instructional materials, or other students. Sometimes, explicit or direct instruction of concepts, principles, and strategies might be needed to improve learning. Remember from Chapter 4 that explicit teaching of concepts and strategies is a part of the explain phase of the learning cycle and the 5-E model of instruction.

Summative Assessment

Summative assessments are assessments that come after instruction. Formative assessments are key elements of inquiry instruction, but they are usually informal and insufficiently documented to answer many of the hard questions posed by teachers, parents, district administrators, and legislators, such as:

* What have students actually learned?
* What evidence demonstrates that they are learning?
* How well are they learning it and at what level of understanding? (National Research Council, 2000, p. 76).

Summative assessments call for more standardized instruments than are typically used in formative assessment. They also require systematic ways of recording, analyzing, and reporting student responses. Decisions about grades typically require high-quality summative assessments.

Large-scale assessments administered at district, state, national, or international levels provide evidence needed to make fair, high-stakes decisions about students, teachers, and a district's need to redesign professional development opportunities for teachers (National Research Council, 2000). Large-scale assessments are usually not classified as formative or summative, because they do not apply directly to what has just been taught in the classroom.

Informal, Traditional, and Performance Assessments

Three types of assessment measures are available to teachers in science, including informal assessments, traditional assessments, and performance assessments.

Informal Assessment

Assessments are generally characterized as informal if they are administered "on the fly" (Duschl et al., 2007) rather than at planned intervals, do not provide for standardized procedures of administration, and do not involve systematic ways to record, analyze, and report student responses. Formal assessments typically involve using traditional items and performative tasks to determine where students are in the learning process.

How to formulate effective questions for inquiry is the subject of Chapter 7.

Informal assessments may involve teachers asking students questions, listening to what they say, watching what they do in learning performance, and examining the products from their performances. Teachers also gather informal assessment data through reading and analyzing what students have written on their record sheets and in their science notebooks. Checklists can be used as a guide in systematically watching and assessing students as they work.

Traditional Assessment

Traditional assessments may be used before, during, or after instruction, but they are most often used after instruction as summative assessments. Traditional assessments typically use multiple-choice, true-false, short-answer, and essay items. Multiple-choice and true-false items are sometimes called *forced-choice* or *selected-response items*, while short-answer and essay items are referred to as *constructed-response items*. These types of assessments offer teachers a number of advantages, but they also have some disadvantages.

Multiple-choice and short-answer items are easy to administer and score. They enable teachers to measure a wide range of knowledge over a short period of time. However, multiple-choice and short-answer items do not usually require students to show their reasoning. Further, traditional multiple-choice items measure more than just knowledge; the reading level, language ability, and vocabulary of students can also affect their choices of answers.

Carefully constructed essay items can assess both the knowledge and understanding of students. Essay items have the advantage of requiring students to generate information in their own words, rather than to just recognize correct answers. Such items can also provide teachers with knowledge about how the student arrived at the answers. A disadvantage of essay items is that poor writing skills can mask the student's science understanding.

Traditional assessments can be used if teachers are careful to follow through and give feedback to students on learning. However, more powerful methods of assessment have been developed to fit the expanded formative and summative purposes of classroom assessment. In recent years, there has been an increasing emphasis on this new type of assessment, called *performance assessment*.

Performance Assessment

Performance tasks provide students opportunities to demonstrate what they know and understand. Sometimes, performance tasks are a natural part of the science lesson. At other times, teachers design special performance tasks that require students to demonstrate their understanding.

When compared with traditional assessment measures, performance assessment offers students a wider range of options for communicating what they know in science and what they are able to do with their knowledge. Students are generally more comfortable with performance assessments, because they are typically set in authentic contexts and often have the look and feel of regular, hands-on learning situations.

Performance tasks can be used to assess conceptual understanding and inquiry abilities. All performance assessment tasks have a performance that can be observed and/or a product that can be examined. Student performances in science assessment tasks might include such tasks as measuring, observing, collecting and organizing data, constructing a graph, making a visual or audio presentation, presenting an oral defense of work, interpreting data, or presenting a how-to explanation of a procedure. Products presented for assessment could include such tangible things as data tables, graphs, models, reports, and written explanations and problem solutions.

Creating a good performance task involves determining the *focus* of the task, setting the *context* for the task, writing *directions*, and developing a *scoring guide* (Kentucky Department of Education, n.d.).

NSES   **Assessment Standard C**

- Assessment tasks are authentic.
- Students have adequate opportunity to demonstrate their achievement.

Focus. The first step in developing a performance assessment is to decide what students are expected to learn and how they can demonstrate that they have learned it. This becomes the *focus* of the performance task. Focus is closely related to learning objectives. In determining the focus, state precisely what you expect your students to know, understand, and be able to do. Once you have determined a focus for the assessment task, a context should be created.

Context. The context of a performance assessment usually includes a background and a question related to the focus objective. The background may be presented in a variety of ways, including in written form and through hands-on activities. The focus question should center on a problem to which students will want to find an answer or solution. The background scenario and focus question represent the "hook" that draws students in and engages them in the task.

The scenario should be made as authentic, or as close to the "real thing," as classroom conditions will allow (Jarolimek & Foster, 1997). Authentic contexts better portray the nature of science, relate classroom learning to the real world, are more intrinsically motivating to students, and serve not only as assessments but also as interesting learning situations.

Directions. Directions for performance tasks should explain what students are expected to do and should describe the final performance or product to be assessed. It is very important to make sure that the directions are clear. You should ask other teachers and some students to review the directions for clarity.

Scoring Guides. The scoring guide provides a means for judging the quality of the assessment performance or product. Begin creating the scoring guide by describing what a high-quality performance or product will look like. The next step is to decide how many performance criteria and performance levels are needed. Descriptions of each criterion and level can then be written.

Scoring of performance assessment typically involves the use of rubrics.

Rubrics. As introduced in Chapter 5, a rubric is a type of scoring guide consisting of a number of evaluative criteria that are precisely described according to level of quality, usually with points assigned to each level. The number of levels should be based on the needs of your class and your observations of what your students are actually doing in science activities. Four-level rubrics are frequently used.

Examples of rubrics for assessing students' mastery of sound and floating and sinking concepts appear in Chapter 5 in Figures 5-5 and 5-8. Figure 6-1 provides examples of criteria and scoring levels for rubrics related to four types of science tasks. You must provide enough information about each performance level to communicate expectations to students and for scorers to distinguish differences in the quality of the students' performances and products.

Include your students in creating rubrics and in the process of scoring task performance. When students are involved in the assessment process, they become more aware of learning expectations and are enabled to take more responsibility for their own learning. Performance assessments have been criticized as being too subjective, but when good scoring guides are used, consistent scoring can be obtained.

Fitting Assessment Methods to Learning Objectives

Your choice of whether to use informal or formal assessments and traditional or performance assessment methods in science will depend largely on the type of objectives you wish to assess.

If you wish to make a quick assessment of where students are in science understanding, informal strategies might be used.

Knowing Science Information

1. Responds only in terms of specific examples experienced in class or presented in instructional materials.
2. Responds in terms of generalizations of these experiences but is unable to show relationships or to go beyond that which was experienced.
3. Demonstrates thorough understanding by applying information in a new context or by explaining relationships, implications, or consequences.

Using Science Concepts and Generalizations

1. Rarely connects previous learning with new situations in which it could be applied unless told what skill or idea is relevant.
2. Uses previous experiences in new situations once the relationship between the new and previous situation has been pointed out.
3. Works out what earlier learning could be applied in a new context by using relationships between one situation and another.

Doing Written Reports and Projects

1. What he writes or says is disorganized and difficult to follow; takes time to understand information in books or verbal directions.
2. Seems to have a clear idea of what he wants to express but does not always find the word to put it precisely or concisely; prefers to seek information orally than to use books.
3. Expresses himself clearly, using words appropriately and economically and at a level which can be understood by whomever receives the message; expands his knowledge through reading.

Experimenting/Investigating

1. Is unable to progress from one point to another in a practical investigation or inquiry without help, failing to grasp the overall plan.
2. Tries things out somewhat unsystematically unless the various steps in a practical inquiry are planned out for him, in which case he uses materials and collects results satisfactorily.
3. Has a clear idea of the reason for the various steps in an investigation; can work through them systematically, making reasonable decisions with only occasional guidance.

Figure 6-1 Criteria and scoring levels for rubric on major science categories.
Source: From Elizabeth Meng and Rodney L. Doran, *Improving Instruction and Learning Through Evaluation: Elementary School Science* (Columbus, OH: ERIC Clearinghouse for Science, Mathematics, and Environmental Education, 1993), 162–163.

If you wish to assess recall of factual or conceptual knowledge, traditional multiple-choice or short-answer items are often suitable. Traditional assessments might also be appropriate to assess student attainment of objectives related to understanding of science knowledge, particularly if you use essay items or combine multiple-choice responses with written explanations of why a particular response was chosen.

You might be able to probe deeper into student understanding and assess inquiry abilities more completely when you use performance assessments that enable students to demonstrate their understanding and investigative abilities during or after a learning task. Finally, performance methods are much more appropriate than traditional assessments when you wish to assess how well students can apply knowledge and plan and carry out inquiry procedures.

Examples of informal assessments, performance assessments, and traditional assessments are given in the following sections. Table 6-2 presents a guide to the assessment examples to help you sort through and keep up with the various assessment procedures illustrated in the chapter. You should begin now to build up a bank of assessment items and sources for each subject you teach. You can find many good assessment examples on the

TABLE 6-2   SCIENCE ASSESSMENT EXAMPLES

Assessment Purpose	Informal Assessment Examples	Performance Tasks Assessment Examples	Traditional Items Assessment Examples
Accessing Recall of Science Knowledge	Teacher questioning: Chapter 7 Student experience charts: Figure 6-2 Science record pages: Figure 6-3 Science notebooks: Figure 6-4 Using a checklist to assess microscope skills: Figure 6-5 Using checklists to assess use of science processes: Figure 6-6 Using checklists to assess investigative procedures: Figure 6-7 Using checklists as a tool for assessing attitudes: Figure 6-8	Oral/written pictorial interpretations: Figures 6-9 and 6-10	Multiple choice: Items 1–3 Short answer: Item 4
Assessing Science Understanding		Concept mapping: Figure 6-11 Electrical circuits performance task: Figure 6-12 Holistic scoring of a performance task: Figure 6-13	Essay: Item 6, 7, 8 Justified multiple choice: Figure 6-22 Essay with investigation data: Items 9, 10, 11 Figure 6-23
Assessing Investigative Procedures and Inquiry Strategies	Watching students as they investigate Examining student products developed in investigation	A leaves task for assessing data-gathering processes: Figures 6-14 and 6-15 Rubric for performance task on growing plants task: Figure 6-16 Scientific processes— Mealworms task: Figures 6-17 and 6-18 Hands-on practical assessment–TIMSS task: Figures 6-19 and 6-20	Multiple choice, short answer: Items 12, 13 Cluster of multiple-choice and essay items with investigation data: Items 14, 15, 16 Essay with application: Item 17
Assessing Multiple Objectives		Models: pp. 165–166 Demonstratons: p. 166 Student Projects: p. 166 Science Fair Projects: pp. 167–168, Figure 6-21	

Internet, in teachers' guides, and in the education literature. In most cases, it is necessary to modify examples from outside sources so that they fit your own learning objectives and classroom situation. And of course, you should begin to create, try out, and revise your own performance and traditional assessments.

Examples of Informal Assessments

Informal methods for assessing students' conceptual knowledge and understanding and their abilities to use inquiry procedures include teacher questioning, student experience charts, student records, student notebooks, and checklists.

Assessing Students' Conceptual Knowledge and Understanding

Teacher Questioning. Teachers' questions are crucial in helping students make connections and learn important science concepts. As an example of how teachers' questions can facilitate understanding, consider the electrical circuits lesson described in Chapter 4. A simple question like "Can you use these materials to make a bulb light?" engages the children in practical activities. By watching the children and listening to them, teachers can begin to assess the students' prior knowledge and current understanding. A follow-up question like "Can you draw a picture of the circuit you made to light the bulb?" reveals the extent to which students understand what they did to light the bulb. As students work on Prediction Sheet 1 in the circuits lessons, the guiding question "In which of these circuits will the bulb light?" discloses how the students conceptualize and generalize what they did to light a bulb. Such questions help to make students' thinking and understanding visible and provide a basis for the continual adjustment and improvement of learning and instruction.

Teacher questioning is treated in more detail in Chapter 7, Effective Questioning.

Experience Charts. At first, you may want students to use a group activity such as the experience chart illustrated in Figure 6-2. When assessing experience charts, consider the following questions (Shepardson & Britsch, 2001):

* Does the drawing or writing relate to and accurately correspond with what was observed or done?
* Does the child label or name the objects used?

Our Trip to the Park		
Things We Saw	**Things We Heard**	**Things We Smelled**
Sally: Branches moving in wind	Birds singing	
Greg: Little bugs crawling		Fresh air
Tom: A bird's nest	An airplane	Flowers
Amy: Yellow flowers in grass	Dog barking	
Juan: Squirrel running	Twigs snapping	Dirt (soil)
Jill: Water drops on grass	Our class laughing	Wet grass

Figure 6-2 Science experience chart.

• Does the drawing or writing elaborate on the details of what was observed or done?
• Does the drawing or writing provide a context of people, materials, and processes from the science activity in which the child was engaged?
• Does the child relate the materials or activity to contexts that might be encountered outside the classroom?

Provide scaffolding to improve learning whenever it is warranted by your assessment data.

Student Record Pages. Record keeping for all students may involve the use of simple data sheets formulated by students or teachers. Record keeping for older students can include brief descriptions of what they did, what they observed, and what they concluded. Prompts to guide investigation and thinking might be included on data sheets.

When your students learn how to give brief descriptions of what they did in groups, they are ready to start their own individual record keeping. You can design a page, such as the one in Figure 6-3, on which your students record their observations and thinking. An example of a more complex data record sheet for organizing data related to activities on white powders is given in Chaper 2, p. 49.

You have been working with things that sink or float. What did you do to find out which objects sink or float? Write a description and draw a picture.

We put objects in the bowl of water. If the object floated, we put it in box with the Float label. If it sank, we put it in box Sink. Then we tried all the objects in the Float box to check if they all floated. We did the same with the objects in the Sink box.

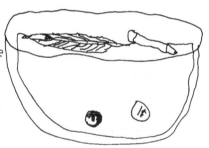

What did you find about which objects sink or float? Record your observations on the chart below.

OBJECT	SPECIAL FEATURES	LARGE OR SMALL	HEAVY OR LIGHT	SINK OR FLOAT
Penny		small	heavy	sink
Styrofoam ball		large	light	float

Figure 6-3 Science record page.

To show their understanding, students might:

* *write* a description of what they did,
* *draw* a picture of the activity, and/or
* *record written observations* in the chart supplied.

Once students become familiar with this strategy, encourage them to devise their own observation formats.

Science Notebooks. Science notebooks are tools for students to grapple with scientific questions and help them make sense of what they have observed through using meaningful recording and organizing strategies. As an example, students often keep notes of their observations. Your examination of observation notebooks can reveal the students' developing knowledge about a topic. Student notes can take many forms, such as drawings, narratives, charts, and graphs.

* *Technical drawings and diagrams with labels.* These are drawings based on careful observations of objects and organisms.
* *Notes and lists.* These are reports of observations used to record information quickly.
* *Charts, tables, and graphs.* These represent different ways to display and view data.
* *Written observations.* These are more detailed accounts of investigations and observations.
* *Additional questions about which students wonder.*
* *Personal judgments and feelings related to activities.*

An example of a student's entry in her science notebook is given in Figure 6-4.

As you assess notebooks, keep your objectives in mind. Content learning may be your main goal, but for students to learn to use different reporting and organizational strategies can also be important. You might teach reporting and organizational strategies in mini-lessons, perhaps in language arts classes, and use later lessons to assess student use of these. Provide feedback to improve reporting strategies whenever appropriate.

More suggestions related to student science notebooks are given in Chapter 9.

Several good articles related to writing to learn science are published in the November/December 2004 issue of *Science and Children*. This topic is also addressed in Chapter 9.

Today we used one wire and one battery to make a bulb light. At first, I didn't think I could do it, but I did! I made the bulb light on my own! I can't wait for more activities on electricity tomorrow. I feel really confident now and like this way of learning.

Figure 6-4 Student science notebook entry.

The *National Science Education Standards* emphasize that students must be provided opportunity to develop both conceptual understandings and abilities of scientific inquiry (National Research Council, 1996; 2000). Assessing inquiry abilities formatively through informal assessment is an important part of science learning.

Checklists. A checklist is simply a list of the specific key elements that a teacher wishes to consider in judging a student performance or product. Scorers observe student performances and examine products and check *yes* or *no* for each element on the checklist. The check mark typically shows only whether the element is observed; no effort is made on a checklist to assess how well the skill is performed. However, space might be added to a checklist for teacher notes or comments. Checklists are easy, quick, and handy to use. They help keep teacher observations focused.

Figure 6-5 is a sample checklist for observing and assessing students' skills in using a microscope. Student results determined with checklists might be used both to provide feedback on learning and to adjust instruction. Be sure to keep a separate record for each student. Review it with students periodically to assess their progress in specific skills.

Hands-on inquiry activities provide an authentic setting for assessing children's developing abilities to do scientific inquiry. Figure 6-6 displays a checklist that can be used to judge students' use of specific science processes. Figure 6-7 shows a checklist for use in assessing investigation procedures. The checklists are best used in informal assessment, since there are no standardized procedures for collecting and reporting this type of student information.

Think about using the checklists over the course of a year. You might

- keep a checklist record for processes and procedures on each student,
- consider each student's performance in a variety of science activities,
- note whether or when each student exhibits the indicated task or behavior,

Student's Name _____									
Behavior/Skills	Date	Yes	No	Date	Yes	No	Date	Yes	No
Is careful in handling microscope									
Cleans lenses properly									
Focuses instrument properly									
Prepares slides correctly									
Orients mirror for correct amount of light									

Figure 6-5　Checklist for observing microscope skills.

Student Name: _____

Process or Skill	Task or Behavior	Task Observed? Date	Comment
Observing	Uses several senses in exploring objects		
	Uses magnifying glasses and other instruments to extend the senses		
	Identifies details in objects, organisms, and events		
	Notice patterns, relationships, or sequences in events		
Inferring	Uses evidence and scientific knowledge in making inferences		
	Explains basis for inferences		
	Makes reasonable inferences that fit the evidence and scientific knowledge		
	Suggests how to test inferences		
Predicting	Uses evidence in making a prediction		
	Explains basis for predictions		
	Makes reasonable predictions that fit the evidence, whether accurate or not		
	Makes interpolations and extrapolations from patterns in information or observation		
	Suggests how to test predictions		
Communicating	Talks freely with others about activities and ideas		
	Listens to others' ideas and looks at their results		
	Reports observations coherently in drawings, writing, and charts		
	Uses tables, graphs, and charts to report investigation results		

Figure 6-6 Checklist for assessing science processes.

- add comments to guide learning and instruction, and
- work with all students to help them improve in their abilities to use each process or inquiry procedure.

A critical part of understanding the nature of science and scientific inquiry is a knowledge of scientific habits of mind, the attitudes that characterize scientists. Although students

Figure 6-7 Checklist for assessing investigation procedures.

Procedure	Task or Behavior	Task Observed?	
		Date	Comment
Questions	Asks a variety of questions, focusing on questions that can be investigated		
	Recognizes differences between questions that can be investigated and questions that cannot be investigated		
Places Priority on Evidence	Has some idea of what evidence to look for to answer the question		
Plans Investigations to Obtain Needed Data or Information	Chooses a realistic way of investigating, measuring, or comparing to obtain results		
	Plans descriptive, classificatory, experimental, and other investigation procedures		
Conducts Planned Investigation	Carries out investigation procedures carefully		
	Works cooperatively with teammates		
	Takes steps to ensure that the results obtained are accurate		
Explains, Interprets, or Make Sense of Data	Gives explanation consistent with evidence and scientific knowledge		
	Explains basis for explanations		
	Shows awareness that other explanations may fit the evidence		
	Asks questions about ways to test predictions and explanations made in activities		
	Suggests how explanations and predictions can be checked		
	Shows awareness that explanations are tentative and subject to change		

Student Name: _____

should attain many affective goals in science, five main attitudes, values, and habits of mind are especially relevant to successful inquiry in elementary and middle school classrooms:

1. being curious,
2. insisting on evidence,
3. seeking to apply science knowledge,
4. being willing to critically evaluate ideas, and
5. working cooperatively.

It is difficult to measure attitudes reliably, but attitudes cannot be improved without an understanding of students' existing attitudes (Shepardson & Britsch, 2001). Figure 6-8 shows a

Student Name: _____

		Behavior Observed	
Attitude	**Component Behavior**	**Date**	**Comment**
Curiosity	Notices and attends to new things and situations		
	Shows interest through careful observation of details		
	Asks questions		
	Uses resources to find out about new or unusual situations		
Respect for Evidence	Searches for evidence to answer questions posed		
	Checks evidence that does not fit the pattern of other findings		
	Challenges conclusions or interpretations where there does not seem to be sufficient evidence		
Predisposition to Apply Knowledge in Problem Solving	Searches for available scientific knowledge to apply in problem solving		
	Uses available knowledge to guide exploration of problem situation		
	Uses available knowledge and evidence in generating explanations and problem solutions		
Willingness to Critically Evaluate Ideas	Changes existing ideas when there is sufficient evidence		
	Considers alternative ideas to her own		
	Willing to examine positive and negative aspects of his own investigations		
	Seeks alternative ideas rather than just the first idea		
	Realizes that it may be necessary to change an existing idea		
Working Cooperatively	Talks freely with other students about topic-related ideas in small group and whole group settings		
	Shows respect for others in groups		
	Considers multiple viewpoints within groups		
	Readily assumes and fulfills assigned role in inquiry group		
	Assists others in investigation and learning tasks when appropriate		

Figure 6-8 Checklist for assessing science attitudes.

Source: From *Assessment in Science: A Guide to Professional Development and Classroom Practice* (pp. 119–147), by D. P. Shepardson, and S. J. Britsch, 2001, Boston: Kluwer. Adapted with permission.

checklist that can be used to gain some understanding of students' science attitudes. The checklist draws on a number of sources, including the work of Shepardson and Britsch (2001). By categorizing attitudes into a number of different components, the checklist allows teachers to watch for specific indicators of these important science attitudes.

As with the science processes and investigation procedures checklists, you might keep an assessment checklist for each student throughout the year, noting when you judge that the child has displayed the attitude or failed to display the attitude when it mattered. Information gained via the checklist should be used formatively to praise and improve attitudes, rather than summatively for grading purposes.

Examine your science program to see where you can use these suggestions to develop informal assessment measures suited to your immediate needs.

Examples of Performance Assessment Items

In this section, we provide a large bank of assessment examples that you can draw on in developing your own performance assessment tasks for use in science.

Performance tasks can be a part of the regular learning activity. The focus, context, and direction of the performance tasks are then derived directly from the learning activities.

The PALS (Performance Assessment Links in Science) website has collected many excellent performance assessment examples. Peruse the PALS website at http://pals.sri.com/index.html.

Using Performance Tasks to Assess Science Knowledge

Conceptual understanding of the natural world is a key goal of elementary and middle school science. When students understand, they are able to do something with their knowledge. They can interpret concepts and principles and use them along with observational evidence in inferring, predicting, analyzing, and explaining. Performance tasks are particularly suited to assessing understanding.

Oral/Written Pictorial Interpretations. Teachers can gain insights into their students' understanding of concepts and principles by using assessments that ask them to respond to pictorial situations. Look for more than mere observations. Assess for hidden meanings, underlying patterns, and explanatory schemas that bring coherence to the students' observations. Such an assessment is intended to determine students' abilities to communicate the trends and sequences of the pictorial situation.

In developing pictorial assessments, decide on the learning objective (the *focus* of the performance task). You might show a science pictorial situation (the *context*), then give *directions* for how to respond to the questions. This can be done orally for younger students or those with limited reading skills, or in written form for others. Figure 6-9 illustrates such an activity.

An example of a *scoring guide* to assess students' responses to the snowman item in Figure 6-9 is given in Figure 6-10. The scoring guide relates to each of the three questions in the pictorial assessment. This scoring guide is similar to a checklist in that the teacher is to examine students' responses for specific criteria. However, points are to be assigned for each relevant response. Teachers must use their own experience to judge the quality of the response and to assign points.

The assessment in Figures 6-9 and 6-10 could be used formatively to guide teachers to improve student understanding or summatively in assigning student grades.

Using Performance Tasks to Assess Science Understanding

Concept maps are useful tools to assess science understanding. Assessing performance on performance tasks through holistic rubrics is another useful tool to assess understanding.

Teacher shows pictures and says to children:

What differences do you see in these three pictures?
Which do you think will happen first? Second?
 Last?
Why do you think the snowman is changing?

Figure 6-9 Pictorial interpretation assessment.
Source: From *Material Objects Student Manual,* Section 5, Chapter 18, SCIS3, 1992, Hudson, NH: Delta Education, Inc. Copyright 1992 by Delta Education, Inc. Reprinted with permission.

Figure 6-10 Scoring guide for pictorial interpretation assessment.

Element	0–8 Points
Differences among pictures	At least three key differences are clearly stated. Differences might relate to the snowman's height, size, position of arms, depiction of eyes. (0–3 points)
Ordering of pictures	Pictures arranged in correct order (picture 1, picture 2, picture 3). (0–1 point)
Reasons for changes	Judge how well the reasons for changes relate to the *evidence* in the pictures and to *knowledge* of heating and melting. Examples: The sun came out and melted the snowman; the longer the sun was out, the more the snowman melted. The snowman melted because he got hot. The snow changed to water because of the sun. (0–4 points)
Scoring	Outstanding 7–8 points Satisfactory 5–6 points Needs improvement 3–4 points Unsatisfactory 0–2 points

Concept Maps. Psychologists theorize that learners organize their knowledge into connected networks called *knowledge structures.* The size of these structures, the number of connections between items of knowledge, and the organization and richness of the connections are all important for processing knowledge, constructing meanings, and solving problems (Rosenshine, 1997).

As discussed in Chapter 3, a **concept map** is a visual representation of a major concept and its connections to subsidiary concepts. Joseph Novak and others (Edmondson, 1999; Mintzes, Wandersee, & Novak, 1998; Novak, 1995) have advocated the use of concept maps in assessing the science understanding of students.

By examining student concept maps before or during instruction, teachers can discover learners' conceptual understandings and their misconceptions. Students' concept maps can then be used by the teacher to provide feedback to students and as a guide to improve instruction.

The concept maps shown in Figure 6-11 provide a means to compare the conceptual understanding of two students on blood circulation. We might judge that the first student

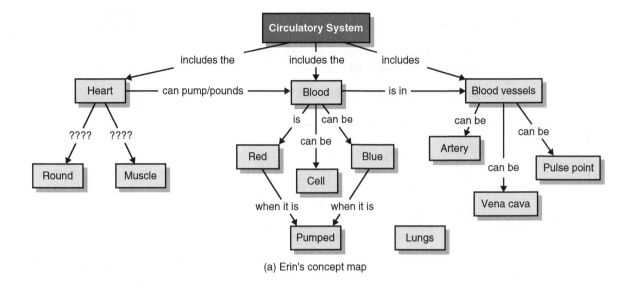

(a) Erin's concept map

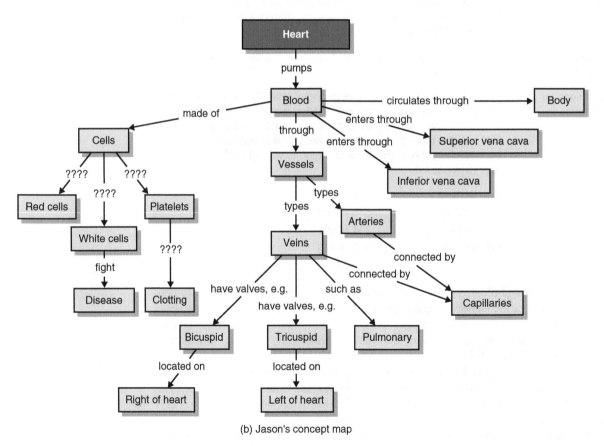

(b) Jason's concept map

Figure 6-11 Two students' concepts maps of the heart and circulatory system. What conceptual organization differences do you note between Erin and Jason?

Source: Figures from Joel J. Mintzes, James H. Wandersee, and Joseph D. Novak, in J. Mintzes, J. Wandersee, and J. Novak (Eds.), *Teaching Science for Understanding: A Human Constructivist View,* copyright © 1998 by Academic Press. Used with permission from Elsevier.

focused more on descriptive aspects of the heart and circulatory system, whereas the second student showed more understanding by focusing on interactions. The concept map assessments in this case might serve as a basis of feedback to students and scaffolding to improve learning.

Performance Tasks and Rubrics. In the performance task shown in Figure 6-12, students make predictions about what happens in an illustrated circuit when switches are either open or closed. Then they construct the circuit and use it to test predictions. Finally, they write explanations of what happens to each of the bulbs in the test. This performance task gauges how well students solve a real-world scientific problem in a laboratory setting. It is appropriate for students in about grade 4 or above. Using what you learned from the 5-E lesson on electrical circuits in Chapter 4, do the performance task in Figure 6-12 for yourself before reading on.

Rubrics could be used in assessing levels of understanding. Two rubrics might be appropriate for the electrical circuits task. One of the rubrics could assess understandings and abilities needed in constructing the circuit. A second rubric could be used to assess students' explanations.

Holistic rubrics might be used with performance tasks, such as an electrical circuits task. Scoring guides are holistic if teachers make judgments about task performance by considering simultaneously all of the criteria that go into a high-quality product or performance. Teachers observe, assess, and evaluate the student's written responses to the questions. The teachers also assess and evaluate the student's performance in constructing and using the test circuit. A holistic scoring guide for the electrical circuits task is shown in Figure 6-13.

Using Performance Tasks to Assess the Application of Inquiry Procedures and Science Processes. A distinctive element of the *National Science Education Standards* is the dual focus on students attaining science understanding and, at the same time, improving their abilities to inquire. Assessing inquiry procedures and science processes, both formatively for learning improvement and summatively for accountability and grading, is an important part of elementary and middle school science programs.

In an inquiry-oriented classroom, there are many opportunities to extend learning activities by making them the centerpiece of performance tasks for assessing science processes and procedures.

Assessing Data-Gathering Processes with a Leaves Task. *Data-gathering* refers to the process of students making observations and recording data about objects, organisms, and events. Figure 6-14 shows a data-gathering task about leaves that can provide teachers with knowledge of students' observing and communicating skills. Figure 6-15 shows a leaves data sheet for use with the leaves task. The leaves task is suitable for use with students from K–8, depending on their prior experiences and developmental levels. It may be adapted for a variety of science topics.

When assessing data-gathering, consider the following questions:

- Does the child use all appropriate senses and instruments such as a hand lens in main observations?
- Are observations reported in writing, labeled drawings, and charts or data tables?
- How well do the written communication and drawings relate to and accurately correspond with what was observed with each sense?
- Does the communication provide details of what was observed?

Performance Task:

A. PREDICT: Study the diagram of the electric circuit. Make a prediction about what will happen to each light bulb if switch 1 is closed and switch 2 is open.

My Predictions:

Bulb 1: Lit   Not Lit   (Circle Lit or Not Lit)

Bulb 2: Lit   Not Lit   (Circle Lit or Not Lit)

Bulb 3: Lit   Not Lit   (Circle Lit or Not Lit)

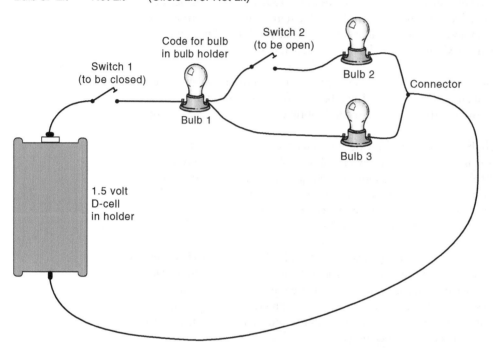

B. CONSTRUCT: Obtain a kit of materials from your teacher. Using the materials, build the circuit illustrated.

C. TEST: Use your circuit to test your predictions. Arrange the circuit so that switch 1 is open and switch 2 is closed. What happened to each bulb?

My Observations:

Bulb 1: Lit   Not Lit   (Circle Lit or Not Lit)

Bulb 2: Lit   Not Lit   (Circle Lit or Not Lit)

Bulb 3: Lit   Not Lit   (Circle Lit or Not Lit)

D. EXPLAIN: Use your knowledge of circuits to explain your observations of what happened to each bulb when you opened switch 1 and closed switch 2 of the test circuit.

My Explanation: (Write out your explanation here.)

_____

_____

_____

_____

Figure 6-12   Electrical circuits task.

Score: 0 Points

The student does not attempt to solve the problem. A 0-point score is characterized by most of the following:

- No predictions are given.
- There is no attempt to build the circuit.
- No observations are made.
- No explanations are given.

Score: 1 point

The overall responses are inconsistent with sound scientific thinking and investigation procedures. The responses indicate the student has little or no understanding of the problem and of circuit ideas. A 1-point response is characterized by most of the following:

- Predictions are inaccurate or missing.
- The student makes a limited attempt to build the test circuit; the circuit, if constructed, has many faults.
- The student's attempts to test the predictions are unsuccessful; the observations are missing.
- Explanations are missing or they are illogical and cannot be supported; understanding of circuit concepts is not demonstrated.

Score: 2 points

The responses represent a limited attempt at applying a sound scientific approach to the problem. Although the responses exhibit errors, incompleteness, and/or omissions, the student demonstrates some understanding of how to predict, how to construct a test circuit, and how to use the circuit to test predictions. Little understanding of the concept of circuits is demonstrated. A 2-point response is characterized by most of the following:

- The student makes two or more inaccurate predictions.
- The student attempts to build a test circuit but it is faulty.
- The students uses the constructed circuit to test the predictions.
- Observations of what happens to the bulbs in the test are inaccurate.
- Explanations are illogical and cannot be supported; clear understanding of the circuit concepts is not demonstrated.

Score: 3 points

The overall response is largely consistent with a sound scientific approach to design. The response indicates that the student has a general understanding of the problem, of how to make predictions, how to construct a circuit, and how to use it to test predictions. The quality of the explanation is good, although minor errors may be present. A 3-point response is characterized by most of the following:

- The student makes generally accurate predictions, with no more than one error.
- The student's test circuit is well constructed with only minor faults.
- The student uses the circuit to test predictions; one or two observations may be inaccurate.
- The explanation is logical and, for the most part, is consistent with observations and shows understanding of circuit ideas.

Score: 4 points

The responses are consistent with a sound scientific approach. The responses indicate that the student has a clear understanding of the problem and of how to predict, construct circuits, and use the circuits to test predictions. The explanation may, in some cases, define additional aspects of the problem or include extensions beyond the requirements of the task. Some inconsistencies may be present, but they are overwhelmed by the superior quality of the responses. A 4-point score is characterized by most of the following:

- The student makes accurate predictions.
- The circuit is well constructed, with no flaws.
- The circuit is successfully used to test the predictions; all observations in the test are accurate.
- The explanation is clear and detailed, and is convincingly supported with the data collected and an accurate presentation of circuit concepts.

Figure 6-13 Holistic scoring guide for an electrical circuits task.

Figure 6-14 Data capture assessment.
Source "Leaves" An Investigation" and "Leaves Data Capture Sheet" (pp. 67–68) in *TCM771 Science Assessment,* 1994 Westminster, CA: Teacher Created Materials, Inc. Copyright 1994 by Teacher Created Materials, Inc. Reprinted with permission.

Observing Leaves

NSES

Science Standards

All students should develop understanding of:

- Characteristics of organisms (K–4).

Investigation

- Collect different kinds of leaves. If possible, allow children to gather their own leaves around their homes and the school.

- Give each group of students a small collection of leaves. Instruct the students to observe the different characteristics (properties, attributes) of the leaves. Ask: *What do you notice about the leaves in your collection? How are they alike? In what ways are they different?* Provide rulers and magnifying glasses for the children to use in observing the leaves. Encourage the children in each group to discuss with one another the similarities and differences among their leaves.

- Let each child choose two leaves to observe and describe. Instruct the students to work individually to compare the leaves according to each of these characteristics: size, color, number of points, and number of veins. Give them the "Leaves Data Sheet" to record their observations.

Assessing Data-Gathering Processes with a Plant Growth Task. One performance task uses a plant growth project to assess ability to apply processes of science. The performance task requires students to observe pairs of growing plants over time and to answer questions about them. During this task, students measure, record data, and determine patterns and trends from the data. The products to be judged are the students' oral or written answers to the questions.

The scorer judges the quality of students' performance in measuring plant heights using a four-point rubric as a scoring guide. The rubric is shown in Figure 6-16. Because the rubric is detailed, teachers will need to adapt it to their particular situations.

A mealworm activity similar to this one was discussed in Chapter 2 as an example of an investigation involving descriptive, classificatory, and experimental procedures.

Assessing Scientific Processes and Investigative Procedures with a Mealworms Task. The assessment of scientific processes and investigation procedures in practical activities can be structured or formalized to guide teacher observations. In one performance task, students are introduced to mealworms, provided necessary materials, including mealworms and different foods, and directed to find out the food preferences of the mealworms.

A student record page, such as the one in Figure 6-17, can be used by students to list observational notes and results on the mealworms task. The teacher may provide a cue, prompt, or question if students are stuck and cannot continue or if the teacher seeks students' thinking or reason for some action.

Figure 6-15 Data sheet for leaves task.

Leaves Data Sheet

Name _____ Date _____

■ Draw a picture of Leaf #1   ■ Draw a picture of Leaf #2

Look at Leaf #1.   Look at Leaf #2.

■ What is its color or colors?   ■ What is its color or colors?

_____   _____

_____   _____

■ How many centimeters long is   ■ How many centimeters long
  Leaf #1?   is Leaf #2?

_____   _____

_____   _____

■ How many points does Leaf #1   ■ How many points does
  have?   Leaf #2 have?

_____   _____

_____   _____

■ Describe the veins in Leaf #1.   ■ Describe the veins in Leaf #2.

_____   _____

_____   _____

The teacher might, for example, make this suggestion: "One way you can try to find the food preference is to make a mark in the middle of the paper. Take some of each food and place it at the same distance from the mark and then put some mealworms on the mark" (Meng & Doran, 1993).

The student inquiry behaviors checklist in Figure 6-18 lists problem-solving skills for the observer to focus on during the mealworms task. If cues or prompts are given, the observer should make a record of them. The checklist spotlights specific behaviors to look for as students progress toward finding answers to the question. Emphasis is placed on observable behaviors such as: "places approximately equal quantities of food on the sections of the paper."

Figure 6-16 Rubric for performance assessment in a unit on plants.
Source From "Scoring Active Assessments: Setting Clear Criteria and Adapting Them to Your Students Are the Key to Scoring Classroom Performance," by Sabra Price and George E. Hein, October 1994; *Science and Children 32*, no. 2 p. 29. Copyright 1994, National Science Teachers Association, 1840 Wilson Blvd., Arlington, VA 22201-3000.

Sample Scoring System

Question One. Students are asked to measure the height of two seedlings and to record their results.

Scoring Rubric for Question One

0 = The student either did not record results or reported measurements that were inaccurate by more than a certain percentage determined by the teacher.
1 = The student did not record results, but did report approximate measurements. The teacher needs to determine the meaning of "approximate." This will depend on such things as the markings on students' rulers and students' classroom experiences.
2 = The student recorded approximate measurements.
3 = The student recorded accurate measurements. The teacher needs to determine the meaning of "accurate."

Question Two. Students are asked to explain their recorded measurements to their teacher.

Scoring Rubric for Question Two

0 = The student provided either no explanation or one that makes no sense to the teacher or is unrelated to any unit activities.
1 = The student's explanation related to unit activities but did not explain the growth pattern.
2 = The student provided an explanation for the growth pattern.
3 = The student gave more than one reasonable explanation for the growth pattern.

Figure 6-17 Example of student record page for mealworms activity.
Source: From Elizabeth Meng and Rodney L. Doran, *Improving Instruction and Learning Through Evaluation: Elementary School Science* (Columbus, OH: ERIC Clearinghouse for Science, Mathematics, and Environmental Education, 1993), p. 93.

Mealworms

Find out if the mealworms prefer some of these foods to others. If they do, which ones do they prefer?

a) Record notes and results as you go along here:

b) Write down what you found about the foods the mealworms prefer here:

☐ Uses hand lens correctly

☐ Hint given for using hand lens

☐ Deliberately provides mealworm with choice; i.e., at least 2 foods at once

☐ Employs an effective strategy such as:
   (i)   uses 6 or more mealworms if all 4 foods compared at once
   (ii)   compares foods in all possible pairs with 1 mealworm
   (iii) tries at least 4 mealworms with one food at a time

☐ Attempts to provide equal quantities of different foods

☐ Places approximately equal quantities of food on the sections of the paper

☐ Attempts to release mealworms at equal distance from all foods *or* arranges mealworms to be randomly distributed around food

☐ Arranges to release mealworms from points equidistant from foods, *or* places mealworms randomly around foods

☐ Arranges for all mealworms to have same time to choose (i.e., puts them all down together or uses a clock)

☐ Uses clock to time definite events

☐ Allows about 4–7 minutes for mealworms to make choice (not necessarily timed)

☐ Examines behavior carefully (to see if food is being eaten)

☐ Counts mealworms near each pile after a certain time (or notes which food the mealworm is on for strategy [ii] above)

☐ Makes notes at (a) on record page (however brief)

☐ Records details such as time of choice and numbers near each food

☐ Can read stop clock correctly (to nearest second)

☐ Makes a record of finding at (b) on record page without prompting

☐ Results at (a) and (b) consistent with evidence (even if only rough)

☐ Results based on and consistent with quantitative evidence

Figure 6-18 Laboratory student behavior checklist. *Source:* From Elizabeth Meng and Rodney L. Doran, *Improving Instruction and Learning Through Evaluation: Elementary School Science* (Columbus, OH: ERIC Clearinghouse for Science, Mathematics, and Environmental Education, 1993), p. 124.

When the checklist is used formatively, scaffolding instruction is provided as needed related to specific checklist criteria to individuals, small groups, or the class as a whole. Consider the checklist as an example that shows how to construct an assessment checklist that uses content (the behavior of mealworms) as the vehicle to gather data on the skills and processes used by students in scientific investigation or problem solving.

Which of your science activities lend themselves to this type of assessment?

Assessing Inquiry Procedures in Science with Performance Tasks: The TIMSS Test. Performance assessments are especially useful for assessing the planning and implementing of inquiry procedures in science. Since the 1980s, assessment data have been collected in the United States and other countries from students in elementary and middle school grades on a series of practical hands-on science activities (Chan, Doran, & Lenhardt, 1999). The 1995–1996 Third International Mathematics and Science Study TIMSS—now The International Mathematics and Science Study—collected data on a

Although interpretations of data from the TIMSS and the earlier international comparisons vary, information from these studies is important for the development of educational policies at national and state levels.

Task	Description	Task	Integrated Tasks (Science and Mathematics)
Pulse	Student investigates changes in pulse rate during exercise, records and analyzes data, and explains results.	Shadows	Student manipulates the position of light source and object to find three positions at which a shadow is twice the width of an object and expresses the relationship of distance of the light and object to the screen as a general rule.
Magnets	Student determines the stronger of two magnets and describes strategies to support the conclusion.		
Batteries	Student determines which of four batteries is worn out, describes strategies, and uses concept knowledge to explain proper arrangement of batteries in a flashlight.	Plasticine	Given only two standard masses, student develops and describes strategies to determine the masses of lumps of various specified masses.
Rubber Band	Student attaches increasing numbers of masses to a rubber band, investigates the effect on the length, and explains results.		
Solutions	Student investigates the effect of different temperatures on rate of tablet disintegration; collects, records, and analyzes data; and explains results.		

Figure 6-19 Description of eighth-grade performance assessment tasks from the Third International Mathematics and Science Study (TIMSS).
Source: From "Learning from the TIMSS," by Alfred Chan, Rodney Doran, and Carol Lenhardt, 1999, *The Science Teacher, 66*(1), p. 20. Copyright 1999 by National Science Teachers Association. Reprinted with permission.

half-million students from 41 nations. U.S. students were well above the average science performance of students worldwide at the fourth-grade level, surpassed only by students from Korea (U.S. Department of Education, 1997). U.S. eighth graders were slightly above the international average in science but trailed the average performance of students in 16 other countries (U.S. Department of Education, 1996).

Figure 6-19 shows seven performance tasks that were included on the TIMSS tests at the eighth-grade level in science (Chan, Doran, & Lenhardt, 1999). These tests used science content and equipment from physics, chemistry, and biology. Students completed the tasks at tables where the necessary materials were provided. Students were asked to manipulate equipment and materials; observe, reason, and record data in test booklets; and interpret data.

Figure 6-20 provides the directions and questions for a TIMSS task called the Solutions Task. In this task, students first planned procedures to determine what effect different water temperatures have on the speed with which effervescent antacid tablets dissolve. The students then carried out tests, measuring water temperatures and corresponding times for the tablets to dissolve. Students were asked to use the evidence from their tests to draw conclusions about the effect of different water temperatures on the speed with which a tablet dissolves. Finally, the students were instructed to explain why different temperatures have different effects. Student activities in this performance assessment closely parallel the tasks of inquiry identified by the writers of the *National Science Education Standards*.

Materials:
Hot and cold water
Several beakers
Effervescent antacid tablets
Stirrer
Clock or watch with a second hand
Thermometer
30 centimeter ruler

Task: Plan an experiment to find out what effect different water temperatures have on the speed with which the tablets dissolve.
 Part one. Write down a plan that includes what will be measured, how many measurements will be taken, and how the measurements will be presented in a table.
 Part two. Carry out the test(s). Make a table and record all measurements.
 Part three. According to the investigation, what effect do different water temperatures have on the speed with which a tablet dissolves?
 Part four. Explain why different water temperatures have different effects.
 Part five. If the plan must be changed, describe the changes and explain why they will be made. If there are no changes, write "no change." Empty all beakers into the waste container, dry them, and leave everything the way it was found.

Figure 6-20 Directions and questions for the TIMSS solutions task. *Source:* From "Learning from the TIMSS," by Alfred Chan, Rodney Doran, and Carol Lenhardt, 1999, *The Science Teacher, 66*(1), p. 20. Copyright 1999 by National Science Teachers Association. Reprinted with permission.

Table 6-3 shows the average percentage scores on each question for the solutions performance assessment. How do U.S. eighth-graders' average percentage scores compare with the international average? On what tasks are they above average? On what tasks are they below average? Why do you think these trends exist? For example, why do U.S. students lag behind in planning investigations but exceed international averages in drawing and explaining conclusions?

Assessing Multiple Objectives Through Performance Assessments

Students can use previously acquired science knowledge and understanding to solve problems and create products in situations that are new or different from those to which they were exposed.

Model Building. Physical models that illustrate students' understanding of natural objects, organisms, structures, and phenomena and that require abilities to use science inquiry processes and procedures are excellent products for assessment. In building models,

TABLE 6-3   AVERAGE PERCENTAGE SCORES ON EACH PERFORMANCE CRITERION FOR THE TIMSS SOLUTIONS TASK

Sample	Overall Task Average	Q1 Plan Investigation	Q2 Conduct Investigation		Q3 Draw Conclusions	Q4 Explain Conclusion	Q5 Evaluate Design
			Presentation	Data Quality			
International	49	44	62	59	77	22	30
United States	48	33	64	59	82	27	24

Source: From "Learning from the TIMSS," by Alfred Chan, Rodney Doran, and Carol Lenhardt, 1999, *The Science Teacher, 66*(1), p. 21. Copyright 1999 by National Science Teachers Association. Reprinted with permission.

students are required to research relevant information, discover what kind of models illustrate the scientific concept(s) to be shown, collect needed scientific supplies and equipment, plan and build the model, and explain it to the class and teacher. Students have successfully accomplished these things for models of the solar system, geological structures, physiological systems of the human body, and so forth.

Student Demonstrations. Students can demonstrate much of what they know and understand about scientific concepts and their interrelationships through planning, manipulating, and demonstrating with scientific supplies and equipment. The audience may be their own classmates and teacher, other classes, their parents, or other persons. Individual students or groups may give the demonstrations, such as showing how electrical circuits work, exhibiting static electricity in everyday situations, or demonstrating what happens when colored lights are mixed.

Student Projects. Student projects may uncover much about students' understanding and thinking. Project assessments provide the teacher with insight into how well students have learned, recorded, and put their knowledge into practical use. The teacher and students should work out expectations of what the projects will encompass *before* students start their projects. Primary grade students often make something as part of their science learning.

In the example of project assessment that follows, groups of students worked together to design an aquarium. The project is built around a "WebQuest" in which students use the Internet to gather information about the habitat and animals selected. A description of the performance task, the detailed rubric, and the WebQuest for the project was originally found online. Websites change and the aquarium project is no longer available on the Internet.

Here is the students' task.

> **Performance Task: You are a zoologist at a city zoo. Many people have suggested adding aquariums to the zoo. Your task as a zoologist is to (a) choose a type of water habitat; (b) choose three animals that can coexist in the water habitat; and (c) design an aquarium so that it is an appropriate habitat for the three animals.**

The students would need to have explored the habitat and food needs of organisms in previous activities. In this activity, they use reference books and the Internet to gather information on the habitat and animals selected. They will need to find information concerning the different components of the habitat, such as plants and rocks, the food that should be available for their animals, and what enables each of the animals to live in a water habitat.

Their aquarium design can be presented to the teacher and the class in the form of a Kid Pix or PowerPoint display or as an actual aquarium. As the teacher, you will be there to assess learning and provide scaffolding and instruction as needed. But do not give too much assistance—this is a student project.

A rubric is used to assess the students' aquarium designs and their performance in oral discussions. The rubric might include these three main criteria:

1. The student identifies and distinguishes between freshwater and saltwater habitats.
2. The student lists at least three animals that live in the chosen water habitat and gives information about each, including the food, shelter, and parts of the body that enable them to live in the environment.
3. The aquarium design includes an appropriate habitat for each of the three animals, including shelter and a source of food for each.

Take some time to develop the aquarium task rubric by writing quality descriptions for three levels: high, medium, and low quality. How does the project call for the development of knowledge and understanding and of science processes and procedures?

Science Fair Projects. Students in many elementary and middle schools are required to develop science fair projects. Projects are usually evaluated by external judges, using a common set of judging criteria. Figure 6-21 shows a composite of the judging criteria used in many science fairs.

The first step in creating a good science fair project is for the student to select an interesting, sufficiently narrow question to investigate. In Chapter 2 we identified and gave examples of three types of scientific investigations: descriptive, classificatory, and experimental. Judging criteria often favor experimental investigations, with hypotheses, responding and manipulated variables, and adequate controls designed into the investigation. Because true experiments are difficult for younger learners, we suggest that school and district science fairs be for students from the fourth or fifth grade up. Younger students might be involved in descriptive and classificatory investigations and the construction of models and demonstrations. These might be displayed in their own classrooms.

Judging Criteria	Indicators
Creativity	• Creativity is shown in the selection of a problem to investigate. • Ingenuity in the design and development of the project is shown.
Scientific Thought	• The problem selected is appropriate. • The question and hypothesis are clear, well formulated, and sufficiently narrow to be investigated empirically. • Experimental variables are clearly defined and appropriate controls are used. • Data are well organized and accurate graphs are shown. • Data collected serve as adequate evidence to support the conclusions formed.
Thoroughness	• The project shows thorough planning. • Review of background information is thorough. • All data are accurate. • All data collected were used in drawing conclusions. • A project notebook sufficiently documents the student's work from beginning to end.
Skill	• The project clearly represents the student's work. • The project is sturdy and well constructed. • The student clearly understands the equipment used. • The project shows continual attention to safety standards.
Clarity	• The student kept and displayed an original, bound logbook. • The project report was well done and easily understandable, with appropriate documentation. • The project display was eye-appealing, with appropriate materials, posters, charts, and graphs. • Lettering, signs, and diagrams are neat and accurate. • Visual aids assist the reader or judge in understanding the project.

Figure 6-21 Science fair judging criteria.
Source: Multiple science fair judging sheets found on the Internet.

In carrying out experimental investigations, students must perform a test to answer their research questions. If they are interested in earthworms, for example, they might perform a test to see if temperature has an effect on how earthworms move. Students would have to get some earthworms, find a way to vary the temperature of the soil in the earthworm container, and measure what happens, related to earthworm movement, at different temperatures.

The question or hypothesis, background information, experiment design, and results might be recorded in a bound notebook. The data collected would be used as evidence to answer the question posed. Students would need to carry out the project with only a little help from parents, teachers, or friends.

The project should be clearly and dramatically displayed, perhaps using show boards. Finally, the students would explain the project in detail through an interview with a judge or team of judges.

For elementary and middle school students, downplay the competitive nature of projects. The goal is for students to improve in their abilities and understanding of science, not necessarily to "win." Thus, you should use the project assessment formatively to improve student learning, rather than summatively for grades. Science fair projects are fun. Students will learn a great deal, and they will display to others what students know and have learned.

Examples of Traditional Assessment Items

Traditional assessment items are useful for assessing students' knowledge, understanding, and abilities to inquire. They have the advantage that they are quicker to construct, administer, and score than performance assessments.

Assessing Science Knowledge with Traditional Items

Traditional multiple-choice, short-answer, completion, and essay items can be useful and effective for assessing science knowledge, understanding, and abilities.

Multiple-Choice Items. You will probably use multiple-choice items frequently in your assessment program to measure the attainment of science knowledge. Multiple-choice items have three parts:

* *Stem:* presents the task or question to your students
* *Distractors:* incorrect responses
* *Correct response*

Item 1. Goal: Students should know that

* water circulates through the atmosphere in what is known as the *water cycle*.

Which of the following is *not* a form of precipitation?
A. hail
B. wind
C. rain
D. snow

Source: 2000 National Assessment of Educational Progress (NAEP), fourth-grade level.

Go to the Homework and Exercises section in Chapter 6 of MyEducationLab and view the video *Science Fair Projects*. In this video clip, students explain projects they have planned and carried out. Through student discussions of their projects, such as Cleaning Golf Balls, Amount of Water Held by Different Kinds of Diapers, and Electrical Conductors, teachers have an opportunity to assess how well students understand and are able to use the tasks of inquiry emphasized earlier in the text (Figure 1-3).

A number of items in this section are from released tests from the National Assessment of Educational Progress (NAEP), a government-sponsored program. Access more NAEP released tests items at http://nces.ed.gov/nationsreportcard/ITMRLS/searchresults.asp.

Item 2. Goal: Students should know that

* the earth is the third planet from the sun in a system that includes the moon, the sun, and the planets.

The moon is
A. always closer to the sun than it is to the earth.
B. always much closer to the earth than it is to the sun.
C. about the same distance from the sun as it is from the earth.
D. sometimes closer to the sun than it is to the earth and sometimes closer to the earth than it is to the sun.

Reference: Stahly, Krockover, & Shepardson (1999).

Item 3. Goal: Students should develop knowledge of scientific inquiry.

Which task would you undertake first in scientific inquiry?
A. collect relevant data
B. ask a question that can be investigated
C. report your investigation and findings to others
D. use data in forming explanations

Source: Released test item from National Assessment of Educational Progress (NAEP), fourth-grade level.

Completion and Short-Answer Items. Short-answer and completion items require students to generate, not just recognize, correct answers, as is shown in the following example. Note that item 4 is a modification of item 1.

Item 4. Name three forms of precipitation.

_____

_____

_____

Score all assessments as quickly as possible, give feedback to students on their results, and use the assessment results to provide feedback to learners and to modify your own instruction to improve student learning.

Assessing Science Understanding with Traditional Items

Traditional assessments can be used to go beyond simple recall to assess student understanding of science concepts and principles. Standard multiple-choice items and justified multiple-choice items can be designed that require students to integrate information and to use knowledge in thinking and problem solving.

Using Standard Multiple-Choice Items to Assess Understanding. Here is an example of a multiple-choice item that measures understanding rather than mere recall.

Item 5. Goal: Students should understand that

* energy is a property of many substances and is associated with heat, light, electricity, mechanical motion, sound, nuclei, and the nature of a chemical.

Go to the Homework and Exercises section in Chapter 6 of MyEducationLab, and select the artifact *Rocks* (6–8) to see an item assessing students' knowledge of the rock cycle. In the item, nine stages of the rock cycle are given out of order. Students are asked to number the stages 1 to 9 to indicate the order in which they occur.

Beans and coal both have stored energy. Where did the energy come from that is stored in beans and coal?

    A. from the earth's gravity
    B. from the sun's light
    C. from the heat in the earth's core
    D. from the airs in carbon dioxide

Source: 2000 National Assessment of Educational Progress (NAEP), fourth-grade level.

This item assesses understanding because it requires students to think about two different examples of stored energy and then to examine each possible source of energy to find one that fits both samples. The item was designed by the NAEP (National Assessment of Educational Progress) project to be used on a national assessment, but it can be used formatively if teachers score it quickly, give immediate feedback, provide opportunity for students to learn from their mistakes, and use the assessment results to modify instruction.

Assessing Understanding with Justified Multiple-Choice Items. In justified multiple-choice questions, students first mark the best answer and then explain in several sentences why they chose that answer. A rubric might be used to assess students' explanations of their answers. An example of a justified multiple-choice item is shown in Figure 6-22.

Figure 6-22 Justified multiple-choice assessment.

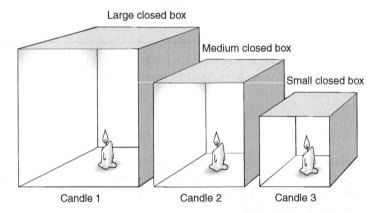

Directions

Three candles, exactly the same size, were put in different boxes like those in the drawing below and lit at the same time. Then the boxes were closed.

Large closed box

Medium closed box

Small closed box

Candle 1   Candle 2   Candle 3

Circle the letter that shows the order in which the candle flames most likely will go out.

    A. 1, 2, 3   C. 3, 1, 2
    B. 2, 3, 1   D. 3, 2, 1

Explain (in two or three sentences) why you think the answer you selected is correct.

Assessing Understanding from Written Responses. Essays, which involve written responses, represent an important way for students to demonstrate understanding. Through an essay, a student might interpret data, describe and explain an event, or show relationships among facts, generalizations, definitions, values, and skills. Like all assessment devices, the written response or essay has disadvantages as well as advantages:

1. Written response (essays) show how well the student is able to organize and present ideas, but scoring may be subjective without firm answers unless you have a clear scoring guide.
2. Written responses show varying degrees of correctness, because there is often not just one right or wrong answer, but scoring requires excessive time.
3. Written responses assess abilities to analyze problems using pertinent information and to arrive at generalizations or conclusions, but scoring is influenced by spelling, handwriting, sentence structure, and other extraneous items.
4. Written responses assess deeper meanings, reasoning, and interrelationships rather than isolated bits of factual materials, but questions may be either ambiguous or obvious unless you carefully construct them.

To offset the disadvantages of essays, you must carefully construct each essay question. Word the question so students will be limited, as much as possible, to the concepts being tested.

Item 6. Goal: Students should develop

- abilities necessary to do scientific inquiry (NSES K–4, 5–8).

A science fair judge asks you, "What is a controlled investigation?" Write out your answer.

_____

_____

_____

Scoring criteria for item 6: The student's answer must show clearly that

- a responding variable and manipulated variable are selected;
- what is investigated is how the responding variable changes in response to changes in a manipulated variable; and
- all other variables are controlled or held constant.

From these three scoring criteria, the teacher might develop a rubric to use as a scoring guide. The rubric would show the quality of the responses relative to each criterion necessary for the student to receive full, partial, or no credit.

Here are two related essay questions to assess your students' ability to interpret scientific concepts in their own words. Item 7 calls for an explanation of a physical phenomenon. Item 8 requires students to describe a test of the explanation given in item 7.

Item 7. Goal: Students should understand that

- unbalanced forces will cause changes in the speed or direction of an object's motion (NSES 5–8).

In the floating and sinking of golf balls task, explain why one golf ball floated and one sank in fresh water.

_____

_____

Items 7 and 8 would fit a fourth- or fifth-grade lesson on floating and sinking similar to the one developed in Chapter 5.

Item 8. How could you test your explanation?

_____

_____

_____

The following set of related items shows written response questions used with an investigation. Items 9 and 10 ask students to interpret data from an investigation. Item 11 requires students to apply the concepts and relationships from items 9 and 10 in a novel situation.

Items 9, 10, and 11. Goals:

   a. Students should understand that energy is transferred in many ways (NSES 5–8).
   b. Students should develop abilities necessary to do scientific inquiry (NSES K–4, 5–8).

One hot, sunny day Sally left two buckets of water out in the sun. The two buckets were the same except that one was black and the other was white. She made certain that there was the same amount of water in each bucket. She carefully measured the temperature of the water in both buckets at the beginning and end of the day. The following pictures show what Sally found.

Look at the pictures of Sally's experiment.

Before sitting
in the sun

After sitting
in the sun

Item 9. What can Sally conclude from her experiment?

_____

_____

Item 10. What is the evidence for Sally's conclusion?

_____

_____

Item 11. How does the experiment help explain why people often choose to wear white clothes in hot weather?

_____

_____

Source: Adapted from released test items, National Assessment of Educational Progress, grade 4, 2000.

Figure 6-23 NAEP scoring guide for essay item 11.

Score and Description

Complete
Student explains that white clothes reflect more heat from the sun than black clothes, or that black clothes absorb more heat from the sun than white clothes.
  a. Black clothes soak up the heat from the sun.
  b. The sun's rays bounce off white clothes.

Partial Student explains that black clothes attract more heat or that white clothes do not attract as much heat.

Unsatisfactory/Incorrect
Student provides little or no explanation that is related to the heat-absorbing properties of dark-colored clothes and light-colored clothes, or gives unrelated answers.
  a. They stay cooler in white clothes.
  b. The sun likes dark clothes better.

You will be able to overcome or minimize subjectivity in scoring answers to written questions by preparing a rubric beforehand and scoring each question separately. If a list of the important ideas you expect is made before scoring, there is less chance for ambiguity while scoring. This list can be developed with your students or at least shared with them when they get the assignment.

Figure 6-23 shows the scoring guide used by NAEP to evaluate responses to item 11. This item proved to be quite difficult for the national sample of fourth-grade students who took the NAEP tests. Only 12% of the national sample wrote complete explanations and 15% supplied partial explanations, while 73% gave unsatisfactory, incorrect, or off-task answers.

Assessing the Application of Science Processes and Inquiry Procedures with Traditional Items

Adding traditional items to your plan for assessing the application of science processes and inquiry procedures can help to achieve balance in assessment. Such items are often easy to construct, are quick to score, and can provide the basis for immediate feedback for the improvement of learning.

Assessing Investigative Procedures with Justified Multiple-Choice Items. Ability to apply scientific procedures can be assessed with standard multiple-choice items, especially if they are combined with essays as is shown in the following examples.

Item 12. Goal: Students should develop abilities to do scientific inquiry.

John cuts grass for several different neighbors. Each week he makes the rounds with his lawn mower. The grass is usually different in the lawns. It is tall in some lawns, but not in others. Which of the following is a suitable hypothesis he could investigate related to this situation?
    A. Lawn mowing is more difficult when the weather is warm.
    B. The amount of fertilizer a lawn receives is important.
    C. Lawns that receive more water have longer grass.
    D. The more hills there are in a lawn, the harder it is to cut.

Item 13. Explain in a few sentences why you think your answer choice in item 12 is better than the other choices.

Complete answers to item 13 should note that

- the variable of interest (responding variable) in the item stem is *length of grass;*
- length of grass is a variable only in answer choice C; and
- answer choice C implies a hypothesis/question that can be investigated: *What effect does the amount of watering have on grass length?*

Items 14, 15, and 16. Goal: Students should develop abilities necessary to do scientific inquiry (NSES K–4, 5–8).

Context: Shannon decided to compare different kinds of popcorn to find out which was the best buy. She bought three kinds of popcorn: regular white popcorn, regular yellow popcorn, and gourmet yellow popcorn. She put 50 kernels of each kind in the popper. She kept the popper running for each batch until the popcorn stopped popping. Then she counted the number of kernels of each kind that popped. She repeated the procedure two more times and averaged the results for each kind of popcorn. Next, she put 25 popped kernels of each kind into a measuring cup to find out which kernels popped the biggest. Then she tasted some of each kind of popcorn. Her results are shown in the following chart.

Kind of popcorn	Average number of kernels that popped	Volume of 25 popped kernels	Price for a 16-ounce bag	Shannon's taste test
Regular white	38	60 ml	$1.19	OK
Regular yellow	46	60 ml	$1.19	BEST
Gourmet yellow	45	80 ml	$1.50	OK

Item 14. Shannon's brother looked at her results and decided that the gourmet popcorn was the best buy. What evidence from the chart supports his decision?
A. There is no evidence from the chart to support his decision.
B. More of the gourmet popcorn popped.
C. There is more popcorn in the bag of gourmet popcorn.
D. The gourmet popcorn kernels popped the biggest.

Item 15. If Shannon's brother repeated the popcorn test, which results would have the greatest probability of being different for the new test?
A. the average number of kernels that popped
B. the volume of 25 popped kernels
C. the price for a 16-ounce bag
D. the results of the taste test

Item 16. Shannon decided that the regular yellow popcorn was the best popcorn to buy. Identify two pieces of evidence from the chart that support her decision.

_____

_____

Scoring guide for item 16:

2 points for two acceptable reasons

1 point for one acceptable reason

0 points for no acceptable reasons

Acceptable reasons include:
- Yellow popcorn had the largest number of popped kernels (46 out of 50 popped).
- Yellow popcorn had the best taste.
- Yellow popcorn is one of the cheaper kinds/is cheap.

Source: Adapted from released test items from the National Assessment of Educational Progress (NAEP), fourth-grade level.

Assessing Application of Scientific Procedures with Essay Items.

Item 17. Goal: Students should develop
- abilities of technological design (NSES 5–8).
- understanding that perfectly designed solutions do not exist; all technological solutions have trade-offs, such as safety, cost, efficiency, and appearance (NSES 5–8).

We have just come back from a field trip to our city's landfill. We were told that there was too much trash being discarded and placed in the landfill. How would you gather information about the amount of different types of trash coming from your school cafeteria? Gather the information and use it to set up a trash management and reduction plan for your school cafeteria.

In developing a scoring guide for this assessment, analyze the problem situation, planning techniques, and communication skills to identify specific things you think should be evident in the students' answers, such as ideas about reducing, reusing, and recycling waste. Use either a rubric or a checklist to guide you in scoring the answers.

What are some topics of interest to you, your students, and the community that might lend themselves to this type of assessment?

Characteristics of Items on State Tests of Science

According to the NCLB legislation, all states had to begin administering statewide assessments in science at the elementary, middle school, and high school levels by the 2007–2008 school year. Although they are ultimately based on similar standards, tests of science differ widely from state to state. It is hardly possible to generalize from such an array of tests and items. State education agencies and local school districts typically provide in-service workshops to familiarize teachers with the tests designed for use in their states. Additionally, many states release test items from previous tests to assist teachers as they work with students to improve performance on the tests.

State assessments of science are designed, administered, and scored outside the specific context of classrooms. Results of these assessments are typically not available to teachers until near the end of the school year. Thus, statewide tests of science learning do not typically provide formative information to be used immediately in improving science learning and instruction. Nor are the statewide tests suitable as summative assessments to determine overall levels of understanding at the end of instruction. Rather, as emphasized in Table 6-1, state measures of student understanding and performance are intended to

provide a basis for policy makers to judge accountability and formulate new regulations. Statewide tests have standardized administration procedures and ways of using assessment results to reliably and fairly judge the levels of understanding of students.

At the elementary and middle school levels, statewide tests are typically administered at grades 4 or 5 and at grade 8. However, helping students prepare for these high-stakes assessments is an imporant task at every grade level, not just the grade at whch the tests are administered.

One of the first steps in understanding test items used for statewide assessment is to examine the specific standards on which they are based.

Science Standards and Statewide Tests

According to Wilson and Berthenthal (2006):

> Standards are the most important element in the science education system because they make explicit the goals around which the system is organized. . . . They guide the development of curriculum, and the choices of teachers in setting instructional priorities and planning lessons. They are the basis for developing assessments, setting performance standards, and judging student and school performance. (p. 54)

As you read the following standards and examine the test items, take some time to complete Activity 6-1.

Activity 6-1: Matching Science Standards and Test Items

Directions

1. Examine the following sample state standards. Note that the standards include *indicators*. These are the evaluation criteria that teachers will use along with standards in lesson planning and test developers will use in writing tests.
2. Examine each of the first four sample test items. Determine which standard each test item is designed to assess.

Sample State Standards

Standard 1. Ask questions that can be investigated scientifically.

Sample Indicators

a. The student identifies appropriate questions that can be answered through scientific evidence and knowledge.
b. The student recognizes the question being investigated by observing the investigation procedures.

Standard 2. Design and conduct a scientific investigation to collect and interpret data about a question.

Sample Indicators

a. The student compares strategies or methods for collecting data.
b. The student selects appropriate method or strategy to collect data.
c. The student determines if an investigation strategy fits the question asked.
d. The student identifies and demonstrates appropriate steps to collect data.
e. The student interprets data collected in an investigation.

Standard 3.   Use appropriate tools and techniques to make observations and gather data.

Sample Indicators

   a. Student uses tools (e.g., hand lens, camera) to extend the senses.
   b. Student accurately uses different measuring instruments, such as rulers, balance scales, graduated cylinders, and thermometers, to collect data.

Standard 4.   Investigate and understand natural phenomena commonly encountered in daily life, including phenomena related to light, heat, sound, electricity, magnetism, life science processes, and earth and space science concepts and models.

Sample Indicators

   a. The student investigates and understands that natural and artificial magnets have certain characteristics and attract specific types of metals.
   b. Student understands that the sun supplies heat and light to the earth and the moon.

Item ST-1

The following chart shows the results of an experiment designed to study how exercise affects heart rate.

Activity Stage	Heart Rate of Person A (Beats per minute)	Heart Rate of Person B (Beats per minute)	Heart Rate of Person C (Beats per minute)
Before Exercise	75	62	70
After Exercise	100	110	130

Which of these statements is the best conclusion for this experiment?

A. Exercise triples a person's heart rate.
B. Exercise decreases a person's heart rate.
C. Heart rate is not affected by exercise.
D. Heart rate is increased by exercise.

Source: Released test item, California Standards Test, grade 5.

Item ST-2

Which of the following systems breaks food into nutrients that can be used by the body?

A. circulatory system
B. digestive system
C. respiratory system
D. reproductive system

Source: Released test item, California Standards Test, grade 5.

Item ST-3

Julie conducted an investigation about seed germination. She kept one group of seeds in a light place. She placed another group of seeds of the same kind in a dark environment.

She kept the seeds moist and observed them for five days. What question was she investigating?

    A. Will seeds germinate in the dark?
    B. Do seeds need soil for germination?
    C. Will seeds germinate better with more moisture?
    D. Do seeds need air for germination?

Source: Constructed by the authors.

You might want to check your answers to the standards-items matches against ours. Our answers are:

    Standard 1 – Item ST-3
    Standard 2 – Item ST-1, Item ST-4
    Standard 3 – Item ST-4

Items often assess more than one standard, so that matching standards and items is not an easy task; you may have good reasons for matching them differently than we have.

Examples of Different Types of State Test Items

Test items on state assessments typically include stand-alone multiple-choice items, items requiring written responses, and clusters of items based on a given scenario.

Stand-Alone Test Items. Many released test items are stand alone, multiple-choice items.

Item ST-4

Which best describes a parallel circuit?

    A. Electricity flows along one pathway.
    B. The flow of electricity comes from one source.
    C. Electricity flows along more than one pathway.
    D. The flow of electricity comes from more than one source.

Source: Released test items for grade 5, 2003–2006, California Board of Education.

Item ST-5

Which of the following is the **BEST** way to investigate the effect of fertilizers on tomato plants?

    A. Put several plants outdoors and several indoors.
    B. Add fertilizer to several plants and change the amount of water given to each.
    C. Grow several plants under the same conditions, but change the amount of fertilizer added to each.
    D. Grow several plants under various temperature conditions, but keep the amount of fertilizer the same for each.

Source: Released test item from California.

Item ST-6

After a rainstorm, Jolanda saw a lot of soil on the sidewalks. Sidewalks next to grassy areas stayed much cleaner. Sidewalks next to areas without grass were covered with soil. Jolanda hypothesized that grass would help protect soil from being washed away. In the classroom, she set up two boxes. She placed grass sod in one box with its roots in the soil. She placed only soil in the second box. Following are some steps (scrambled) that Jolanda carried out.

 A. Tilt the boxes the same amount.
 B. Draw conclusions from her data.
 C. Add moisture to the soil.
 D. Observe and measure the amount of erosion of soil in each box.

What should be the order of steps in this investigation?

 A. a, c, d, b
 B. b, c, a, d
 C. c, d, b, a
 D. d, b, c, a

Source: Adapted from a series of released test items from the Washington State Assessment Program, 2006.

Items Requiring Written Responses. States also include many written response items in which students might write descriptions and explanations or plan investigations to answer questions. Detailed rubrics are typically provided to facilitate and standardize scoring.

Item ST-7

While observing birds in the neighborhood, James noticed that the birds pecking in the grassy areas had different beaks than the birds feeding at the bird feeder in a tree. Explain why birds have different beaks.
 In your description, be sure to:

- Identify **two** different types of bird beaks.
- Describe **why** birds need these different types of beaks.

Use words, labeled pictures, and/or labeled diagrams in your answer.

(Source: Based on released test item from the Washington State Assessment Program, 2006.

Clusters of Related Test Items. Some states use clusters of items related to a scenario. Both multiple-choice and written responses are used with the clusters.

Information for Items ST- 8-12

Jose and Maria noticed the grass in one part of the yard was growing better than in other areas. They thought this happened because parts of the yard received more light than other parts. They did the following investigation with *grass sod* (a layer of grass with its roots in soil).

Hypothesis:
Grass that receives more light will grow taller.

Materials:

grass sod cut into three equal pieces
meter stick
water
200 ml beaker
three trays of the same size
three grow lights connected to timers

Procedure:

1. Set the three pieces of grass sod into the three trays and put the trays in a dark place with the lights above them.
2. Measure the average height of the grass in each tray and record as starting heights.
3. Set the timers to turn the lights on daily: one light for 2 hours, one light for 6 hours, and one light for 12 hours.
4. Water each tray with 200 ml of water every 4 days.
5. Measure the average height of the grass at the end of each week.
6. Record the average heights in the data table for 3 weeks.

Item ST-8

What question were Jose and Maria asking in their investigation?

  A. How does the amount of light affect the color of grass?
  B. How does the amount of light affect the thickness of grass?
  C. How does the amount of light affect the height of grass?

Item ST-9

Why is soil important to the plant in Jose and Maria's investigation?

  A. The soil prevents dust from getting to the leaves.
  B. The soil provides support and nutrients for the grass.
  C. The soil provides a place for insects and worms to live.

Item ST-10

Which variable did Jose and Maria change (manipulate) in their investigation?

  A. The amount of light
  B. The amount of water
  C. The amount of grass sod

Item ST-11

Name **two** needs besides sunlight that Jose and Maria must provide for the grass so that it can grow healthy and tall. Explain why grass needs these things.

Item ST-12

Jose and Maria noticed that three different types of soil—black soil, sand, and clay—were found in their neighborhood. They decided to investigate the question, "How does the type of soil (black soil, sand, and clay) under grass sod affect the height of grass?"

Plan an investigation that could answer their new question.

In your plan, be sure to include:

* Hypothesis about the outcome of the investigation
* Materials needed to do the investigation
* Procedure that describes:
  * logical steps to do the investigation
  * the variables kept the same (controlled variables)
  * the variable that was changed (manipulated variable)
  * the variable that responds to the changes (responding variable)
  * any variables being measured, and recorded
  * how often measurements are taken and recorded

Source: Items 8–12 are from 2004 test items released by Washington State.

Using Released Tests to Help Students Prepare for State Tests

Preparing students for tests at a specific grade level, say fifth grade, is a responsibility of K–5 teachers, not just fifth-grade teachers. An examination of the sample items given shows that items measuring inquiry procedures also measure conceptual knowledge and understanding. Thus, science lessons from the earliest grades should be designed to build conceptual knowledge and understanding as well as inquiry procedures.

A group of teachers from the same district might work together to study items released from their own state tests. The information gained through this process can then be used to plan instruction.

Released test items from your own or other states can be directly used to help your students prepare for future statewide tests. One way to use the items is to break the test up into four- or five-item mini-tests, and administer the mini-tests to your students periodically (only after the concepts or inquiry abilities to be assessed have been taught and mastery expected). Have your students complete the mini-tests individually and turn in their answer sheets to you. Students keep a copy of their answer sheets. While you score answer sheets, students should work together in small groups to develop a "key" for the test. Record student scores on the mini-tests. Ask them to keep a copy of their answer sheets and compare their answers with yours. When students have developed answer keys that are satisfactory to them, go over the items one by one with them. Through this procedure, students have an opportunity to receive immediate feedback on their work, to think through their answers more completely, to learn from one another, and to better prepare for the high-stakes statewide examinations.

Effective assessments in science require thorough planning, skillful execution, and careful, constant review and modification. Learning to use assessment effectively will help you become a better teacher and your students better learners. It is clearly worth the effort.

SUMMARY

• Various principles form the foundation for assessment; they critically affect the *what, how,* and *how well* of your science teaching/learning. Assessments can be *diagnostic* (before starting teaching), *summative* (after teaching), and *formative* (during teaching).

• Assessment is focused on two questions: *Where are learners going?* and *Where are they now?* In answer to the first question, local, state, and national standards define the science facts, concepts, and principles, and the inquiry processes and procedures students should know, understand, and be able to apply. A wide variety of traditional assessment items and performance assessment tasks can be used to determine where learners are now. The results of assessments can then guide teachers as they work with individual students to help them reach learning goals.

• Authentic performance assessments are particularly relevant for inquiry science. Performance assessment tasks are authentic whenever they simulate tasks that scientists, students, or other citizens might be called on to perform in real-world contexts. Developing performance assessment tasks involves determining the focus, context, directions, and scoring guides for the tasks. Types of scoring guides discussed included holistic scoring guides, checklists, and rubrics. Rubrics are particularly important in performance assessment. Keep these things in mind as you write your own rubrics:

  • Set clear assessment standards to interpret the specifics of your students' work.
  • Determine levels of rubric scoring—often on a four-point scale—that are applicable to the unique scientific processes, skills, content, and attitudes you are assessing.

• A large bank of traditional items, performance assessment tasks and techniques, checklists, and rubrics have been provided as resources for you to draw on in developing your own assessment program.

• Assessment is a critical component of inquiry learning and instruction. The assessment revolution is here to stay.

ONLINE PROFESSIONAL DEVELOPMENT

Pre- and post-tests to assess your knowledge of chapter content, along with exercises to enhance your understanding, can be found on MyEducationLab at www.myeducationlab.com.

Video Guides

The video clip on MyEducationLab selected for this chapter is *Science Fair Projects.*

Accessing the Video

1. Go to the Homework and Exercises section in Chapter 6 of MyEducationLab to select and view videos for this chapter.
2. The video might be viewed individually, by small groups of colleagues, or by the whole class.
3. As you watch the video, use the **Questions for Reflection** to guide your thoughts and note taking for personal use and group discussion.
4. Discuss your answers to the questions about the video with classmates.

Video: Science Fair Projects

Overview

In this video excerpt, we watch as students explain projects they have planned and carried out. Through student discussions of science fair projects, such as Cleaning Golf Balls, Amount of Water Held by Different Kinds of Diapers, and Electrical Conductors, teachers have an opportunity to assess how well students understand and are able to use the tasks of inquiry (Figure 1-3) emphasized earlier in the text.

Questions for Reflection

1. What examples of students asking questions and planning and conducting investigations do we see in the video?
2. What different kinds of records that students have made do we see in the video?
3. How do students communicate their investigations and results to teachers and others?
4. How could science fair projects be used for summative assessment?

Annenberg Videos

Video Series: Learning Science Through Inquiry
Video: Assessing Inquiry

To access Annenberg videos, follow the instructions given in the Online Professional Development section in Chapter 1 on page 26.

7

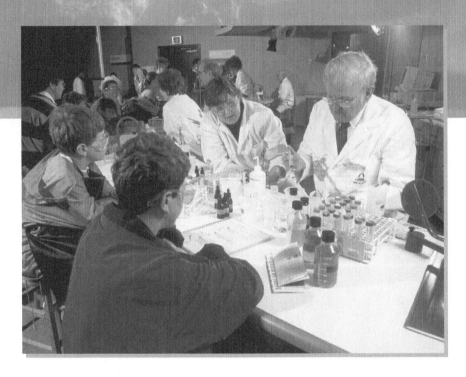

T*eachers' questions are crucial in helping students make connections and learn important mathematics and science concepts. Effective questioning—the kind that monitors students' understanding of new ideas and encourages students to think more deeply—was relatively rare in the mathematics and science classes we observed. . . . Unfortunately, teachers more often used low-level, "fill in the blank" questions asked in rapid-fire fashion with an emphasis on getting the right answer and moving on rather than helping students make sense of the concepts.*

(Weiss and Pasley, 2004, pp. 24–25)

Effective Questioning

ASKING THE RIGHT QUESTION is at the heart of doing science. It is also at the heart of learning and teaching science as inquiry. Science teachers who use inquiry methods ask questions to focus investigations, probe prior knowledge, stimulate reflective thinking, shift the focus from observation to explanation, encourage creativity, and develop student understanding.

Just as important as asking the right question at the right time is the way you respond to and promote student discourse. *Discourse*—expressing one's own questions, observations, and meaning making and listening to and reflecting on the ideas of others—is a normal part of science. It is also an essential part of children's inquiry. Making meaning from investigations and experience requires that you guide student dialogue, encouraging your students to make connections, draw conclusions, and ask new questions.

Does the way you respond to students open a discussion up, or does it close it down? Do your responses acknowledge student ideas, probe for deeper understanding, and serve to scaffold inquiry?

This chapter is intended to provide some guidelines as you use questioning strategically, respond to student ideas, and promote understanding.

Here are some questions to guide you as you study the chapter:

- *What is meant by open-ended and closed questions, and what are their functions in teaching science?*

- *How can you help children formulate productive questions to initiate investigation?*

- *What types of questions can teachers ask to facilitate children's inquiry and promote understanding?*

- *How can you respond to children to promote deeper thinking and improved science learning?*

Questioning: An Essential Tool for Teachers

Questions are among the most important tools teachers have. Teachers use questions for many purposes: to manage classroom activities, discourage inattentiveness, and cut down on disruptive behavior; to initiate inquiry; to guide student organization of data; and to encourage students to reflect on their data and use it as evidence in constructing explanations.

Go to the Homework and Exercises section in Chapter 7 of MyEducationLab and select the article, "What Is High Quality Instruction?" In this interesting article, Weiss and Pasley (2004) observed and analyzed 364 science and mathematics lessons to assess the quality of science and math instruction in schools. Factors that distinguished more effective lessons related to student engagement with content, culture conducive to learning, equal access by all students, effective questioning, scaffolding assistance to help students make sense of content, and teacher decision making.

Teachers' questions are widely accepted as crucial in helping students make connections and learn important science concepts. However, as is indicated in the chapter-opening quote, in a series of classrooms observations of science teachers' questionng behavior, Weiss and Pasley (2004) found that effective questioning was relatively rare. Teachers must learn to use questions strategically and be committed to using strategic questioning.

Strategic questioning involves selecting and using specific types of questions with well-defined functions. A specific questioning skill, such as asking open-ended questions, is like a tool used by a master carpenter. Tools have unique purposes. Carpenters use different tools to drive a nail, cut a board, or square off the end of a piece of lumber. The master carpenter plans ahead by keeping a well-stocked toolbox and becoming proficient in using each tool. Similarly, master teachers need different questioning tools for specific educational tasks, such as setting the cognitive level of inquiry, promoting discussion by class members, stimulating deeper thought on the part of students, and building meaningful explanations that connect investigative evidence to what students already know. Teachers, like carpenters, need well-honed tools that they know when and how to use.

Closed and Open-Ended Questions

One important tool in your questioning toolbox is the skill of knowing how and when to ask open-ended and closed questions. Both types of questions are important for assessing prior knowledge and promoting new learning, but in very different ways. A **closed question** has a single correct answer, while **open-ended questions** can be answered in a number of ways (Texas A&M Center for Mathematics and Science Education, 2005, 2006).

Closed questions require students to think *convergently*—that is, to focus on a single fact, define a particular term, or attend to specific objects or specific aspects of events. Children's responses to closed questions help you assess their factual recall and observation skills and allow you to adjust your teaching accordingly.

In contrast, open-ended questions enable all students to make useful contributions to a discussion. Open-ended questions require children to engage broad portions of their schemas. They also trigger *divergent* thinking. In thinking divergently, children consider a wide array of possibilities.

Figure 7-1 provides a series of closed and open-ended questions about a pictorial riddle. The closed questions in Figure 7-1 focus on specific observations and recall of prior knowledge and experience. The open-ended questions are broader questions that can engage students reflectively and build toward understanding.

In typical classrooms in every subject, the large majority of teachers' questions are closed, calling for factual knowledge and convergent thinking. Research indicates that even a slight increase in the percentage of open-ended questions by teachers yields a significant increase in divergent productivity by students; that is, a larger number of students respond, and their responses are more thoughtful and exhibit higher levels of thinking. These types of responses, in turn, stimulate further discussion among students (Carin & Sund, 1978).

Students learn from teachers how to ask good questions. If teachers' questions are open-ended, with no one right answer, students can learn to ask open-ended questions. Teachers should ask and encourage questions such as *What would happen if . . . ?* , *What will happen next?*, and *Why did that happen?*

In the following sections we describe some questioning strategies for inquiry discussions.

A glossary containing definitions of important terms used in this chapter can be found on MyEducationLab.

Questioning to Guide Inquiry Discussions

Duschl and colleagues (2007) described a *formative assessment scaffolding* "feedback loop" proposed by Furtak and Ruiz-Primo (2005). In this loop:

1. Teachers ask questions to elicit levels of student understanding.
2. Students respond to the questions orally, in writing, or through diagrams and drawings.
3. Teachers recognize and acknowledge student responses.
4. Teachers provide scaffolds to improve learning and understanding.

According to Duschl et al. (2007), when the strategies of formative assessment and scaffolding are applied together, continuous improvement in student understanding, as well as modifications in teaching approaches, can be achieved.

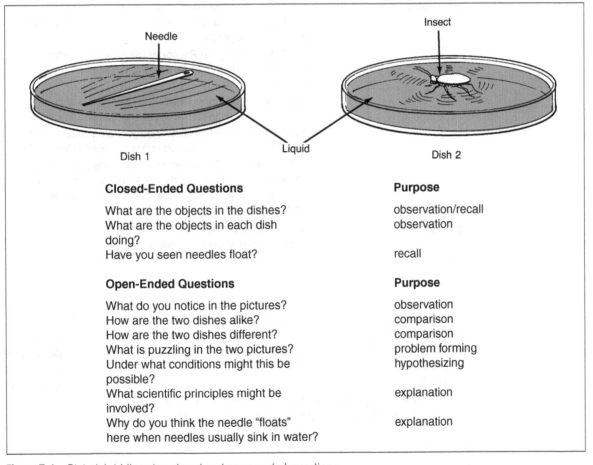

Figure 7-1   Pictorial riddle using closed and open-ended questions.

TABLE 7-1 TEACHER QUESTIONS FOR GUIDING SCIENCE DISCUSSIONS

Phases of 5-E Model	Descriptions and Purpose of Question
1.1 Engage	**1.1.1. Building Intrinsic Interest.** Ask questions to focus thought on puzzling events and to build intrinsic motivation.
	1.1.2. Prior Knowledge. Ask questions to assess students' prior knowledge and conceptions.
	1.1.3. Focusing Questions. Ask questions to initiate and focus inquiry.
1.2 Explore	**1.2.1. Observing.** Ask questions to focus students' thoughts on investigations, observations, and data.
	1.2.2. Reflecting on Data. Ask questions to guide students in reflecting on data.
	1.2.3. Patterns and Relationships. Ask questions that require students to identify patterns and relationships in their data.
1.3 Explain	**1.3.1. Student Theories.** Ask questions that invite students to offer their theories and explanations of why an event took place.
	1.3.2. Reflecting on Personal Ideas. Ask questions that encourage students to examine and reflect on their theories.
	1.3.3. Scientific Knowledge. Ask questions that invite students to relate evidence to prior and existing knowledge.
	1.3.4. Developing New Knowledge. Ask questions that prepare the way for instruction on new scientific knowledge.
	1.3.5. Scientific Explanations. Ask questions that guide students to build on their theories, use prior and new knowledge, and construct new scientific explanations that relate to observational evidence.
1.4 Elaborate	**1.4.1. Apply.** Ask questions that require students to apply new knowledge in new situations.

Tables 7-1 and 7-2 provide a strategy for such a formative assessment scaffolding loop. Table 7-1 focuses on asking questions strategically. The strategy follows the 5-E model of instruction. It involves asking questions that can initiate inquiry discussion (engage), guiding discussions of information and data obtained through observation and experiments (explore), assisting students to make the transition from observaton to explanation (explain), and applying new ideas in new situations (elaborate).

Consider first how to use questioning to engage students in inquiry.

1.1. Engage: Using Questioning to Initiate Inquiry

In science inquiry, we want students to be intrinsically motivated to pursue a learning task and to engage in it for intrinsic reasons, rather than because of grades or teacher approval. Nothing creates intrinsic motivation in students more than presenting them with novel events.

Novel or discrepant events, such as the ones presented in Chapter 5, can be presented through hands-on student investigations or through a teacher demonstration using science materials. If time and resources are constrained, you could show a film segment or use a pictorial riddle instead.

Here is an example of a discrepant event that might build interest and initiate inquiry about the earth's magnetic field.

Place a needle on a styrofoam chip floating in a container of water. What do you see happening? (Nothing special.) Stroke the needle several times in one direction with a bar magnet. Lay the needle on the styrofoam chip again. Regardless of how you orient the needle, it always swings around and points in the same direction.

Ask, *What do you see happening?*

After a discussion of what is observed, refocus the discussion on what was puzzling here. Ask, *What is unexpected or puzzling in the event observed?*

If you had appropriate prior experiences and scientific knowledge about magnetism, you might have inferred that the needle was not initially a magnet. (*What observations support this inference?*) However, stroking it with a bar magnet served to magnetize the needle. When the magnetized needle was placed on the styrofoam chip, it swung around until it was oriented along the direction of the earth's magnetic field. The needle pointed along a magnetic north-south direction.

Demonstrating discrepant events is certainly a good way to arouse curiosity and promote interest in the topic you plan for them to investigate.

For students to construct understanding of a discrepant event, they must have relevant prior knowledge. To help your students build and strengthen their scientific concepts, you must be aware of what they know or do not know at the start of any study. You might assess children's prior knowledge by simply asking them what they already know about a topic. However, discrepant events, such as the magnetized needle demonstration, provide a natural context for you to discover what they already know.

In the needle demonstration, children display their prior knowledge of magnetism as they talk about the event and respond to your questions:

- What is happening to the needle?
- What have you seen that is like this?
- What is puzzling here? What needs explaining?
- What might cause the needle to point in a particular direction?

When building toward understanding of descrepant events, students are called on to observe objects and events, form a question about why something happens, and recall relevant knowledge to be used in explaining the event. As children conduct an investigation or watch a demonstration, they typically talk about what they observe and think. By listening and interacting with the students, you will be better able to assess their prior knowledge and conceptions.

When students are ready, ask questions or lead them to ask questions to initiate and focus inquiry. Of course, the questions asked should be ones that students are able to investigate through their own inquiries.

In Chapter 1, we discussed and gave examples of a variety of kinds of investigation questions that can initiate and focus inquiry.

1.2. Explore: Using Questioning to Guide Discussions of Observations

One way children seek answers to their questions is through using the senses or instruments that extend the senses to observe what happens in an investigation or demonstration activity.

Through questioning, students try to infer the contents of the mystery box.

Observing what happens familiarizes children with the natural world and provides evidence for understanding it.

An important key to inquiry teaching is to lead children to think about their observations. You can guide children in thinking about their observations through the questions you ask. In general, observation questions should be open-ended. An open-ended question such as *What are some of the things you noticed during the demonstration?* allows many students to contribute useful information during inquiry.

When working with small groups or the class as a whole, do not seek closure on a question until a number of responses have accumulated. Such a strategy not only gives more students a chance to enter into the discussion but also ensures that all students will have a variety of descriptive information from which to later build explanations. Observational information from students might be recorded on the chalkboard or through electronic media.

When getting responses from several students on the same question, it is generally not necessary to repeat or rephrase the question. After one student has supplied an answer, you may redirect the question to another student by asking a question such as, *Juan, would you like to add anything else?*

Following are some suggestions you might follow and some sample questions you might ask or train students to ask to focus their attention on observing and describing.

A. If you seek descriptions of objects in a discrepant event or investigation, ask such questions as:
   • *What objects were involved in the investigation (demonstration)?*
B. If you seek *descriptions of events* in an investigation or demonstration, ask such questions as:
   • *What did you do?* (or, *What did I do?*)
   • *What happened in the experiment (demonstration)?*
   • *What are some of the changes you noticed in the . . . ?*
   • *What did you see that surprised you?* (that you liked? that startled you?)

By focusing on the aspect of an event that is puzzling, the last question begins to lay the groundwork for explanations.

Often discussion about observations occurs when children report their observations and data to the class. When groups report, train them to consider two kinds of questions about observational information (Rowe, 1973, p. 347):

- *What was observed?*
- *In what sequence did events happen?*

Then, ask students to compare their observations:

- *Were the observations of all groups the same? Are the reported sequences the same? How are they alike? How are the observations different?*

Differences among groups in reports of what they observed or the sequence of events observed can lead to disagreements. To resolve these disagreements, students must think more carefully about their data and sometimes repeat an activity. If students are unclear about what happened in an investigation, they will not have adequate evidence for constructing explanations for why it happened.

If the observations reported by groups represent numerical data and you want children to make and compare measurements (quantitative observations), you might ask:

- *Which of the reported measurements is highest? Which is lowest?*
- *Why do you think there is variation (differences) in the class's measurements?*

Discussing differences in the data reported by groups gives you an opportunity to discuss the nature of science with your students. According to the *Benchmarks for Science Literacy* (American Association for the Advancement of Science, 1993, pp. 6, 10), by the end of second grade, students should know that

- science investigations generally work the same way in different places; and
- when people give different descriptions of the same thing, it is usually a good idea to make some fresh observations instead of just arguing who is right.

Sometimes you want children to compare measurements and notice changes that occurred:

- *What changes in the temperature of the water did you notice?*

It is important that children spend considerable time at the *observation* level before beginning to search for problem *explanations*. Unless sufficient time is spent in developing an adequate foundation at the lower cognitive level, students are often not able to sustain discussion at higher levels of thought.

Go to the Homework and Exercises section in Chapter 7 of MyEducationLab to read the article "Helping Students Ask the Right Questions" by Richetti and Sheerin. They have developed a questioning strategy to help students integrate their thinking and produce a logical, well-considered conclusion or point of view that builds on previous thinking.

1.3. Explain: Using Questioning to Guide Discussions of Explanations

At some point in the discussion, you should shift the thinking of students from *observation* to *explanation*. Explaining is the counterpart of observing. In observing, students are directly involved with objects and events. Explanations require students to go beyond observations, to reason about their experiences, and to make up and test interpretations of them. Careful observations determine *what* happens. Explanation is concerned with *why* it happened.

When you are ready to shift instruction from an observation or exploration phase to explanation, let children help you decide which aspects of an investigation might need explaining. Find out what *they* want to know about the results of an investigation or why a puzzling event occurred. List the children's questions where they can see and think about them. Make sure that all children have a chance to frame their own questions.

In leading students to identify problems, you might ask:

* What do you think needs explaining here?
* What surprised you?
* What is most puzzling to you?

When attempting to focus thought on interpreting and explaining, a good approach is to start with the simpler problems that have been identified, gradually gather interpretative ideas, and build toward the more difficult problems.

The transition from observation to explanation can be a difficult process for students. One of your jobs in inquiry teaching is to facilitate the process of *making meaning* from data. To facilitate the meaning-making process, you might begin by asking students, *Do you notice any pattern in your data (in your moon observations)?*

At some point, you will want to shift the thinking of students to making sense of the data and patterns in the data. You might begin to facilitate the process of explaining by asking: *What ideas do you have about why this happened?*

The *National Science Education Standards* (National Research Council, 1996, p. 145) emphasize that in constructing explanations, students must think critically about evidence, considering which of their observations constitute evidence and which are irrelevant. They must also have adequate subject matter knowledge. Finally, they must be able to link their evidence with their knowledge in a reasonable way to explain why something happened.

Learners in grades K–2 observe the world using all of their senses and offer their theories about why an event happened. Typically, grade 1 and 2 learners do not construct consistent explanations of events in the world. It is not until late second grade or third or fourth grade that children begin to distinguish between observations and interpretations (or inferences) and to construct simple explanations involving effects and their causes. Complex explanations involving chains of causes and effects are not formed until about grades 5 or 6. Yet learners at every grade level can profit from considering why an event happened and how the world works.

A first step in developing explanations is for students to organize their data or observations in some way. To *organize* means to fit individual parts into a whole. Discussion of data and organization might take place as groups build data tables or report their findings to the class or perhaps in a whole class discussion.

Research suggests that understanding is enhanced when students actively integrate information in various ways. To help students see their data holistically rather than as fragmented parts, teachers might ask them to

* describe to others what they did and what they found out,
* summarize their data,
* organize their data/information into tables and graphs,
* elaborate information by adding details,
* generate relationships between the new material and information already in memory, and
* recognize patterns in observational data.

For example, in developing ideas about relationships, ask such questions as:

* *How is this situation like (different from) the other one?*
* *What similarities (differences) do you see in these situations?*

Viewing data holistically is not enough, however. According to Duschl and colleagues (2007), research evidence indicates that children and adolescents had particular problems in coordinating evidence and theories. Through strategic use of questions, science teachers can help children reflect on and represent evidence more completely, think at deeper levels, and connect evidence and knowledge more logically in explaining events in the natural world.

Students may need considerable scaffolding assistance in accessing prior knowledge to make sense of observations. Sometimes, as is emphasized in the 5-E model of instruction, relevant scientific knowledge must be taught to students.

Here are some sample questions that focus on accessing knowledge and constructing explanation.

A. If you seek suggestions about scientific knowledge that might be involved in an explanation, ask such questions as:
- *What principles that we have learned do you think may come into play here?*
- *What do we already know that might help us here?*
- *What principles (rules, laws, concepts) do you think are needed in solving this problem?*
- *How do you think that the principles of floating and sinking apply to this problem?*

B. If you seek ideas about the possible cause of an event, ask questions such as:
- *Why do you think the raisins sank (the puzzling event happened)?*
- *What ideas do you have about why this happened?*
- *What suggestions (theories) do you have about the cause of this?*
- *Can you explain why it might have happened?*
- *What do you think is the cause of . . . ?*

Questions that focus on interpretation and explanation should be open-ended and divergent and should be pursued for a sufficient time to get responses from several students. This strategy helps to ensure that ideas and explanations at a variety of levels of abstractness are at hand for students of different abilities to consider.

Note the use of the personal pronoun *you* in the examples of explanation questions. Framing questions in this way helps to make them more open-ended, allowing children to respond at their own level of thought. An explanation question such as *What ideas do you have about why . . . ?* (rather than *Why did this happen?*) focuses more on the act of thinking than on correct answers. This questioning approach frees children from the burden of knowing in advance why something took place. It encourages them to think about possible reasons for the cause of a puzzling event and to offer suggestions or theories to build on. Their initial responses need not be absolutely correct. The teacher, through sensitive listening, careful and caring questioning, and appropriate scaffolding, can help the class as a whole formulate a satisfying response that is age and grade level appropriate. Practical experience demonstrates that children can learn to go beyond their observations and construct scientific explanations for why things happen.

"We really want children to be explorers and investigators and we want them to try to dictate for themselves what is the problem they should be exploring and what ways they are going to go about exploring that problem."

Dr. Thomas M. Dana, Pennsylvania State University, Annenberg Video Case Study, Erien (Year One) (Annenberg Foundation, 1997)

1.4. Elaborate: Questioning to Guide Discussions of Applications to New Situations

In building understanding, children need opportunities to apply or transfer new knowledge and understanding in many problem-solving situations (Bransford, Brown, & Cocking, 1999). Problems can be generated in various ways. For example, you may plan the problem situations, or they may arise from students' creative ideas and interests. As they work on fresh problems, students try out their recently learned ideas by transferring them to the new situations, thereby refining and extending their developing understanding. In a 5-E model of instruction, the elaborate (application) phase of a lesson allows students to make new connections and construct more useful schemas from the knowledge they gained in previous activities.

To elicit thinking about how new knowledge and understanding might be extended to different phenomena, ask such questions as:

* *How do you think . . . applies to . . . ?*
* *In what ways does this idea compare/contrast with . . . ?*
* *How can we use this principle to explain . . . ?*
* *What new problems does this suggest?*
* *What might happen if . . . ?*

Especially good problems for the elaborate phase can be found from applications of science in technology. Application opens up the opportunity for students to explore the natural and technological world more deeply and to realize how extensively science and technology affect people.

In an Annenberg video entitled *Case Studies in Science Education: Greg,* Greg challenged his sixth-grade students to design and constuct a bridge that was tall enough for a radio-controlled car to pass under it and sturdy enough for the car to ascend to the top of the bridge and cross over on it.

In constructing their bridges, the students followed the design cycle. As a test of their bridges, the class watched as each group successfully passed the robot car under the bridges. However, in all cases, the approach to the bridge was too steep for the robot cart to climb. By applying what they had learned previously about inclined planes, the student groups decided they needed longer approaches to the bridges that were not too steep for the robot car.

Next we look at how teachers use strategic responding to encourage and guide discourse.

You can find the video *Case Studies in Science Education: Greg* on the Annenberg website. Instructions for accessing this website are provided in the Online Professional Development section of Chapter 1.

Responding to Student Ideas

By responding strategically, teachers encourage critical discourse and communication of procedures, data, and explanations. Instructional research indicates that student growth is influenced by teacher actions that involve students in the development and extension of ideas (King, 1994).

There are three main ways you can respond strategically to nurture and extend children's ideas during inquiry. You can *accept* or recognize student responses without judging them; you can *extend* student responses by adding something new to what was said; and you can *probe* student responses by asking questions based on their responses. Extending and probing represent two different ways to scaffold student understanding. Table 7-2 shows what is involved in applying these three teacher responses strategically. (Note that Table 7-2 extends the taxonomic numbering system of Table 7-1.)

2.1. Accept Student Responses

Your inquiry teaching repertoire should incorporate an attitude of initial *acceptance* of student ideas, even when they contain errors, mistakes, and alternative conceptions. Students should feel that they have the "right to be wrong." Because the very process of inquiry involves the challenge of trying the unknown, it necessarily must result in mistakes. The need to be always right, whether imposed by teachers, peers, or self, is a limiting and threatening position. Teachers have a major responsibility to help students explore new experi-

TABLE 7-2 TEACHER RESPONSES THAT ACCEPT, EXTEND, AND PROBE STUDENT IDEAS

Teaching Purpose	Description of Response
2.1 Accepting	**To accept student responses, teachers:** **2.1.1. Acknowledge.** Teacher statements or actions that acknowledge or recognize student responses. **2.1.2. Reinforce.** Teacher statements that reinforce or praise student responses. **2.1.3. Repeat.** Teacher statements that repeat, restate, or paraphrase student responses.
2.2 Extending	**To extend student responses, teachers:** **2.2.1. Build on Student Ideas.** Teacher statements that add to and build on student ideas. **2.2.2. Compare Ideas of Students.** Teacher statements that compare and contrast student responses. **2.2.3. Apply Student Ideas.** Teacher statements that apply or relate student ideas to explanations or problem solving. **2.2.4. Summarize Student Responses.** Teacher statements that summarize or review what a student or class has arrived at so far through thinking and discussion.
2.3 Probing	**Teacher questions that ask students to:** **2.3.1. Build on Ideas.** Ask questions that call for students to build on and follow up on their own and other students' ideas. **2.3.2. Clarify.** Teacher questions that call for students to clarify or explain their ideas. **2.3.3. Justify.** Teacher questions that ask students to justify or give reasons for their ideas. **2.3.4. Verify.** Teacher questions that ask students to test their ideas or to give evidence to support their ideas.

ences and new meanings without penalizing the mistakes and wrong turns that are certain to accompany the process of inquiring. By accepting children's ideas without initially judging or evaluating them, the teacher helps establish a climate in which students feel they can risk their ideas.

Teachers can show acceptance of student ideas by acknowledging, repeating, and reinforcing them. When *acknowledging,* you should refrain from evaluating students' responses. This leaves the door open for further discussion. For example:

- *OK.*
- *All right.*
- *Let's list your idea on the board.*
- *Let's keep your idea in mind.*

You might also use nonverbal behaviors such as a nod to tell students that their responses have been heard and accepted.

Simply repeating a student idea is another way to acknowledge and accept it. You can show that you accept a student's idea by repeating it almost verbatim or by paraphrasing the idea, without changing or adding to it significantly. For example:

Student: Maybe it's the air leaking.
Teacher: OK. You think it may be the air leaking. (Repeating); or,
Teacher: OK. You think the bubbles may be caused by escaping air. (Paraphrasing)

Blosser (1991) cautioned against the overreliance on repeating student responses. If students know you are going to repeat responses, they may tend not to listen to one another but wait for your repetition. If you think the whole class has not heard a response, you might say something like:

Teacher: That's an interesting idea. I don't think the whole class heard it, though. Would you say it again so everybody can hear?

Another type of accepting behavior is *reinforcing* student ideas. It is an established principle of behavioral psychology that a person's tendency to display an action is dependent on events that follow the action (Ormrod, 2004). These special events are called *reinforcements*. In order to encourage student participation in discussion, a teacher may need to reinforce the act of responding. Teachers may also wish to reinforce both good thinking and good ideas.

One way of reinforcing student responses is with praise. For example:

- *Good!*
- *Fine!*
- *Excellent!*

A stronger way of reinforcing children's responses is through praise followed by an explanation of the reason for the praise:

- *Great! I like the way you are contributing.*
- *Good job! Your idea is particularly good because it relates your theory to your observations.*
- *Fine! I like the way you compared your idea to Celeste's idea.*

Praise is important, but it should not be given in such a way that students think the idea praised is the only possible one. Other children might thus give up on their own lines of thought. Even when the idea you are seeking is voiced by a student, reinforce the child but let the class know there is more to be done. For example,

Teacher: Great thinking! Your idea is one we will have to consider. (Then, to the class) What other ideas do you have on why this happened?

Reinforcement is more effective if it follows an unpredictable schedule. If students can predict that the teacher will say "very good" after every response, this form of praise loses its effectiveness. For best results, the teacher should vary the type of reinforcements.

Reinforcement is, of course, more than a matter of what the teacher says. Both research and practice show that students are less inhibited about making responses and show more productivity and achievement when their teachers tend to be approving, to provide emotional support, to express sympathetic attitudes, and to accept their feelings.

2.2. Extend Student Responses

When students give vague, incomplete, unorganized, or partially correct responses or when they are on the right track but need assistance, the teacher may act to nurture and extend their ideas. Perhaps the best reinforcement for students comes when they see their own ideas used by the teacher. Several techniques for extending student responses are described next.

To help move the discussion along it is sometimes appropriate to focus on an idea suggested by one or more students and to build on it. For example.

- *All right! I believe we are on the right track here. We might also consider what we learned last week in science. Remember . . .*

To help clarify a student idea, a teacher may restate the idea in simpler terms, reorganize the idea, or perhaps summarize it. For example, suppose a student has given an unclear and unorganized response. The teacher may reply:

- *In other words, the air takes up more space when heated.*
- *If I understand you correctly, you are saying that the air takes up more space when it is heated.*

When two or more students make suggestions that have significant similarities or differences, the teacher may wish to extend the ideas by comparing or contrasting them:

- *Your idea is similar to Jamal's in that . . .*
- *Notice the difference in Kenesha's suggestion and Sean's suggestion. Kenesha said the wire would expand when it was heated; Sean said it would expand when it cooled. Both are good suggestions. How could we test these two hypotheses?*

There is uncertainty among teachers about how to handle incorrect ideas and misconceptions held by students. On the one hand, a student who is told that his idea is all wrong may be reluctant to participate in discussions again. On the other hand, misconceptions left unchallenged can cause confusion and interfere with understanding. Teachers need tactful ways of helping students confront and change wrong notions. One possibility is to plan lessons to lead students to challenge their own misconceptions, as is illustrated in Chapter 3 with the moon-watching lesson.

Sometimes a teacher wishes to directly correct an incorrect notion and move on. In that case, the teacher might determine if part of the student's answer is correct and reinforce this part. For example:

Teacher: *Yes, heat does play a part in the expansion of the copper rod, but melting does not take place. Remember, in melting, the solid rod would become a liquid. Can you make another suggestion?*

Applying an idea suggested by a student in building an explanation is an excellent method of extending student ideas. However, teachers should be careful not to shift from extending student ideas to simply giving the desired information through lecture.

To move the inquiry along, occasionally summarize the group's discussion and assess the various suggestions. This will not only extend students' ideas but also promote further inquiry. When the concepts involved are abstract or vague, when there are many responses, when student answers have been lengthy, or when some investigations have taken a great deal of time, you might briefly summarize what has been said or identify and restate the main ideas discussed.

2.3. Probe Student Responses

After a student has contributed an idea to a discussion, the teacher may attempt to produce greater critical awareness by *probing*. Probing is a strategy in which the teacher reacts to student responses by asking penetrating questions that require students to go beyond superficial, first-answer responses.

Probing differs from extending. In *extending,* the teacher does the clarifying, comparing, and contrasting of student ideas; in *probing,* the teacher asks students to look deeper at their own ideas or those of others. Let's consider a variety of probing techniques.

A good way to probe student ideas is to ask questions that build on those ideas. Here the teacher builds on a student response by asking a question based on it. For example:

- *You have said that the bubbles are caused by escaping air. What do you think happens to the air pressure in the tube when some of the air escapes?*

A teacher may probe students' responses by asking them to clarify the response by giving more information, explaining a term used, or restating the response in other words. For example:

- *What do you mean by melting?*
- *Was the wicked witch who claimed "I'm melting . . ." actually melting, or was she dissolving? What do you think?*
- *How could you restate that to make clearer what you mean?*
- *How could you explain that further?*
- *What do you mean by the term . . . ?*

The following interaction illustrates the clarification technique:

Teacher: What do you think is the relationship between the pressure of the air and its volume?
Student: The pressure got more and the gas condensed?
Teacher: What do you mean by condensed? (Or) How would you restate that in terms of volume?

You can also probe to seek justification of student ideas. In asking a student to justify a response rationally, you might say:

- *What are you assuming here?*
- *Why do you think that is so?*
- *I'm not sure I follow your reasoning. Tell us how you arrived at that answer.*
- *What evidence supports your idea?*

Sometimes you might probe by asking students how they would test and verify ideas or confirm a theory. For example, you may say:

- *You have suggested that the heaping effect might involve both adhesive and cohesive forces. Can you think of a way to test your idea?*
- *What would you do to test your idea?*
- *What would it take for that to be true?*
- *What evidence (additional information, data) would we need to support your explanation (suggestion)?*
- *What experiment could we do to test your idea?*

Go to the Homework and Exercises section in Chapter 7 of MyEducationLab to watch the video *Properties of Air in First Grade Science,* excerpts from which appear on the next page. Spend some time watching and listening to this delightful example of first graders' ideas about air.

Questioning Strategies in the Classroom: Properties of Air in First Grade

In a video of first-grade science produced by Merrill Education, Ms. Newhall is preparing to teach her students that "air" is a real material substance. In front of her, she has a fish bowl about three-quarters full of water and a small, transparent glass. She plans to push the small glass, open-end down, all the way under the water, as in Figure 7-2, and asks the chil-

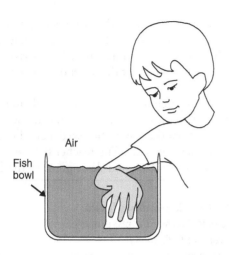

Figure 7-2 What happens when a glass is pushed open-end down into a container of water?

Air

Fish bowl

dren what they saw and why they think it happened. Before beginning the actual demonstration, Ms. Newhall questioned the children to ascertain their prior knowledge.

Teacher: I'm going to push this glass into the water until it is all the way under the water. What will happen? Terry, what do you think?
Terry: It's going to stay at the bottom . . . sink.

Ms. Newhall wanted the children to focus on the air and the water rather than the glass. So, with a nod acknowledging Terry's answer, she turned to another student who had her hand up.

Teacher: Samantha.
Samantha: Me and my dad took a glass into the pool one time. We put the glass under the water. We kept it straight, and if you keep it straight, no water will come in. The air will stay in there, but if you tip it up, the water will come in.
Teacher: Interesting.

Samantha's answer revealed that she had significant prior experience and knowledge about what would happen in the demonstration. Some of her knowledge came from personal discoveries. She had also acquired some knowledge from discussions with her father. Samantha used the term *air* appropriately, but Ms. Newhall was not sure what she really *understood* about the concept.

Ms. Newhall acknowledged Samantha's answer and filed it away for later use. But she wanted to know what the other children knew about air and what they thought would happen in the demonstration. So she turned to the class again.

Teacher: Is there anybody else who thinks if you put this whole glass under the water, nothing is going into the glass? What do you think, Michelle?
Michelle: Water may go in the glass.

After giving the rest of the class time to offer opinions, Ms. Newhall polled the students to see which of the two ideas they supported. There was about equal support for Samantha's idea that water would not come into the glass and Michelle's idea that the glass may fill up with water. Then the teacher continued with the demonstration.

Teacher: OK. We have two ideas. Let's test these ideas.

Ms. Newhall called on a student to help her with the demonstration. First, she asked the student to check to make sure the glass was dry. To encourage careful observation, she told the students to "watch with your eyes." Then she pushed the glass open end down all the way under the water. Most students noted that the water did not get into the glass, but one student was not sure.

Ms. Newhall then dried the glass carefully, took a paper towel, and crumpled it into the bottom of the dry glass. She pushed the glass with its open end down under the water again. When she removed the glass from the water, she asked a child to examine the paper towel, and the child observed that it was dry. The teacher then attempted to lift the children's thoughts from a level of observation and description to the higher cognitive level of explanation.

> Teacher: Why did it stay dry? What do you think, Jessica?
> Jessica: Because it was inside that glass and the rest is outside.
> Teacher: But what kept the water out? Anthony?
> Anthony: A water seal. It was pooled up. There was water on the bottom, but not on the inside.
> Teacher: But if there's all that water around the outside, why didn't it go in here (pointing to the inside of the glass)?
> Student: Because the air was in there.
> Teacher: The air. . . . Oh . . . Is that what kept the water out?

The initial answers to Ms. Newhall's question about why the paper towel stayed dry indicated that the children did not yet have a good understanding of air. Although they knew the term *air* and had connected it to some physical situations such as wind and breathing, they had difficulty applying the concept in interpreting the demonstration. When one child said that the air kept the water out, Ms. Newhall decided to extend Samantha's earlier contribution.

> Teacher: Samantha said something earlier. When she put the glass down straight, the glass stayed dry, but when she pushed it down and tipped it, the glass got wet.

Ms. Newhall then demonstrated that when she tilted the glass, bubbles came from the glass and rose in the water. She tried to get the children to describe the bubbles as bubbles of air. However, the children described the bubbles as "water bubbles" and in other ways, but no one used the term "air bubbles." So, the teacher attempted to extend the children's thinking by giving them a hint.

> Teacher: In the bottom half of the glass is water; in the top half of the glass is . . .
> Student: Dry.
> Teacher: What is in there?

No answers were forthcoming, so the teacher further extended the dialogue by giving an explanation.

> Teacher: When I tip it (a small amount), the water keeps the air in. When I tilt it far enough, the air can come out.

There is much for you to learn about questioning from the teacher in this lesson. She strategically used some exceptional science questioning techniques.

- First, she asked questions to ascertain the students' prior knowledge.
- Then, she asked observation questions to get the children to focus on what happened and to help them improve their observational skills.

- Only after sufficient evidence had been introduced into the discussion did she ask explanation questions, focusing on why the events happened.
- She did not immediately acknowledge that Samantha's initial answer was correct but kept the discussion open so that all children could enter in and possibly construct knowledge about air for themselves.
- Also, she asked her questions before calling on a student by name, thus helping to ensure that all students would have to listen to and think about their answers to the questions.
- She kept the discussion orderly, asking students to raise their hands when they wished to volunteer an answer.
- She called on a diversity of students, making sure she included both boys and girls and children of all ability levels.

Despite the teacher's use of model teaching techniques, the children had difficulty constructing notions about air and its properties that would be useful in *understanding* why the paper in the glass remained dry. That is, the children still had problems in *applying* their knowledge to *explain* or make sense of the demonstrations involving air.

From the perspective of child development theory presented in Chapter 3, most of these young students have simply not yet developed the conceptual structures and types of relational thinking that will support the construction of complex explanations. Nevertheless, through their discoveries and discussion, the children are building knowledge to apply in future knowledge construction experiences when they are more developmentally ready.

Some Considerations in Questioning

Through your questioning, your body language, your treatment of students, and your general demeanor, you are establishing the climate of your classroom. Here are some general considerations to think about as you guide students in questioning, listening to them, and responding.

Increase Your Wait-Time

Elementary and middle school teachers often feel pressured to cover everything in the few hours that students are in the classroom each day. So it is no surprise that teachers try to rush through many of the things they do, even question-and-answer times. Rowe (1973, 1987) found that most teachers usually wait less than a second for a response after asking a question! These very brief intervals, or **wait-times**, encourage rote, verbatim recall, usually of textbook or teacher-made information. In contrast, inquiry requires time for students to reflect, make connections, and construct inferences and explanations.

What differences in student responses do you think were found with longer teacher wait-times? Rowe found that when teachers waited 3 seconds or longer student responses included greater speculation, conversation, and argument than when wait-times were shorter. She also found that when teachers are trained to wait an average of more than 3 seconds before responding, the following positive student behaviors happen:

- The length of student response increases by 400 to 800%.
- The number of unsolicited but appropriate responses increases.
- Failure to respond decreases.
- Confidence increases.
- The number of questions asked by students increases.
- Academically challenged students contribute more.

- The variety of types of responses increases. There is more reacting to each other, structuring of procedures, and soliciting.
- Speculative thinking increases by as much as 700%.
- Discipline problems decrease.
- Achievement improves in cognitively complex items on written tests.

Rowe also found that teachers trained to prolong wait-time changed their teaching behavior in the following ways:

- The number of teacher questions decreased, because more students responded and the responses of students became longer.
- The number of teacher questions that called for reflection and clarification increased.
- Teacher expectations for student performance were modified. (Teachers were less likely to expect only the brighter students to reply and viewed their class as having fewer academically challenged students.)
- Teachers changed the direction of discussion from teacher-dominated to teacher-student discussion.

There are two types of wait-time. **Wait-time 1** is the pause that follows a question by the teacher. The students may answer quickly, but if they do not, the teacher waits. **Wait-time 2** is the pause that follows a burst of responses by the students. The teacher waits before responding or asking another question to see if the students will continue to talk.

Of the two, Rowe (1987) indicated that wait-time 2 is more important for a teacher to develop. She found an increase of 500 to 700% in student responses when teachers used it. Furthermore, the responses from the academically challenged students increased significantly when teachers increased their wait-time after student talk.

Instructors need to increase their wait-time tolerance so learners have more opportunities to think, create, and fully demonstrate their potential.

Gradually Fade Your Questioning Support

Teachers model, coach, and scaffold thinking behaviors through their questions. But gradually, students should come to ask self-regulatory questions themselves as teachers fade their support (Bransford et al., 1999). This approach highlights the importance of students' **metacognition** in planning, monitoring, and adjusting their own learning and inquiry behaviors. Thus, as teachers use questioning strategies, they are not just scaffolding student understanding, they are teaching students how to formulate productive inquiry questions for themselves.

Listen to One Another

Listening carefully and sensitively—not only to the answer but to the thinking behind the answer—provides you with much information about your students. The way teachers perceive their roles is undoubtedly related to their listening skills. If you see your function as mainly to develop or achieve some subject matter concept or principle, you naturally will focus on its achievement. However, if you perceive your role as helping students develop cognitively and construct their own concepts and understanding, you will tend to focus on the students, as well as on the students' thinking processes.

To help students make discoveries and use their own developing thought processes, listen intently to what they have to say. Formulate questions and responses only when they have finished. There is no substitute for a teacher who is primarily interested in people and really listens to them.

Try not to analyze, evaluate, or judge what students are saying until after they have completed their thoughts about the questions. Unfortunately, some teachers start to dissect what students say before they have had a chance to finish. Many students' ideas are good, but they suffer from poor verbalization. If you wait until students finish their answers before reacting, you will grasp their ideas better and be more likely to convey in nonverbal ways that you are sincerely interested in their ideas. If you are not clear about what the children are saying, you can engage them in discussion to clarify their meanings by asking a probing question.

Students often do not learn and achieve as well as they could because they have not developed their own listening skills. By modeling good listening yourself, you can help your students become better listeners.

Consider Cultural Implications of Your Questions

Because of students' diverse backgrounds, questions may take on different meanings for different students (Bransford et al., 1999). For example, research indicates that many African American parents engage in different patterns of questioning with their children than do their white counterparts. African American parents are likely to emphasize metaphorical questions ("What is that like?") rather than fact-gathering questions ("What is that?"). Thus, African American students may not understand the purposes of white teachers' inquiry questions. According to Bransford and colleagues (1999), the answer to cultural mismatch between schools and communities "is not to concentrate exclusively on changing children or changing schools, but to encourage adaptive flexibility in both directions" (p. 99).

Some Native American students are averse to responding when called on in class. It may be that they perceive the traditional classroom, where teachers control all activities and interactions, as very different from their community social events, where there are no clear leaders and no clear separation between performers and audience. These students usually perform better one-on-one with the teacher or in cooperative settings with small groups of classmates (Vasquez, 1990).

You must know your students well so that your manner of questioning and presentation does not conflict with their cultural backgrounds.

Remember, We All Need Strokes!

Research indicates that teachers should use praise judiciously when they guide discussions. Praise can provide a signal to students that their contributions to discussion are appropriate. But praise of one student's answer might also tend to stop discussion. Other students may think that the purpose of the inquiry discussion is to find the right answer, not to probe more deeply into nature. Students look to their teacher for guidance and approval.

However, it is important to recognize students during individual work and group work for specific things they have done well. Teachers who try to look for good in every student and who inform them specifically and privately about these things are effective. They also are more likely to enjoy teaching. It is possible to look for something good to say to each individual, when they come into class or in private discussions, for example. As Abraham Maslow indicated in his theory of human needs, we all need to be recognized as valuable persons so our self-concepts continue to grow positively (Maslow, 1987).

SUMMARY

* Questioning is at the heart of inquiry teaching. By questioning effectively, you can ascertain what students already know, guide them in establishing questions for inquiry and collecting relevant data, help them construct explanations, and lead them to apply their new knowledge in different situations.
* Open-ended questions are more likely to promote inquiry than closed questions.
* Questions can be used to assess the prior knowledge and conceptions of students. Questions can also be used to engage the interest and motivation of students, to guide them in exploring systems, and to lead them in building explanations. Questions are also important in leading students to apply what they are learning to new situations, including societal issues and concerns.
* How you respond to students' answers is important in ongoing inquiry discussion. To keep students involved, be accepting of all their (relevant) answers; to keep them on target and supply needed information, extend their answers by adding to them; to lead them to think about their own ideas more deeply, probe their responses by building additional questions on them.
* After asking a question and calling on a student, teachers often wait only a second or two for students to compose and state their answer. When teachers wait just a little longer, 3 seconds or more, students tend to think more deeply, give longer answers, provide a wider variety of answers, and respond to one another more often.
* Learning to use questions effectively and productively in inquiry teaching takes practice, feedback, and reflection. Keep honing your questioning and responding tools to better guide children's inquiry.

 ONLINE PROFESSIONAL DEVELOPMENT

Pre- and post-tests to assess your knowledge of chapter content, along with exercises to enhance your understanding, can be found on MyEducationLab at www.myeducationlab.com.

Video Guides

Video clips on MyEducationLab selected for this chapter include: *Effective Questioning* and *Investigating Recycling—Parts 1, 2,* and *3.*

Accessing the Videos

1. Go to the Homework and Exercises section in Chapter 7 of MyEducationLab to select and view videos for this chapter.
2. Videos might be viewed individually, by small groups of colleagues, or by the whole class.
3. As you watch each video, use the **Questions for Reflection** to guide your thoughts and note taking for personal use and group discussion.
4. Discuss your answers to the questions about each video with classmates.

Video: Effective Questioning

Overview

In this video we return to three lessons we saw previously: goldfish at kindergarten, water wheels at third grade, and moon phase observations at fifth grade. This time around, the focus is on how teachers use questions to guide children in engagement and exploration tasks.

Questions for Reflection

1. Open-ended questions invite students to think more deeply about observations, observation records, and activities. Do you think the teachers' questions are primarily open-ended or closed in these three lessons?
2. What questions did the teacher use to guide students in engagement and exploration in each of the three lessons?
3. How did the teacher respond to children's answers to her questions in the different lessons?

Video: Investigating Recycling—Parts 1, 2, and 3

Overview

In this video we see how a teacher uses questions with third graders in activities on recycling.

Questions for Reflection

1. How did the teacher use questions to engage students in this unit and guide them through it?
2. What did the teacher do to *redirect* questions from one student to other students?
3. What were some of the things the teacher did to *acknowledge* the children's responses to a question?
4. How did the teacher use questions to guide the activity on classifying the materials of the different packages?

8

N ew technological developments can help transform schools if these developments are used to support new models of teaching and learning, models that characterize sustained community-centered, constructivist classrooms for learner investigation, collaboration, and construction. The Internet and educational software can support a collaborative culture in "doing science."

(Ebenezer and Lau, 1999, p. 17)

Technology Tools
and Resources
for Inquiry Science

ADVANCES IN EDUCATIONAL TECHNOLOGY certainly have much to offer science students and teachers. The Internet offers a gold mine of opportunities for classroom use, such as pictures, videos, and animations to pique curiosity, online data sources, web-based lessons, and worldwide connectivity. Software, ranging from simple instructional programs to sophisticated interactive, multimedia learning environments, present endless possibilities for learning. Data sensors connected to your computer enable the collection of data about temperature, motion, light intensity, air pressure, and more that can be displayed in real time through tables or graphs. Application programs from desktop publishing to multimedia presentation packages enhance the art of communication. Spreadsheets and graphing software facilitate the organization and display of data. Digital cameras and image processing software expand opportunities for observations and measurements of scientific phenomena. These imaginative products of the information technology age provide innovative ways to expand the classroom walls to encompass the universe.

This chapter provides a framework and some suggestions for using technology tools and resources to support science teaching and learning. Because technology changes rapidly, however, you will need to continue to take advantage of professional development opportunities to keep up with the latest innovations.

As you study the chapter, consider these questions:

- *How does educational technology fit within the broader context of inquiry and constructivist learning of science?*

- *What Internet sites, telecommunications resources, commercial instructional software, and data collection and analysis tools are available to enhance the teaching and learning of inquiry science in your classroom?*

- *How should the hardware and software available in your classroom be managed?*

- *How can you stay on the cutting edge of learning technology throughout your teaching career?*

Are you prepared to use educational technology in the most effective way in your science instruction? This chapter will help you see possibilities of incorporating educational technology into hands-on, inquiry science programs in your classroom.

Educational Technology

Educational technology is a prime example of technology in general. As discussed in Chapter 1, technology refers to any process or product that has been invented to assist humans in adapting to their natural, constructed, and social environments. Technological advances have certainly changed the way people do science, handle personal affairs, and run businesses, and they have the potential to enhance the way schooling takes place.

Innovative technology can facilitate science teaching and learning. The technology shown here allows the teacher to place a slide on a microscope so the whole class can view it at once by video.

Content Standards

Children in grades K–4 should develop skills in the use of computers and calculators for conducting investigations (National Research Council, 1996, p. 122).

Students in grades 5–8 should be able to use computers to access, gather, store, retrieve, and organize data using hardware and software designed for these purposes (National Research Council, 1996, p. 145).

In 1999, the National Science Teachers Association adopted a position statement about the use of computers in science education. The position statement presents the following rationale:

> Just as computers play a central role in developing and applying scientific knowledge, they can also facilitate learning of science. . . . Computers have become an essential classroom tool for the acquisition, analysis, presentation, and communication of data in ways which allow students to become more active participants in research and learning. In the classroom the computer offers the teacher more flexibility in presentation, better management of instructional techniques, and easier record keeping. It offers students a very important resource for learning the concepts and processes of science through simulations, graphics, sound, data manipulation, and model building. . . .These capabilities can improve scientific learning and facilitate communication of ideas and concepts.

Using educational technology tools, such as the Internet, DVDs and CD-ROMs, data sensors, digital microscopes, and digital cameras, enables students to practice science and technology in ways similar to professionals in the field, leading to a deeper understanding of concepts and improved thinking and problem-solving capabilities (see Figure 8-1).

Let us examine in more detail how these technology tools and resources can enhance learning at the various phases of inquiry.

You can read the complete NSTA Position Statement on "The Use of Computers in Science Education" at http://www.nsta.org/about/positions.aspx.

The National Educational Technology Standards describe what it means for students and teachers to be technology literate. You can learn more about these standards at http://cnets.iste.org/. On the website, look especially at NETS-S: The Next Generation.

Technology Tools and Resources

The Internet
CD-ROMs
DVDs
Digital Images
Databases
Computer- or Calculator-Based
    Laboratory Systems
Virtual Field Trips
Simulations
Computer-Enhanced Instruction
Spreadsheets
Graphing Software
Presentation Software
Global Information Systems
Global Positioning Systems

Figure 8-1 Technology resources and tools for inquiry science.

The Internet as a Technology Resource for Inquiry Science

The Internet is an important resource for teaching and learning in all subject areas. It consists of a vast connection of computers that was initially developed for communication among scientists and now is used by businesses, governments, homes, and schools around the globe (Stull, 1998). If your computer is connected to the Internet, you can access and exchange information with millions of computers worldwide. The World Wide Web, which was developed in 1989, allows users to access text, visual images, video, and audio presentations. Web browsers, such as Internet Explorer and Safari, enable users to navigate along the electronic superhighways that crisscross the Internet.

Suppose you wish to find out what is available on the Internet about a specific topic. You can use a search engine, such as Google, to find hundreds of sites related to the topic. To use a search engine, type in a descriptor of the topic in the appropriate space and begin.

Following are some suggestions of Internet sources for science lessons and how to use them.

A glossary containing definitions of important terms used in this chapter can be found on MyEducationLab.

Use Internet Images to Engage Students in Inquiry into Volcanoes

The best way for elementary or middle school students to learn something is through first-hand experiences. However, this is not always practical, cost-effective, or safe. Simulating the experience by computer can be an effective substitute. Simulation follows the constructivist idea that learners construct their own unique concepts through active participation.

High-speed Internet access makes downloading of still and video images from the World Wide Web a practical approach to supplementing teaching with visual material. Picture yourself teaching elementary or middle school students about volcanic action. To engage students in the investigation of volcanoes, you would love to have them experience the sights, sounds, and other sensory aspects of these dramatic forces of nature. But how will you do that? Take them to a volcano? That is not practical for most of us, and it is potentially dangerous.

Fortunately, you can take students via the Internet to the sights and sounds of an erupting volcano. Go on the Internet to http://mam.ngdigitalmotion.com/SearchRes.aspx. This site, sponsored by *National Geographic,* shows actual motion picture footage of active volcanoes at different stages of eruption.

Using a search engine, you will be able to find many different pictures and videos of other exciting natural phenomena, including earthquakes, tornadoes, and hurricanes and exotic animals such as whales and sharks. By investing a little bit of time in Internet searches, you can enable your students to observe not just the immediate world around them, but exciting things that happen far away in both distance and time.

Use Archived Data on Whale Movements in 5-E Lessons

Whales never cease to fascinate children and adults alike. Judith Hodge (n.d.) writes:

> Whales are monarchs among the animals of the ocean. They are some of the most enormous—and most intellgent—animals on earth. The blue whale, for example, is the largest animal that has ever lived. Full grown, it can be nearly one hundred feet long and weigh one hundred and fifty tons.

Although they live in the oceans, whales are not fishes. They are mammals, like humans. As mammals, whales must come to the surface to take in air, they are warm-blooded, and they give birth to their young.

Due to the whaling industry in the 19th and early 20th centuries, whales of virtually all species are scarce today (Hodge, 1997). For example, there are fewer than 300 right whales living today. Right whales inhabit the Atlantic Ocean along the eastern seaboard of the United States. Despite their great size, right whales are very slow swimmers, averaging less than 4 miles per hour. Consequently they are often hit by boats and become entangled in fishing gear.

Preserving whales from danger and extinction is a global problem. One way to preserve right whales is to warn fishermen and boat captains when right whales are likely to be in their area. Thus, scientists are intent on finding patterns in the movements of right whales. By tagging several right whales with radio transmitters, marine biologists can collect data on the movement of these whales.

The following 5-E lesson is designed to introduce students to the right whale named *Metompkin* and to find patterns in Metompkin's movements.

An Internet-Based Lesson Plan on Right Whales

* Access the Internet and go to: http://whale.wheelock.edu/whalenet-stuff/metompkin. html.
* There you will find the exciting story called *Metompkin: Entangled and Heading for Home*. To engage students in the plight of Metompkin, read this brief story aloud.
* Ask: *Why would scientists want to attach a radio tag to Metompkin? Why would they wish to use the radio tag to track her movements?*
* Ask your class: *What questions might you ask about the pattern of Metompkin's movements?* Here are some suggested questions about Metompkin's movements that students might investigate:
  1. How far does Metompkin travel in a day? (Average)
  2. How far did Metompkin travel between Jan. 6, 1996, and March 10, 1996?
  3. Why do you think Metompkin is traveling from a south to north direction?
  4. Why do whales migrate?
  5. What is Metompkin's average rate of travel per hour? Per day?

* Ask: *What data would you need to collect to answer your selected question?*
* Show students the resources on the website so they are able to use the map of Metompkin's route north. The map is at http://whale.wheelock.edu/whalenet-stuff/ images/GOES_map6.GIF.
* Allow the students to work in small groups to use the Metompkin data and map to collect data to answer the questions they are investigating.

Use the data the students bring from the explore phase of the lesson, the WhaleNet site, and other Internet sites to answer these questions:

* Why was Metompkin in the coastal waters off of Florida in January 1996?
* Does Metompkin tend to move day after day in one main direction? Why do you think this is so?
* What do you think Metompkin did in April and May 1996? Why do you think this is so?

Engage

An Annenberg video entitled *The Journey North* is available for viewing on the Internet. The video documents and explains the movement of different animal species from south to north. To access the Annenberg Internet site and this video, follow the instructions given in the Online Professional Development section in Chapter 1.

Explore

Explain

Elaborate

Use the WhaleNet site and other related sites to answer these additional questions:

- What is a whale? How large are whales? What are some varieties of whales? Are whales fish or mammals?
- What are the distinguishing characteristics of right whales? How many of these endangered right whales are there now in the Atlantic?

Explore Space Through the Internet

To see a collection of space–science related games, projects, animations, and amazing facts, visit The Space Place (http://spaceplace.jpl.nasa.gov/do.htm). There you will find a variety of memory and matching games, puzzles of images, crosswords, word finds, and so on. Go to Space Place Live to hear what NASA scientists say about their jobs, how they became scientists, and what they do from day to day. Participate in the Space Place Quiz Show and assess your own knowledge of space.

Earth Observing 1 (EO-1 for short) is a satellite with some great instruments for taking images and gathering other information about Earth. It can take such a clear picture you can make out an airplane sitting on a runway from 430 miles away! Satellite data can help scientists and others understand and deal with all sorts of problems, such as

Volcanoes
Earthquakes
Floods
Droughts
Forest fires
Forest diseases
Erosion of beaches
Melting of polar ice sheets
Oil spills
Planning cities
Farming (agriculture)
Making maps

The possibilities for data taking to support investigations are almost limitless.

Come to Space Place and check out the games, animations, projects, and fun facts and images about Earth, space, and technology. The site is maintained by NASA.

Take a Virtual Field Trip

Consider what you do when you organize a traditional field trip. You pick a location, plan the day's schedule, and guide the group from one spot to the next (Dockterman, 1997). You are creating an educational experience that supports your curriculum objectives and classroom activities. On a real field trip—whether to a local pond, aquarium, wetlands area, museum, zoo, planetarium, or any one of dozens of other exciting places—students experience new things and relate the experiences to concepts previously encountered in the classroom. Taking an electronic field trip can offer many of the same advantages as real field trips. Additionally, virtual field trips can enhance students' skills in using word processors, spreadsheets, databases, presentation programs, and the Internet (Bitner, Wadlington, Austin, Partridge, & Bitner, 1999).

Visit Science Exhibits Online

The Internet provides opportunities for children to take virtual field trips to museums, zoos, or science centers without ever leaving the classroom (Ebenezer & Lau, 1999). For example, visit the Exploratorium, a San Francisco–based interactive science museum, at http://www.exploratorium.edu. An "exhibit cam" captures live views of Exploratorium visitors interacting with featured exhibits in the hall. The "roof cam" provides real-time images of the surrounding area, and you can select the direction it points. It is almost like being there. Additionally, "on-line exhibits" featuring optical illusions let students try out some of the museum's exhibits through interactions with their computer.

To find current links to virtual field trips on the Internet, just search for "virtual field trips" using Google or another search engine. You will discover many sites that provide links to places to visit.

Take a Factory Tour via the Internet

How Everyday Things Are Made, published online by Alliance for Innovative Manufacturing (AIM) in cooperation with Stanford University, provides links to narrative video clips and collections of still images of manufacturing processes ranging from the production of airplanes and golf clubs to jellybeans and denim (http://manufacturing.Stanford.edu/). The links on this page can take you to forty different virtual factory tours. Students interested in engineering and how familiar products are made will be impressed with the diversity of products included. Those with a sweet tooth will be satisfied, too, since eight of the links are to candy factories.

Successful electronic field trips that support your curriculum need to be well planned (Dockterman, 1997). You can choose what your students will visit and what you expect them to learn, or you can let your students plan their own pathways through the software. Alternatively, you can let the Internet serve as a guide through the virtual landscape.

Use Commercially Available Multimedia Packages to Enhance Science Inquiry

CD-ROMs and DVDs can provide some of the same types of sensory experiences found on the Internet. A single CD can store more than 600 MB of data, the equivalent of about 250,000 pages of text or 20,000 images.

CD-ROMs embellish science teaching and learning by dispensing instant individual illustrations and sound for hard-to-grasp material. They invite creativity for teachers and students. Best of all, they are easy to use. It is little wonder they are among the most popular teaching and learning technologies. For example, to use CD-ROMs to explain the concept of phototropism, select time-lapse shots and slides of plants growing toward the light to make the learning more dramatic and meaningful. These technological tools allow you to pause at critical points, show entire sequences in slow motion, speed up action that is very slow, and review important concepts quickly and easily.

CD-ROMs provide a library of images and text for students as they research, study, and present reports. Your students can use the materials stored on CD-ROMs just as they would an encyclopedia. When they are ready to present their reports, they can display pertinent images to dramatically illustrate their understanding.

Many computers also have DVD (digital video disk) drives allowing direct access to digital information stored on this even more powerful medium. DVD players can be connected to a television to enable viewing of a DVD without a computer. DVDs enable students and teachers to use menus to quickly select certain topics or segments of the presentation to view.

Computer simulations have great potential as a teaching tool. NSTA's position statement about the use of computers in science education states,

> Simulation software should provide opportunities to explore concepts and methods which are not readily accessible in the laboratory, e.g., those that require: expensive or unavailable materials or equipment; hazardous materials or procedures; levels of skills not yet achieved by the students; and more time than is possible or appropriate in a real-time classroom.

Simulated activities that are difficult or impossible to do in your classroom include visits to the planets of our solar system, investigations of ocean wave properties, studies of population growth of various organisms in an ecosystem, dissections, and monitoring of the inheritance of traits. Students enjoy engaging with the colorful, animated displays. While engaging with colorful, animated displays, students are placed in a situation where they control an environment by interacting with the computer. They collect data, correlate results, and learn skills, attitudes, and concepts. Your job is to help your students understand the relationship of the simulation to reality.

The Great Solar System Rescue: A Simulation for Science Classes

Tom Snyder Productions has developed a space simulation in which students search for a probe lost somewere in space:

Mi and her three teammates watch the monitor closely as the lost space probe sends back images of the planet where it has crashed. They can see craters, so they know the planet is terrestrial rather than gaseous. But which one is it?

"Temperatures here range from very mild to –135° Celsius," the probe informs them.

Mi, the meteorology expert on the team, quickly searches her data to learn more about the weather on the terrestrial planets. "Only Earth and Mars have mild weather," she tells her teammates, "and only Mars has temperatures as low as –135°C. The probe must be on Mars!"

After listening to information from the probe in their areas and consulting their own expert data, they concur: The lost probe crashed on Mars.

"I'm going to check it out," Cassie says. She clicks the mouse on the Mars symbol on the screen to test her team's hypothesis. The screen confirms their inference: The probe is on Mars!

"But," Gerald says, "where on Mars?" Gerald and Cassie decide from their collective historical data that there are only four possible locations where the probe could have landed. Angelo, the team's geology expert, clicks the mouse on the probe's elevation detector. The probe informs the team that its location is 4 km deep. Angelo quickly searches through his geological database. "The probe must be either in Valles Marineris or Argyre Basin," he tells his teammates. "The other two locations aren't that deep." Then Angelo tries a rock analysis. He clicks on the rock analysis label on the probe. The probe tells the team that it senses violent activity within Mars's crust.

"It has to be Valles Marineris!" Angelo tells them. "That's where there's folding and faulting of the surface due to Marsquakes!"

Take Your Case to Science Court

Science Court (for grades 4–6) and Science Court Explorations (for grades 2–4) are innovative series of programs developed by Tom Snyder Productions (http://tomsnyder.com) on such topics as friction, sound, work and simple machines, flight, electrical current, and the water cycle. Each episode engages students in a scientific question presented in a humorous, animated video. The case ends up in Science Court, where lawyers and expert witnesses seek the answer to the question. Before the case is decided, students form hypotheses and test them through hands-on activities. They then use their findings to predict the verdict in the Science Court trial.

For example, in the case of the electric circuit, I. M. Richman refuses to relinquish his ping-pong trophy to the new champion, Mary Murphy. But he does agree to let her look at it. On the way into Richman's mansion, Mary trips and breaks the wire for Richman's alarm system. He repairs the break by inserting his dog's leash in the circuit, but later discovers that his alarm system is not working. Did Mary attempt to steal the trophy, or does the broken alarm system have to do with the way the wiring was repaired? The case is argued before the Science Court. Before the answer is revealed on the CD-ROM, students discuss the case, form hypotheses, and test them through hands-on activities with electric circuits.

Many other good simulation programs are available that let your students explore an unknown universe.

Explore the Skies with Planetarium Programs

Voyager 4 by Carina Software (2006) is a planetarium simulation that displays the sun, moon, planets, and stars in their correct spatial positions for any day of the year, from the distant past, through the present, to the future. As a dynamic simulation, *Voyager 4* allows students to do compressed time studies of motions of objects in the sky. In a few seconds, students can watch the circumpolar constellations as they revolve about the North Star throughout a 24-hour period, follow the moon on its cycle around the earth, or keep track of a planet as it moves through the night sky.

Planetarium programs can be used to understand sky relationships. For example, the positions of sunrise along the horizon for different days throughout the year might be measured using *Voyager 4*. Students would note that the sun rises along the northeastern horizon around June 21, due east around September 21, along the southeastern horizon around December 21, and due east again around March 21. Through studying the sun's movements, students can construct a better understanding of the causes of the seasons. Further, students can better understand and appreciate the annual movements of the sun along the horizon, a means people thousands of years ago used to establish a solar calendar. *Voyager Stargazer* even allows students to map the changing areas of day and night on the earth's surface at different times and dates to help them explore the reasons for seasons.

Use Virtual Laboratories

Some simulation programs allow learners to conduct experiments in a virtual setting. *Virtual Labs: Light* allows students to use virtual lasers and optical tools to safely investigate the nature of light, reflection, refraction, and color, rather than setting up light beams, mirrors, and lenses in a laboratory. *Virtual Labs: Electricity* enables students to construct virtual circuits by clicking and dragging labeled icons that specify electrical components, including batteries, bulbs, motors, resistors, and wires. Students can discover the basic properties of a circuit and the purpose of devices such as switches and fuses without the expense or potential safety issues of exploring with electrical components in the laboratory. The school version of this program includes structured learning activities, opportunities for open exploration, thinking questions and challenges, and embedded assessment activities. For example, "Broken? Fix It!" requires students to alter two circuits that do not work to make them functional.

Another quality computer planetarium simulation appropriate for the classroom is *Starry Night EDU* by Space Holding Corp. This program has many of the same features as *Voyager Stargazer* and is packaged with a printed teacher's manual with reproducibles. Visit http://www.starrynight.com to learn more about this program's features.

A wonderful library of online simulations that power inquiry and understanding can be accessed at http://www.explorelearning.com. Here you will find nearly 400 *Gizmos* designed to develop lasting conceptual understanding in science and mathematics at the middle and high school levels. All Gizmos have certain things in common. They are visual and interactive, have greath depth, and encourage student inquiry. Gizmos appropriate for grades 3 through 5 are being added to the collection. One allows users to investigate the growth of three common garden plants: tomatoes, beans, and turnips. The amount of light, the amount of water, and the type of soil in which the seed is planted can be varied. The plants' height, mass, leaf color, and leaf size can be observed. Tables and graphs of height and mass data can be displayed. Investigators can use this simulated greenhouse to answer such questions as: *What type of soil will produce the best tomato plant?* Or *How much should we water a turnip planted in garden soil?* A thirty-day free-trial enables users to explore this award-winning site, read research articles about the effectiveness of this approach to teaching and learning, and try out Gizmos that correlate with their instructional standards.

Use Instructional Software Packages

A variety of innovative instructional packages, often incorporating interactive multimedia activities and presentations, are currently available to schools from commercial sources.

Learn with Computer-Assisted Instruction Packages

Computer-assisted instruction (CAI) packages may range from text-based drill and practice or tutorial software to open-ended multimedia environments that support student's exploration of information (Reynolds & Barba, 1996). Tutorials present information to students, often like an electronic textbook. Drill and practice, or review and reinforcement, programs provide opportunities for students to rehearse their knowledge and get immediate feedback about the accuracy of their answers. Though both of these approaches have developed negative connotations over the years, they can be effective learning tools when used in conjunction with other learning approaches.

In their book *Technology for the Teaching and Learning of Science*, Reynolds and Barba (1996) present a concise review of the research into the effectiveness of CAI, then summarize the research-based implications for computer-assisted instruction as follows:

> From the research of the past two decades, we have learned that computer-assisted instruction is a powerful learning tool for improving students' knowledge of science concepts at the knowledge and comprehension levels. Drill-and-practice packages help students decrease learning time, while increasing their achievement levels. Students enjoy working in electronic environments and enjoy learning in electronic microworlds. Computer-assisted instruction provides science teachers with supplementary resources to enrich basic science instruction. (p. 41)

Computer presentations can enhance the learning of science topics such as the circulatory system, the organs in the respiratory system of a fish, the parts of a microscope, and constellations and star names.

Explore the World with Global Information Systems

ArcView is a global information systems (GIS) software package that is being used in middle and secondary schools. A license and training for using this software tool are available for purchase through the Internet. The book *Mapping Our World: GIS Lessons for Educators* by Malone, Palmer, and Voigt (2002) provides a 1-year license for ArcView, a teacher

An example of a program that explores human anatomy (basic organization and terminology, bones and body organs, and body systems and how they relate to each other) is *A.D.A.M. The Inside Story* from A.D.A.M. Software (http://www.adam.com).

resource CD, and lesson plans for a variety of science and geography investigations. For example, "The Earth Moves: A Global Perspective," can engage students in investigating patterns of earthquake and volcanic activity on the earth's surface and the relationship of those patterns to the location of diverse landforms, plate boundaries, and the distribution of population. Based on their exploration of these relationships, students will form a hypothesis about the earth's distribution of earthquake and volcanic activity and identify world cities that face the greatest risk from those phenomena (p. 49).

Explore the Potential of Digital Cameras and Digital Microscopes

Digital and video cameras are now affordable tools for schools. Their availability makes it possible for teachers and students to electronically record images of objects and events in their environment. This capability adds a real-world connection to science learning. Visual and written and drawn observational records can be stored for future analysis. A photographic record of the seasonal changes in the school yard, the growth of plants in a classroom investigation, or the position of shadows at different times during the day can provide familiar visual data for students to observe, sequence, and analyze.

In a Mississippi elementary school, students worked with a partner in a parklike setting to collect digital photographs of at least 10 different leaves and the bark of the trees from which the leaves came (Carter, Sumrall, & Curry, 2006). The students downloaded the photographs onto computers and used a special program to edit the images. They were encouraged to explore and edit the pictures using the color, contrast, brightness, and cropping features of the program.

The students used a variety of sources to identify the trees from which the leaves and bark came. The URLs of Internet sites they used in the identification process included:

http://www.fw.vt.edu/dendro/forsite/key/intro.htm
http://www.uwsp.edu/cnr/leaf/treeid.htm

You should be able to find other identification keys through Internet and literature searches and visiting bookstores.

Digital microscopes are also useful tools in elementary and middle school classrooms. They make it possible to display magnified images of objects and organisms on a computer monitor, television screen, or video projection device. A huge advantage of displaying the image for the whole class to see is that the teacher knows that all students are looking at the same thing, so questions can be asked, observations can be discussed, and parts of the object or organism can be pointed out, described, and identified. Digital microsopes eliminate a common problem that occurs when students are each looking through their own microscopes, that the teacher doesn't know for sure whether each student is observing the object being investigated or simply seeing their eyelashes as they gaze through the microscope's tube.

Some digital microscopes are simply small digital video cameras that magnify the image when postitioned close to an object because the image is displayed on a screen with a greater area than the object being imaged. These can be placed at the end of a traditional microscope tube, where your eye would normally be, to display what is on the microscope's stage for all to see. Other digital microscopes have a variety of lenses that can be attached to change the magnification of the displayed image. Computer software can enable students to capture images they see on the computer screen and save them for future use in written or oral reports.

A simple editing program for digital photos, Microsoft Office Picture Manager, is part of the Microsoft Office suite of programs.

Contribute to and Use Computer Databases

Useful data collected over long periods of time are available to students and scientists today on the Internet and CD-ROMs. Your science classroom computer can be used to search through database materials from throughout the United States and other parts of the world. **Databases** (electronically stored information) exist in all curricular areas, including science. For instance, if your students are studying the interrelationships between wind direction, speed, and weather conditions, they can instantly gather information from a variety of geographic locations without leaving your classroom. This not only motivates students and encourages them to use higher-thinking processes but also helps students learn how to effectively select and secure information.

Students can use a computer to:

* access commercial databases and information services;
* do collaborative research with other teachers and students locally or around the world;
* get up-to-the-minute weather and other science-related data;
* use computer based laboratories to collect and process data for addition to databases; and
* communicate with other investigators using e-mail.

Contribute to and Use Regional Databases

Dotty is a participating teacher in the Tennessee Valley Project, which was designed and funded to improve science education in eight rural school districts in eastern Tennessee. In an Annenberg video entitled *Case Studies in Science Education: Dotty*, we see Dotty's students collecting and testing water samples for pH and dissolved oxygen. They use the one computer in their classroom and telecommunications to exchange data with students from other schools in their area. In this way, they both contribute to and use a common database of water quality in the eastern Tennessee region. The students also send e-mail messages to students in all 50 states asking for water samples.

Telecommunications allow these students from rural Tennessee to feel connected to students in other parts of the state, the nation, and the world. The video *Case Studies in Science Education: Dotty* is available to view on the Annenberg website. Take some time to view the video on Dotty and her students and learn more about the potential for using computers in school science.

Participate in the GLOBE Project

Global Learning and Observations to Benefit the Environment (GLOBE) is a model for international cooperation in monitoring the environment. GLOBE is an Internet-based research program involving scientists, students, and teachers worldwide (Ebenezer & Lau, 1999; Rock, Blackwell, Miller, & Hardison, 1997). GLOBE students learn to observe the environment by taking scientific data, such as the maximum and minimum temperature of the atmosphere, precipitation, cloud cover, cloud type, and the temperature, pH, dissolved oxygen, and alkalinity of bodies of water. Protocols for data collection are specified by GLOBE and some require specific instruments to be purchased by the participating school. Students send their data via the Internet to the GLOBE, student data archive. Environmental and earth scientists use the data to accurately map such features as rivers, lakes, reservoirs, forest types, wetlands, and urban areas. The data are then available for students to use in their own research projects.

Though many projects are designed for middle and high school participation, there are several designed specifically for elementary students to contribute to and learn from

You can access the GLOBE website at http://www.globe.gov.

worldwide data. One GLOBE research project that requires no special equipment, focuses on light pollution and its effect on viewing stars in the night sky. Known as *GLOBE at Night,* this investigation, which happens each spring during a period when the moon is not in the night sky, challenges observers to match a card showing the part of the sky where the constellation Orion is found with the way this region of their sky appears. In areas with a lot of light pollution, only the brightest stars are visible; when there is little light pollution, many stars both bright and dim are visible in the sky. Observers input their location (longitude and latitude), time and date of viewing, and indicate the which card is the closest match for their sky. Data from around the world is assembed and displayed at the GLOBE website so that patterns of light pollution can be analyzed geographically and from year to year.

Collect Observational Data on Clouds

NASA's S'COOL (Students' Cloud Observations On-Line) project provides another opportunity for students to contribute to real scientific research by making and sharing their observations. Classes provide *ground truth* measurements to assist in the validation of the CERES (Clouds and the Earth's Radiant Energy System) instrument. Students make visual cloud observations at the same time the satellite does and share their findings electronically with NASA. Then the two observations are compared to validate the analysis of the satellite data. Students can also compare the surface- and space-based observations to learn more about clouds and climate.

The S'COOL project is suggested for students in fourth grade or above, but classes of younger students have also participated successfully. Instructional materials and all materials necessary for participating in S'COOL are free. If you are teaching about clouds and weather, consider using the S'COOL materials.

The S'COOL Project has recently been revised for classrooms. For more information, visit the S'COOL website at http://asd-www.larc.nasa.gov/SCOOL.

Use Archived Data to Discover Weather Patterns

Scientific databases are also available on CD-ROMs. Michael Passow (1996) and his eighth grade science students have used a CD-ROM called the *Global Tropical/Extratropical Cyclone Climatic Atlas* to study historic storms. The *Climatic Atlas* CD-ROM was produced by the National Climatic Data Center of the National Oceanic and Atmospheric Administration (NOAA).

In one activity, Passow's class (1996) studied storms along the East Coast of the United States. Selecting a North Atlantic option on the CD-ROM allowed them to view a list of storms that occurred between 1871 and 1992. From the list, they found that most of the storms (21) in the North Atlantic occurred in 1933. They chose a particular 1933 storm and used the CD-ROM data to map its path from its beginning to its ending dates. The storm formed in the Atlantic Ocean, moved along the East Coast, and struck land in North Carolina on August 23, 1933.

Another CD-ROM in the NOAA series allowed students to study historical climatic data from more than 2,000 stations worldwide. Thus, they could select a station near their city and determine such things as annual temperature and wind patterns.

Passow (1996) concluded that CD-ROMs and other technologies

> lie at the heart of the Standards' vision of "Science as Inquiry," where students sharpen observing, inferring, and experimenting skills while increasing their knowledge and using scientific reasoning and critical thinking. (p. 23)

To find more information on the Internet about weather and weather patterns over long periods of time, type "Weather Data" into Google or another search engine and begin your search.

Use Computer-Based Laboratories to Collect and Process Data

Nothing adds to student excitement and links to real-world science like **computer-based laboratory (CBL)** systems. These electronic systems use data sensors and software programs to collect, organize, display, and process real-world data automatically. Data sensors need not replace direct measurements of temperature, time, force, air pressure, and so on. The direct measurement of variables in your classroom science program is still very important. However, the use of electronic data taking can help shift the focus from mechanical procedures to higher-level and more creative scientific processes, such as analyzing and hypothesizing. CBLs allow students to focus on thinking about data, not merely gathering it (Nachmias & Linn, 1987; Price, 1989).

The website of Vernier, a CLB supplier, features a lesson plan for using a temperature probe to investigate temperature. In the investigation, students use temperature sensors and computers to compare temperature readings from two different cups when hot or cold water is added to them. Through these data-taking and analysis procedures, students determine which material is a better conductor and which is a better insulator.

Caniglia (1997) has pointed out that the exchange of ideas and results is just as important in science as collecting and analyzing data. When engaging in CBL activities, students do more than just look for patterns in graphs. They also argue about experimental procedures, discuss inconsistencies, draw conclusions, and make connections to the physical processes underlying the data. These are core activities in both science and mathematics. CBL investigations offer exciting opportunities for students to model real-world events and make needed connections between science, mathematics, and engineering design.

TERC (formerly, Technical Education Research Center, now simply TERC) has been a leader in developing the potential of computer-based laboratories since 1984. The *Hands-On Elementary Science Project Leader's Manual* developed by TERC (1993) states that a computer-based laboratory provides

> more opportunity for learners to pay attention to the data—to interpret it, redisplay it, and analyze it to inform their understanding of the phenomenon. Since the time span between changing a variable in their investigation and seeing the results is shortened, learners can ask more 'what if' questions and are more likely to revise their test design and try it again. (p. A-21)

TERC (1993) suggests that CBL systems also introduce learners to some standard representations of science data, including bar graphs and line graphs, and assists them in acquiring the "language of graphing" (p. A-22). This instructional technology is especially applicable when trying to measure events that happen very slowly or very quickly, that change over a very small range, or that must be measured indirectly.

A variety of computer-based lab packages is available commercially (see Table 8-1).

Here is a sample lesson using CBL activities. As part of their study of measurement, a third-grade class was monitoring the temperature of their room every school day. Each hour, a student read the thermometer and posted the temperature on the class chart. At the end of each day, Ms. Winter worked with the class to construct a graph showing how the temperature changed during the school day. After a week or so, during a discussion of that day's graph, Suzy wondered, "But what does the temperature do while we are at lunch?" Then Ben said, "You know, we really don't know how it changes between the times we check it." Yelana added, "Sometimes the heater comes on and it gets hot in here but we aren't measuring then." Ms. Winter asked, "Would that show up on the graph?" "No, we don't have data for it," replied Heather.

Teachers are continually searching for ways to help students make connections among subject areas. Using data sensors and computers can be a critical way to help students tie mathematics and science together.

Several lessons using the GO! Temp probe are available online at the Vernier website. Go to http://www.vernier.com/cmat/cmatdnld.html and select an indented title from the drop-down menu under "Elementary Science."

TABLE 8-1 SOME COMPUTER-BASED LAB SUPPLIERS	
Company	**Website**
Acculab Products	http://www.sensornet.com
Data Harvest Company	http://www.dataharvest.com
EyeThink Station Probeware System	http://www.eyethinkcorp.com/
Pasco	http://www.pasco.com/probeware/
Vernier Go! Lab	http://elementary.vernier.com/

The next day, Ms. Winter attached the GO! Temp probe to her computer and set it up to collect temperature data all day long. Meanwhile, the students didn't really notice the metallic rod attached to a wire that was near the thermometer they continued to read each hour. In the afternoon, after the hourly data was graphed as usual, Ms. Winter turned on the projector attached to her computer, and a graph appeared on the screen. She asked the class to compare the two graphs, then do an "I Notice/I Wonder" chart in their science journals before they left for the day. As she looked over the journals after school, she discovered that most students noticed that both displayed time on the X axis and temperature in degrees Celsius on the Y axis. A few of the students noticed that the graph on the screen was shaped somewhat like the class graph, but was smoother. Several of the children commented that the starting temperature and the ending temperatures on both graphs were the same.

The next day, Ms. Winter showed the class the GO! Temp probe and explained that it was a temperature sensor connected to the computer, basically a digital thermometer. Joey said, "You mean like the barbeque fork that tells you when the meat is done?" Ms. Winter agreed, then went on to say that the data from the Go! Temp probe was stored in the computer and displayed as a graph as it was collected. She told the class, "Today when we check the thermometer, we'll also check the thermometer shown on the computer screen. Then in the afternoon, we'll compare graphs again."

During the afternoon discussion, connections between the graphs were made. The students were all excited about what else they could do with this new tool. They discussed what the GO! Temp probe would let them do that would be hard to do with just the thermometer. Ben said, "We don't have to keep checking the thermometer all the time, the probe and the computer can do it for us." Suzy said, "We can collect data even when we aren't here, then look at it later!" Heather suggested, "Could we set it up to see what happens to the temperature in the room tonight?" "Sure," Ms. Winter replied. "Why don't you all predict what the graph will look like tomorrow morning, then I'll show you how to set up the computer to collect our data."

The next morning, Ms. Winter's students could hardly wait to see how the temperature changed in their classroom the night before.

Use Spreadsheets to Organize and Analyze Data

Spreadsheets can facilitate and extend the organization and analysis of real data taken by students. A **spreadsheet** is a computer program for organizing data in rows and columns, then manipulating it in various ways through the use of mathematics. **Graphing software** contained within spreadsheet programs enables students to display data in different types of graphs. This software tool is especially useful in processing directly measured data if probes are not being used for data collected from Internet databases.

One of the most commonly used spreadsheet programs is Microsoft® Excel. Its inclusion in Microsoft® Office packages has made it available on many home and school computers. This powerful program can be used successfully by teachers and students alike with proper training.

Another spreadsheet and graphing program, Inspire Data, appropriate for grades 4 and higher, applies research-based strategies of visual learning to data literacy. It is designed to inspire students to discover meaning as they collect and explore data in a dynamic inquiry process. Using data they have collected or from databases included with the program, students formulate questions and make connections between data and its visual representations to interpret information, solve problems, and draw conclusions. This helps students develop deeper content knowledge and stronger critical thinking skills.

Communicate Through Multimedia Presentations

Multimedia software programs such as PowerPoint, Kid Pix, and Kidspiration enliven presentations, reports, and projects for both teachers and students. With these multimedia programs, users can build colorful and creative slides and combine them into the desired presentation product (Lee & Patterson, 1997). Program users have access to prebuilt graphic templates, word processing and drawing tools, built-in graphics, and high-quality clip art. Kid Pix includes movie clips as well. All three programs enable the user to insert items from other sources, including the Internet.

Teachers can create motivating slide shows that capture students' attention for instruction and model how students can present their own ideas through technology. In science instruction that follows the 5-E model, teachers might use a graphics presentation program to

- add catchy, animated graphics to the engage phase;
- list directions for the explore phase and project them onto a screen for students to view and follow;
- build concept maps and augment invention of new concepts and ideas in the explain phase;
- assist students in the elaborate phase to develop understanding by linking invented concepts to previous activities and to new investigations; and
- present tests, rubrics, and other assessment items to students in the evaluate phase of instruction.

Using teacher-developed slide shows as models, students might construct reports of their investigations and prepare interesting presentations for the class. The very act of creating products with a multimedia program forces students to clarify, extend, and refine their ideas and thus helps them in constructing understanding.

Additionally, teachers and students might use a multimedia program to create single slides to illustrate a point, to create theme files, to construct and print displays for bulletin boards and projects, to design and produce safety and lab procedure posters, or to create announcement flyers to post in the classroom or send home to parents.

Earlier in the book, concept maps were introduced as effective tools for planning, teaching, and assessing science lessons. Inspiration®, a program designed for learners in sixth grade and up, can be used to create graphic organizers such as concept maps and expand topics into writing. For younger students, Kidspiration® provides an easy way to apply the proven principles of visual learning. Students build graphic organizers by combining pictures, text, and spoken words to represent thoughts and information. For more information about both of these programs, visit http://www.Inspiration.com.

For more information about Inspire Data, visit http://www.inspiration.com

Go to the Homework and Exercises section in Chapter 8 of MyEducationLab and view the videos for this chapter, *Technology and Science Learning, Parts 1* and 2. In these videos we see teachers and students in third and fifth grades using a variety of educational technologies, including PowerPoint presentations and the Internet, to enhance students' understanding. We return to the videos on water wheels, recycling, and explaining moon phases with a focus on the educational technology tools that are used in the lessons.

So far in this chapter, we have looked mostly at isolated uses of educational technology in teaching. Refer to the science and social studies lessons presented in Chapter 9 on weather and on river ecology for sample technology-supported lessons that can address standards from science and other disciplines.

Successfully using technology in science and other classes requires that classroom technology resources be managed effectively.

Managing Educational Technology in the Science Classroom

The success of using computers to enhance science learning of your students depends on a number of considerations.

Using Different Arrangements of Computers in Your School

Educational technology resources in schools are usually arranged in one or more of these ways: (1) technology resources may be housed in a centralized computer center or lab with computers for every student in the class, (2) classrooms may have only a single computer, or (3) classrooms may be equipped with several computers.

The One-Computer Classroom. If you have one computer in your classroom, like Dotty in the video case study described previously in this chapter, you may have a problem (Brown, 1998). How are you going to use the computer? Will it be used primarily for presentation by the teacher, or as a tool for students in creating projects? How often will students use the computer? Will you encourage cooperative learning with the computer?

Fortunately, there is advice available for the teacher in a one-computer classroom. Dockterman (1997) has compiled some good ideas in his *Great Teaching in the One Computer Classroom*. Kahn (1998) has also written a versatile and practical guide, *Ideas and Strategies for the One-Computer Classroom*, which provides many suggestions for teachers. Additionally, *Learning and Leading with Technology (L&L)*, a journal of the International Society for Technology in Education, includes a periodic section on teaching in the one-computer classroom.

In the October 1998 issue of *L&L*, Cindy Brown suggested that an important use of a single computer in a classroom is for teacher and student presentations. If you use the computer for instructional presentations, your computer will need to be connected to a large-screen monitor or liquid crystal display (LCD) projection system. You or your students work at the computer, and images are displayed on-screen for the entire class to view. Interaction can take place as students view the screen and discuss what they see.

According to Brown (1998), another important way to use a single computer in a classroom is as a learning center. Mary Ellen Swadley, an innovative sixth-grade teacher of science, mathematics, and social studies, uses the computer as one of several ongoing learning stations for her two classes of about 20 students. Each class meets for a 3-hour block of time. Students work in the learning stations—on science, math, or social studies content—in small cooperative groups. All computer activities are related to the topic being taught in the class. For example, students may engage in *The Great Ocean Rescue* as part of a study of oceans, or they might use a multimedia package to develop a report or prepare a presentation on a topic being learned.

Every child in Ms. Swadley's classes uses the computer at least 20 minutes each day as a member of a cooperative group. Additionally, students might work on the computer on their own at different times during the day, including before and after school. Although

Ms. Swadley started her adventure into educational technology with only one computer in her classroom, she has found creative ways to add five more.

More Than One Computer. It is possible that you will have more than one computer in a multimedia arrangement in your self-contained classroom. Here are some guidelines for setting up and managing computers and other electronic technology equipment for a class of 20 to 25 students:

1. Use a variety of educational technologies to accommodate the range of learning styles and backgrounds of your students (e.g., texts, videos, hands-on materials, computers, computer-based laboratory systems, software, and Internet connections).
2. Arrange tables so students can work in cooperative learning groups.
3. Consider setting up the following learning stations for groups of four students: a listening station, video station, hands-on materials station, word processing station, computer-based laboratory station, and writing station. Figure 8-2 presents a suggested floor plan for a science/technology-oriented classroom incorporating these stations.

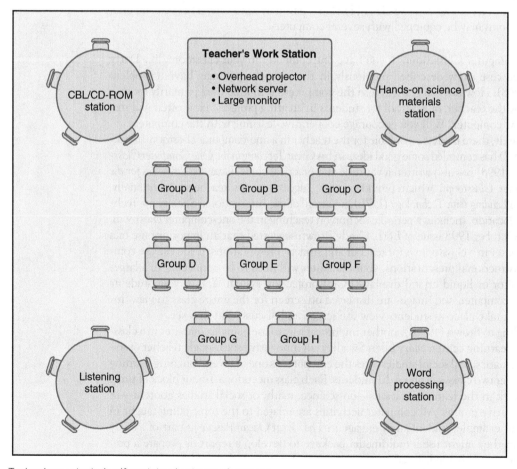

Figure 8-2 Technology-oriented self-contained science classroom.
Source: Based on *Designs for Elementary School Science and Health* (p. 50), A cooperative project of biological Science Curriculum Study (BSCS) and International Business Machines (IBM),© 1989, Colorado Springs, Co. Reprinted by permission.

4. Equip the teacher's workstation with a computer with Internet access, an LCD projection system or large-screen monitor, an electronic writing board, and a printer.
5. Consider establishing these types of computer stations in your classroom:
   - Student computer workstation with multimedia presentation software and Internet capability for data collection and sending science e-mail and bulletin board/newsgroup correspondence
   - Computer-based lab systems for student-conducted science activities
   - A videocassette, DVD, and CD-ROM station for viewing and using in the videos and software
6. Arrange to lock the computers when they are not used. Many schools engrave the name of the school on all components and bolt them to tables or portable carts.
7. Arrange your classroom schedule so that students who are responsible can use the computers on a sign-up basis when they have completed their other classroom responsibilities. You will find that computers are popular and can positively motivate students to complete assignments. Encourage this.
8. Periodically assess technology literacy content and skills with simple tests, and introduce your students to new software as it becomes available.

You should set up computer learning stations where students can work on learning software, word processing, and multimedia presentations. These would be similar to the learning centers described earlier in the text where collections of materials are arranged for students to work on individually or in small groups. Follow these guidelines:

1. Locate your computer learning stations so you can see them from anyplace in your classroom.
2. Post specific directions related to the station for easy reference.
3. Select two or three students who have used computers, and train them to be peer computer experts. They will have to know the hardware and software in your room, how to operate the computer, and how to positively help their classmates. Post the names of these students and assign them specific times when each one will be available for help.
4. Set up a schedule so students can sign up for computer time at the computer station. Include some open or free times. Your schedule should record time spent on the computer by each student, so you can ensure that everyone gets computer time.

Schoolwide Computer/Multimedia Center or Lab. Some elementary and middle schools set up computer or technology centers or labs for class-sized groups. Classes are scheduled into the technology center, and either an educational technology specialist conducts computer lessons or individual teachers work with their own classes there. It is often quite difficult to connect educational technology to the ongoing curriculum with centralized technology centers.

Selecting Science Software and Internet Sites

Computer programs and Internet sites vary greatly in suitability for use with elementary and middle school students. Many programs are designed to supplement or be an integral part of science programs and textbooks. You may be called on to suggest which software your school should buy in the coming years or to screen and select websites for student use. In the selection process, start with your instructional objectives, not the mass of available software and websites. First decide what you want to do with educational technology; then it is relatively easy to determine what hardware and software you will need.

Here are some questions to guide you in selecting and evaluating software for your elementary and middle school science program:

1. Does the program support your instructional objectives?
2. Does the software provide a better way to teach this content or skill than some other instructional approach?
3. Is the program well designed and easy to use?
4. Is the program design flexible?
5. Is the menu complete?
6. Is the program content accurate and at an appropriate developmental level for your students?
7. Does the program offer a complete learning package, including a teacher's guide that suggests integration into your science curriculum?
8. Are follow-up or enrichment science activities or demonstrations offered?
9. Is the reading level appropriate for your students?
10. Are the graphics correct, attractive, and appropriate?
11. Is there a program purchase warranty?
12. Has the software been reviewed or recommended?

There are a multitude of appropriate and inappropriate sites available on the Internet. Here are some questions to ask when selecting Internet sites for student use (Gray, 1997):

1. Do the instructional objectives and content of the site provide a high degree of correlation to your science curriculum and to national, state, and local standards?
2. Does the site's use of unique Web features, such as communication and information access, promote a significantly broader and deeper understanding of ideas, concepts, and theories than more traditional instructional materials?
3. Does the online resource facilitate person-to-person interactivity and increased understanding through the use of telecommunications?
4. Are learners able to link to additional online resources that provide related information?
5. Is the site rich in content and aesthetically pleasing? Is text easy to read, and do graphics enhance the basic instructional design of the site?
6. Is the online resource well structured and easy for students to work with?
7. Is the site without cultural, gender, or racial bias in content and format?

Another important issue related to Internet use is the determination of the information's credibility. Everyone can learn to detect dubious assertions, strategies that are particularly applicable to assessing scientific claims and information students may encounter on the Internet. Students can detect less credible information by looking for the following signs:

* Premises of arguments are not explicit.
* Evidence does not lead logically to conclusions.
* Fact and opinion are not clearly distinguished.
* Celebrity is quoted as authority.
* Specific references are vague or missing.
* Graphs are misleading.
* Measures taken to guard against distortion in self-reports are not described.
* Percentages are given without stating total sample size (Kreuger & Sutton, 2001).

According to Kreuger and Sutton (2001), scientifically literate students will respond appropriately to the barrage of information that technology provides. Separating sense from nonsense is a critical response skill that must be developed in all students.

In some cases, you will be able to download free software or programs from Internet sites. You can also join online discussion groups to find out what other teachers think of the programs, websites, or materials you are considering for your classroom. Some descriptions list schools where computer-based materials and learning models have been field-tested or reviewed. In addition, some software companies offer previews of their products and encourage teachers to return products that do not meet their needs. Be sure to explore the programs, packages, and approaches that can help you and your students take advantage of information technology.

Acceptable Use Policies for the Internet

Soholt (1999) has cautioned that "the Internet is wide open. There are sites which no child should see" (p. 43). You need to protect your students and yourself. Thus, every school should have acceptable use policies in place for children and the Internet. These policies should relate to such things as e-mail use, responses to requests for information by different sites, actions students should take when they confront an inappropriate image or site, and times when students can use the Internet. Figure 8-3 shows an acceptable use policy for one school.

Internet Standards at Sandia Elementary

The following standards must be adhered to by all students and staff at Sandia Elementary. Violation of **any** of these standards will result in immediate suspension of Internet privileges. Continued and habitual violations will result in permanent suspension of Internet privileges.

1. Students and staff must have on file a signed Acceptable Use Policy in order to use any network services at Sandia Elementary, including e-mail and Internet access.
2. Students may not have individual e-mail accounts. All accounts will be in the teacher's name.
3. Students must have specific permission from their teacher to conduct a search on the Internet.
4. Students may not add "Bookmarks" without specific permission from a teacher.
5. Students may not give the following information out on the Internet without prior permission of their teacher.
   - your last name
   - a picture of yourself or any other students
   - your home address
   - your telephone number
   - any personal information asked for by someone you do not know
6. If you ever find an inappropriate site or image, immediately hit the back key and contact an adult.
7. If you ever feel uncomfortable about a certain site or message, contact an adult immediately.
8. No chat rooms!
9. There will be no Internet or e-mail access when a substitute teacher is in the room.

Figure 8-3 A school policy for acceptable Internet use.
Source: Using Technology Effectively in Your Classroom (p. 44), by Gordon Soholt, 1999, Bellevue, WA: Bureau of Education and Research , P.O. Box 96058, Bellevue, WA 98009.

Take the Plunge—Join the Information Age

Change is taking place so rapidly in the educational technology field that it is easy to feel overwhelmed by all the new products and resources. Fortunately, help is available. A number of professional magazines review computer-based materials and provide articles that guide you through the technology maze. The NSTA journals *Science and Children* and *The Science Teacher* regularly feature articles related to educational technology. *Learning and Leading with Technology* and *Multimedia Schools* are devoted specifically to the what, how, where, and how well of incorporating technology into teaching and learning. In addition, the Eisenhower National Clearinghouse for Mathematics and Science Education (http://www.goENC.com) offers an online catalog that provides extensive information about available curriculum resources, including prices.

Computers and other electronic multimedia technology open many vistas for teaching science in the elementary and middle schools. Consider them another tool in your teaching arsenal. Be curious, but critical. Attend instructional technology workshops, conferences, and exhibitions. Keep up with the latest advances in educational technology by reading widely. Most importantly, take the plunge and find out why students are so enthusiastic about computers and other electronic technologies. Learn to share their enthusiasm.

SUMMARY

• A variety of technology tools and resources are available to enhance inquiry learning and instruction in elementary and middle school classrooms.

• Each phase of inquiry science activities can be enriched with Internet sources. Using the Internet can be beneficial, but you must also use caution and should establish an Internet use policy. Follow the suggested guidelines for evaluating software and Internet sites for your elementary and middle school science programs. There are also many sources for learning what other teachers think of specific resources.

• Other electronic resources available for teaching and learning science include computer-based lab systems, CD-ROMs and DVDs, databases, digital cameras, liquid crystal display (LCD) projection systems, interactive TV, and the Internet.

• This chapter is only introductory, opening up for you the many possibilities of using technology to enhance learning and motivation in your science classroom. Take advantage of the multiple opportunities available to foster your technological literacy.

ONLINE PROFESSIONAL DEVELOPMENT

Pre- and post-tests to assess your knowledge of chapter content, along with exercises to enhance your understanding, can be found on MyEducationLab at www.myeducationlab.com.

Video Guides

Video clips on MyEducationLab selected for this chapter include *Technology and Science Learning—Parts 1* and *2*.

Accessing the Videos

1. Go to the Homework and Exercises section in Chapter 8 of MyEducationLab to select and view videos for this chapter.

2. Videos might be viewed individually, by small groups of colleagues, or by the whole class.

3. As you watch each video, use the **Questions for Reflection** to guide your thoughts and note taking for personal use and group discussion.

4. Discuss your answers to the questions about each video with classmates.

Video: Technology and Science Learning—Parts 1 and 2

Overview

In these videos we see teachers and students at third and fifth grades using a variety of educational technologies, including PowerPoint presentations and the Internet, to enhance students' understanding. We return to the videos on water wheels, recycling, and explaining moon phases with a focus on the educational technology tools that are used in the lessons.

Questions for Reflection

1. What examples of the use of PowerPoint do you see in the lesson on recycling?

2. What does the teacher say is the advantage of using PowerPoint presentations in science lessons?

3. What examples of the use of the Internet in the moon phase lessons do you see? (The NASA photos of the moon used by the class are among the many Gizmos found at http://www.explorelearning.com.)

4. According to one of the teachers, Cindy Shofner, how does the 2-D model of moon phases found on the Internet help students connect the 3-D model to what they actually saw in their moon observations?

9

*S*tudent achievement in science and in other school subjects such as social studies, language arts, and technology is enhanced by coordination between and among the science program and other programs. . . . As an example, . . . a coordinated social studies and science unit is natural. Oral and written communication skills are developed when students record, summarize, and communicate the results of inquiry. . . . Science requires the use of mathematics in the collection and treatment of data and in the reasoning used to develop concepts, laws, and theories.

(National Research Council, 1996, p. 214)

Connecting Science with Other Subjects

ALTHOUGH THE CURRICULUM AND THE SCHOOL DAY are often neatly divided into separate subjects, real-world approaches to problems and issues cut across disciplinary lines. Scientists, for example, use mathematics as a tool to explore, represent, and explain patterns in data from investigations. They draw on their language and literacy skills as they read scientific literature, formulate problems, write proposals, plan investigations, record data, and communicate findings and conclusions to others. Furthermore, scientists as well as other citizens enter into discussions and make decisions about societal problems and issues arising from the applications of science and technology. In the real world, then, science, mathematics, reading, writing, social studies, and other disciplines are not isolated from one another, but connected.

Just as scientists use mathematics and language arts as tools, children should have opportunities to apply and enhance their mathematics, reading, and writing skills while investigating the natural world. This heightens the relevance of mathematics and language arts, enhances their usefulness, and promotes greater learning in science. Similarly, in their studies of both science and social studies, children should have the opportunity to examine the cause-and-effect relationships among science, technology, and societal change. Students might, for example, identify the impact of new technologies on communities around the world or study and offer solutions to environmental problems in the local community or other communities.

In this chapter, we help you confront and begin to develop answers to questions about curriculum connections between science and other subjects. As you study the chapter, consider the following questions:

- *How can mathematics and science be connected in practical instructional activities so that knowledge, understanding, and skills in both subjects are enhanced?*

- *How can reading and writing be used in the service of science learning? How can science be used to promote and improve children's abilities to read and write?*

- *How do events and issues studied in social studies connect to science and technology?*

- *How can science, social studies, mathematics, reading, writing, and other subjects be integrated to promote learning of the essential knowledge and skills of each of these subjects?*

Let us start by examining connections between science and mathematics.

NSES   You can review the *National Science Education Standards* online. Go to http://www.nap.edu/readingroom/books/nses/html. For an overview of the *Principles and Standards for School Mathematics*, go to http://nctm.org/standards/overview.htm

Connecting Science and Mathematics

Mathematics has been called the language of science. It is the ultimate human method for exploring, representing, and expressing patterns. Thus, mathematics is an indispensable tool used to investigate, discover, model, and communicate the order and patterns found in the real world (Activities That Integrate Mathematics and Science, 1999).

Both the *National Science Education Standards* (National Research Council, 1996) and the *Principles and Standards for School Mathematics* (National Council of Teachers of Mathematics, 2000) emphasize that students must learn to view mathematics as a practical subject that can be applied to real-world situations and to problems arising in other disciplines. Science is a natural place for students to develop this view of mathematics.

Table 9-1 shows the array of mathematical concepts, operations, and skills that can be emphasized in both mathematics and science classes in elementary and middle schools. Figure 9-1 depicts a connections model for science and mathematics, which graphically relates the mathematical ideas of Table 9-1 to scientific inquiry. In the following sections, we will expand on the connections model and show you a variety of ways that mathematical ideas can be used and enhanced in scientific inquiry.

TABLE 9-1	WAYS OF APPLYING MATHEMATICS IN SCIENTIFIC INQUIRY
I. Quantifying the Real World	• Identifying variables • Counting objects and events • Estimating number and size • Measuring all sorts of things using standard and nonstandard units
II. Organizing and Interpreting Data	• Depicting data in pictures and diagrams • Constructing data tables • Constructing different kinds of graphs: bar graphs, histograms, line graphs • Searching for and expressing patterns in graphs, including linear, proportional, geometirc, and other relationships
III. Using Patterns and Relationships	• Using patterns and relationships from tables and graphs in explaining events and making predictions • Using ratios, rates, proportionalities, and formulas in explaining events and making predictions
IV. Operating on Numbers	• Adding, subtracting, multiplying, dividing • Using fractions, decimals, and percentages • Calculating averages • Estimating probabilities • Calculating products, ratios, and rates • Recognizing equalities and inequalities • Constructing proportionalities

Sources: Adapted from *Curriculum and Evaluation Standards for School Mathematics,* National Council of Teachers of Mathematics, 1989, Weston, VA: NCTM; and an analysis of the Third International Mathematics and Science Study (TIMSS) in *Splintered Vision: An Investigation of U.S. Science and Mathematics Education,* by William H. Smith, Curtis C. McKnight, and Senta Raizen, 1997, Boston: Kluwer Academic Publishers.

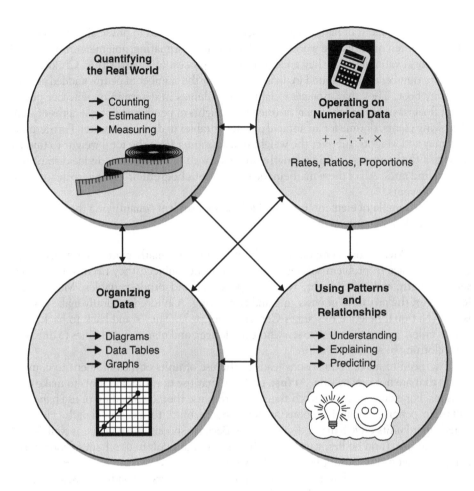

Figure 9-1 A connections model for science and mathematics.
Sources: Principles and Standards for School Mathematics, National Council of Teachers of Mathematics, 2000, Weston, VA: NCTM; *Splintered Vision: An Investigation of U.S. Science and Mathematics Education,* by William H. Smith, Curtis C. McKnight, and Senta Raizen, 1997, Boston: Kluwer Academic Publishers.

Quantifying the Real World

Expressing and thinking about the real world in terms of numbers is the first step in connecting science and mathematics (see Figure 9-1). By examining how infants respond to different stimulus situations, researchers have shown that number concepts are used to organize physical arrays and repetitive events as early as 5 to 7 months of age, if the arrays or events vary from two to four. From as early as 5 months, children can use concepts of addition and subtraction to recognize when objects have been added to or subtracted from a small array (Bransford, Brown, & Cocking, 1999, p. 89).

Program Standard C

The science program should be coordinated with the mathematics program to enhance student use and understanding of mathematics in the study of science and to improve student understanding of mathematics.

The development of mathematics concepts is often rooted in physical experiences. In school, children quantify the world through counting, estimating, and measuring all kinds of real-world variables that they encounter in the process of investigating. Children may *count* the number of seeds found in different fruits or the number of pennies added as cargo to a clay boat. They may *estimate* weights and volumes in determining whether objects might float or sink. And they may *measure* the weights of pendulum bobs, lengths of stems of growing plants, or time for an antacid powder or tablet to dissolve in water. Furthermore, they may add weights, subtract the weight of a container from the total weight to find the weight of the contents, multiply lengths and widths to find areas, and divide distances by time to find rates. All of these mathematical operations help children begin to quantify objects and events.

As an example of elementary and middle school students quantifying the world, consider the task of measurement.

Measuring. Measuring is emphasized in both science and mathematics standards. When children engage in problem-solving activities in either subject, they need skills for measuring length, volume, weight, time, temperature, and other variables. Measuring is founded on the processes of observing and comparing. "Children naturally make comparisons" (National Science Resources Center, 1996, p. 3). They stand back to back to see who is taller, line up their feet to see whose are longer, and match their bodies to different-sized clothing to see what will fit.

The need to make comparisons leads to the use of units of measurement to compare things that are not side by side. At first, children may use nonstandard units to make comparisons. For example, they stretch their own arms, use their own bodies, or use handy objects like pencils or plastic spoons as nonstandard units to measure length. However, nonstandard units have a major disadvantage. Because spoons and pencils, as well as children's arm spans and bodies, vary in length, it is often difficult to use them to consistently compare objects that cannot be held side by side.

By second grade, children use standard units—centimeters, seconds, grams, and degrees Celsius or Fahrenheit—marked on different kinds of scales to measure in their investigations. Standard units enable consistent descriptions and comparisons of measured objects.

A glossary containing definitions of important terms used in this chapter can be found on MyEducationLab.

Mathematics standards were first developed in 1989 and updated in 2000. Check out the newest version of the measurement standards at http://standards.nctm.org/document/appendix/meas.htm.

Mathematics Standards for Measurement

Throughout programs in grades pre-K through 8, the study of measurement should enable students to

- understand measurable attributes of objects and the units, systems, and processes of measurement, and
- apply appropriate techniques, tools, and formulas to determine measurements.

For example, in grades pre-K through 2, students should

- recognize the attributes of length, volume, weight, area, and time;
- compare and order objects according to these attributes;
- understand how to measure using nonstandard and standard units; and
- select and use an appropriate unit and tool for the attribute being measured.

Reference: *Principles and Standards for School Mathematics*. National Council of Teachers of Mathematics, 2000.

As an example of measuring, we will examine length.

The logic of length measurement is deceptively complex. It encompasses such ideas as the conservation of length, the notion of standard units, unit iteration (counting the number of standard units in a length), and knowledge of how to use standard measuring instruments, such as rulers. According to research by Clements (1999), however, children do not have to master all of these logical complexities to learn to measure the lengths of objects using a ruler, if the teacher provides appropriate scaffolding.

When length measurements are set within the contexts of real-world investigations and a *need to know* is established, even young children can learn to use rulers successfully. Learning to use a ruler, even by rote, provides a framework for children to begin to understand the logical complexities of length measurement.

Real-world measurements often present a challenge to children. For example, measuring the length of plant roots in germination bags (as discussed in Chapter 2) can be difficult because the roots are not straight, but curved and twisted. A simple ruler cannot be used to directly measure the roots. Children must invent ways to measure them with nonstandard measuring devices, perhaps by laying a curving string along the roots, then straightening out the string and measuring it with a ruler.

The process of measuring length in science contexts provides children an opportunity to rehearse, and consequently enlarge, their measurement knowledge. Practice and rehearsal are important concepts in learning theory. *Practice* means to do something over and over again the same way to improve a performance (Ormrod, 2007). What is learned in practice is a specific skill applicable in a specific context. As discussed in Chapter 3, *rehearsal*, in contrast, takes place "when people do something again in similar but not identical ways to reinforce what they have learned while adding something new" (Lowery, 1998, p. 28). When using measurement and other mathematics skills in science, children not only practice what they have already encountered in mathematics classes, but add something new to it. Mathematics schemas are expanded with the new additions from science activities. Children's mathematics skills are then less likely to be bound to specific tasks and are more likely to be transferable and useful in a variety of ways.

A number of innovative elementary science programs emphasize connections between mathematics and science, including AIMS (Activities That Integrate Mathematics and Science), GEMS (Great Explorations in Mathematics and Science), FOSS (Full Option Science System), and Science and Technology for Children (STC). STC has produced a series of very good lessons for first grade classes on comparing and measuring length. Through the 16 lessons of the STC unit *Comparing and Measuring* (National Science Resources Center, 1996), children begin to understand that

- comparing involves observing similarities and differences;
- one way to make comparisons is by matching;
- a common starting line is required to make fair comparisons;
- using beginning and ending points and placing units end to end are important factors when measuring;
- nonstandard units of measure can be used in comparing; and
- standard units of measure produce more consistent results than nonstandard units (p. 2).

> Addresses for AIMS, FOSS, GEMS, STC, and other exemplary science programs are provided in Appendix F.

Science, Mathematics, and the Metric System. The metric system, termed the International System of Units (SI), is used exclusively in science. It is also used exclusively in daily life in all English-speaking countries except the United States. Although use of units such as feet and pounds is customary in the United States, the need for SI units has already affected machine tools, packaging, and temperature measurements. Competition with the rest of the world will continue to accelerate the use of SI in business, science, and government.

The metric system is convenient because it is based on the mathematics of place value and uses decimals rather than fractions. Thus, the metric system is often easier to use than U.S. customary units. It is easier for children to add 4.5 cm and 4.2 cm, for example, than to add 1¼ and 1⅓ inches.

American children must continue to learn and be familiar with both metric and customary units, but programs should de-emphasize the memorization and use of conversion factors between the two systems. When a student measures something 6.5 cm long, for example, accept that as a description of its length. Do not ask how many inches it is. Students' concepts of a unit of length will be just as good without knowing the exact equivalent in the U.S. standard unit system.

More on metric and customary units can be found in Appendix B.

Organizing and Interpreting Data

In science activities, once data have been obtained through measurements, they must be organized and interpreted. Organizing data into diagrams, tables, and graphs is another key step in scientific inquiry portrayed in Table 9-1 and Figure 9-1. Data tables display numerical data in column form. Graphs provide visual displays of data. Putting data obtained from scientific investigations into tables and graphs better enables students to

Chapter 8 on educational technology provides a discussion of the use of graphing programs to facilitate the construction of charts and graphs from investigative data.

- relate their data to their investigative procedures;
- make comparisons among data;
- see relationships and patterns; and
- communicate their data to other people.

A data table is one communication medium that links math and science.

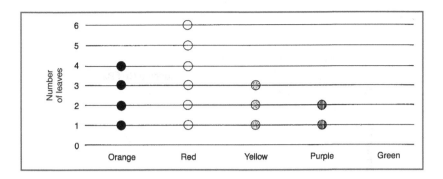

Figure 9-2   Bar graph of collected fall leaves of different colors.

Using Graphs to Organize and Interpret Data. The FOSS K–6 science program developed at the Lawrence Hall of Science provides many opportunities for children to construct and interpret graphs (Full Option Science Sysem, 1991). In the FOSS program, graphs are prepared at three levels of abstraction:

* *Concrete:* organizes real objects to facilitate comparisons and reveal patterns
* *Representational:* uses organization of pictorial representations to reveal relationship
* *Symbolic:* uses numbers and data points to reveal relationships and facilitate interpretation

There are different types of graphs. The graphs most often used in scientific applications in elementary and middle schools are bar graphs, histograms, and line graphs. Each of these was discussed in Chapter 2, but we will supplement that discussion here.

Bar graphs vividly show differences between groups in data collected. Bar graphs can be used, for example, to show the number of children in a class with each different type of eye or hair color. Comparisons of the number of students in each group are easy to see because of the relative lengths of the bars.

A bar graph at the *representational* level is shown in Figure 9-2. This graph depicts the number of leaves of different colors collected by children. The left side, or *vertical axis* of the graph, shows the number of leaves. The bottom line, or *horizontal axis*, shows leaf color. Students stack gummed dots of the appropriate color, creating a series of dots representing the number of leaves collected. Thus, this graph shows that four orange, six red, three yellow, and two purple leaves have been collected.

Histograms display the number of times a number event occurs in a large set. Histograms differ from bar graphs in that the *x* axis on a bar graph simply names a category, while the *x* axis on a histogram is a number line representing a variable. An example of a histogram of the number of unshelled peanuts of different lengths in a group of peanuts is shown in Figure 2-4.

Line graphs are more advanced; students from about grade 4 can learn to construct and interpret them. With line graphs, your students can graphically show numerical data that are continuous. A line graph typically displays visually the changes in a *responding* or *dependent variable* in an investigation corresponding to changes in the values of a *manipulated* or *independent variable*. Figure 9-3 shows an example of a line graph depicting the bounce height versus the drop height of golf balls. In collecting data for the graph,

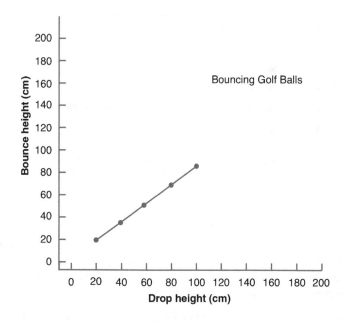

children varied the drop height of a golf ball systematically and recorded the rebound height of the ball for each drop height. Criteria for line graphs are given in Figure 9-4.

It is scientific convention to plot the manipulated or independent variable on the horizontal (x) axis and to plot the responding or dependent variable on the vertical (y) axis. The mnemonic DRY MIX is helpful for remembering this convention:

> The **D**ependent or **R**esponding variable is plotted on the **Y** axis.

> The **M**anipulated or **I**ndependent variable is plotted on the **X** axis.

Study the line graph in Figure 9-3 to see how the graphing conventions of Figure 9-4 are applied. For example, if students are studying bouncing golf balls, the vertical axis shows bounce height (the responding variable in centimeters) and the horizontal axis shows drop height (the manipulated variable, also in centimeters). Using the whiteboard, chalk board, or overhead, show your students how to place a point on the graph to represent the data, as well as how to draw smooth, best-fit lines indicating the pattern or relationship of the data.

Figure 9-4 Criteria for constructing line graphs in science.

1. The manipulated variable is graphed on the horizontal axis, or x axis.
2. The responding variable is graphed on the vertical axis, or y axis.
3. The name of each variable is placed along the appropriate axis.
4. The unit of measurement of each variable is included along with its label.
5. The axes are uniformly scaled and numerals are placed at regular intervals along each axis.
6. The graph is given a descriptive title.
7. Data points are plotted on the graph.
8. A smooth line, either straight or curving, is drawn through or near each point on the graph to show the best-fit pattern of the data.

Students should understand that in using mathematics in scientific investigations, they will "encounter all the anomalies of authentic problems—inconsistencies, outliers, and errors—which they might not encounter with contrived textbook data" (National Research Council, 1996, pp. 214, 218). Thus, if certain data points do not fall on a projected trend line, students should consider whether the points might be anomalies or errors and retake that data.

In connecting mathematics and science, it is important that students not only construct tables and graphs but also interpret them.

Using Patterns and Relationships

Science and mathematics can also be connected through finding mathematical patterns and relationships and using them in interpreting physical situations (see Table 9-1 and Figure 9-1). Patterns and relationships found in tables and graphs enable students to

- make predictions from collected data;
- formulate and test possible relationships between variables in the science/mathematics activities performed;
- construct hypotheses about possible patterns of change in their obtained data; and
- draw conclusions and inferences from data (Curcio, 1989).

Let us look at some examples of using charts and graphs to make interpretations in science.

Making Predictions from Graphs Predicting is an excellent way for students to use their data and for you to assess student understanding. Predictions can be made, for example, from the bouncing ball graph in Figure 9-3.

After some time investigating the bouncing ball and constructing graphs (as described in the previous section), ask students to predict what they think the rebound height will be for, say, a 200 cm drop height. To do this, students should first extend the graph line, making sure that it follows the pattern of the graphed data. Next, they should locate the 200 cm point on the *x* axis and draw a vertical line straight up from it until it intersects the graph line. Students can then read across to the *y* axis to predict the rebound height for a ball dropped from 200 cm. With appropriate safety precautions, teams should check their predictions by dropping the ball from the new height and measuring the rebound height.

For golf balls, children should find that their measured rebound height for a 200 cm or greater drop height is very close to their predicted rebound height. Interestingly, this is not the case for Ping-Pong balls. Why do you think this is so? The answer has to do with the air resistance experienced by the very light Ping-Pong balls.

Another investigation that can promote data collection and graphical analysis concerns the swing time for pendulums.

Swingers The Full Option Science System (1990) has provided an interesting activity on pendulums, in which collected data are displayed on a concrete line graph. In the activity, students are given long strings and directed to attach a small weight to one end of each string. Students then trim each string to a specific length, such as 13 cm, 15 cm, 17 cm, 18 cm, 20 cm, and so on. The students determine the number of swings in 15 seconds for their particular pendulum lengths. Next, they hang their pendulums from pushpins arranged along a number line to uniformly display the number of swings in 15 seconds for different

> Recall from Chapter 2 that a prediction is a forecast of an outcome based on knowledge of patterns or trends. A line graph visually displays the pattern of the relationship between two variables.

Figure 9-5 A concrete line graph depicting the number of swings pendulums of different length take in 15 seconds.
Adapted from FOSS® (Full Option Science System®) Variables, Investigation 1: swingers. © The Regents of the University of California and published by Delta Education. Adapted with permission.

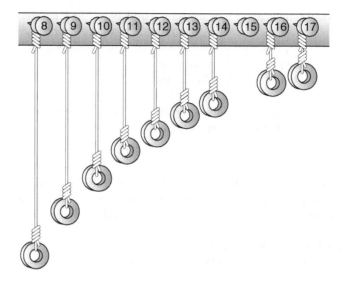

An interesting research study investigating how students with special needs and regular education students form generalizations from pendulum data is described in Chapter 10.

length pendulums. The strings have been cut so that there are whole numbers of swings in 15 seconds, for example 13 swings in 15 seconds.

When all of the data have been collected and the pendulums hung from the number line, the pendulum strings are seen to form a gentle curve (see Figure 9-5). The curve shows a relationship that can be detected and expressed by students: The longest length pendulums have the fewest number of swings in 15 seconds, and the shortest pendulums have the most swings in 15 seconds. That is, the longer the pendulum length, the fewer the number of swings in 15 seconds.

As part of the pendulum swingers activity, the students are given a swing rate for which swing data have not been collected, for example, 15 swings in 15 seconds or 6 swings in 15 seconds. They are asked to use their graph to predict the length of the pendulum that would produce that swing rate. In making predictions, the students simply hold a new string up to the graph and fix the new string length so that it will continue the gentle curve pattern established. Students then test their predictions by counting the number of swings in 15 seconds for their new pendulums to see if the length they chose produces the desired swing rate.

Operating on Numerical Data

Table 9-1 and Figure 9-1 show that operating on numerical data is another way to connect mathematics and science. Numbers obtained in scientific investigations through counting and measurement processes often need to be operated on mathematically. Lengths may need to be *added*, and weights of containers may need to be *subtracted* from total weights to determine the weights of contents. Areas might be calculated through *multiplication*; ratios, such as densities, and rates, such as speeds, must be obtained through *division*; averages must be determined through *addition* and *division* operations; and so on. Understanding mathematical operations on numbers is essential for students in understanding concepts in prealgebra and algebra.

Children encounter mathematical relationships from a very early age, for example, when pulling a wagon uphill. From experience, the child might predict that more force will be needed to pull a wagon up a steeper hill. An upper elementary or middle school student may take data on the required force to pull a cart up planes of different angles of inclination, put the data in a chart of ordered pairs, and graph the data.

At upper middle school grades, the student may search for an equation to model the mathematical relationship. Once an equation is developed, it may be manipulated through algebraic and arithmetic operations to predict the exact amount of force required to move an object of a given weight up inclined planes of different heights. The equation is connected back to the real world through the graphs, tables, measurements, verbal descriptions, and physical manipulations that serve to represent the mathematical relationship at different levels of thought. Historically, one of Galileo's great contributions to modern science was his pioneering use of mathematics to describe physical situations (Sobel, 2000). By using mathematics to summarize (or model) past experiences and to analyze real-world situations, students demonstrate true mathematical understanding.

Mathematics of the Balance. Children experience balancing from very early ages. For example, young children physically balance themselves as they walk on narrow rails, play on seesaws, or learn to ride a bicycle. Children's actions reveal the ways they think about balancing. When they start to fall to one side when walking on balance boards, they shift their weight to the other side by extending an arm or leg. A lighter child might balance a heavier child on a seesaw by sitting further out toward the end of the seesaw board. These actions show that young children are implicitly using mathematical ideas in understanding and adapting to physical reality. The seeds of mathematical thinking are present in the children's mental and physical actions.

In one FOSS (Lowery, 1998) investigation of balancing, students attempt to balance a cardboard cutout figure on the end of a finger. Children quickly discover several ways to balance the figure. They are then challenged to place clothespins at different points on the figure (to shift its center of gravity) and to discover new ways to balance it. Children solve the problem by finding a balance point that enables the weights to be distributed around it.

Qualitative Thinking About the Balance. The NSES and the NCTM standards emphasize the importance of the qualitative dimensions of children's mathematical learning. When children think qualitatively, they compare and make judgments about whether variables are equal, or one is greater or less than another, without regard to exact numbers or measurements. According to the mathematics standards,

> The mathematical ideas that children acquire in grades K–4 form the basis for all further study of mathematics. Although quantitative considerations have frequently dominated discussions in recent years, *qualitative* considerations have greater significance. (NCTM, 1989, p. 16. Emphasis added)

Children's success with quantitative thinking and problem-solving activities in mathematics and science programs at later grade levels depends largely on the qualitative foundations established in the earlier years of school.

Inhelder and Piaget (1958) have carried out a detailed study of children's mathematical thinking about the balance. Around ages 8 or 9, at the concrete operational level, balance is seen to be a function of four variable factors working together:

- weight on one side
- distance of that weight from the middle
- weight on the other side
- distance of the other weight from the middle

The Invicta Math-Balance, sold by various science education equipment companies, is an excellent tool for studying balancing from kindergarten through middle school. Addresses for science education equipment companies are given in Appendix C.

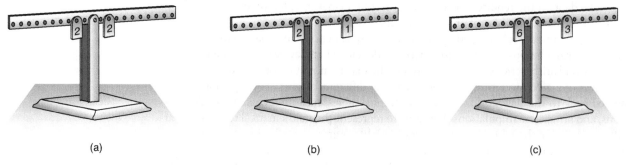

Figure 9-6 (a) Qualitative Rule #1: Equal weights at equal distances will balance. (b) Qualitative Rule #2: Heavier weights close in can balance lighter weights farther out. (c) Quantitative Rule: When the product of the weight and distance on one side of the pivot is equal to the product of weight and distance on the other side, the balance bar will be horizontal.

Through discovery activities and teacher instruction, these four variables can be coordinated into rules, though the rules are qualitative or nonnumerical at this stage. Two main rules are learned initially:

* Equal weights at equal distances will balance [see Figure 9-6(a)].
* Heavier weights close in can balance lighter weights further out [see Figure 9-6(b)].

The first rule is a symmetry rule. Children predict that, for an equal-arm balance, if weights are equal and distances are equal, the crossbar will balance. Younger children may implicitly know the symmetry rule, but they tend to focus on either the weights *or* the positions, not both at the same time. Thus, younger children may take incomplete data and fail to apply the symmetry rule appropriately. Children in third or fourth grade who are at the concrete operational level can consider the weights and distances simultaneously and use the symmetry rule to consistently predict balance.

The second balance rule, placing heavier weights closer to the center, is also a qualitative rule. It involves a nonnumerical combination of weights and distances. In making qualitative comparisons using the rule, children may note, for example, that one weight is considerably heavier than the other. If the two weights are to balance, the first one must be much closer to the central pivot-point than the second one.

The children's qualitative rules govern their trial-and-error learning as they add and take off weights and move them to different positions. This reversible and flexible way of thinking about qualitative relationships makes complex thought about numerical operations truly possible.

Quantitative Thinking About the Balance. Around fifth or sixth grade, many children can extend their qualitative rules through using exact numbers to represent weights and distances. When one side of a balance beam has more weights, the young mathematical scientist goes beyond qualitative questions about more and less and asks such questions as:

* How much heavier is it? How much farther out is it?
* What is the proportion? Is it twice as much or three times as much?

If the weight on one side is twice as much, for example, then to compensate, either the weight or the distance on the other side has to be twice as much for balance. If this type of thinking is to be useful, it must build on the qualitative thinking at an earlier level.

At some point in the formal operational stage, the student begins to understand the use of formal mathematics to coordinate the four numerical variables. The quantitative rule of the balance can then be understood and applied [see Figure 9-6(c)]. Stated in the form of an equation, the quantitative rule of the balance is:

$$WL \times DL = WR \times DR$$

where W = weight, D = distance, L = left side, and R = right side of the balance. Thus, the product of the weight and distance on one side is equal to the product of weight and distance on the other side. Try the equation for yourself using Figure 9-6(a), (b), and (c). The products of the weights and distances on the left side will equal the products on the right side for each of these three cases.

This equation summarizes experiences at the qualitative level; for example, heavy weights must be placed closer to the pivot for balance. The quantitative rule, however, tells the child exactly how much closer to the pivot the heavier weight would need to be for balance.

The principle governing equal-arm balances also governs the operation of levers. Using a small force far out from a fulcrum, a person can lift a heavy load that is closer to the fulcrum. Using the equation, students can predict how much force is needed to lift a load of a given weight when the distances involved are known. By using mathematics to summarize (or model) past experiences and to analyze real-world situations students develop and demonstrate true mathematical understanding.

Balances and other hands-on materials provide students opportunities to personally bridge from the concrete world to the abstract world of mathematics. In so doing, students must talk about concrete objects and their actions on them, find qualitative ways to represent their thinking, and eventually construct ways of coordinating numerical variables that describe the real world. When they learn to think about mathematics and its applications in this way, students are better prepared to negotiate the complex ideas of advanced mathematics and science in later grades.

There are many more opportunities for you to integrate mathematics into your science program. To augment your own creativity, examine the abundance of excellent lessons in contemporary nationally funded science programs and on the Internet that connect science and mathematics. For exemplary activities, see FOSS (Full Option Science System) and STC (Science and Technology for Children). The URLs for the websites for these and other programs are given in Appendix F.

Next, we will discuss connections between science and language arts.

Connecting Science and Literacy

Teachers of all subjects should be engaged in language instruction. As stated in the *Standards for the English Language Arts* (International Reading Association, 1996),

> Language is the most powerful, most readily available tool we have for representing the world. . . . Language is not only a means of communication, it is a primary instrument of thought. . . . Encouraging and enabling students to use language effectively is certainly one of society's most important tasks. (p. 12)

Literacy instruction in schools generally includes four areas: reading, writing, speaking, and listening. These critical elements of language learning occur in all curricular areas and should not be separated from substantive content in science, mathematics, social studies, and other subjects. An emphasis on literacy across the curriculum is a natural way for students to learn and use language skills to communicate and reason in specific domains, as well as in their everyday lives.

A teacher of science can do many things to help students enhance their language abilities and, at the same time, enrich their science learning. The elements of literacy are valuable for students in doing science and should be promoted through science instruction as well as in language arts classes. For example, in helping students develop language and thinking processes, teachers of both science and language arts are called on to

- develop, extend, and refine the knowledge base of students;
- assist students to organize knowledge into useful schemas or networks;
- learn vocabulary that is related to topics being studied;
- provide students with opportunities to use reading, listening, and viewing behaviors; and
- supply many opportunities for practice and rehearsal in communicating through writing, speaking, and representing things visually (Ormrod, 2007).

Let us focus first on reading. How can science and reading be connected for students?

Science and Reading

A helpful collection of articles on the why and how to use science texts in instruction can be found in *Science Learning: Processes and Implications* (Santa & Alvermann, 1991). This volume, with contributions from reading and science specialists, is sponsored by the International Reading Association.

Santa and Alvermann (1991) noted, "Science and reading teachers have very similar goals for their students. Foremost is the pursuit of meaning" (p. vi). In science, students construct meaning from the natural world; in reading, they construct meaning from text. Although investigative processes in science and comprehension processes in reading are quite different, processing strategies remain at the heart of both disciplines. Both science and reading teachers want their students to be able to describe events, make inferences, interpret information, draw conclusions, and make and test predictions (Padilla, Muth, & Padilla, 1991; Tompkins, 2006).

Contemporary learning theories in both science and reading follow a constructivist view. In the traditional view of reading, meaning resided in the text; the reader's task was to ferret it out. In the constructivist view, the reader creates meaning based on the text, and her or his existing knowledge about its content, language, and structure (Tompkins, 2006).

A key element in the construction of meaning from text by students is their existing or prior knowledge.

An instructional tool often used to teach reading, a K–W–L chart can help you assess students' prior knowledge before beginning a new topic of study. (K–What Do You Know? W–What Do You Want to Learn? L–What Did You Learn?)

Prior Knowledge and Comprehending Science Text. Science text materials, whether in activity guides, laboratory manuals, or textbooks, are notoriously difficult for students at every level to read. In successfully comprehending a topic presented in science texts, a student's existing knowledge must be extensive, accurate, and consistent with the information presented in the text. Finley (1991) has suggested that teachers must make sure that readers have sufficient prior knowledge of terms, facts, concepts, and relationships to understand an assigned text selection. Thus, it makes sense to follow the dictum suggested in Chapter 4: *investigation first; reading later* (Lowery, 1998).

Students need extensive and repetitive experiences with hands-on, minds-on activities to develop connected, accurate, and useful knowledge. It is this type of knowledge that students must be able to draw on in reading science books.

Access to Prior Knowledge. To be able to comprehend written information, students must have prior existing knowledge, access what they know, and apply it appropriately. Students differ in the degree to which they use potentially available knowledge to learn and understand (Brown, Bransford, Ferrara, & Campione, 1983). Science teachers should scaffold learning to assist students in accessing and using what they know in comprehending text material.

Finley (1991) and others have suggested various ways that science teachers can help students draw on and use their existing knowledge. Teachers can help students assess prior knowledge by having them

- write initial descriptions and explanations of phenomena;
- construct concept maps of what they know;
- draw pictures and labeled diagrams of events, accompanied by written explanations; and
- present their ideas to the class so that alternative descriptions and explanations might be considered.

All of these examples portray the student as an active learner, both in acquiring new knowledge and in accessing it in reading. In addition to helping students acquire and use prior knowledge, teachers can help students approach reading more strategically.

Strategies for Comprehending Science Textbooks. Teachers should assist students in prereading, reading, and postreading strategies to help them make sense of what they read (Yopp & Yopp, 2006).

Prereading Strategies. In beginning a reading assignment in science, students should be clear about what they are expected to learn from the text. The teacher might begin by having students make predictions about the text content before reading (Padak & Davidson, 1991; Tompkins, 2006). When making predictions about text, children might first examine the illustrations and pictures given in the text. They close the text and make their predictions about words that might appear in it.

For example, in a selection on butterflies, children might predict from a butterfly illustration and their prior knowledge that caterpillars would be a word in the text (Yopp & Yopp, 2006). This prereading process helps students think about the relationships between the text information and their own prior knowledge.

In a case study reported by Padak and Davidson (1991), students who learned to predict text content before reading were able to read for a wider variety of purposes than before. Rather than reading simply to answer the teacher's questions or questions in the passage, they read to learn more about science concepts, to verify predictions that they or others had made, and to connect text presentations to their own prior knowledge.

Using Strategies During Reading.　Students should be taught to use comprehension-monitoring strategies during reading. Comprehension-monitoring strategies include such tasks as raising questions about the text, clarifying terms, identifying main ideas and supporting statements, paraphrasing and summarizing text meanings, and making and verifying inferences and predictions about text meaning. Such strategies are not easily learned from direct instruction or from teacher modeling, because the learner tends to be a passive observer in both cases (Brown et al., 1983).

King (1994) has adapted *reciprocal reading* procedures to science teaching and learning. In King's adaptation, two children work cooperatively in reading a science text, with the children alternating in the roles of dialogue leader and student. King has used prompt cards to successfully teach fourth- and fifth-grade children to deliberately ask themselves and one another questions to access prior science knowledge, comprehend what they have read, and make connections in constructing science explanations. A sample prompt card, which students may keep in front of them during the process of reading for understanding, is shown in Figure 9-7.

Postreading Strategies.　Discussion of the text is an important way to help students check on their comprehension. In discussion, go beyond asking factual questions about what was read. Rather, you should focus on helping students:

- Link text ideas with their prior knowledge and experience.
- Make connections between main ideas and supporting details.
- Recognize and think about text statements that conflict with their own ideas.
- Work to resolve conceptual confusion.
- Use concepts presented in text to explain other real-world phenomena (Roth, 1991).

These prereading, reading, and postreading strategies help readers pay attention to how they create meaning based on the text, their own existing content knowledge, and their knowledge about language.

Next, we will examine ways science and writing can be connected.

DIRECTIONS:

Discuss the lesson with each other.

Ask each other questions.
Answer each other's questions by giving explanations.

Comprehension questions
　Describe . . . in your own words.
　What does . . . mean?
　Why is . . . important?

Connection questions
　Explain why . . .
　Explain how . . .
　How are . . . and . . . similar?
　What is the difference between . . . and . . . ?
　How could . . . be used to . . . ?
　What would happen if . . . ?
　How does . . . tie in with . . . that we learned before?

Figure 9-7　(a) A sample prompt card for interactive reading procedures.　(b) Prompt card given to students to facilitate understanding of science texts.

Writing in Science

The writers of the *Standards for the English Language Arts* (International Reading Association, 1996) assert that

> Reading and writing are intertwined. . . . Just as students need an array of strategies to comprehend . . . text written by others, so too do they need to apply an array of strategies as they write. (p. 34)

To build these strategies, students need frequent opportunities to write on different topics and for different purposes. Science provides students with many opportunities to write.

Writing in science forces students to consider their audience, clarify their questions, organize and present their data more clearly, and form more secure links among data, prior knowledge, and conclusions. Organizing and presenting their findings and conclusions to others helps students make new information their own and connect it to their prior understandings. Furthermore, according to the *National Science Education Standards,*

> Oral and written communication skills are developed in science when students record, summarize and communicate the results of inquiry. . . . Coordination suggests that these skills receive attention in the language arts program as well as the science program. (National Research Council, 1996, 214).

Writing might take place in journals or on prepared investigation sheets. Observation journals, sometimes referred to as *science notebooks*, provide an opportunity for students from primary grades through middle school to enhance both their science learning and writing approaches (Santa & Havens, 1991). Journal writing in science might also routinely include labeled illustrations as well as narrative descriptions and explanations. Journals may contain observations of a demonstration, personal explanations of a discrepant event, data collected through investigations, reactions to a film or oral presentation, and personal notes from reading an assignment. Journals allow students to write informally and personally explore content.

Connecting Science and Social Studies

Making connections between science and social studies helps students create a more complete picture of the world. While science emphasizes how the natural world works, social studies addresses the multiple roles of humans as they adapt to their surroundings and reorganize ways they relate to each other.

Social studies cuts across and combines several disciplines. According to the National Council for the Social Studies (1994),

> Social studies is the integrated study of the social sciences and humanities to promote civic competence. Within the school program, social studies provides coordinated, systematic study drawing upon such disciplines as anthropology, archaeology, economics, geography, history, law, philosophy, political science, psychology, religion, and sociology, as well as appropriate content from the humanities, mathematics, and natural sciences. The primary purpose of social studies is to help young people develop the ability to make informed and reasoned decisions for the public good as citizens of a culturally diverse, democratic society in an interdependent world. (p. 3)

Interactions between science and technology play a vital part in helping students understand their relationship to the world around them.

Go to the Homework and Exercises section in Chapter 9 of MyEducationLab and view the videos for this chapter, entitled *Science and Literacy: Parts 1* and *2*. In these videos, we return to the excerpts on goldfish (grade 1), recycling (grade 3), particles (grade 3), and pin-hole cameras (grade 5). The focus this time around is on children's writing and drawing as they keep records of what they notice and what they wonder about.

Go to the Homework and Exercises section in Chapter 9 of MyEducationLab, access the artifact called *Variables,* and study a student's reaction in his journal to a control of variables problem.

The national social studies standards can be found on the National Council for Social Studies (NCSS) website at http://www.socialstudies.org.

Plan Lessons Around Science/Technology/Society Themes

One of the 10 themes of the NCSS standards is science, technology, and society. This theme is also found in various state-level frameworks for social studies, which draw on the standards. In one state (Texas Education Agency, 1999), for example, social studies standards include a strand for each grade level called Science, Technology, and Society. Throughout the elementary and middle school grades, students are challenged to understand how science and technology have affected human life past and present. Appropriate to their levels of development, students are expected to

* describe how science and technology have changed transportation, communication, medicine, agriculture, industry, and recreation;
* explain how science and technology have changed the ways people meet their basic needs;
* analyze environmental changes brought about by scientific discoveries and technological innovations;
* give examples of the contributions of scientists and inventors that have shaped society;
* explain how resources, belief systems, economic factors, and political decisions have affected the use of technology from place to place, culture to culture, and society to society; and
* make predictions about future social, economic, and environmental consequences that may result from future scientific discoveries and technological innovations.

In state-level frameworks for both science and social studies, student expectations are often closely related. Both types of frameworks call for students at different grade levels to study common topics such as the use of natural resources, the history of science and scientists, the effects of physical processes on the environment, and the societal impact of energy usage. Social studies processes shared with science include representation, problem solving, decision making, data collection, data interpretation, and critical thinking.

Weather: A Science and Social Studies Lesson for Grade 3

Investigating weather provides an excellent way to merge social studies and science expectations. The following lesson on weather combines ideas from a number of sources to illustrate connections between science and social studies.

In the lesson, students work in groups to design and construct wind socks to determine what directon the wind is blowing and rain gauges to measure the amount of rainfall in a period of time. They also use thermometers to measure the outside temperature. In using these weather instruments, students have to determine what readings to take and when to take them. This lesson is included in the Annenberg video, *Bring It All Together: Processing for Meaning During Inquiry,* which is featured in the Chapter 3 Online Professional Development section.

Each day, students take data and record their data in writing on data record sheets or in their science notebooks. Through group and class discussion, students reflect on and synthesize their data to describe the local weather. In connecting to social studies, students work in groups to access Internet weather data and record the weather in different geographic regions, such as Argentina, Cambodia, Australia, Mexico, Canada, Portugal, South Africa, and Russia. Web information available to students includes physical and weather maps of each region and pictures that give identity to each area. A compendium of web resources for weather worldwide can be found on the Franklin Institute website at http://www.2.fi.edu/.

In order to apply weather information in decision making, each student describes how people in each region dress for their local weather conditions. The students write daily journal entries about the weather, the people, and unique features of the region.

As the lesson progresses each day, students develop both science and social studies concepts by exploring how humans collect weather data and how they deal with the physical processes related to weather and climate. Students also use current events to determine how weather affects the way people live. Further, students develop essential computer skills as they become weather watchers.

In concluding the lesson, students answer questions such as: *What weather instruments are used to measure weather conditions? How can weather data best be recorded? How does the weather change? How is weather different in various regions? Why is weather important to us? Why is it helpful to predict the weather?* These questions get to the heart of social studies and science because they lead students to understand the characteristics of weather, the instruments and processes real scientists use to describe and explain weather, the effects weather has on humans, and the many ways humans cope with constantly changing weather phenomena.

A River Ran Wild: A Science and Social Studies Lesson for Grades 3–5

An example of connecting science and social studies at grades 3–5 centers on a study of the book *A River Ran Wild* by Lynne Cherry (1992). The goal of this learning experience is to guide students in understanding that the history of a given environment can reveal how humans have affected an ecosystem in both responsible and irresponsible ways. In this study, students expand their understanding of the environment and its relationship to humans by merging the theme of science, technology, and society with other social studies themes, including people, places, and environment, time, continuity, and change, civic ideals and practices, and culture.

The class is divided into five groups, with each group assigned to answer one of these five guiding questions:

1. In what ways have humans historically affected particular ecosystems?
2. How do cultural beliefs and practices affect the quality of the environment?
3. What physical and human factors cause an environment to change over time?
4. How can humans help change a polluted environment?
5. How can industry exist and progress within an ecologically sound environment?

Each group researches their question and illustrates their answer by making posters or creating a multimedia presentation. The presentations include the portion of *A River Ran Wild* that deals with their question as well as answers from two other sources such as the Internet, resource books, newspaper articles, or interviews.

After students have presented their answers to the first five questions, a sixth question is posed for all students:

6. What do people in my community do to preserve our environment?

A community expert is enlisted to guide the students in answering this question. Before the expert comes to class, students write a letter summarizing what they have learned from the class presentations. This informs the expert about the students' background knowledge and also gives the students an opportunity to demonstrate understanding of all the issues raised in the guiding questions. The expert not only talks to students and answers their questions but also may arrange field trips or other appropriate means for students to

For some creative ideas about using community resources to extend this study, see Lois R. Stanley (1995), "A River Runs Through Science Learning: Tap Community Resources to Create an Integrated Science and Social Studies Unit," *Science and Children,* 52(4), 12–15, 58.

attain information. As a culminating activity, once students have answered the sixth question, they develop a rubric for an ecologically balanced community and rank their community on the basis of the rubric. Where there are problems, students may write a request to state, county, or city officials asking them to address the situations. Where there are environmentally sound practices, students write letters thanking the people who are responsible for creating a safe environment for all living things.

Through their encounter with *A River Ran Wild* and by being engaged in the lesson's procedures, students meet the expectations outlined in the national standards and grow as informed, environmentally aware, and responsible citizens.

The lessons about weather and *A River Ran Wild* illustrate how science and social studies fit together well for effective student understanding of the earth and its systems. Students benefit when teachers merge science and social studies concepts, processes, and approaches to learning on appropriate occasions and in a manner that fosters learning the essential elements of both science and social studies.

The Environment and Native American Culture: A Science/Social Studies Lesson for Upper Grades

You can view the video on *Case Studies in Science Education: Donna* on the Annenberg website. Instructions for accessing Annenberg videos are given in the Online Professional Development section of Chapter 1.

Donna, a fifth-grade teacher featured in the Annenberg video *Case Study in Science Education: Donna*, has integrated the curriculum for her students around the themes of the environment and Native American cultural heritage. In Donna's classroom, 25% of the students are Native American, while another 25% are Hispanic. One of Donna's main goals for her students is that they all "feel they have a very important heritage . . . all people have contributed to the body of knowledge we call science."

As part of a study of native plants and animals, Donna asks students to study and retell Native American myths and folktales. She emphasizes that these myths and folktales are not true stories, but they incorporate various accurate observations about nature. Donna wants her students to understand that the observations expressed in the myths often have scientific understandings at their foundation. The students share the stories with their class members using various means, including narratives, plays, and puppet shows.

The students take field trips to two ancient Native American sites and participate in an ongoing archaeological dig, using their mathematics skills to document the precise location of artifacts they discover. They also write stories that reveal their ideas about why people living in the area centuries ago might have abandoned their settlements.

In a culminating activity, students complete a chart identifying elements that are common to different cultures, such as food, shelter, medicine, and transportation. Then they construct shoe-box middens in which they have buried household items that represent their own "clan." Middens are exchanged between groups, who "excavate" the shoe-box middens to study the past as evidenced by the artifacts.

SUMMARY

- National standards in every discipline support connections between subjects in the school curriculum. There are important connections to be made between science and mathematics, language arts, social studies, and other school subjects.
- Connections between science and mathematics can center on four main themes: quantifying the world, organizing

and interpreting data, using patterns and relationships, and operating on numbers.

- Children begin to quantify the world through counting, estimating, and measuring all kinds of real-world variables that they encounter in the process of investigating. Measuring should be emphasized in both science and mathematics. When children encounter measurement in problem-solving activities in science, they go beyond practice to engage in rehearsal. Through rehearsal, they not only develop skills, they add something to them.

• Organizing data into diagrams, tables, and graphs is a key step in scientific inquiry. The types of graphs most often used in elementary and middle schools are bar graphs, histograms, and line graphs. Putting data obtained from scientific investigations into tables and graphs better enables students to relate data to their investigative procedures, make comparisons among data, see relationships and patterns, and communicate their data to other people.

• Science and mathematics can also be connected through using mathematical patterns and relationships in interpreting physical situations. Patterns and relationships found in tables and graphs enable students to make predictions, formulate and test hypotheses, and draw conclusions and inferences from data.

• Operating on numerical data is another way to connect mathematics and science. Understanding mathematical operations on numbers obtained from investigations is an essential prerequisite for understanding the use of functions in prealgebra and algebra, and in high school science courses. In science and mathematics, quantitative treatments of data should be preceded by qualitative, nonnumerical investigations.

• Connecting science to reading and writing is critically important in the elementary and middle school classroom. Science teachers can help students succeed in reading through helping them acquire necessary prior knowledge, guiding them in using comprehensive strategies, and following up after science reading assignments. There are also many opportunities in science for learners to use and improve their writing skills as they communicate their inquiries to others.

• Science, technology, and society themes are common to science and social studies standards. Lessons built around such topics as weather and the environment show how science and social studies can be linked. There are many opportunities for students to connect these two disciplines as they embark on re-creations of this fantastic voyage of discovery.

ONLINE PROFESSIONAL DEVELOPMENT

Pre- and post-tests to assess your knowledge of chapter content, along with exercises to enhance your understanding, can be found on MyEducationLab at www.myeducationlab.com.

Video Guides

Video clips on MyEducationLab selected for this chapter include: *Science and Literacy—Parts 1 and 2*.

Accessing the Videos

1. Go to the Homework and Exercises section in Chapter 9 of MyEducationLab to select and view videos for this chapter.
2. Videos might be viewed individually, by small groups of colleagues, or by the whole class.
3. As you watch each video, use the **Questions for Reflection** to guide your thoughts and note taking for personal use and group discussion.
4. Discuss your answers to the questions about each video with classmates.

Video: Science and Literacy—Parts 1 and 2

Overview

In these videos, we return to the excerpts on goldfish (grade 1), recycling (grade 3), particles (grade 3), and pin-hole cameras (grade 5). The focus this time around is on children's writing and drawing as they keep records of what they notice and what they wonder about.

Questions for Reflection

1. What kinds of records do you see children using in the classroom excerpts? How do the children blend writing and drawing in keeping observational records?
2. What does the teacher do to guide the children's writing about what they notice about goldfish?
3. How is the I Notice/I Wonder chart used in the goldfish and recycling lessons?
4. In the goldfish excerpt, how does the teacher use children's literature to promote student understanding?
5. There is no audio in the first part of the particles lesson, but what do you infer about the teacher's goals in using the vocabulary cards?
6. How does the teacher in the recycling lesson use PowerPoint?

10

T he increasing diversity of the school age population, coupled with differential science performance among student demographic groups, makes the goal of "science for all" a national challenge.

(Lee, 2002, p. 23)

Science for All Learners

YOUR ELEMENTARY OR MIDDLE SCHOOL SCIENCE CLASSROOM will include a diverse group of students. In addition to general education students, you will be responsible for teaching students with disabilities, students from different cultural and linguistic backgrounds, and students with special gifts and talents. The *National Science Education Standards* emphasize that science must be for all students: All students—regardless of race, gender, cultural or ethnic background, disabilities, aspirations, or interest and motivation in science—should have the opportunity to attain high levels of scientific literacy (National Research Council, 1996, p. 20). This principle is one of equity and excellence. It challenges science teachers to meet the needs of all students, requiring them to recognize the diversity of students and to prepare science experiences to address these differences.

All children are unique. They will achieve understanding in different ways and at different depths as they explore answers to questions about the natural world (National Research Council, 1996, p. 20). Some children have special learning needs. You may need to adapt science activities for students who have disabilities, or you may need to work much more closely with them to scaffold learning. Students who are English Language Learners (ELLs) may need special instructional strategies, or they may need to work with other students who can help them access material more readily. Gifted and talented students may challenge you to find ways to lead them to ever-deeper understanding.

Whatever adaptations you need to make, you will want to consider the following questions to help you plan for the diverse backgrounds and abilities of your students:

- *Who are the students with special learning needs? What are likely to be the learning challenges and special needs of individual students in your science classroom?*
- *What are the goals of science for students with special learning needs?*
- *What special modifications in materials, equipment, instruction, and assessment strategies should be made in science for students with special learning needs?*
- *How can you meet the learning needs of students in your science classroom who are gifted and talented?*
- *What are the learning challenges and special needs of ELL students in your science classroom? What is sheltered instruction? How can you best help students acquire science knowledge and skills and learn English at the same time?*

NSES You can review the *National Science Education Standards* online. Go to http://www.nap.edu/readingroom/books/nses/html.

The following sections will help you begin to build a bank of resources from which you can draw as you teach science in an inclusive classroom.

Students with Special Learning Needs

Who are the learners with special needs who will likely be included in your classroom? Although we run the risk of losing sight of individual values and differences when we categorize students, it is useful with the enormous numbers of students in public education to group diverse learners into these categories (Mastropieri & Scruggs, 2004):

- Students with disabilities
- Gifted and talented student
- Students with linguistically and culturally diverse backgrounds

Although students in each of these groups may exhibit special learning needs, federal legislation addresses educational modification for only the first category—students with disabilities. Various states have passed laws relating to the identification and education of students in other categories. However, in many cases funding for accommodations is inadequate or not provided.

Grouping students according to their special learning needs can mask an essential truth: All of us are unique. Even within the same culture, community, or family, we are all different. Your students will have varying intellectual abilities and learning styles, diverse language and cultural backgrounds, and physical, social, and emotional differences. All will enter your classroom having experienced life differently. Thus, their understanding of the world will be different. The varied experiences, background knowledge, and abilities of your students should influence how you plan for and teach science.

Common Standards, Common Assessments, Diverse Pathways

Although different learning pathways and modifications in teaching approaches may be necessary for individuals and special groups, the goals of science instruction are the same for all learners. The *National Science Education Standards* (National Research Council, 1996) state that

> The understandings and abilities described in the content standards are for all students; they do not represent different expectations for different groups of students. (pp. 221–222)

The standards assert that all students should be expected to achieve the same science knowledge and inquiry standards, though learning approaches and levels of achievement may vary.

The No Child Left Behind Act of 2001 requires adherence to this principle. Although there will be modifications in materials, instruction, and testing conditions, students with disabilities and students who are learning English must take the same statewide assessments and be included in statistical analyses.

Planning for individual student needs in science requires knowing the general characteristics of students with different disabilities. The Individuals with Disabilities Education Act (IDEA) recognizes about a dozen disabilities. Data from the National Center for Education Statistics (http://www.nces.ed.gov) indicate that in 2003–2004, students with disabilities represented 13.7% of the public school student population. Approximately 6.6 million students with identified disabilities require special education services.

Statistics from the National Center for Education Statistics indicate that in 2003–2004, 42.7% of students with disabilities were categorized as having specific learning disabilities. Four categories of disabilities—specific learning disabilities, speech or language impairments, mental retardation, or emotional disturbance—account for 80.7% of all students with disabilities. Statistics from the center indicate that in 2003–2004, 49.9% of students with disabilities spent at least 80% of the school day in regular education classrooms, a figure that was up noticeably from the 31% of 1988–1989.

IDEA, which governs the education of students with disabilities, directs that all students have the right to a full, free public education in the *least restrictive environment*. This means that schools are required to educate students with disabilities with nondisabled students to the maximum extent appropriate for the students with disabilities.

Making Modifications for Students with Special Learning Needs

There are a variety of considerations to remember as you plan learning experiences, make modifications, and implement instruction for students with disabilities.

Use Individualized Education Plans (IEPS). Some students with disabillities will enter your classroom with an IEP (individualized education plan) in place. You should view the IEP as a dynamic, working document intended to improve student learning, rather than a set of legalities to be fulfilled. Recorded on each IEP are learning goals and objectives designed for an individual student. Once a student with special needs has been assigned to your class, you will want to review her IEP goals and objectives to see what science activities or experiences will help to meet these goals. For example, one goal in an IEP might read: *Develop communication skills and interactions with peers.*

Science teachers can help to meet this individual learning goal by including the student in a cooperative learning group. Within this group students may be asked to engage in an inquiry activity that requires meaningful student interaction to discover and communicate findings revealed by the data. The student with a disability could be required to communicate her understanding of the phenomena she observes to her peers, and together they could determine how to report these findings.

Even though the IEP lists general goals to advance the education and socialization of the student with special needs, you should develop specific science objectives that will move the student from what she knows to learning new concepts and inquiry strategies called for in state and district standards and curriculum frameworks. Just as you would strive to do this for nondisabled students, based on their abilities, so you would do this for your students with disabilities. Ascertain their areas of interest and the conceptions they have of science knowledge, and plan instruction for them accordingly.

The following sections provide concrete ideas for working with students who have varied cognitive differences, students with emotional or behavioral disorders, students with orthopedic disabilities, students who are blind or have low vision, and students who are deaf or hard of hearing.

Science for Students with Specific Learning Disabilities

Defined by IDEA, the term *specific learning disability* means a disorder in one or more of the basic psychological processes involved in understanding or in using language, spoken or written. A disorder may manifest itself in imperfect ability to listen, think, speak, read, write, spell, reason, or do mathematical calculations.

Students with learning disabilities (LD) are commonly in the normal range of intelligence. Sometimes, in fact, they are gifted intellectually. However, students with learning

---

Since the passage of IDEA in 1997, schools have been striving toward the inclusion of students with physical, mental, sensory, and emotional challenges in the classroom. Still, students with disabilities too often experience barriers to science learning. The NSTA Position Statement on Students with Disabilities identifies some of these barriers and makes recommendations about how teachers and administrators can address them (available online at http://www.nsta.org/about/positions.aspx).

NSES *"Teachers of science guide and facilitate learning; recognizing and responding to student diversity and encouraging all students to participate fully in science learning."*
(*National Science Education Standards*, Teaching Standard B)

A very useful and well-organized compilation of strategies for teaching science to students with learning disabilities and other disorders is available online. Go to http://www.as.wvu.edu/~scidis/sitemap.html.

disabilities are generally achieving below their current grade level, or are several grade levels below where they should be, in one or more basic academic skill areas such as reading, written language, or math.

What Teaching Approaches in Science Are Most Appropriate for Students with LD? Students with learning disabilities are a heterogeneous group and can have overlapping problems. This makes it difficult to classify their learning discrepancies and prescribe learning activities and approaches for them. However, research and practical experience support some general strategies to enhance science instruction. These include the use of

- activities-based science;
- intensive scaffolding;
- learning strategies;
- visual presentations and multimedia in general; and
- mnemonics and graphic organizers.

Select an Inquiry Approach.   Tom Scruggs and Margo Mastropieri, a husband-wife team at George Mason University, have conducted a variety of research studies to investigate the most appropriate methods of teaching science to students with special needs. With two colleagues (Scruggs, Mastropieri, Bakken, & Brigham, 1993), they carried out a controlled investigation comparing textbook and activities-based, inquiry approaches to teaching science to students with learning disabilities.

In the study, 26 seventh- and eighth-grade students with LD received instruction on two science topics—(1) rocks and minerals and (2) electricity and magnetism. All students received instruction through an activities approach on one of the topics and a textbook approach on the other. Lessons for the activities-based approach were from FOSS (Full Option Science System) modules. For example, in exploring electricity and magnetism, students constructed and investigated circuits, switches, an electromagnet, and a telegraph.

In the activities approach, teachers first presented problems to be investigated by students (the *engage,* phase of the 5-E model). Students then performed activities in small groups of three to five students (*explore*). The lesson was concluded with a whole class session, in which the activities were summarized and discussed (*explain*). FOSS materials were available for students to use in describing and recording their observations.

Lessons for the textbook approach paralleled the activities approach in content. In the textbook approach, teachers presented information, and students read text materials and examined pictures (such as pictures of circuits, switches, electromagnets, or telegraphs). The children engaged in independent and guided practice activities using worksheets.

Both approaches were well structured and involved daily review, active engagement by students, formative evaluation of student products, and questioning. Teachers in the activity approach raised questions and guided students to raise questions about what happened and why, but generally refrained from directly answering them. Instead, they encouraged and challenged students to answer questions for themselves. Questions in the textbook approach were most often directed toward promoting student attention and prompting direct recall of information provided.

Tests were given individually to students in both conditions for the lessons covering the two science topics. The tests emphasized recall of what students did in the science lesson, recall of facts and vocabulary, and application of concepts, principles, and procedures. Students were also asked four questions related to their enjoyment of the two approaches.

Working cooperatively with their general education peers assists students with exceptionalities to learn science effectively.

Interestingly, these modules on electricity and magnetism were designed for much lower grade levels (grades 3 and 4). Many science actvities can be adapted to the grade level you are teaching.

Results strongly favored the activities-based approach to science. Students in the activities approach scored significantly higher on the tests at the end of instruction. Additionally, almost all of the students enjoyed the activities approach more. Scruggs and colleagues (1993) concluded:

> Results of the present investigation suggest that activity-based, inquiry-oriented approaches, when appropriately structured, may facilitate the acquisition of content knowledge of students with LD. . . . In the present context, when students were taught by experiential, more indirect methods, they learned more, remembered more, and enjoyed learning more than when they were taught by more direct instructional methods. (pp. 10–11)

Fradd and Lee (1999) have suggested that, rather than debate about whether a textbook or inquiry approach is best, it may be more fruitful to consider how to use the two approaches in a complementary way to meet students' needs.

Use Questioning to Guide Active Thinking. An advantage of inquiry science for diverse learners, according to Mastropieri (Brownell & Thomas, 1998) is that it facilitates the efforts of classroom teachers to make appropriate modifications to accommodate different learning needs.

One modification teachers often make is to provide more scaffolding assistance to certain learners. Consider this example in which a teacher uses questioning to provide support for a group of seventh grade students with learning disabilities and mild mental retardation to help them draw conclusions from their observations. The students have participated in an activity in which white flowers were placed in water containing food dye and were observed over a period of time:

> *Teacher: . . . What do you think happened? I have a flower in blue water and a flower in green water, a white flower, right? Ken, what is the color of this flower?*
> *Ken: Blue.*
> *Sam: White.*
> *Teacher: White and blue. Julie, what color is this flower? (designating the second flower)*
> *Julie: Green.*
> *Teacher: White and green. How did I get the colors there? How did I get the colors there, Shawn?*
> *Shawn: That's from a stain in there like . . .*
> *Teacher: A stain? What do you think? Ken, how did this blue get here?*
> *Ken: . . . Oh, you watered it with food coloring.*
> *Teacher: But I didn't put any up here, did I?*
> *Ken: You put it in the dirt.*
> *Teacher: But there's no dirt.*
> *Ken: Oh.*
> *Teacher: OK, Jimmy, what do you think?*
> *Jimmy: It went all the way up to here.*
> *Teacher: Went all the way through water? The what, Mary?*
> *Mary: A stem.*
> *Teacher: The stem. It went all the way through the stem, you're right. (Scruggs, & Magnuson, 1999, p. 243)*

This example shows us how difficult it can be for some students to generalize from real-world experiences and form new science concepts. The students in the example did not initially generalize from their observations that water was transferred through the plants along stems. The children answered the teacher's questions only through a highly structured questioning approach.

Use Scaffolding to Enhance Understanding.   How well, compared to their general education peers, can special education students form generalizations from their science experiences? How much coaching will general education students and special education students need to make generalizations? These were questions addressed in an informative study by Mastropieri, Scruggs, and Butcher (1993).

A total of 54 junior high students participated in the study, including 20 general education students, 18 students with LD, and 16 students with mental retardation (MR). Students were seen individually by a teacher-examiner. Each student was shown a pendulum and taught how to count the number of complete back-and-forth swings the pendulum made in 10 seconds. Then, the pendulum was set in motion and the student counted the number of swings while the teacher-examiner kept the time.

The first pendulum made 10 swings in 10 seconds. The examiner recorded the number of swings on a sticker below the pendulum. The student and examiner then took data on three more pendulums. The number of swings each pendulum made in 10 seconds was recorded on a sticker below the appropriate pendulum. When the four pendulums were displayed together, the labeled number of swings read, from left to right, 10, 6, 12, and 8. The corresponding lengths of the pendulums, from left to right, were second longest, fourth longest (shortest), longest, and third longest.

Inductive reasoning is the process of generalizing, or drawing general rules based on a number of specific observations. In the 5-E approach to science teaching, students are often required to generalize during the explain phase from data taken during the explore phase of instruction. The task of students in the pendulum study was to generalize from observations of four instances that the longer a pendulum, the fewer number of complete back-and-forth swings it makes in 10 seconds.

Participants in the study were provided a graded series of five prompts as needed to assist them to make the correct generalization about pendulum length and rate of swing. Here are the prompts:

1. The examiner asked, "Thinking about these pendulums, can you think of a general rule about pendulums?" If the student was not successful, the examiner went to the next prompt.
2. Students were asked to compare the number of swings in 10 seconds for the shortest and longest pendulums and then make a generalization.
3. Students were asked to sequence all of the pendulums from the shortest to the longest, compare the number of swings in 10 seconds for the pendulums, and then form a generalization.
4. The teacher pointed out that when the pendulums were sequenced, the strings got longer and the rates got smaller; based on this direct information, students were then asked to form a generalization.
5. Finally, if needed, the examiner gave the generalization, saying, "Isn't it that, as the string gets longer, the number of swings they make get smaller?" The examiner then demonstrated the rule until the students expressed understanding.

The number of prompts needed for a student to be successful on the task was taken as a measure of inductive reasoning. As shown in Table 10-1, the results indicated that 75% of the nondisabled students were successful after the first prompt and 100% were successful by the fourth prompt. For students with LD, 50% were successful with the first prompt, while 72% were successful after the fourth prompt. For students with mild mental retardation, no students were successful with one prompt, while only 19% were successful after four prompts.

TABLE 10-1 CUMULATIVE PERCENTAGE OF STUDENTS MAKING CORRECT INDUCTION OF THE PENDULUM PROBLEM IN RESPONSE TO NUMBER OF PROMPTS

Number of Prompts	Nondisabled	Learning Disabled	Mild Mental Retardation
1	75%	50%	0%
2	95%	61%	6%
3	95%	67%	12%
4	100%	72%	19%
5	100%	100%	100%

Source: From "How Effective Is Inquiry Learning for Students with Mild Disabilities?" by M. A. Mastropieri, T. E. Scruggs, and K. Butcher, 1993, *The Journal of Special Education, 31*(2), pp. 199–211. Copyright 1993 by PRO-ED, Inc. Reprinted with permission.

Additionally, students were asked to apply the rule to a new pendulum problem. The students were shown a new pendulum intermediate in length between the 8-swing pendulum and the 10-swing pendulum and asked how many swings it would make in 10 seconds. On this application problem, 90% of the nondisabled students, 50% of students with LD, and none of the students with MR provided the correct answer.

According to Mastropieri and colleagues (1993), general education junior high school students may readily make generalizations from data, with only a moderate amount of scaffolding assistance. Students with LD may also succeed on an induction task, but may need more assistance. "On the other hand," the investigators concluded, "the very low performance of students with MR on this task suggests (but does not prove) that inquiry-based teaching methods and tasks that are appropriate for normally achieving students may not be developmentally appropriate for similarly aged students with MR" (Mastropieri et al., 1993, p. 208). But this certainly doesn't imply that students with MR are better off with a text-based approach!

Teach Learning Strategies. Successful students develop many skills and strategies that they use when integrating, remembering, and using information. However, students with special needs may require explicit instruction in the use of these strategies.

Dr. Edwin Ellis (2002), a professor at the University of Alabama, advocates "watering up" rather than "watering down" instruction. He has developed a teaching/learning model referred to as Makes Sense Strategies (MSS). The MSS model is an approach to teaching based on three fundamental instructional principles:

1. Students learn better when they are actively engaged in processing new information in meaningful ways.
2. Increasing the learn-ability of information or skills is preferable to dumbing it down.
3. Students should not waste time learning trivia.

Approaches to instruction based on these principles can result in more effective learning by students with LD.

One important strategy in learning is *elaboration*. Elaboration of an idea occurs when one transforms an idea without losing the essence of its meaning. Ellis (2002) notes that students with LD often lack the language-based cognitive skills necessary to engage in effective elaboration but can be taught to use elaboration strategies. In teaching students

An informative article by Professor Ellis on teaching/learning strategies is available on the Internet. Access the article at http:// www.ldonline. org/article/5742.

with or without LD to elaborate, teach them how to create a visual image of an idea, how to paraphrase and summarize information about an idea, how to raise a series of questions about the idea, and how to use the idea in drawing inferences and forming predictions.

Another important strategy in learning is reflection. According to Ellis (2002), reflection is a powerful tool for developing deep knowledge structures, but promoting it can be considerably more challenging than creating situations that require students to memorize answers for tests. Important reflective processes for learning and performing include activating background knowledge, forecasting, anticipating and predicting, establishing goals, relating ideas, and recognizing manifestations of ideas as they appear in other forms and how ideas might be applied in various contexts.

Students with LD may have particular difficulties in collecting, organizing, and using data skills that are critical in science inquiry. Thus, they may benefit from explicit instruction on how to record data and how to construct and interpret charts and graphs.

Cawley and Foley (2002) have emphasized the importance of teaching students with exceptionalities the inherent relationships involved in data tables. Help your students learn to recognize relationships by involving them in connecting data to measurement procedures, describing data, filling in blank spaces in data tables, and using data to make predictions of new measurements.

In the pendulum data interpretation study described previously, for example, students with LD benefited from prompts related to examining the data, arranging it in order to form a concrete graph, and interpreting the graph to form a generalization about pendulum length and time for 10 swings. Nondisabled students in general did not need these prompts, presumably because they had learned to analyze data on their own. Students with LD may need to be provided explicit instruction in constructing and working with tables, charts, and graphs.

To teach students with disabilities to use charting and graphing strategies (Mastropieri & Scruggs, 2004), prefamiliarize them with graph paper and various types of charts and graphs, such as bar graphs, histograms, and line graphs. Use concrete examples in your instruction. For example, create a class bar graph based upon students' favorite foods, colors, or television shows. Talk with the class about what might be learned from the graph. Is each person's favorite displayed? Is there a "class favorite"? Use pictures of the objects being graphed to help reinforce what the graph represents.

Consider grouping students with and without disabilities together and allow them to record and graph data cooperatively. Peers may be able to assist with some of the more difficult components of the task. As students work together, take time to teach specific cooperative skills, such as turn taking and listening. In teaching cooperative skills, use explicit instruction procedures, such as modeling, pointing out examples and nonexamples, role playing, and providing feedback. In this way, students with and without exceptionalities can learn to actively and successfully be part of cooperative learning groups.

Procedural facilitators, such as "think sheets" and semantic maps, can assist students with special needs in the use of learning strategies. Procedural facilitators assist performance by reminding students of options, strategies, and questions to ask themselves as they attempt to learn and solve problems. Students with and without disabilities may also benefit from metacognitive training to better monitor and regulate their own learning efforts (Mastropieri & Scruggs, 2004).

Teach Mnemonics. Students with LD often have difficulty with short-term memory. One of the strategies identified for assisting students with LD is mnemonics. In their research, Mastropieri and Scruggs (1993) found the use of mnemonics very effective with students

Figure 10-1 Pegword mnemonic strategy for classes of levers.
Source: From *A Practical Guide for Teaching Science with Special Needs in Inclusive Settings* (p. 154), by M. A. Mastropieri and T. E. Scruggs, 1993, Austin, TX: PRO-ED. Copyright © 1993 by Purdue Research Foundation. Reprinted with permission of author.

who have LD. Figure 10-1 is an example of a mnemonic strategy. In this example, a pegword strategy (rhyming words) helps students remember the three classes of levers. The figure of an oar is an example of a first-class lever because it has the fulcrum at the middle and the force and load or resistance at opposite ends. To remember that an oar is an example of a first-class lever, students were given a picture of an oar with a package of buns (pegword for one) at the fulcrum. To remember that a wheelbarrow is an example of a second-class lever (with the fulcrum at one end and the force at the other), a picture of a wheelbarrow on a shoe (pegword for two) was depicted. Finally, a rake was used as an example of a third-class lever (with the fulcrum at one end and the force at the middle), to provide a picture of a rake leaning against a tree (pegword for three).

Use Graphic Organizers. A variety of graphic organizers are available to aid students with LD in visualizing how to order or sequence conceptual ideas. Figure 10-2 is one example. In using this graphic organizer, students fill in the blank spaces about the phases of the water cycle as the information is presented or as they engage in relevant activities.

Activities-based approaches are quite appropriate for students with LD, but may not be the most beneficial method for teaching science to students with mental retardation. Let us examine the characteristics of students with MR and approaches to science that may be more beneficial for them.

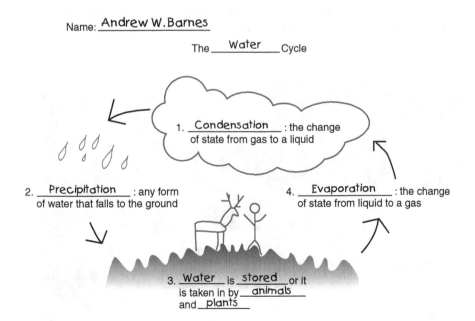

Figure 10-2 Graphic organizer modified for a student with a disability.
Source: From *The Inclusive Classroom: Strategies for Effective Instruction* (p. 514), by M. A. Mastropieri and T. E. Scruggs, 2000. Upper Saddle River, NJ: Merril/Prentice Hall. Copyright © 2000 by Merrill, an imprint of Prentice-Hall, Inc. Reprinted by permission of Pearson Education, Inc. Upper Saddle River, NJ.

Science for Students with Mental Retardation

Students with mental retardation show greater cognitive discrepancies than students with learning disabilities. To improve functioning of persons with MR, science teachers might provide learning experiences that promote self-care, home living, community use, communication, self-direction (problem-solving and decision-making skills), and functional academics as appropriate. Still, unless you emphasize and teach to the science standards that all students are expected to master, they will not be prepared to pass the state science test.

Research indicates that students with mild MR learn concepts better when they are guided to construct them through questioning than when the information was presented directly to them. Additionally, a study of the thinking of fourth-grade students with mild disabilities during an ecology unit indicated that they can actively engage in such processes as observing, describing, comparing, recording, and predicting—with appropriate assistance (Scruggs & Mastropieri, 1994).

Science for Students with Emotional/Behavioral Disorders

According to IDEA, students with emotional/behavioral disorders (EBD) exhibit one or more of these characteristics:

* an inability to learn not due to intellectual, sensory, or health factors;
* an inability to exhibit appropriate behavior under ordinary circumstances;
* an inability to maintain relationships with peers or teachers;
* an inappropriate effect such as depression or anxiety; and/or
* an inappropriate manifestation of physical symptoms or fears in response to school or personal difficulties (Turnbull, Turnbull, Shank, & Smith, 2004, p. 80).

Because students with EBD may be included in your classroom, a few words of wisdom may be helpful. Consider that labels often get in the way of seeing these students as children. Even as they are aggressive, antisocial, or disruptive, you could also identify them as smart, good soccer players, lively, helpful, creative, tenacious, and daring. Picture the student(s) in your class exhibiting these positive characteristics and choose carefully the words you use to describe them. Finally, as you review the strategies in this section that will

An excellent compilation of strategies for teaching science to students with behavioral disorders is available online. Go to http://www.as.wvu.edu/~scidis/sitemap.html.

Working cooperatively with their general education peers assists students with exceptionalities to learn science effectively.

help you work with students who have EBD, note that your utmost concern is to provide a safe and supportive environment for all of your students.

Behavior Modification. A behavior management strategy called *behavioral modification*, which was described in Chapter 5, is one approach that systematically applies behaviorist principles to classroom practices and therapeutic settings. Hundreds of research studies reveal that behavior modification improves not only classroom behaviors but academic performance as well (Ormrod, 2007). Behavior modification is often effective when other techniques are not, because (1) students know exactly what is expected of them; (2) through the gradual process of shaping, students attempt to learn new behaviors only when they are truly ready to acquire them; and (3) students find that learning new behaviors usually leads to success.

These four steps are routinely used in behavioral modification:

1. Identify problem behavior to be modified.
2. Log behavior with regard to how often and under what conditions it occurs.
3. Reinforce desired behavior(s) by initiating a system that reinforces or rewards appropriate, positive behavior.
4. Determine the type of positive reward or reinforcer to use: manipulatives (computer games, interactive videos, games); visuals (videos, CD-ROMs); physical (extra gym or recess privileges, dance); social (praise, attention, status); tactile (art time); edibles (food and drink); auditory (music as choices of audiotapes or CDs); and others selected by students. Positive (or negative) reinforcers can vary.

Science for Students with Visual Impairments

You may have students with visual impairments in your classroom from time to time. The severity of the disability determines further classification. Students with low vision might need special aids or instruction to read ordinary print. Those who are functionally blind typically use Braille for efficient reading and writing. Those who who are totally blind do not receive meaningful input through the visual sense. These individuals use tactile and auditory means to learn about their environment.

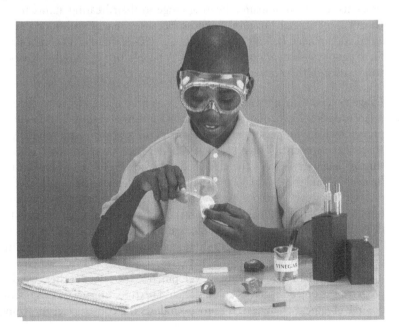

Inquiry science programs help schools to meet the needs, interests, and expectations of students.

Adapting Learning Materials. One of your main tasks if you have a student with visual impairments is to figure out how to adapt classroom materials to make them accessible. Textbooks, blackboards, whiteboards, handouts, and science instruments are not generally accessible for students with visual impairments. Thus, you may need to create alternative formats for printed materials (handouts and textbooks) and computer-based materials, and you may even have to adapt science instruments or tools. Currently, using alternative formats remains an imperfect process, but audiotapes, enlarged print, Braille, and some computer text are somewhat viable.

You may want to find out how to access printed science materials in Braille or prepare grades in Braille that you can affix to lab reports, papers, or quizzes. Students' needs will be identified on their IEP, and school or district specialists in special education should be able to assist you. In addition, there is now software that can produce synthetic speech from text and other software that can convert speech into text. Technological advances such as these offer students who are blind greater levels of independence.

Activities like those developed by the Center for Multisensory Learning, Lawrence Hall of Science, Berkeley, California, are especially appropriate. The materials published by the Lawrence Hall of Science for students with visual or physical disabilities are called SAVI/SELPH. SAVI represents Science Activities for the Visually Impaired, and SELPH represents Science Enrichment for Learners with Physical Handicaps. These programs have been combined and reworked into a single program, mostly for upper elementary school and beyond, but nine modules are adapted for primary grade students.

SAVI/SELPH consists of sets of activity folios, with a section overview, background, purpose, materials, anticipating (what to do before starting), doing the activity, and follow-up. For an example of a running summary of how the program developers provided metric measurement activities for visually impaired students, see Figure 10-3.

In addition to SAVI/SELPH, other curriculum developers have created science materials for students who are blind or have low vision, such as Adapting Science Materials for the Blind (ASMB).

Science for Students with Hearing Impairments

Students who have impaired hearing range in their hearing ability from hard of hearing (use of amplification) to total deafness. Because there are substantial differences between aided and unaided hearing (Turnbull et al., 2004), there is no consensus about how to refer to people with hearing impairments. A people-first approach—persons who are deaf—will be used in this section.

Language and Concept Development. One of the major problems of persons who are deaf is language development. Just as incidental learning accounts for the lack of certain kinds of prior knowledge for persons who are blind, persons who are deaf generally struggle with language development. Thus, psychosocial development—an interaction with the world through language—is a key need for students who are deaf or hard of hearing. Sign language, lip reading, and the reading of body and facial movements help these students with communication. However, without intervention, there are increasing gaps in vocabulary, concept formation, and the ability to understand and produce complex sentences for people who are deaf. Without intervention, both language and intellectual development may be affected.

Hands-on activities can help show students differences in the meanings of words. Begin with familiar objects from the students' everyday environment. Stress handling the objects during language/concept development. Introduce other words related to the properties of objects, such as color, size, and texture. Engage older students in activities to observe chemical changes. This process follows the constructivist learning cycle in which

Science Education in the Balance

During the past spring and fall, SAVI answered the cry for metric measurement activities for visually impaired students with the SAVI **Measurement Module.** The six hands-on activities contained in this module introduce youngsters to standard units of metric measurement.

To develop the concept of *mass,* we needed a measuring tool that would be suitable for use by the visually impaired. We finally decided to use a balance instead of a spring scale or other device and this decision resulted in some unexpected dividends for the project.

We looked at a lot of balances before we made the decision and even built a few of our own. Finally, we chose a simple, vacuum-formed model that is commercially available at a reasonable price. Then, we went to work on it!

First, we cut the bottoms of the two balance pans so that a paper or plastic cup could be dropped securely into the hole and then removed easily. Then, we added a tactile balance indicator. These slight modifications made it possible for blind students to determine weight to an accuracy of one gram!

The removable cup was the breakthrough we need to make accurate weighing easy for visually impaired students. Both the weights (20 g, 10 g, 5 g, 1 g plastic pieces) and the objects or substances to be weighed automatically centered in the cups, thus eliminating discrepancies due to the position of objects in the cups. An object, substance, or liquid can be removed from the balance—cup and *all;* a new cup can then be inserted and a new material weighed. There's no more trouble "getting all the powder out," or "transferring the beans"; the objects stay in the cups.

The students use the balances to verify that 50 ml of water (measured with a modified SAVI syringe) weigh 50 g, thereby establishing the relationship between volume and mass.

Since its introduction, the SAVI balance has crept into other modules. The forthcoming **Kitchen Interactions Module** will feature an activity that focuses on the concept of *density.* Density is defined operationally using the SAVI balance: equal volumes of two different liquids are compared on the balance and the heavier one is identified as the denser liquid.

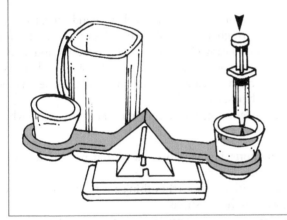

Figure 10-3 Science activity for students with visual impairments.
Source: Reprinted by permission of The Center for Mutisensory Learning, Lawrence Hall of Science, University of California, Berkeley, CA 94720.

the learner manipulates materials and then the teacher introduces or "invents" words for the scientific concepts.

In addition, use pictures, drawings, models, text, and closed-captioned TV programming or videotapes for your students who are deaf.

Science for Gifted and Talented Students

Ten-year-old Alan developed an unlikely interest in Einstein's theory of relativity. Alan's teacher invited a college professor to the classroom to talk about the theory with the boy. The child said to the professor, "I understand that Einstein described the universe in terms of four variables, but I can only think of three of them." As they discussed the problem, the professor told Alan that at age 16, Einstein set this puzzle for himself: *What would happen if I traveled along at the speed of light and held up a mirror to my face? What would I see?* The professor explained that Einstein needed the three variables of space and an additional variable of time to eventually answer this question at age 26. Somehow, this information helped Alan to bring together a variety of things he had read and thought about. He then took up the explanation, laying out Einstein's problem and solution in such an insightful way that the astounded professor began to understand them more deeply himself.

Students such as Alan provide a different kind of challenge for teachers. These students have above average intelligence and possess unusual skills, interests, talents, and attitudes about learning. Words such as *creativity*, *vitality*, *potential*, *motivation*, and *joy* tend to describe their approach to learning (Armstrong, 1998). Such students are identified as having special gifts or talents.

As a teacher, you will quickly learn that there is no typicality associated with students who are gifted, but most have general intellect, specific academic ability, creative and productive thinking, leadership ability, or abilities in visual and performing arts that stand out from their classmates. Students who are gifted or talented love to participate in many activities and usually enjoy being challenged with meaningful enrichment activities. The following suggestions may prove useful.

Make Real Inclusion a Goal

Make gifted and talented students in your classroom feel welcome and accepted. Previously, these students were accelerated to higher or special pullout classes. Currently, greater emphasis is placed on inclusion, incorporating changes in science content and activities to introduce higher levels of abstract and independent thinking and problem-solving skills. Your challenge is to help your gifted and talented students modify, adapt, and learn how to discover new skills and concepts for themselves.

Most highly motivated, bright students need little encouragement. For those who do, try these suggestions:

- Provide recognition for their efforts, but be wary of gifted students with know-it-all tendencies. Encourage cooperative efforts.
- Challenge students to come up with questions they think are difficult and then work in small groups to find answers to the questions.
- Encourage student-initiated projects and alternative activities sometimes in lieu of standard kinds of class activities.
- Introduce elementary and middle grade students to research methods.
- Encourage students to use a variety of media to express themselves in creative ways such as drawing, creative writing, drama, and role playing.
- Help students organize and publish a classroom or school science magazine.

A caution is in order: Students who are gifted must also acquire basic knowledge, understandings, and procedures, even as they are given more freedom to move in their own directions.

Stimulate Gifted Students by the Way You Teach

Your teaching methods can encourage students who are gifted and talented. In our society, students' thinking is often trained to focus on the right answer, which sometimes discourages them from taking risks in academic situations. Students may be confused or feel threatened with failure when they are faced with tasks in which there are either no clear answers or a variety of correct answers. Be sure to use some of these techniques to encourage them:

1. Use a series of questions rather than giving information.
2. Use hypothetical questions beginning with "What if . . . ?"
3. Ask students to develop open-ended situations where no one answer is correct.

4. In science tasks involving mathematics, where specific answers are usually required, encourage students to estimate their answers.

5. Instead of information, emphasize concepts, principles, relationships, and generalizations.

6. Provide opportunities and assignments that rely on independent reading and research as appropriate. Ask students to report on their research and experimentation; this helps them acquire a sense of sharing knowledge.

7. Provide students multiple opportunities to learn how to use technology to research information and gather data from a variety of global resources.

8. Challenge students to engage in, and perhaps design or originate, more openended, hands-on inquiry activities.

   - Start by working with the entire class or a group. Later, when routines are established, invite individuals to explore on their own.
   - Keep the experimentation within the limits of time, talents, and available apparatus. Explore these limitations before suggesting problems.
   - Be alert to the open-endedness of this type of exploration. Expect questions to arise such as, "Suppose we vary the experiment in this way. What will happen?"
   - Do not assume that the gifted student will have a sustained interest in the problem. You must continually check on progress.

Connecting science and mathematics is important for all students, particularly gifted students. Challenge them to go beyond describing what happens and why and to explore *how much* or what *quantitative relationships* exist between variables. Ask students to quantify their findings, and encourage them to use graphing when communicating their findings.

Learn with and from Your Gifted and Talented Students. Most elementary school teachers have not majored in science and therefore find that some of their students know more about certain areas of science than they do. Feeling somewhat incompetent with science should not stop you from encouraging gifted and talented students to do more advanced work than the rest of the class. Students enjoy seeing their teachers get excited about the results of their work. Facilitate the academic environment of students who are gifted by posing challenging questions and offering constructive feedback. Also, identify community people who are available to work with gifted and talented students in a mentor program. Be sure to provide some guidance to those who are knowledgeable in their fields but do not know how to motivate and teach students.

Remember that for all their knowledge and abilities, gifted students are still elementary or middle school students whose social, emotional, and physical development mirrors the development of their peers. They need your mature adult guidance, professional training, and practical experience. They will seek caring and emotionally stable adults. That's you!

Science for Students from Linguistically and Culturally Diverse Backgrounds

Our nation's motto is *e pluribus unum*, "out of many, one." Nowhere in our society is the rich mosaic of people that embodies the United States better represented than in our schools. Meeting the needs of children from diverse backgrounds in our classrooms has become an important issue in education.

Many students from diverse ethnic backgrounds are in the process of acquiring the U.S. mainstream language, culture, and discourse patterns in schools. For many of these students, a language other than English is spoken at home.

TABLE 10-2 PERCENTAGE OF PUBLIC ELEMENTARY AND SECONDARY STUDENTS BY RACE/ETHNICITY FOR THE 2005–2006 SCHOOL YEAR	
Race/Ethnicity	Percent
White, non-Hispanic	57.1
Black, non-Hispanic	17.2
Hispanic	19.8
Asian/Pacific Islander	4.6
American Indian/Alaska Native	1.2

Source: National Center for Education Statistics (http://nces.ed.gov/pubs2007).

Hispanic students make up the large majority of the English Language Learners (ELLs) or limited-English-proficient (LEP) students in American schools. Statistics change continually, but according to the National Center for Educational Statistics, in the 2005–2006 school year, Hispanic students made up 19.8% of the nearly 49 million students enrolled in public elementary and secondary schools (see Table 10-2). Statistics from the 1999 U.S. census indicate that 57% of Hispanic students in grades K–12 spoke mostly English at home, 25% spoke mostly Spanish, and 17% spoke English and Spanish equally. This translates to more than 4 million Hispanic students who are encountering English as a second language in U.S. public schools. Providing equal educational opportunities to students who are not proficient in English is a special challenge.

Inquiry science programs, with their emphasis on exploring, investigating, and manipulating concrete materials, are especially valuable for students who wrestle with the development of a new language, customs, friendships, and less advantageous community environments. Providing inquiry activities equalizes the opportunity for success because success is not generally dependent on the students' ability to read a textbook, answer questions from the textbook, or complete worksheets that depend on students' understanding of what they have read. Hands-on, inquiry activities help all students span the gap between their past experiences and the development of language within their immediate environment.

View the NSTA position statements on multicultural science education and other issues at http://www.nsta.org/about/positions.aspx#list.

English Language Learners and Inquiry Science

Learning language is much more than learning vocabulary. Language learning is a complex process of developing relationships among ideas, terms, and meanings (Lee & Fradd, 1998). A great deal of language can be learned in the context of science and other subjects. Context enables children to build on what they already know to infer the meaning of new words and verbal constructs. According to Lapp (2001, p. 2), "For children who are learning science by means of an inquiry-centered approach, classroom investigations and the activities surrounding them can provide context. These experiences can be springboards for growth in verbal fluency and literacy."

In learning science through inquiry approaches, students have opportunities to develop verbal fluency as they talk about what they are doing, record their observations, summarize their findings, and create written explanations that draw on their understanding of science concepts. They also read science articles and books, write essays and stories, and do library and Internet research to complement their classroom work (Lapp, 2001).

Language is only one of the internal learning systems students need to learn science and other subjects. Students also need knowledge of facts, concepts, and principles and knowledge of how to apply them in making sense of problem situations (Bransford, Brown, & Cocking, 1999). Inquiry science can help students learn how to construct understanding through teaching them the scientists' approach to solving problems—an approach that has proved successful in every culture.

One method of teaching science and English to ELL students is called **sheltered instruction**. Sheltered instruction involves a minimum dependency on language for concept development. Freeman and Freeman (1998) have presented well-thought-out general strategies for using sheltered instruction with ELL students. Lee and Fradd (1998) and Fradd and Lee (1999) have discussed the uses of sheltering within inquiry science lessons. Many of these strategies are also useful for teaching science to all students.

Following is a presentation of using sheltered instruction for ELL students within the context of the 5-E model of inquiry.

Sheltered Instruction and the 5-E Model of Inquiry

With minimum dependency on language, sheltered instruction focuses on concept development and nonlanguage cues and prompts. Sheltered instruction methods are organized in this section under Preparation and All 5-E Phases: engage, explore, explain, elaborate, and evaluate.

Preparation.   Critical to effective sheltered instruction is the preparation of targeted learning objectives. In addition to science objectives, language objectives should be developed in alignment with state language proficiency benchmarks or language arts standards (Lee & Fradd, 1998).

All 5-E Phases.   Sheltering teachers are careful to integrate listening, speaking, reading and writing skills into science lessons. ELLs are called upon to process, manipulate, and display large amounts of new material at a rapid pace in a foreign language. Visual aids, allowances for processing time, and opportunities for clarification provide support in this demanding process. Sheltered lessons guide the learning of content information, including inquiry strategies, in ways that ELLs can comprehend.

During all phases of 5-E lesson teachers should modify their speech and use concrete referents so that ELLs can grasp important science questions, facts, concepts, principles, and procedures. In modifying their speech, teachers should:

- speak clearly and slowly;
- employ pauses, short sentences, simple syntax, few pronouns, and idioms;
- use redundancy and discourse markers, keywords, and outlines;
- provide examples and descriptions, not definitions; and
- use visuals, hands-on resources, gestures, and graphic organizers.

Successful students develop many skills and strategies that they use when integrating, remembering, and using information. Successful sheltering teachers explicitly teach learning strategies that enable ELLs and other students to develop a toolkit for accomplishing difficult learning tasks. Such strategies might include how to relate new science terms to observed objects, organisms, and events; how to access and use prior knowledge as a context for new learning; how to record new terms and their meanings in science journals; and how to keep initiating questions in mind as inquiry proceeds.

Sheltering teachers also provide ample opportunities at each phase for students to interact with others in English around tasks that are meaningful to them. Teachers should:

- facilitate frequent pair and small-group activities focused on meaningful tasks;
- model and assign tasks requiring turn taking, questioning, supporting/disagreeing, and clarification; and
- model and discuss ways of communicating respect.

Engage. Use simple words and simple sentences. Use body language or concrete objects while you explain what you are saying. Ask clear questions designed to elicit students' current conceptions. Their answers will help you know about previous related experience your students have had.

Explore. During this phase students are often involved in small group activities and are observing and manipulating objects and/or organisms. Sheltering teachers strive to make the goals of the activities clear to all of their students. Cooperative group strategies with assigned tasks can supply structure that can help students stay focused on the investigation. Small group discussions give students opportunities to practice taking turns, asking and answering questions is a reduced risk environment, respectfully supporting and/or disagreeing with peers and clarifying their thinking. As appropriate for the age level of your students, challenge all class members to keep journals in English.

Explain. Sheltering teachers encourage ELLs to contribute to the class discussion about their findings from the explore phase. Summarize what has been presented at frequent intervals. Print the key points on the board, display them with a projector, or refer to a wall chart. As new science terms are introduced in the context of the experiences of the explore phase, post the words on your "word wall," pronounce them clearly, and have your students repeat the pronunciation together.

Elaborate. Sheltering teachers provide opportunities for students to apply their new knowledge to new tasks that involve concepts and skills students have learned. English language learners have opportunities in the classroom to practice and apply the language skills and content knowledge they have acquired.

Trying out new knowledge and practicing new skills in a safe environment, supported by teacher and peer feedback, leads to mastery. Students can reflect on and adjust their performance, initially with assistance and ultimately independently.

Evaluate. Formative and summative assessments of science understandings and English language usage are used. In this way of learning, teaching and assessment are integrated into an ongoing process that provides feedback to students and informs future instruction.

In conjunction with formative and summative assessments, teachers might gather information for evaluative decision making through:

- conferences
- take-home reflections
- oral retelling
- learning logs
- graphic organizers

Use a scoring guide or performance rubric aligned with learning objectives to collect evidence of content learning.

Go to the Homework and Exercises section in Chapter 10 of MyEducationLab and select the Article *Teacher Skills to Support English Language Learners*. Short and Echeverria have written an informative article on using sheltered instruction with English Language Learners. The article effectively refines and extends the discussion of sheltered instruction given in this chapter.

Perhaps the best way to include ELL students in your classroom is to view these students as an asset to the learning of all students. ELL students can contribute language enrichment for native English-speaking students and abundant occasions for cross-cultural teaching and learning.

Students from Culturally Diverse Backgrounds and Inquiry Science

Meeting the needs of students from diverse cultural backgrounds has become an important issue in education (Lee, 2002). The National Science Teachers Association recognizes and appreciates the strength and beauty of cultural pluralism. In its 2000 Position Statement on Multicultural Science Education, NSTA asserted that

- children from all cultures are to have equitable access to quality science education experiences that enhance success and provide the knowledge and opportunities required for them to become successful participants in our democratic society;
- curricular content must incorporate the contributions of many cultures to our knowledge of science; and
- science teachers are knowledgeable about and use culturally related ways of learning and instructional practices.

Additionally, science teachers have the responsibility to expose culturally diverse children to career opportunities in science, technology, and engineering.

The NSTA statement on multicultural science education calls for you to become knowledgeable about the learning styles of your students from diverse cultures and how their cultures aid or hinder their science learning. The prior cultural experiences of some students may actually interfere with inquiry science. For example, newly arrived students may experience difficulties with scientific inquiry in school because they have not been previously encouraged to ask questions or devise plans for investigation. Students from cultures that respect authority may be more receptive to teachers directing and telling them than to inquiry, exploration, and seeking alternative ways (Lee & Fradd, 1998).

Students unfamiliar with more exploratory approaches to learning may need explicit instruction to acquire the skills for effective participation. Fradd and Lee (1999) suggested, "With teachers' encouragement, students learning English can also learn to pose questions, devise plans, test hypotheses, collect and analyze data, engage in science discourse, and construct theories and explanations" (p. 15).

In teaching science, you should employ a wide range of content and teaching strategies to meet the learning needs and interests of students with special needs and those from different cultural backgrounds. You should also build on and broaden the prior knowledge of students by deepening their learning experiences.

SUMMARY

- The *National Science Education Standards* emphasize that science is for all students. Students come to your classroom with a wide range of learning abilities and styles, diverse cultural backgrounds, and physical, social, and emotional differences. Some have a limited proficiency using the English language, and all have had different sensory experiences and prior knowledge. It is your challenge to provide worthwhile science learning activities for every student.

- The Individuals with Disabilities Education Act (IDEA) mandates that individuals with disabilities from birth to age 21 have the right to a full, free public education in the least restrictive environment. This has led to the current trend of inclusion, which means that all students, including those with a wide range of disabilities (physical, social, and cognitive), are in regular classrooms for the entire school day.

• Practical teaching and learning techniques provide for the needs of students who have learning disabilities, are mentally retarded, have emotional disturbances, have orthopedic disabilities, or have sensory impairments. More important than the individual means by which you can adapt instruction is your attitude and expectations for working with each of these students to provide a sensitive and supportive learning community.

• Gifted and talented students present different kinds of challenges for teachers. Students who have unusual talents or are intellectually gifted can benefit from doing rel-atively unstructured explorations, engaging in enrichment activities such as studying abstract topics to integrate connections, and observing how math and science are connected.

• A National Science Teachers Association position paper recognizes and advocates a quality science education for students from diverse cultural and linguistic backgrounds. This challenges all science teachers to employ a wide range of science content and teaching methods to meet the learning needs and interests of students with different cultural backgrounds. Hands-on science teaching and learning activities have many benefits for students from diverse backgrounds, especially those with limited English proficiency.

ONLINE PROFESSIONAL DEVELOPMENT

Pre- and post-tests to assess your knowledge of chapter content, along with exercises to enhance your understanding, can be found on MyEducationLab at www.myeducationlab.com.

Video Guides

The video clip on MyEducationLab selected for this chapter is *Dual Language Classrooms: Science in English and Spanish.*

Accessing the Video

1. Go to the Homework and Exercises section in Chapter 10 of MyEducationLab to select and view videos for this chapter.
2. Videos might be viewed individually, by small groups of colleagues, or by the whole class.
3. As you watch each video, use the **Questions for Reflection** to guide your thoughts and note taking for personal use and group discussion.
4. Discuss your answers to the questions about each video with classmates.

Video: Dual Language Classrooms: Science in English and Spanish

Overview

Two teachers discuss the concept of dual language classrooms. We see the two teachers working together to guide an investigation on skimmers, with one teacher delivering instruction in English and the other teacher delivering instruction in Spanish.

Questions for Reflection

1. What are the respective roles of the English language teacher and the Spanish language teacher in guiding the investigation?
2. How effective for students do you think this method of instruction is?
3. What is the evidence that the dual language lessons were effective?

REFERENCES

Activities That Integrate Mathematics and Science. (1999). *AIMS programs and product catalog.* Fresno, CA: AIMS Education Foundation.

American Association for the Advancement of Science (1993). *Benchmarks for science literacy.* New York: Oxford University Press.

American Association for the Advancement of Science. (2007). *Atlas of science literacy,* Volume 2. Copublished by AAAS Project 2061 and the National Science Teachers Association.

American Association for the Advancement of Science. (2001). *Atlas of science literacy.* Copublished by AAAS Project 2061 and the National Science Teachers Association.

Anderson, C. W. (1987). Strategic teaching in science. In B. F. Jones et al. (Eds.), *Strategic teaching and learning: Cognitive instruction in the content areas.* Alexandria, VA: Association for Supervision and Curriculum Development.

Annenberg/CPB (Corporation for Public Broadcasting). (1997). *Case studies in science education: Rachel.* Washington, D.C.: Annenberg/CPB Foundation.

Annenberg Foundation. (1997). *Annenberg video case studies in science education, Linda.* South Burlington, VT: Annenberg Foundation.

Annenberg/CPB (Corporation for Public Broadcasting). (1997). *Case studies in science education: Jean.* Annenberg/CPB Foundation.

Armstrong, T. (1998). *Awakening genius in the classroom.* Alexandria, VA: Association for Supervision and Curriculum Development.

Baron, E. B. (1992). Discipline strategies for teachers. *Fastback, 344.* Bloomington, IN: Phi Delta Kappa Educational Foundation.

Biological Sciences Curriculum Study. (1989). *New designs for elementary school science and health: A cooperative project of Biological Sciences Curriculum Study (BSCS) and International Business Machines (IBM).* Dubuque, IA: Kendall/Hunt.

Bitner, N., Wadlington, E., Austin, S., Partridge, E., & Bitner, J. (1999). The virtual trip. *Learning and Leading with Technology, 26*(6), 6–9, 25.

Blosser, P. (1991). *How to ask the right questions.* Arlington, VA: National Science Teachers Association.

Bransford, J. D., Brown, A. L., & Cocking, R. R. (Eds.). (1999). *How people learn: Brain, mind, experience, and school.* Washington, DC: National Academy Press (also available at http://www.nap.edu).

Brown, A. L., & Campione, J. (1994). Guided discovery in a community of learners. In K. McGilly (Ed.), *Classroom lessons: Integrating cognitive theory and classroom practice.* Cambridge, MA: The MIT Press.

Brown, A. L., & Campione, J. C. (1998). Designing a community of young learners: Theoretical and practical lessons. In N. L. Lambert & B. L. McCombs (Eds.), *How students learn: Reforming schools through learner-centered education.* Washington, DC: American Psychological Association.

Brown, A. L., Bransford, J. D., Ferrara, R., & Campione, J. C. (1983). Learning, remembering, and understanding. In J. H. Flavell & E. M. Markman (Eds.), *Carmichael's manual of child psychology* (Vol. 3). New York: Wiley.

Brown, A. L., Bransford, J., Ferrara, R., & Campione, J. (1983). Learning, remembering, and understanding. In J. N. Flavell & E. M. Markman (Eds.), *Handbook of child psychology* (Vol. 3, 4th ed., pp. 79–166). New York: Wiley.

Brown, C. A. (1998). Presentation software and the single computer. *Learning and Leading with Technology, 26*(2), 18–21.

Brownell, M. T., & Thomas, C. W. (1998). An interview with Margo Mastropieri: Quality science instruction for students with disabilities. *Intervention in School and Clinic, 34*(2), 118–122.

Bybee, R. W., Buchwald, C. E., Crissman, S., Heil, D. R., Kuerbis, P. J., Matsumoto, C., & McInerney, J. P. (1989). *Science and technology education for the elementary years: Frameworks for curriculum and instruction.* Washington, DC: National Center for Improving Science Education.

Caniglia, J. (1997). The heat is on! Using the calculator-based laboratory to integrate math, science, and technology. *Learning and Leading with Technology, 25*(1), 22–27.

Carin, A. A., & Sund, R. B. (1978). *Creative questioning and sensitive listening techniques: A self-guided approach.* Upper Saddle River, NJ: Merrill/Prentice Hall.

Carina Software (2006). *Voyager 4.* San Ramon, CA.

Carter, L., Sumrall, W., & Curry, K. (2006). Say cheese! Digital collections in the classroom. *Science and Children, 43*(8), 19–23.

Cawley, J. F., & Foley, T. E. (2002). Connecting math and science for all students. *Teaching Exceptional Children, 34*(4), 14–19.

Champagne, A. L., & Kouba, V. L. (2000). Writing to inquire: Written products as performance measures. In J. J. Mintzes, J. H. Wandersee, & J. D. Novak (Eds.), *Assessing science understanding: A human constructivist view* (pp. 223–248). New York: Academic Press.

Chan, A., Doran, R., & Lenhardt, C. (1999). Learning from the TIMSS. *The Science Teacher, 66*(1), 18–22.

Cherry, L. (1992). *A river ran wild.* New York: Harcourt Brace Jovanovich.

Clements, D. (1999). Teaching length measurement: Research challenges. *School Science and Mathematics, 99*(1), 5–11.

Curcio, F. R. (1989). *Developing graph comprehension: Elementary and middle school activities.* Reston, VA: National Council of Teachers of Mathematics.

Dockterman, D. (1997). *Great teaching in the one computer classroom.* Watertown, MA: Tom Snyder Productions.

Duschl, R. S., Schweingruber, H. A., & Shouse A. W. (2007). *Taking science to school: Learning and teaching science in grades K–8.* Washington, DC: National Academies Press.

Ebenezer, J., & Lau, E. (1999). *Science on the Internet: A resource for K–12 teachers.* Upper Saddle River, NJ: Merrill/Prentice Hall.

Edmondson, K. M. (1999). Assessing science understanding through concept maps. In J. J. Mintzes, J. H. Wandersee, & J. D. Novak (Eds.), *Assessing science understanding: A human constructivist view* (pp. 223–248). New York: Academic Press.

Ellis, E. S. (2002). Watering Up the Curriculum for Adolescents with Learning Disabilities, Part II: Goals for the Affective Dimension. *LD Online*. Retrieved June 2007, from http://www.ldonline.org/articles/5742.

Finley, F. N. (1991). Why children have trouble learning from science texts. In C. M. Santa & D. E. Alvermann (Eds.), *Science learning: Processes and applications* (pp. 22–27). Newark, DE: International Reading Association.

Fradd, S. H., & Lee, O. (1999). Teachers' roles in promoting science inquiry with students from diverse language backgrounds. *Educational Researcher, 28*(6), 14–20.

Freeman, D., & Freeman, Y. (1998). *Sheltered English instruction* (ERIC Digest).

Full Option Science System. (1990). *Swingers*. Berkeley, CA: Lawrence Hall of Science.

Full Option Science System. (1991). *Graphs in the elementary science program*. Berkeley, CA: Lawrence Hall of Science.

Full Option Science System. (2000). *Overview: Physics of sound*. Nashua, NH: Delta Education.

Fulton, L., & Campbell, B. (2004, November–December). Student-centered notebooks. *Science and Children, 42*(3), 26–29.

Furtak, E. M., & Ruiz-Primo, M. A. (2005, January). Questioning cycle: Making students' thinking explicit during scientific inquiry. *Science Scope*, 22–25.

Gerlovich, J.A. (1996). Developments in laboratory safety. In J. Rhoton and P. Bowers (Eds.). *Issues in science education*. Arlington, VA: National Science Teachers Association.

Grahame, K. (1981). *The wind in the willows* (E. Shepard, Illus.). New York: Charles Scribner & Sons.

Gray, T. (1997). ED's Oasis (Guidelines for evaluating educational web sites). *Learning and Leading with Technology, 25*(1), 44–45.

Hand, B., & Keys, C. W. (1999). Inquiry investigation: A new approach to laboratory reports. *The Science Teacher, 66*(4), 27–29.

Harlen, W., & Jelly, S. (1990). *Developing science in the primary classroom*. Portsmouth, NH: Heinemann.

Haury, D. L. (1993). Teaching science through inquiry. *ERIC CSMEE Digest* (March Ed 359 048).

Hodge, J., & Brocker, S. (1997). *Animals of the oceans: Whales*. Hauppauge, N.Y.: Barron's.

Hogan, K., & Pressley, M. (1997). Scaffolding scientific competencies within classroom communities of inquiry. In K. Hogan & M. Pressley (Eds.), *Scaffolding student learning: Instructional approaches and issues*. Cambridge, MA: Brookline Books.

Hunter, M. (1984). Knowing, teaching, and supervising. In P. A. Hosford (Ed.), *Using what we know about teaching* (pp. 169–192). Alexandria, VA: Association for Supervision and Curriculum Development.

Inhelder, B., and Piaget, J. (1958). *The growth of logical thinking from childhood to adolescence*. New York: Basic Books.

International Reading Association. (1996). *Standards for the English language arts* (a project of the International Reading Association and the National Council of Teachers of English). Newark, DE: Author.

Jarolimek, J., & Foster, C. D., Sr. (1997). *Teaching and learning in the elementary school* (6th ed.). Upper Saddle River, NJ: Merrill/Prentice Hall.

Jones, M. G., & Carter, G. (1997). Small groups and shared constructions. In J. J. Mintzes, J. H. Wandersee, & J. D. Novak (Eds.), *Teaching science for understanding: A human constructivist view*. New York: Academic Press.

Judson, H. F. (1980). *The search for solutions*. New York: Holt, Rinehart & Winston.

Karplus, R., & Thier, H. (1974). *SCIS teacher's handbook*. Berkeley, CA: Science Curriculum Improvement Study.

Kentucky Department of Education. (n.d.). *Designing a performance assessment*. Frankfort, KY: Author.

King, A. (1994). Guiding knowledge construction in the classroom: Effects of teaching children how to question and how to explain. *American Educational Research Journal, 31*(2), 338–368.

Klahr, D., & Nigam, M. (2004). The equivalence of learning paths in early science instruction: Effects of direct instruction and discovery learning. *Psychological Science*.

Klentschy, M., (2005). Science notebook essentials: A guide to effective notebook components. *Science and Children, 43*(3), 24–27.

Koch, J. (1999). *Science stories: Teachers and children as science learners*. Boston: Houghton Mifflin.

Kreuger, A., & Sutton, J. (Eds.). (2001). Instructional technology in science. In *EDThoughts: What we know about science teaching and learning* (pp. 69–79). Aurora, CO: Mid-continent Research for Education and Learning.

Kwan, T., & Texley, J. (2002). *Exploring safely: A guide for elementary teachers*. Arlington, VA: NSTA Press.

Kwan, T., & Texley, J. (2003). *Inquiring safely: A guide for middle school teachers*. Arlington, VA: NSTA Press.

Lapp, D. (2001). Bridging the gap. *Science Link (Newsletter of the National Science Resources Center), 12*(1), 2.

Lee, J. R., & Patterson, W. R. (1997). It's show time! Six hints for PowerPoint presentations. *Learning and Leading with Technology, 24*(5), 6–11.

Lee, O. (2002). Promoting scientific inquiry with elementary students from diverse cultures and languages. In W. C. Secada (Ed.), *Review of research in education* (Vol. 26, pp. 23–69). Washington, DC: American Educational Research Association.

Lee, O., & Fradd, S. H. (1998). Science for all, including students from non-English-language backgrounds. *Educational Researcher, 27*(4), 12–19.

Loucks-Horsley, S., Hewson, P., Love, N., & Stiles, K. (1998). *Designing professional development for teachers of science and mathematics*. Thousand Oaks, CA: Corwin Press.

Lowery, L. (1998, November). How new science curriculums reflect brain research. *Educational Leadership*, 26–30.

Lowery, L. (1998a). How new science curriculums reflect brain research. *Educational Leadership*, November, 26–30.

Lowery, L. F. (1998b). Classroom arrangements and teaching. *FOSS Newsletter, 11*, 6–9.

Lowery, L. F. (Ed.). (1997). *Pathways to the science standards: Elementary school edition.* Arlington, VA: National Science Teachers Association.

Malone, L., Palmer, A., & Voigt, C. (2002). *Mapping our world: GIS lessons for educators.* Redlands, CA: ESRI Press.

Maslow, A. H. (1987). *Motivation and personality* (3rd ed.). New York: Harper and Row.

Mastropieri, M. A., & Scruggs, T. E. (1993). *A practical guide for teaching science to students with special needs in inclusive settings* (p. 154). Austin, TX: PRO-ED.

Mastropieri, M. A., & Scruggs, T. E. (2004). *The inclusive classroom: Strategies for effective instruction.* Upper Saddle River, NJ: Merrill/Prentice Hall.

Mastropieri, M. A., Scruggs, T. E., & Butcher, K. (1993). How effective is inquiry learning for students with mild disabilities? *Journal of Special Education, 31*(2), 199–211.

Mechling, K. R., & Oliver, D. L. (1983). *Handbook I: Science teaches basic skills.* Arlington, VA: National Science Teachers Association.

Meng, E., & Doran, R. L. (1993). *Improving instruction and learning through evaluation: Elementary school science.* Columbus, OH: ERIC Clearinghouse for Science, Mathematics, and Environmental Education.

Minnesota Mathematics and Science Teaching Project. (1970). *Overview: Minnesota mathematics and science teaching project.* Minneapolis: Minnemast Project, University of Minnesota.

Mintzes, J., Wandersee, J., & Novak, J. (1998). *Teaching science for understanding: A human constructivist view.* San Diego, CA: Academic Press.

Nachmias, R., & Linn, M. C. (1987). Evaluations of science laboratory data: The role of computer presented information. *Journal of Research in Science Teaching, 24*(5), 491–506.

National Academies of Science. (2006). *Rising above the gathering storm.* Washington, DC: National Academy Press.

National Aquarium in Baltimore. (1997). *Living in water: An Aquatic science curriculum.* Dubuque, IA: Kendall/Hunt.

National Council for the Social Studies. (1994). *Expectations of excellence: Curriculum standards for the social studies.* Washington, DC: Author.

National Council of Teachers of Mathematics. (1989). *Curriculum and evaluation standards for school mathematics.* Weston, VA: Author.

National Council of Teachers of Mathematics. (2000). *Principles and standards for school mathematics.* Weston, VA: Author.

National Gardening Association. (1992). *GrowLab: Activities for growing minds.* Burlington, VT: Author.

National Research Council. (1996). *National science education standards.* Washington, DC: National Academy Press.

National Research Council. (2000). *Inquiry and the national science education standards: A guide for teaching and learning.* Washington, DC: National Academies Press.

National Research Council. (2001). *Classroom assessment and the national science education standards.* Washington, DC: National Academy Press.

National Science Resources Center. (1996). *Science and technology for children: Comparing and measuring.* Burlington, NC: Carolina Biological Supply.

National Science Teachers Association (2000). Safety and school science instruction: A position statement. Arlington, VA: National Science Teachers Association (Available online at http://www.nsta.org/about/positions/safety.aspx)

Novak, J. (1995). Concept mapping: A strategy for organizing knowledge. In S. Glynn & R. Duit (Eds.), *Learning science in the schools: Research reforming practice.* Mahwah, NJ: Erlbaum.

Ormrod, J. (2004). *Human learning.* Upper Saddle River, NJ: Merrill/Prentice Hall.

Ormrod, J. (2007). *Human learning, 5th ed.* Upper Saddle River, NJ: Merrill/Prentice Hall.

Ostlund, K., & Mercier, S. (1999). *Rising to the challenge of the national science education standards: The process of science inquiry.* Squaw Valley, CA: S&K Associates.

Padak, N. D., & Davidson, J. L. (1991). Instructional activities for comprehending science text. In C. M. Santa & D. E. Alvermann (Eds.), *Science learning: Processes and applications* (pp. 76–85). Newark, DE: International Reading Association.

Padilla, M. J., Muth, K. D., & Padilla, R. K. (1991). Science and reading: Many process skills in common? In C. M. Santa & D. E. Alvermann (Eds.), *Science learning: Processes and applications* (pp. 14–19). Newark, DE: International Reading Association.

Passow, M. (1996). Storm studies. *The Science Teacher, 63*(3), 21–23.

Paulu, N., & Martin, M. (1991). *Helping your child learn science.* Washington, DC: U.S. Department of Education, Office of Educational Research and Improvement.

Piaget, J. in Gruber, H.E. & Voneche, J.J. (1977). *The Essential Piaget.* New York: Basic Books.

Price, C. L. (1989). Microcomputer applications in science. *Journal of Science Education, 1*(2), 30–33.

Reynolds, K., & Barba, R. (1996). *Technology for the teaching and learning of science.* Needham Heights, MA: Allyn & Bacon.

Rezba, R. J., Sprague, C., Fiel, R. L., & Funk, H. J. (2003). *Learning and assessing science process skills.* Dubuque, IA: Kendall/Hunt.

Rock, B. N., Blackwell, T. R., Miller, D., & Hardison, A. (1997). The GLOBE program: A model for international environmental education. In K. C. Cohen (Ed.), *Internet links for science education: Student-scientist partnerships.* New York: Plenum Press.

Rosenshine, B. (1997). Advances in research on instruction. In J. Lloyd, E. Kameanui, & D. Chard (Eds.), *Issues in educating students with disabilities* (pp. 197–221). Mahwah, NJ: Lawrence Erlbaum.

Roth, K. (1991). Reading science texts for conceptual change. In C. M. Santa & D. V. Alverson (Eds.), *Science learning: Processes and applications.* Newark, DE: International Reading Association.

Roth, K. (1993). *What does it mean to understand science? Changing perspectives from a teacher and her students.* East Lansing: Center for the Learning and Teaching of Elementary Subjects, Institute for Research on Teaching, Michigan State University.

Rowe, M. B. (1973). *Teaching science as continuous inquiry*. New York: McGraw-Hill.

Rowe, M. B. (1987). Wait-time: Slowing down may be a way of speeding up. *American Educator, 11*(1), 38–47.

Rowe, M. B. (1996). Mounting and maintaining an elementary science program: What supervisors can learn from research. In J. Rhoton & P. Bowers (Eds.), *Issues in science education* (pp. 162–166). Arlington, VA: National Science Teachers Association.

Rutherford, F. J., & Ahlgren, A. (1989). *Science for all Americans*. New York: Oxford University Press.

Santa, C. M., & Havens, L. T. (1991). Learning through writing. In C. M. Santa & D. E. Alvermann (Eds.), *Science learning: Processes and applications* (pp. 122–133). Newark, DE: International Reading Association.

Santa, C. M., & Alvermann, D. E. (Eds.). (1991). *Science learning: Processes and applications*. Newark, DE: International Reading Association.

Scruggs, T. E., & Mastropieri, M. A. (1994). The construction of scientific knowledge by students with mild disabilities. *Journal of Special Education, 28*(3), 307–321.

Scruggs, T. E., Mastropieri, M. A., Bakken, J. P., & Brigham, F. J. (1993). Reading versus doing: The relative effects of textbook-based and inquiry-oriented approaches to science learning in special education classrooms. *Journal of Special Education, 27*(1), 1–15.

Shapiro, B. (1994). *What children bring to light: A constructivist perspective on children's learning in science*. New York: Teachers College Press.

Shepardson, D. P., & Britsch, S. J. (2001). Tools for assessing and teaching science in elementary and middle schools. In D. P. Shepardson (Ed.), *Assessment in science: A guide to professional development and classroom practice* (pp. 119–147). Boston: Kluwer.

Sobel, D. (2000). *Galileo's daughter*. New York: Penguin Books.

Soholt, G. (1999). *Using technology effectively in your classroom* (p. 44). Bellevue, WA: Bureau of Education & Research.

Stahly, L. L., Krockover, G. H., & Shepardson, D. P. (1999). Third grade students' ideas about the lunar phases. *Journal of Research in Science Teaching, 36*(2), 159–177.

Stokes, N. C., & Hull, M. M. (2002, May). Every drop counts! *The Science Teacher, 69*(5), 40–44.

Stull, A. T. (1998). *Education on the Internet: A student's guide* (adapted for Merrill Education by R. J. Ryder). Upper Saddle River, NJ: Merrill/Prentice Hall.

TERC. (1993). *Hands-on elementary science project leader's manual*. Cambridge, MA: TERC Communications.

Texas A&M Center for Mathematics and Science Education. (2006). *Texas science initiative meta-analysis of national research regarding science teaching: Executive summary*. Austin: Texas Education Agency (available online at http://72.14.209.104/search?q=cache:AWfRsosvXPIJ:www3.science.tamu.edu/cmse/tsi/ExecutiveSum).

Texas A&M Center for Mathematics and Science Education (2005). *Effective research-based science instruction*. Austin: Texas Education Agency (available online at http://72.14.209.104/search?q=cache:q4rfHv7MDMYJ:www3.science.tamu.edu/cmse/tsi/).

Texas Education Agency. (1999). *Texas social studies framework, kindergarten–grade 12*. Austin, TX: Author.

Tompkins, G. E. (2006). *Literacy for the 21st century*, 4th ed. Upper Saddle River, NJ: Pearson/Merrill.

Trowbridge, L., & Bybee, R. (1996). *Teaching secondary school science* (6th ed.). Upper Saddle River, NJ: Merrill/Prentice Hall.

Turnbull, A., Turnbull, R., Shank, M., & Smith, S. J. (2004). *Exceptional lives: Special education in today's schools* (4th ed.). Upper Saddle River, NJ: Merrill/Prentice Hall.

U.S. Department of Education. (1996). *Planning excellence: A study of U.S. eighth-grade mathematics and science teaching, learning, curriculum, and achievement in international context*. Washington, DC: U.S. Department of Education, Office of Educational Research and Improvement.

U.S. Department of Education. (1997). *Introduction to TIMSS: The third international mathematics and science study*. Washington, DC: U.S. Department of Education, Office of Educational Research and Improvement.

Vasquez, J. A. (1990). Teaching to the distinctive traits of minority students. *The Clearing House, 63*, 299–304.

Vitale, M. R., & Romance, N. R. (2000). Portfolios in science assessment: A knowledge-based model for classroom practice. In J. J. Mintzes, J. H. Wandersee, & J. D. Novak (Eds.), *Assessing science understanding: A human constructivist view* (pp. 167–196). New York: Academic Press.

Vygotsky, L. S. (1962). *Thought and language*. Cambridge, MA: The MIT Press.

Watson, S., and Marshall, J. (1995). Effects of cooperative incentives and heterogeneous arrangements on achievement and interaction of cooperative learning groups in a college life science course. *Journal of Research in Science Teaching, 32*, 291–299.

Weiss, I. R., & Pasley, J. D. (2004, February). What is high-quality instruction? *Educational Leadership, 45*: 24–29.

Wiggins, G., & McTighe, J. (1998). *Understanding by design*. Alexandria, VA: Association for Supervision and Curriculum Development.

Wilson, M. R., & Berthenthal, M. W. (2006). *Systems for state science assessment*. Washington, DC: National Academies Press.

Wiske, M. S. (Ed.). (1998). *Teaching for understanding*. San Francisco: Jossey-Bass.

Wolfinger, D. M. (2000). *Science in the elementary and middle school*. New York: Longman.

Yopp, H. K., & Yopp, R. H. (2006, November). Primary students and informational texts, *Science and Children, 44*(3), 22–25.

Appendixes

Safety Requirements and Suggestions for Elementary and Middle School Inquiry Activities

Consult your state's classroom safety and health manual for specific state policies, requirements, and suggestions.

Safety Guidelines for Teachers

1. Review science activities carefully for possible safety hazards.
2. Eliminate or be prepared to address all anticipated hazards.
3. Consider eliminating open flames; use hot plates where possible as heat sources.
4. Be particularly aware of possible eye injuries from chemical reactions, sharp objects, small objects such as iron filings, and flying objects such as rubber bands.
5. Consider eliminating activities in which students taste substances; do not allow students to touch or inhale unknown substances.
6. Warn students of the dangers of electrical shock; use small dry cells in electrical activities; be aware of potential problems with the placement of extension cords.
7. Maintain fair, consistent, and strictly enforced discipline during science activities.
8. Instruct students in the proper care and handling of classroom pets, fish, or other live organisms used as part of science activities.
9. Instruct students to report immediately to the teacher
   * any equipment in the classroom that appears to be in an unusual or improper condition,
   * any chemical reactions that appear to be proceeding in an improper way, or
   * any personal injury or damage to clothing caused by a science activity, no matter how trivial it may appear.
10. Post appropriate safety rules for students in the classroom, review specific applicable safety rules before each activity, and provide occasional safety reminders during the activity.

Safety Rules for Students

1. Always follow the safety procedures outlined by your teacher.
2. Never put any materials in your mouth.
3. Avoid touching your face, mouth, ears, or eyes while working with chemicals, plants, or animals.
4. Always wash your hands immediately after touching materials, especially chemicals or animals.
5. Be careful when using sharp or pointed tools. Always make sure that you protect your eyes and those of your neighbors.
6. Wear American National Standards Institute approved safety goggles (with Z87 printed on the goggles) whenever activities are done in which there is a potential risk to eye safety.
7. Behave responsibly during science investigations.

REFERENCES

The University of the State of New York, *Elementary Science Syllabus*, 49, 1985, Albany, NY: The State Education Department, Division of Program Development; Ralph E. Martin, Colleen Sexton, Kay Wagner, and Jack Gerlovich, *Teaching Science for All Children*, 1994, Boston: Allyn & Bacon; Full Option Science System (FOSS) Teacher's Guides, 1994, Washington, DC, National Academies of Science.

Measuring Tools, Measuring Skills

In elementary and middle school science and mathematics, students should have many opportunities to

- use a variety of types of measuring instruments;
- measure length, area, volume, mass, and temperature; and
- make comparisons using different systems of units.

Metric Prefixes

milli = .001 (one thousandth)
centi = .01 (one hundredth)
kilo = 1000 (one thousand)

Measuring Length
Length is a linear measure.

Metric Units

millimeter = 0.001 meter (one-thousandth of a meter; the thickness of about 20 pages)
centimeter = 0.01 meter (one-hundredth of a meter; width of a little fingernail)
kilometer = 1000 meters (about 10 city blocks)

Some Conversions

1 inch = 2.54 centimeters
1 centimeter = 10 millimeters
100 centimeters = 1000 millimeters = 1 meter
1 meter = 39.37 inches = 3.28 feet
1000 meters = 1 kilometer = 0.621 mile
100 meters = 109 yards
1 yard = 3 feet

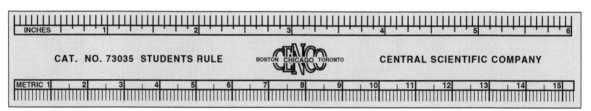

Use the ruler to convert lengths between units.

1 in. = _____ cm = _____ mm
3 in. = _____ cm = _____ mm
10 cm = _____ mm = _____ in.
140 mm = _____ cm = _____ in.

Use the ruler to measure lengths.

Length of dollar bill = _____ in. = _____ cm = _____ mm
Diameter of quarter = _____ in. = _____ cm = _____ mm
Thickness of quarter = _____ in. = _____ cm = _____ mm

Measuring Area
Area is a surface measure.

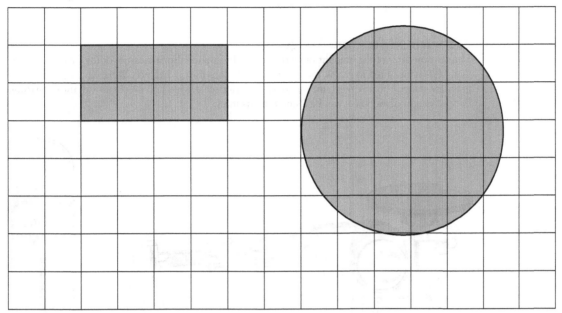

The area of each small square in the figure is 1 square centimeter = 1 cm^2.

Determine the area of the shaded rectangle

- by counting squares. _____
- by formula ($A = L \times W$). _____

Determine the area of the shaded circle

- by counting squares. _____
- by formula ($A = \pi r^2$). _____

Measuring Volume
Volume is three-dimensional.

1 cubic centimeter (cm^3 or cc) is the volume of a cube that is 1 centimeter on each side.

Some Conversions

1 cm^3 = 1 cc = 1 milliliter (ml)
1000 cm^3 = 1000 ml = 1 liter
1 liter = 1.06 quarts

Determine the volume of the large solid in the figure

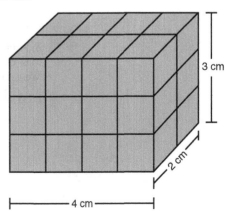

- by counting unit cubes.
- by using the formula, $V = L \times W \times H$. _____

Estimate the volume of a golf ball in cubic centimeters. A golf ball has a diameter of about 4 cm.

[*Answer:* Estimate how many unit cubes (1 cm³) might fit inside a golf ball if it were hollow. A good estimate of its volume might be between 25 and 40 unit cubes. By formula, the volume of a golf ball is about 33.5 cm³.]

Measuring Mass and Weight

Mass is a measure of the amount of matter in an object and, also, a measure of the inertia of an object. Mass is measured in grams, milligrams, or kilograms using a balance. Weight is a measure of the gravitational pull on an object, measured with a spring scale. Mass and weight are not the same thing, but the weight of an object can be found from its mass.

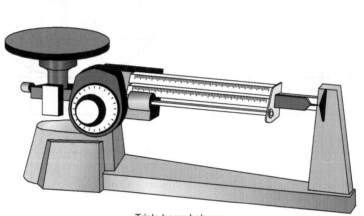

Triple beam balance

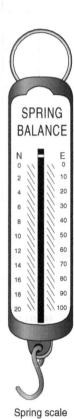

Spring scale

Some Conversions

1000 grams (g) = 1 kilogram (kg)
1 milligram = 0.001 gram (one-thousandth of a gram)
1 gram = 1000 milligrams (mg)
1 kg-mass weighs 2.2 pounds on the surface of the earth

Some Masses and Weights

Mass of nickel = 5 g
Mass of small child weighing about 60 pounds on earth = 27.3 kg (divide 60 by 2.2)
Weight on moon of small child of mass 27.3 kg = 10 pounds (1/6 of weight on earth)

Food labels tell how many grams and milligrams of different substances are in a food product.

Measuring Temperature

Temperature is a measure of how hot or cold a substance is. Temperature is measured with a thermometer in degrees Celsius or degrees Fahrenheit.

Some Equivalent Temperatures: Use the Fahrenheit/Celsius thermometer to convert from one temperature unit to the other.

Boiling point of water 100°C = _____ °F
Normal body temperature _____ °C = 98.6 °F
Room temperature 22°C = _____ °F
Freezing point of water 0°C = _____ °F
Slush of crushed ice, water,
   and ice cream salt _____ °C = 10°F
A really cold day in Alaska _____ °C = −15°F

Nutrition Facts

Serving Size 2/3 cup (55g)
Servings Per Container 12

Amount Per Serving

Calories 210
   Calories from Fat 25

% Daily Value*

Total Fat 3g	**5%**
Saturated Fat 1g	**4%**
Polyunsaturated Fat 0.5g	
Monounsaturated Fat 1.5g	
Cholesterol 0mg	**0%**
Sodium 140mg	**6%**
Potassium 190mg	**5%**
Total Carbohydrate 44g	**15%**
Other Carbohydrate 23g	
Dietary Fiber 3g	**13%**
Sugars 18g	
Protein 5g	
Vitamin A	0%
Vitamin C	0%
Calcium	2%
Iron	6%
Thiamine	10%
Phosphorus	10%
Magnesium	10%

* Percent Daily Values are based on a 2000 calorie diet. Your daily values may be higher or lower depending on your calorie needs.

	Calories	2,000	2,500
Total Fat	Less than	65g	80g
Sat Fat	Less than	20g	25g
Cholesterol	Less than	300g	300g
Sodium	Less than	2400mg	2400mg
Potassium		3500mg	3500mg
Total Carbo		300g	300g
Dietary Fiber		25g	30g

Calories per gram:
Fat 9   •   Carbohydrate 4   •   Protein 4

Temperature in °C and °F

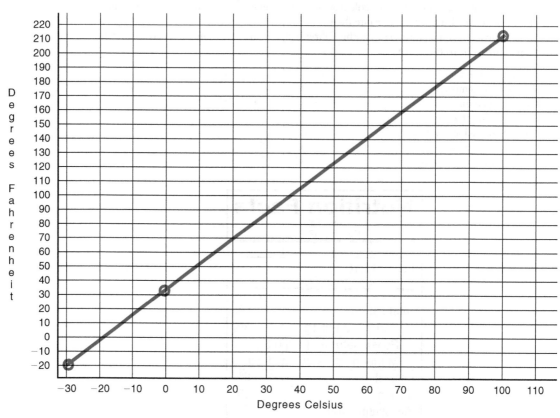

Use the graph to find equivalent temperatures.

0°C   = _____ °F
212°F = _____ °C
40°F   = _____ °C
180°F = _____ °C
50°C   = _____ °F

Selected Sources of Science Supplies, Models, Living Things, Kits, and Software

Brock Optical

Microscopes—rugged enough for small children
E-mail: magiscope@aol.com
URL: http://www.magiscope.com

Carolina Biological Supply Company

Instructional materials for all sciences; Science and Technology for Children (STC) guides and materials
E-mail: carolina@carolina.com
URL: http://www.carolina.com

Delta Education

Materials, kits, and activities for hands-on science programs, including FOSS, SCIS 3+, and DSMIII (Delta Science Modules)
E-mail: ecurran@delta-edu.com
URL: http://www.delta-education.com

Discovery Scope

Small, handheld microscopes
E-mail: dscopes@aol.com
URL: http://www.discoveryscope.net

Educational Innovations

Heat-sensitive paper, UV-detecting beads, Cartesian diver, super-absorbent polymers, and other science supplies
E-mail: info@teachersource.com
URL: http://www.teachersource.com

Educational Products, Inc.

Science fair display boards and materials
E-mail: kdavis@educationalproducts.com
URL: http://www.educationalproducts.com

ETA/Cuisenaire

Hands-on science materials
E-mail: info@etacuisenaire.com
URL: http://www.etacuisenaire.com

Fisher Science Education

Instructional materials for all sciences
E-mail: info@fisheredu.com
URL: http://www.fisheredu.com

Forestry Suppliers, Inc.

Orienteering compasses, water, soil, and biological test kits, tree borers, soil sieves, rock picks, weather instruments, and other materials for interdisciplinary science teaching
E-mail: fsi@forestry-suppliers.com
URL: http://www.forestry-suppliers.com

Ken-A-Vision Manufacturing Co., Inc.

Microscopes
E-mail: info@ken-a-vision.com
URL: http://www.ken-a-vision.com

Lab-Aids, Inc.

Single-concept hands-on kits for chemistry, biology, environmental science, and earth science
E-mail: customerservice@lab-aids.com
URL: http://www.lab-aids.com

Learning Technologies, Inc.

Portable planetariums and other materials for astronomy teaching
E-mail: starlab@starlab.com
URL: http://www.starlab.com

Mountain Home Biological

Living materials, barn owl pellets, skull sets
E-mail: mtnhome@gorge.net
URL: http://www.pelletlab.com

NASCO

Science materials and supplies
E-mail: info@enasco.com
URL: http://www.nascofa.com

National Gardening Association

GrowLab guides for kids' gardening, professional development materials on plant science
E-mail: MK@garden.org
URL: http://www.kidsgardening.com

NSTA Science Store

Books, posters, software, CD-ROMs
URL: http://www.nsta.org

Ohaus Corporation

Balances and measurement aids
E-mail: cs@ohaus.com
URL: http://www.ohaus.com

Pitsco LEGO Educational Division

LEGO construction kits, model hot air balloons, educational technology products
E-mail: pitsco@pitsco.com
URL: http://www.pitsco-legodacta.com

Rainbow Symphony, Inc.

Lesson kits for the study of light and color, specialty optics materials, diffraction gratings, 3-D lenses, solar eclipse safe-viewing glasses
E-mail: kathy@rainbowsymphony.com
URL: http://www.rainbowsymphony.com

Sargent-Welch

GEMS materials, materials for all sciences
E-mail: Sarwel@Sargentwelch.com
URL: http://www.Sargentwelch.com

TOPS Learning Systems

Science lessons using simple available materials
E-mail: tops@canby.com
URL: http://www.topsscience.org

Source: Compiled by authors from advertisements and Web searches.

Selected Science Education Periodicals for Teachers and Children

American Biology Teachers

National Association of Biology Teachers
http://www.nabt.org/

Audubon Magazine

National Audubon Society
http://www.Audubon.org/nas/

Journal of Research in Science Teaching

*National Association for Research in Science
    Teaching*
http://www.narst.org

National Geographic

National Geographic Society
http://www.nationalgeographic.com/

National Geographic Kids

National Geographic Society
http://www.nationalgeographic.com/kids/

Natural History

American Museum of Natural History
http://www.amnh.org/naturalhistory/

Ranger Rick

National Wildlife Federation
http://www.nwf.org

School Science and Mathematics

School Science and Mathematics Association
http://www.ssma.org

Science

*American Association for the Advancement
    of Science*
http://www.aaas.org

Science and Children

National Science Teachers Association
http://www.nsta.org

Science Education

John Wiley & Sons
http://www.wiley.com

Science Scope

National Science Teachers Association
http://www.nsta.org

Scientific American

http://www.sciam.com

Sky and Telescope

Sky Publishing Corp.
http://www.skyandtelescope.com

Super Science (for grades 3–6)

Scholastic
http://teacher.scholastic.com

The Science Teacher

National Science Teachers Association
http://www.nsta.org

Your Big Backyard

National Wildlife Federation
http://www.nwf.org/kidszone/

Professional Societies for Teachers of Science, Science Supervisors, and Science Educators

American Association for the Advancement of Science (AAAS)

http://www.aaas.org

American Association of Physics Teachers (AAPT)

http://www.aapt.org/

American Chemical Society (ACS)

http://www.acs.org/

Association for Educators of Teachers of Science (AETS)

http://theaste.org/

Association for Supervision and Curriculum Development (ASCD)

http://www.ascd.org/

Council for Elementary Science International (CESI)

http://unr.edu/homepage/crowther/cesi.html

International Society for Technology in Education (ISTE)

http://www.iste.org/

National Association of Biology Teachers (NABT)

http://www.nabt.org/

National Association of Geoscience Teachers (NAGT)

http://www.nagt.org/

National Geographic Society (NGS)

http://www.nationalgeographic.com

National Science Education Leadership Association (NSELA)

http://www.nsela.org

National Science Teachers Association (NSTA)

http://www.nsta.org

National Wildlife Federation (NWF)

http://www.nwf.com/

School Science and Mathematics Association (SSMA)

http://www.ssma.org

Contemporary Elementary Science Projects and Programs

Name	Grades	Contact Information	Characteristics
AIMS	K–9	AIMS Educational Foundation http://www.aimsedu.org	*Activities Integrating Math and Science* are hands-on activities that supplement science programs; available as content-themed or state-specific collections of student and teacher pages; supported by professional development workshops; strong math integration, especially in areas of organization and graphing of data.
Bottle Biology	K–8	Department of Plant Pathology, College of Agricultural and Life Sciences, University of Wisconsin, Madison Available from NSTA Science Store http://www.nsta.org	*Bottle Biology* is an ideas book for exploring environmental interactions using soda bottles and other recyclable materials. The book contains more than 20 scientific investigations using bottle constructions, including the Ecocolumn, the Predator-Prey Column, the Niche Kit, and the TerrAqua Column.
BSCS Science Tracks: Connecting Science and Literacy	K–5	Biological Science Curriculum Study, Attn: BSCS Science Tracks, 5415 Mark Dabling Blvd., Colorado Springs, CO 80918-3842 http://bscs.org Available from: Kendall/Hunt Publishing http://www.kendallhunt.com	*BSCS Science Tracks: Connecting Science and Literacy* is a comprehensive, modular, kit-based elementary science program. Developed with the help of NSF funding it features: standards-based content, teaching, and assessment; the 5-E learning cycle; guided inquiry; focus on conceptual understanding; collaboration; student journals and continuous assessment.
FOSS	K–8	Lawrence Hall of Science, University of California, Berkeley http://www.lhs.Berkeley.edu Available from: Delta Education http://www.delta-education.com	*Full Option Science System* is an inquiry-based science program, funded in part by the NSF. This comprehensive, modular, kit-based program features: developmentally appropriate materials and concepts; informative teacher guides, FOSS Readers that provide reading in the content area practice through a variety of literary genres; suggestions for science notebooking; and newly developed formative assessment tools.
GEMS	K–10	Lawrence Hall of Science, University of California, Berkeley http://www.lhs.Berkeley.edu/	*Great Explorations in Math and Science* includes more than 70 teacher guides and handbooks. Materials kits for the stand-alone and supplementary units can be purchased. Easy to use, well organized teacher guides, support teachers with limited science background. Typical units can be completed in 2 to 4 weeks.
GrowLab	K–8	National Gardening Association Burlington, VT http://kidsgardening.com	*GrowLab: Activities for Growing Minds* is an innovative curriculum guide to support plant-related instruction though indoor gardening. Activities are inquiry-based and follow GrowLab's version of the 5-E instructional model. A workshop toolkit titled, *Growing Science Inquiry*, was also developed with the support of NSF.
Insights	K–6	EDC Center for Science Education http://cse.edc.org Available from: Kendall/Hunt Publishing Company http://www.kendallhunt.com	*Insights: An Inquiry-Based Elementary School Science Curriculum* is designed to meet the needs of all children in grades K–6 while specifically addressing urban students. Insights is a core curriculum of seventeen, 6- to 8-week kit-based modules. This NSF supported program focuses on key science concepts, creative and critical thinking, problem solving through experiences in the natural environment, developing positive attitudes about science, bridging science concepts to current social and environmental events; and integration with language arts and mathematics.

Name	Grades	Contact Information	Characteristics
Peaches	Preschool	Lawrence Hall of Science, University of California, Berkeley http://www.lhs.Berkeley.edu	*Preschool Explorations for Adults,* Children, and Educators in Science consists of 10 teacher's guides for children's activities and teacher workshops. Topics include Ant Homes Under the Ground, Homes in a Pond, and Ladybugs.
SAVI/SELPH	3–8	Lawrence Hall of Science, University of California, Berkeley http://www.lhs.Berkeley.edu	*Science Activities for the Visually Impaired/Science Enrichment for Learners with Physical Handicaps* is an interdisciplinary, multi-sensory science enrichment program designed to be used with students who are blind or visually impaired, physically disabled, learning disabled, hearing impaired, or developmentally delayed. There are nine modules, each focusing on a specific content area; teacher guides to the activities; teacher preparation videos; and specially designed equipment that allow students with disabilities full access to science investigations.
SCIS 3(+)	K–6	Lawrence Hall of Science, University of California, Berkeley http://www.lhs.Berkeley.edu Available from: Delta Education http://www.delta-education.com	*Science Curriculum Improvement Study,* one of the elementary science projects developed with NSF support in response to the launch of Sputnik, is now available (after multiple revisions) as SCIS 3(+). Its modules are organized around a hierarchy of science concepts. Science process skills are integrated into the materials centered modules, which use an inductive instructional approach at the three-phase learning cycle which evolved into the 5-E instructional model.
Seeds of Science	2–5	*Seeds of Science/Roots of Reading,* Lawrence Hall of Science, University of California, Berkeley, CA 94720 seeds@berkeley.edu Available from: Delta Education http://www.delta-education.com	*Seeds of Science/Roots of Reading* is a research-based, field-tested curriculum that integrates inquiry science with content-rich literacy instruction. This developing project, funded in part by the NSF, addresses the urgent need for materials that help students make sense of the physical world while addressing foundational dimensions of literacy. The program will include 12 concept-focused, kit-based modules two text series: a collection of integrated science and literacy units, and a parallel collection of literacy units. Both series feature delightful 4-color student books that are central to each of the units.
STC	1–8	National Science Resources Center, Smithsonian Institution Available from: Carolina Biological Supply Company http://www.carolina.com	*Science and Technology for Children* is a comprehensive, modular, kit-based science program featuring inquiry-centered science education curricula that can be used by school districts to construct core instructional programs. Developed using a rigorous research and development process, STC modules provide age-appropriate opportunities for children to expand their conceptual understanding of important science concepts, acquire problem-solving and critical-thinking skills, and develop positive habits of mind toward science.
The Young Scientist Series	Preschool	Education Development Center, Inc. Available from: Redleaf Press http://www.redleafpress.org	*The Young Scientist Series* is an NSF supported science curriculum for children who are three to five years old. Each of the three teacher's guides (*Discovering Nature with Young Children, Building Structures with Young Children,* and *Exploring Water with Young Children*) provides background information and detailed guidance for incorporating science into preschool programs using materials typically found in an early-childhood classroom.

Index

,